MEXICO'S UNEVEN DEVELOPMENT

Mexico and the United States may be neighbors, but their economies offer stark contrasts. In *Mexico's Uneven Development: The Geographical and Historical Context of Inequality*, Oscar J. Martínez explores Mexico's history to explain why Mexico remains less developed than the United States. Weaving in stories from his own experiences growing up along the U.S.–Mexico border, Martínez shows how the foundational factors of external relations, the natural environment, the structures of production and governance, natural resources, and population dynamics have all played roles in shaping the Mexican economy. This interesting and thought-provoking study clearly and convincingly explains the issues that affect Mexico's underdevelopment. It will prove invaluable to anyone studying Mexico's past or interested in its future.

Oscar J. Martínez is a Regents' Professor of History at the University of Arizona. His previous books include *Troublesome Border* and *Mexican-Origin People in the United States: A Topical History*.

MEXICO'S UNEVEN DEVELOPMENT

The Geographical and Historical Context of Inequality

Oscar J. Martínez

NEW YORK AND LONDON

First published 2016
by Routledge
711 Third Avenue, New York, NY 10017

And by Routledge
2 Park Square, Milton Park, Abingdon, Oxon OX14 4RN

Routledge is an imprint of the Taylor & Francis Group, an informa business

© 2016 Taylor & Francis

The right of Oscar J. Martínez to be identified as author of this work has been asserted by him in accordance with sections 77 and 78 of the Copyright, Designs and Patents Act 1988.

All rights reserved. No part of this book may be reprinted or reproduced or utilised in any form or by any electronic, mechanical, or other means, now known or hereafter invented, including photocopying and recording, or in any information storage or retrieval system, without permission in writing from the publishers.

Trademark notice: Product or corporate names may be trademarks or registered trademarks, and are used only for identification and explanation without intent to infringe.

Library of Congress Cataloging-in-Publication Data
Martínez, Oscar J. (Oscar Jáquez), 1943– author.
  Mexico's uneven development : the geographical and historical context of inequality / Oscar J. Martínez.
     pages cm
  Includes bibliographical references and index.
  1. Mexico—Economic conditions. 2. Mexico—Social conditions. 3. Mexico—Politics and government. 4. Mexico—History. 5. United States—Economic conditions. 6. United States—Social conditions. I. Title.
  HC133.M36 2015
  330.972—dc23
  2015009268

ISBN: 978-1-138-84022-5 (hbk)
ISBN: 978-1-138-84023-2 (pbk)
ISBN: 978-1-315-73265-7 (ebk)

Typeset in Bembo
by Apex CoVantage, LLC

For Virginia

CONTENTS

List of Maps ix
List of Tables xi
List of Figures xiii
Acknowledgments xv
Prologue xvii

Introduction 1

PART I
The Mexico–U.S. Divide 17

  1 Divergent Pathways 19

  2 Affluence and Poverty 53

PART II
Context: Nature and People 69

  3 The Power of Geography 71

  4 Landforms, Transportation, and Cities 101

  5 Mexico's Fabled "Riches" 138

  6 People and the Economic Pie 162

PART III
Context: External Relations — 181

   7 So Far, So Close — 183

   8 Chasing Capital — 208

   9 Legal and Illegal Trade — 230

  10 Drugs, Liquor, Tobacco, and Migrants — 260

Conclusion: Lessons Learned — 277

Bibliography — *289*
Index — *311*

MAPS

2.1	Location of municipios with poverty rates of 75 percent or more, 2010	58
3.1	Contemporary Mexico	80
3.2	Major climates of Mexico (simplified)	83
3.3	Topography of Mexico	85
3.4	Central Mexico	88
4.1	Major navigable inland and intracoastal waterways of the United States, 1960s	105
4.2	Railroad networks of the United States, 1860, 1890, and 1960	108
4.3	U.S. national highway system, circa 2000	110
4.4	Major urban areas, United States, 1920 and 1980	112
4.5	Megalopolises and urban corridors in the United States, circa 2000	115
4.6	Evolution of Mexico's railroad network, 1880–1963	124
4.7	Mexican highways, mid-1940s and 1960s	127
4.8	Location and population of Mexican cities, 1940 and 2000	131
4.9	Ten largest metro areas in Mexico, 2010	132
6.1	Population density of the United States, 2010	164
6.2	Population density of Mexico, 2005	170
7.1	The political geography of North America in 1783	185
7.2	Territorial expansion of the United States and the absorption of Spanish and Mexican territories, 1795–1853	186
7.3	Republic of Mexico, 1824	189

TABLES

6.1 Regional Distribution of U.S. Population and GDP, 1900–2010   164
6.2 Population of Mexico, by Ethnicity (for Select Years), 1500–2010   168
6.3 Regional Distribution of the Population and GDP in Mexico, 1900–2010   169

FIGURES

Introd.1 Foundational Factors of National Economies 6
2.1 Evolution of Mexico's Real Minimum Salary, 1980–2012 60

ACKNOWLEDGMENTS

I am indebted to many people who, over the course of two decades, have helped me bring this book to fruition. In particular I thank John M. Hart, Richard Rhoda, Amanda B. Krause, and the Routledge anonymous reviewers for their careful reading of the entire manuscript and for passing along valuable suggestions that have improved the final product. James Peach, Ed Williams, Christopher Brown, David Gibbs, David Ortiz, and Kathy Staudt read portions of the manuscript and generously offered insightful comments. Al Bergesen kindly shared materials that proved helpful in my own formulation of geographic interpretations, while Jared Diamond graciously gave me ideas on how to make an academic book more reader-friendly.

I express my gratitude to Chris Miller, Becky Eden, and Geronimo García for their superb cartographic work, and to numerous librarians who assisted me in locating hard-to-get source materials, especially staff at the University of Arizona, the University of Texas at El Paso, and Yale University. My appreciation as well to Molly Molloy, whose postings on her frontera-list proved vital for gathering data on current conditions in Mexico.

My thanks to Ignacio Medina Nuñez and Manuel Flores Robles for the invaluable information and leads they provided during my research visit to Guadalajara, Mexico.

And to my children, Jamie, Gabriel, Daniel, David, and Andy, *muchas gracias* for having the patience to listen to my views on Mexico and the United States, and for taking time to read chapters and offering commentary. I owe the greatest debt to my wife, Virginia, whose support over the years, as well as insights, research assistance, and editorial help have contributed so much to shaping the book.

Oscar J. Martínez

PROLOGUE

While growing up in Ciudad Juárez, Chihuahua, Mexico, during the 1950s, I frequently crossed the international border into El Paso, Texas, United States, and noticed the differences between the two cities. El Paso had an impressive skyline. Modern buses and automobiles circulated in an orderly fashion along the city's wide streets and avenues. Large numbers of El Pasoans lived in attractive, spacious homes in nice neighborhoods. By comparison, Juárez had no tall buildings, traffic was chaotic, many streets were unpaved, old smoking buses and trucks rumbled on the roadways, horse-drawn wagons competed with motorists on major streets, impoverished *colonias* (neighborhoods) took up much of the space in the city, and there were few middle- and upper-class neighborhoods. Many marginalized *juarenses* (Juárez residents), including my own family, yearned to live in the United States because of its higher standard of living and greater economic opportunities. After many trips back and forth—both legally and illegally—between the two countries, in 1957 my parents and their six children finally became permanent legal U.S. residents.

The contrast between Juárez and El Paso then, as well as now, mirrors the gulf that has separated Mexico and the United States historically. Juárez, reflecting many of the problems that have afflicted Mexico as a whole, has been predominantly poor and heavily dependent on foreigners for its economic well-being. El Paso, despite having large numbers of poor immigrants as part of its population, has enjoyed a much higher standard of living than Juárez and has been the dominant partner in an interdependent but asymmetrical twin-city economic relationship. Juarenses have been particularly vulnerable to the vagaries of the U.S. and global economies. Economic downturns have occurred with regularity, bringing devastation to their city.[1]

Why is El Paso so much more prosperous than Juárez? Most people whom I have interviewed informally on both sides of the border feel that El Paso is more affluent because it is a part of the United States, which they believe is a forward-looking, "progressive" country, and that Juárez is poorer because it is a part of Mexico, which "lacks" energy and dynamism. If asked for specifics regarding the sources of Mexico's "backwardness" and Juárez's poverty, some respondents usually mention government incompetence, others bring up corruption, and still others claim that Mexicans suffer from cultural deficiencies. Such negative views about Mexico and Mexicans are shared by many public figures, analysts, and even scholars.

I, however, have come to much different conclusions regarding the roots of the deep dissimilarities between Juárez and El Paso, as well as the inequalities between Mexico and the United States. What ails Juárez ails much of Mexico: an economy that provides mostly low-paying jobs, scarce resources to meet overwhelming needs and, of late, massive lawlessness fueled by the drug trade. My view is that these maladies, and many others, derive from unfavorable circumstances linked to the larger historical and geographical context that have shaped both Juárez and Mexico.

El Paso's fundamental advantage over Juárez is simply that it is tethered to the powerful U.S. national system and thus has access to the resources, support structures, and protections that are available to many U.S. cities. The large permanent federal military and law enforcement presence in El Paso enhances the city's ability to shield itself from the devastation that has tormented Juárez and other parts of Mexico. As a resident of El Paso, I sometimes feel like I live in a fortified space reminiscent of old European castles, which were protected by well-armed guards, walls, and moats. Juarenses live but a short distance away beyond the militarized international border known as the Rio Grande. Much like drug-consuming suburbanites in large U.S. cities who shield themselves from drug-related violence because such lawlessness is concentrated in inner-city neighborhoods, the violence connected with illegal drug trafficking in El Paso finds its outlet beyond the boundary—in Juárez. Drug traffickers have no need to take risks with U.S. authorities because they can commit crimes with impunity in Mexico, where the police, the army, and the legal system have proven ineffectual in fighting criminals. Such institutional weaknesses have their roots in lack of resources. In contrast to El Paso, Juárez receives far fewer material benefits from the Mexican national system because that system is built on scarce public revenues and can only provide limited support to the country's municipalities. With more than double the population of El Paso, the Juárez city budget in 2011 was only about a third of that of El Paso. Such meager resources allow the Juárez authorities to meet only a small part of the needs of juarenses.

In the early and mid-1970s, during my graduate studies at Stanford University and UCLA, I developed a strong interest in identifying the root causes of Mexico's problems. I wrote my doctoral dissertation on the history of Juárez, and

I subsequently began drawing comparisons and contrasts between Mexican and U.S. metropolitan areas, eventually looking more broadly at differences between the two countries. Visits to numerous regions within both Mexico and the United States reinforced my belief that the great divergence in the natural environment of each nation played important roles in the vast economic gap between them. What caught my eye most was the extraordinary difference in the physical geography of each country. In Mexico, other than the fertile Central Highlands, green areas were largely confined to woodlands in the high country, scattered river valleys, and rain forests in the Gulf and Pacific coastlands and the flatlands of Yucatán. The landscape was predominantly brown and arid. Mexico's inland plains did not have waterways in any way comparable to the Mississippi River or large bodies of water like the Great Lakes, or like European rivers such as the Rhine and the Danube. Cities on Mexico's coasts were much smaller than those in the country's interior, a pattern that departed sharply from the urban systems in much of the United States and Europe. The dramatic differences between Mexico and the continental United States became apparent to me when I ventured frequently beyond the arid U.S. Southwest, where I had lived most of my life. I was struck by the ever-present green vegetation and the woodlands in large parts of the United States, and as well by the location of many large cities adjacent to the ocean and to navigable rivers and lakes. My feeling grew stronger that geography had to be central to the explanation as to why the two countries had evolved so differently. The combination of direct observation and traditional research made it clear to me that in the United States an astonishingly favorable natural environment had greatly facilitated economic growth and promoted national cohesion, whereas in Mexico difficult geography had not only conspired to place myriad limitations on economic activity but had also undermined political and societal integration. In short, nature had been generous with Americans and stingy with Mexicans.[2]

But, I knew that other important factors needed to be considered to properly understand the prosperity achieved by the United States versus the uneven development that has long bedeviled Mexico. I needed to venture deeply into Mexican history. I needed to know how Mexico's relationship with the United States had affected the Mexican economy. I also had to take into account the role of such things as Mexico's resource endowment, demography, economic organization, and government institutions. Delving into these different subjects would prove to be a daunting task, but I kept searching for answers. This book is the result of that decades-long journey of discovery.

I have no illusions that my findings will be satisfying to everyone. For example, those who explain Mexico's problems in terms of presumed cultural "deficiencies" or "flawed" governmental institutions will not find support here. In the Introduction and in Chapter 1, I explain why cultural norms, although insightful, are not deterministic factors for promoting or retarding economic development, whether in Mexico, in the United States, or in any other country. And, while I am cognizant of corruptive practices in Mexican society and policy mistakes made by Mexican governments over the years, I do not consider such aberrations that unusual or fundamental to understanding the root causes of Mexico's uneven development. The origins of Mexico's big economic problems lie elsewhere. "Defective" institutions, for example, represent outcomes (rather than causes) of deep-seated unfavorable conditions inherent in the natural and human environment in which Mexico has functioned historically. Mexican leaders, as awful as many of them might be, are no worse than their nonsocially conscious counterparts around the world. Many Mexican oligarchs have behaved as self-indulgent oligarchs usually do, monopolizing economic and political power and doing little to alleviate the needs of the masses. The current crop of greedy U.S. oligarchs and their political protectors actually have much in common with Mexican oligarchs and their political puppets.

Readers who feel that individuals and societies absolutely control their own fates and that it is entirely up to them to shape their own destinies may be reluctant to accept one of the central messages in this book, which is that building and improving national economies are far from being just matters of human choice. Whether in Mexico or anywhere else, the reality is that, because of geography, world conditions, or sheer luck, a good deal of what happens around us is beyond our ability to shape, manage, or direct. Thus there are limits to what the leaders at the helm of countries can do to achieve prosperity for all citizens. In the case of Mexico, powerful forces over which Mexicans have had limited control have seriously undermined the country over the centuries. Mexico is not unique in that respect. Similar forces have been present in many countries, with the impacts varying in accordance with the contextual frameworks of their respective settings. It is that big picture milieu that is my primary concern in this book.

Notes

1 The boom and bust cycles characteristic of the economy of Juárez and other Mexican border cities are documented in Martínez (1978, 2006).
2 Even though the term *American* rightfully belongs to people everywhere in the Americas, in this book I use it specifically to refer to citizens and long-term residents of the United States and those whose way of life is predominantly reflective of mainstream U.S. society. This choice is based simply on the reality that *American* is widely used and understood that way, and there is no good alternative term. The term *Mexican* refers to a person of Mexican birth and/or long-term residency in Mexico or elsewhere whose culture is predominantly Mexican.

INTRODUCTION

Acquiring a good understanding of either the past or the present requires familiarity with *context*, meaning knowledge of the totality of conditions, settings, and circumstances in which evolution takes place or in which events unfold. Historical facts and comparisons are essential for building context. Ignoring or underestimating context inevitably leads to partial or simplistic answers or, worse, misleading or wrong interpretations. Thus the serious study of countries necessitates recognition of the complex forces that shape human societies. Deconstruction of the general milieus in which nation-states function aids in the identification of the backwinds that propel progress and the headwinds that stall it. Comparisons of the experiences of different countries are especially helpful for shedding light on why some countries go in one direction and others travel a different path. I have endeavored to follow that approach in this book. My thesis is that the vast differences that separate Mexico from the United States are rooted in profoundly different national contexts.

Mexico is a land of great contrasts. The upscale, modern side of the country is readily apparent to visitors from other countries who spend time in the bustling downtown areas or affluent suburbs of Mexico City, Guadalajara, Monterrey, or other major urban centers. In these metropolises, broad avenues lined with high-rise buildings, businesses of all types, and modern commercial districts resemble many boulevards found in large U.S. cities. Affluence is ubiquitous, especially in centrally located or suburban malls and shopping centers that house an array of upscale establishments as well as iconic U.S. retail brands such as Sears, Best Buy, Walmart, Sam's Club, Costco, Office Max, Home Depot, 7-Eleven, and Circle K. Restaurant choices similar to those available in the United States abound, including fast-food eateries such as McDonalds, Burger King, Carl's Jr., and Pizza Hut, fashionable coffee shops such as Starbucks, and Häagen-Dazs ice cream parlors. The other, much less dazzling side of Mexico is not as visible to outsiders; it is found in impoverished sprawling neighborhoods, located usually on the periphery of cities, as well as in thousands of small towns and villages in the countryside. In those locales, legions of *mexicanos/as* live in poor urban *colonias* (neighborhoods) or isolated *pueblitos* (small towns), *rancherias* (rural communities), and *comunidades indígenas* (indigenous communities). Life is hard in such spaces. Many of the poor live in slum dwellings; lack access to safe drinking water, sanitation, medical care, and decent schools; and face the prospect of premature death because of exposure to deadly diseases. These are the two striking faces of Mexico—half of the people living in affluence and the other half living in poverty.

The dual nature of Mexican society accounts for Mexico's designation as a developing country, rather than a developed nation.[1] From the perspective of low-income people, the major problem is that Mexico's externally dependent, erratic economy has historically not delivered enough good jobs that pay decent wages. Millions of Mexicans have simply abandoned their country in search of opportunities abroad, while a large percentage of those who have stayed home continue to labor in the informal sector, taking on self-created jobs such as street peddling or engaging in illegal activity such as selling contraband goods or trafficking drugs. One estimate for 2010 put Mexico's underground or nontax-paying economy at 36 percent of the country's GDP.[2] The extant high poverty rate and the large size of the informal economy provide striking evidence that despite the fact that Mexico has the fourteenth largest economy in the world (as measured by nominal GDP), the level of human deprivation remains quite high. Using real GDP per capita, actually a better measure of living standards, Mexico ranks sixty-seventh among 185 countries, according to the World Bank.[3]

In contrast to Mexico, the neighboring United States is not only a highly developed country, but it is the world's superpower, possessing the largest and most modern economy and boasting high ratings on standard-of-living measures such as life expectancy, literacy, formal education, and income. While poverty and wealth inequality have always existed in the United States, the percentage of people living in a state of underdevelopment has been much lower than in Mexico. But why is there such an overwhelming development gap between the two countries?

The Search for Answers

During my years as a college undergraduate in the 1960s, I sought to learn about the causes of economic backwardness in Latin America and discovered the different theoretical approaches that dominated the literature at the time. Modernization theory was much in vogue then as an explanation for shortcomings in the Third World.[4] According to this perspective, underdevelopment was rooted in outmoded political policies and economic organization. The answers to backwardness and impoverishment in Latin America, said the modernizers, lay in adopting the values and institutions of the Western industrial countries and discarding the "entrenched" and "retarding" influences inherited from Spain and, in the case of Mexico and other countries that practiced state-directed economics, eliminating protectionist and socialistic policies. I read in works that reflected the modernization perspective that Latin Americans lacked an entrepreneurial ethic and that they shunned business, engineering, and science in favor of such fields as philosophy, religion, literature, and law. Further, Latin Americans allegedly were not interested in commerce and industry, fields that were obviously central to promoting economic growth. The message of the modernizers was that Latin Americans had chosen to remain poor because they avoided hard entrepreneurial work. By contrast, Americans and Europeans allegedly had achieved spectacular development by investing in science and technology, by building efficient institutions, and by remaining faithful to free market economics. If Latin Americans really wished to get ahead, they must emulate the ways of the advanced western countries. Economist Walt Rostow even provided a model of the evolutionary journey that underdeveloped countries could undertake once they made the commitment to have their economies "take off" in the pursuit of development and modernity.[5] The modernization approach implied that by simply following a set formula, countries in one part of the world could duplicate results achieved by countries in another part of the world. Modernizers ignored environmental differences, disparities in natural resource endowments, and contrasting population dynamics among countries. It troubled me in particular that modernization theorists seldom took into account the profound effect that unequal international relationships had on the Third World.

When I hit upon dependency theory, at long last I had what struck me as a fitting explanation of cross-national inequalities. *Dependistas* asserted that wealth disparities were rooted in long-standing global economic asymmetries. They stressed that poor countries were locked in a condition of subordination and diminished capacity to determine their own destinies. Dependistas argued that underdevelopment in the Third World had its roots in conquest, colonization, and exploitation perpetrated by imperialistic countries. That certainly had the ring of truth in the case of Mexico and the Central and South American countries whose histories I had studied. Interpretations offered by Raúl Prebisch, Fernando Cardoso, Paul Baran, André Gunder Frank, and others proved useful in crystallizing where and how external interventions, manipulations, unequal terms of trade, and corporate exploitation had subordinated economies in the southern portion of the western hemisphere to the will of the advanced countries of Europe and North America.[6] No reasonable person with a basic knowledge of history could deny the damages inflicted on the Third World by imperialist states and predatory corporate interests bent on taking natural wealth and extracting commercial profits from poor countries while simultaneously tapping their markets and exploiting the labor of impoverished peoples.

I embraced a good deal of what the dependency model offered, but I remained dissatisfied with the dependistas because of their overwhelming emphasis on external blame. Were the countries of the Third World mere victims in a global political and economic chess game? Could there also be significant internal or domestic reasons for underdevelopment? The dependistas neglected to provide persuasive answers to these questions. Moreover, the radical leftist agenda promoted by dependency's staunchest proponents, as well as their advocacy of isolating poor countries from the international free market system as the way of stopping external exploitation, struck me as extreme and unrealistic. Despite my reservations about dependency as a grand theory of underdevelopment, I remain convinced that dependence as an objective economic condition is a highly significant factor that continues to be central to the persistence of poverty in many Third World countries, including Mexico. The historical record clearly reveals that, for much of its history, Mexico has been heavily reliant on the much stronger United States, meaning that the Mexican economy has been conditioned and shaped to a significant degree by the U.S. economy. Although at various points in history Mexico has practiced self-determination and defied American policy on some international issues, in economic matters Mexicans have persistently needed the United States. U.S. loans and investments, as well as extensive cross-border trade and human migration, have all played central roles in shaping the Mexican economy.

As dependency theory waned in academic circles by the 1980s, an updated version of modernization theory now called "neoliberalism" swept across the globe as the advanced countries' answer to the intense economic crisis then gripping the developing world. The United States in particular aggressively promoted free market economics and limited government as the way out of the morass. That strategy was developed in Washington, D.C., by members of the World Bank, the International Monetary Fund, and other organizations. Desperation in the time of economic emergency meant many poor nations saw no alternative to accepting the prescriptions of the "Washington Consensus." In exchange for rescue loan packages from international banks, countless debt-ridden Third World countries, including Mexico, abandoned quasi-socialist practices, downsized their governments, privatized state enterprises, cut social programs, and opened up their economies to external investment and trade. Conservative policy analysts and scholars jumped on the neoliberal bandwagon and produced a new body of literature that trumpeted the message that the adoption of freewheeling capitalism would bring unprecedented growth and progress to any society.

My doubts about the ability of the market system to deliver on such grand promises in the Third World grew stronger as the societies that adopted the neoliberal model actually made little headway in diminishing poverty among their masses. While some countries experienced growth and some sectors of their populations saw their incomes rise, the shocking expansion of the already wide gap between rich and poor wherever neoliberalism was practiced cast serious doubt as to whether this ideology provided the best road map to help bring about balanced development.[7] What I have learned from history is that, regardless of the ideological paradigm embraced by poor countries, the choice alone, no matter how well the selected model is implemented, is not enough to achieve success. Third World countries need much more than paradigms to overcome deeply rooted problematic domestic contexts and unequal playing fields in the global economy. Innate disadvantages in the Third World combined with innate advantages in the First World have created and sustained vast disparities among nation-states.

Foundational Factors and the Development Process

As I considered the general conditions that have shaped the economies of Mexico and the United States, I sought answers to basic questions about wealth and poverty on a global scale. How different have the challenges faced by poor countries been from those faced by the now rich countries? Have poor countries had the same opportunities to achieve development that the now advanced countries have had? Have the highly industrialized countries had natural assets that Third World countries have lacked? To what degree have natural or environmental success-promoting factors in the United States been present, or absent, in Mexico? Has Mexico faced geographic and human circumstances not encountered in the United States?

Even a cursory comparison of the histories of Mexico and the United States will show that each country has functioned in very different contexts, especially in the geographic sense. Mexico is one-fifth the size of the United States, its location is less favorable, its shape is more contorted, its topography is much more mountainous, its resource endowment is significantly smaller, its coastlines have far fewer good harbors, and its rivers and lakes have almost no navigation possibilities. These basic physical differences provide a logical starting point for understanding the divergent economic trajectories of each country, but of course there is much more to the story than geography.

In my estimation, the level of development in Mexico, as well as that in the United States, can best be understood by considering the effects of five overarching "foundational factors" that have long been present in each country. My contention is that these factors have been much less favorable for Mexico than for the United States. They are as follows: (1) the natural environment, (2) natural resources, (3) population dynamics, (4) relations with other countries, and (5) the structure of production and governance. These are the paramount building blocks or, in their totality, the mega contexts that I believe determine the size, character, and capacity of any national economy. Because every nation's context is different, the weight given to each factor depends on particular circumstances. In the cases of Mexico and the United States, among the five factors, the natural environment and foreign relations have been the most decisive in the overall construction of each economy; these two factors have also greatly influenced the shaping of the structure of production and governance. The other two building blocks, the

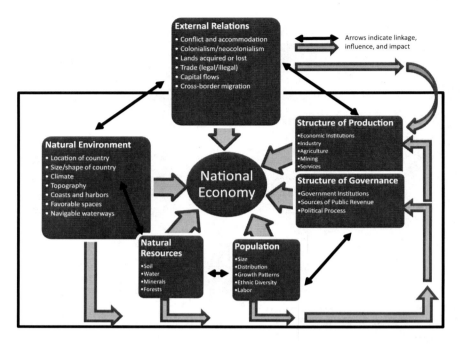

FIGURE INTROD.1 Foundational Factors of National Economies

resource endowment and population dynamics, have played lesser roles in determining the economic fate of each country. Figure Introd. 1 illustrates the different weights assigned to each foundational factor as well as the connections among them, with specific reference to the economies of Mexico and the United States.

The main purpose of this book is to explain Mexico's substandard economic activity by applying the foundational factors approach primarily to Mexico and, for purposes of comparison, secondarily to the United States. The argument is that, unlike the United States, Mexico has been shaped by an inherently difficult context. Formidable environmental or geographic impediments in Mexico—that is, disadvantages linked to locational, climatic, and topographical circumstances—have seriously thwarted domestic economic activity. Despite Mexico's robust natural endowment, shortages of key raw materials essential for agriculture and industry have held back production, and problematic population dynamics have had various negative impacts historically. Additionally, unfavorable external factors, such as disadvantageous international conditions and/or the existence of problematic interactions and unequal relationships with other countries, have impacted Mexico in an extraordinary manner. And finally, long-standing weaknesses in the structure of production and governance in Mexico have contributed to slow, inefficient, and uneven growth and have promoted the maldistribution of wealth. Institutions linked to such sectors as agriculture, mining, trade, commerce, and manufacturing have historically performed at subpar levels, while governance has been erratic and inefficient. Moreover, public policies have favored the rich and the powerful and have neglected the impoverished masses.

The roles played by these five foundational factors in Mexico cannot be adequately understood without viewing them in historical and comparative contexts, and for that reason this book utilizes a framework that compares Mexico's evolution to that of the United States. History itself is an indispensable foundational force, and a comparative approach is necessary because it reveals the differences in the quality of the foundational factors that have shaped each country.

Individual chapters assess the impact of specific foundational factors—with the exception of the means of production and governance, whose significance is pointed out in many places throughout the book. But because political economy figures so prominently in the literature on Mexico's uneven development, at this juncture it is important to place this subject in proper perspective and to consider its relationship to the other foundational factors.

Assessing the Structure of Production and Governance

One of the major similarities between Mexico and the United States is that the organization and functioning of economic and governmental institutions in both societies are rooted in the same economic system—that is, capitalism. But capitalism has not functioned the same way in each nation. This is partly explained by differences in policy, but the divergence is best understood by considering the profoundly dissimilar internal and external contexts that have impacted each society. These contexts have given rise to disparate institutional frameworks. In Mexico, highly problematic domestic and external circumstances spawned a more monopolistic and exploitative form of capitalism, along with less political democracy, than in the United States. Mexicans have had much less success than Americans in reducing undesirable side effects of capitalism such as regional economic disparities, power concentration, wealth accumulation among the few, and social inequality, though interestingly, while the problem of wealth disparity has historically afflicted Mexico more than the United States, since the 1980s inequality has become as great an issue among Americans as it always has been among Mexicans.[8] In both countries recent powerful global tendencies and internal political changes have decisively modified each economy and each government to the detriment of large numbers of middle- and working-class Mexicans and Americans. A less-regulated system of capitalism—that is, the neoliberal version—has become entrenched in both countries, appreciably increasing the divide between people at the top of the social pyramid and those below.

To a significant extent, then, Mexico's underdevelopment needs to be understood in relation to the workings of capitalism. Capitalism inevitably creates inequalities and unbalanced development. It naturally favors those with capital and disadvantages those without it, and it naturally produces uneven growth across landscapes and among population groups. The standard remedies for moderating the predictable negative effects of capitalism include government regulation and oversight of the means of production, enactment of laws and policies intended to lessen the power gap between capital and labor, equitable taxation, and creation of social security programs and safety nets for the population at large. Historically Mexico has fallen far shorter than the United States when it comes to mitigating the maladies associated with capitalism.

Mexico's structure of production and governance is seen by many people as based on ideas and methods introduced by Spaniards centuries ago, and the U.S. system is assumed to rest on the English model traceable to the time of the thirteen colonies. Such interpretations are simplistic. Without a doubt Spain and England played important roles in molding Mexico and the United States during the early histories of these New World societies. But European influences are in reality secondary to the much more decisive parts played by country-specific natural environments, resource endowments, population patterns, and international relations in the eventual shaping of both Mexico and the United States. The mega contexts under which these countries have evolved are fundamentally different than the mega contexts that shaped Spain and England in bygone eras.

The work of Stanley L. Engerman and Kenneth L. Sokoloff is especially helpful in understanding the crucial roles played by environmental forces, especially physical geography, climatic conditions, the quality of the land, and available labor forces in the molding of institutions and national economies. In their comparison of North and South America, Engerman and Sokoloff write that geographical factors directly affect the form, quality, and performance of both economic and governmental institutions and, thus, on a larger scale, the general level of development. Owing to their more favorable natural endowments, the United and Canada built economies whose means of production fostered more equitable wealth distribution and allowed for greater societal participation in the political process than in Latin American countries, where less favorable geographic features naturally encouraged higher levels of wealth disparity and concentration of political power. Further, the natural advantages of Canada and the United States predisposed them to develop commerce and industry more extensively than anywhere in Latin America, including Mexico.[9]

The nature of a country's external relations is just as important as the interplay between its people and their natural environments. In other words, human decisions pertaining to the selection and building of institutions are conditioned by prevailing circumstances in the broader environmental and international contexts in which countries function. Institution selection is predominantly an outcome of economic possibilities offered by surrounding physical environments and trade interaction with other countries. Thus institutions function as interdependent entities, with the overall context determining their quality and capacity. For these reasons institutions are not fundamental in the development process; they are derivative.

At a broader level, national economies and attendant governmental structures likewise are dependent on the attributes of the natural environment and the circumstances that govern external relations, as well as on available natural resources and extant population dynamics. Favorable contexts tend to produce strong and efficient institutions as well as strong and efficient structures of production and governance. Conversely, problematic contexts tend to produce deficient and, more often than not, extractive and exploitative institutions, as well as deficient structures of production and governance.

In Mexico, the deficient side of a decidedly mixed natural endowment has played a powerful role in predisposing the country to develop societal structures and institutions that spawned an unhealthy concentration of political and economic power early on, which in turn fostered great wealth inequality. Illustrative classic extractive Mexican institutions include *encomiendas*, a form of labor exploitation practiced during the Spanish colonial period that sprang from settlement patterns among indigenous people and what agricultural possibilities the land had to offer, and the equally exploitative private estates known as *haciendas* and plantations, which were also derived from the available land and labor. These agricultural institutions, along with similarly extractive institutions in the mining industry, generated economic, governmental, and societal effects detrimental to the overall development of Mexico. Such effects include the concentration of land in few hands, the persistence of low wages, and the slow growth of the domestic market. Other economies in Latin America had similar antecedents.

To some analysts, the long-term presence of inequality-promoting and undemocratic institutions in Mexico constitutes evidence that Mexicans have made many bad choices in organizing their economy and building state institutions. Such bad choices presumably account for the underdevelopment readily apparent throughout Mexico. For example, Daron Acemoglu and James A. Robinson (2012) place the lion's share of the blame for underdevelopment in Mexico and other poor countries on the adoption of inadequate or bad governmental and economic institutions. The path to progress, these authors argue, is to have good institutions.

Such an interpretation is not convincing. Acemoglu and Robinson not only ignore the impact of the mega context on nations in general but on the shaping of national institutions in particular. If many poor countries lack strong institutions, it is not for lack of want, but rather because such countries do not have the means to support the desired institutions. For instance, to have healthy populations, countries need good health care institutions (clinics, hospitals, pharmaceuticals, doctors, etc.); to have an educated citizenry, countries need good educational institutions (schools, universities, research laboratories, teachers, etc.); and to have good rule-of-law systems, countries need good judicial and law enforcement institutions (judges, clerks, courtrooms, administrative resources, computers, prosecutors, policemen, police academies, detectives, weapons, crime labs, cars, jails, etc.). The crucial issue is how poor countries get such beneficial institutions.

The reality is that health, educational, and rule-of-law institutions are not easy to acquire because they are very costly. If it were simply a matter of human choice, then practically every country would have strong institutions of the type referenced above, but most do not. Poor countries lack the necessary revenues to sustain good institutions because underdeveloped economies do not produce the robust revenues that can be channeled to that end.

In their work Acemoglu and Robinson reference the U.S.–Mexico border, pointing out differences in living standards in Nogales, Sonora, versus Nogales, Arizona. The Mexican side, the authors say, is poorer than the U.S. side because Mexico's institutions do not work as well as those in the United States. It is a fact that Mexico is less prosperous than its northern neighbor and, indeed, that Mexico has weaker institutions. But to conclude that those weaker institutions alone account for Mexico's profound economic problems is a stretch. To back up their claim that Mexico is just another country whose self-serving leaders have passed up opportunities to adopt good institutions, Acemoglu and Robinson recount some historical events and what they believe to be instances of poor decisions by Mexican elites. Anyone who knows the history of Mexico, however, will quickly see that Acemoglu and Robinson rely on cherry-picked and uncontextualized history. Three examples ignored by these authors come to mind of the reduced institutional capacity of Mexico to achieve desired economic outcomes as a consequence of unfavorable external circumstances. First, in the 1880s, president Porfirio Díaz, apparently worried about continuous economic pressures originating in powerful U.S. circles—including continuous advocacy of annexation of Mexican territory among U.S. political and business leaders—felt compelled to discard long-standing national policies regarding state ownership of the country's natural resources. Díaz diffused the external threats by granting generous concessions to foreign investors, allowing them to exploit Mexico's land and minerals as they saw fit. By following a strategy of modifying the law to suit foreigners, Mexico protected its political sovereignty; however, Mexico lost substantial *economic* sovereignty.[10] Second, between 1917 and 1930, Mexico adopted a new constitution, passed new laws, and built new institutions designed to reduce the excessive property rights acquired by foreigners in prior eras. The Mexican government also sought to collect more taxes on company profits. In opposition, powerful U.S. and British oil and mining firms rendered such initiatives largely ineffectual through political influence, control over commodity markets, monopoly of specialized technology used in resource industries, and strong pressures against Mexico applied by their home governments. Third, in the 1980s, economically distressed Mexico had little choice but to radically change its economic institutions and drastically shrink its governmental apparatus as a result of unfavorable international market conditions, high indebtedness to foreign banks, and pressures exerted by the World Bank and the International Monetary Fund. What these three examples show is that dependent countries like Mexico are not totally free to shape their institutions. Mexican leaders learned long ago that the interests of foreigners, especially Americans, must always be taken into account in making significant decisions. Ignoring the reality of Mexico's pronounced external dependence, Acemoglu and Robinson cite select fragments of the past as their major source of "evidence" for Mexico's and other countries' alleged poor institutional choices to make their case that bad institutions are the deterministic causes of underdevelopment. It will be up to historians of all the countries cited as examples by Acemoglu and Robinson to check the efficacy of their arguments.

Many other authors besides Acemoglu and Robinson have placed the blame for Mexico's uneven growth on defective economic organization, inefficient institutions, and faulty government policies. To be sure these maladies have long existed in Mexico but, viewed in context, it becomes clear that they are actually outcomes of underdevelopment rather than its causes. Favorable internal and external economic circumstances need to be present if meaningful advances are to be made in governance and policy making. As economist Ha-Joon Chang has pointed out, it took decades, even generations, for institutions in advanced countries to become sufficiently strong and efficient enough to remove impediments, uncertainties, and arbitrariness from the economic arena so that entrepreneurs and investors could be guaranteed fair treatment by government bureaucracies, legal systems, and financial organizations.[11]

But the belief has often been expressed that Mexican leaders somehow have lacked the vision, or the will, or the ambition, or the stamina, or the entrepreneurship to steer the economy toward successful development. For example, in 1964 economic historian Marvin D. Bernstein characterized Mexican economic actors as being too traditional, passive, and "hampered by fatalism and indifference. They are made cautious by the tradition of violence and arbitrary government, and they are hobbled by their nation's technological backwardness."[12] No doubt lethargic, selfish, and inept Mexicans have stood in the way of progress throughout the country's history, and many policy errors have been made by incompetent government officials. But stereotyping distorts reality. There is little hard evidence to sustain the proposition that the predominant tendency among those in power in Mexico over the last two centuries has been simply to coast along and to derive self-benefit while totally casting aside the national interest.

With respect to corruption, undeniably such behavior has been rampant in Mexico for a long time. But corruption has existed in many countries, rich and poor. In any case, the view that corruption is the cause of underdevelopment in Mexico or anywhere else is not sustainable.[13] Further, the fact that many Mexican officials have used their positions to enrich themselves does not mean that at the same time they have failed to pursue rational policies on behalf of the state and for the benefit of the country. Plenty of serious works document the continuous existence over time of sensible approaches to governing and policy-making among most Mexican officials.[14] Yes, Mexico has produced an abundance of greedy, venal, and unsavory politicians and bureaucrats. But the same can be said about the United States and many other countries.

Culture Is Not the Problem

The view expressed by Marvin D. Bernstein in the quote cited above reflects an explanation long propagated by many observers that places the blame for underdevelopment in the Spanish-speaking world squarely on culture. According to this perspective, "defects" associated with governing and with the conduct of economic affairs are rooted in the "backward" societies that have predominated in Mexico and other countries in Latin America. The region is said to abound with negative values and customs inherited from three centuries of Spanish colonialism. However, proponents of the cultural interpretation do not provide hard evidence to substantiate the theory. Rather, they make assumptions and draw inferences based on simplistic correlations and old prejudices that presume the superiority of European and North American cultures and institutions over those found in Latin America, Africa, and Asia. In reality, empirical data do not exist that convincingly substantiate the allegations made against the cultures of Third World peoples. Cultural explanations are speculative at best and ideologically and racially suspect at worst.

Much like foreign scholars who have been critical of Mexican culture while routinely ignoring or underplaying the effect of external factors and internal environmental and resource constraints on the national economy or on governmental structures, a number of Mexican writers have turned to theorizing about Mexico's national character to explain their country's shortcomings. In a recent book, scholar and former diplomat Jorge G. Castañeda discusses Mexico's shortcomings within a pseudo-psychological/cultural genre first popularized in the 1930s and 1940s by Samuel Ramos and Octavio Paz.[15] In highly imaginative essays on the Mexican "personality," philosopher Ramos, poet/writer Paz, and others have hypothesized that the violent Spanish conquest and subsequent 300-year colonial domination of Mexico left deep wounds in the hearts and minds of Indians and *mestizos* (racially mixed people; more specifically Spanish/Indian offspring). A culture of victimization supposedly emerged among the Mexican citizenry, exemplified by the wearing of invisible personality masks to conceal pain, distress, and feelings of inferiority. Unhealthy and self-destructive attitudes and behavioral patterns purportedly became central to the Mexican character, a development that damaged Mexico's prospects for success. Castañeda continues the tradition of attributing endless negative value orientations to Mexicans as he gives credence to highly suspect and controversial interpretations. He argues that, as a result of its history, Mexico continues to be held back by an alleged national obsession with past tragedies, a fear of foreigners, excessive individualism, an aversion to conflict and competition, and a tendency toward risk avoidance, corruption, and disrespect for the law. According to Castañeda, Mexico can achieve its potential economically and politically "only if its soul ceases to be a burden for its people, if its character and culture become instruments of change, and no longer of immobility."[16]

The ideas espoused in the works of Castañeda and his predecessors are interesting, but their validity is highly questionable for several reasons. First, there is the matter of nonexisting hard evidence to back up the claims, and such speculative interpretations ignore the foundational factors detailed in this book, which, in reality, are the genuine determinants of Mexico's uneven economic circumstances. Castañeda's elucidations rest on the extremely shaky supposition that negative personality traits are found throughout Mexico and among all social and economic groups. Not to mention, character studies confuse cause and effect, assuming that negative economic and politically related value orientations result in underdevelopment, when, in reality, it is underdevelopment itself that gives rise to economically related negative cultural traits; cultural norms shaped in the context of underdevelopment, after all, merely reflect the adaptation of humans to their surroundings. Cultural claims also disregard the fact that traits attributed exclusively to Mexicans are actually found throughout the world, especially among peoples who live in economic contexts that manifest dependence, colonialism, and social marginalization. Examples of such contexts abound in Latin America, Asia, Africa—and, alas, even in the United States itself, as the externally exploited and chronically depressed region of Appalachia illustrates.[17] The interpretations of Castañeda and others explicitly or implicitly assume that the prosperity of developed countries such as the United States rests on national characters that are imbued with wholly positive cultural traits and that, because of those supposedly prevailing wholesome values, the governments of those countries function efficiently and, as a matter of course, are necessarily structured to promote the common welfare. The fallacy of such assumptions is readily revealed in recent acute economic downturns in the United States brought about by the unethical behavior of Wall Street firms and the dysfunctional nature of the U.S. Congress, both obviously major national institutions.

Economists and other social scientists have as a rule rejected psychological and cultural interpretations of development and underdevelopment because of the liberties that culturalists have taken in making broad generalizations based on far-fetched hypotheses. If, as Castañeda argues, Mexicans are obsessed with tragic history, fear of foreigners, individualism, aversion to conflict and competition, avoidance of risk, corruption, and disrespect for the law, they are far from alone in thinking that way. Plenty of Americans, for example, have been equally obsessed with the lingering effects of sectional divisions caused by the Civil War of the 1860s; or have had irrational fears of socialism and communism; or have been haunted by the terrorist attacks of September 11, 2001; or have felt threatened by other religions, especially Islam; or have been frightened by immigrants, especially Mexicans; or have shaped their political ideology based on the myth that "rugged individualism" (versus collectivism) is at the root of the American "character." Arguably Americans have engaged in disrespect for the law and practiced massive corruption to an equal or even greater degree than Mexicans. Such deviant behavior has been widespread in Washington, D.C., on Wall Street, and most predominantly on Main Street, where for generations many have been involved in the unlawful sale, purchase, and consumption of illegal drugs and, more recently, in the ubiquitous surreptitious downloading of music and movies from the Internet.[18] And yet, as widespread as deviancy has been present in the United States, it must be emphasized that behavior such as disrespect for the law and everyday corruption has had little effect on the country's dynamic economic development. That is a lesson apparently lost on adherents of psychological or cultural explanations.

The negative economic-related values present in Mexican society are explained by the simple reality that Mexicans have long lived and functioned in a decidedly mixed economic context. The adverse side of that milieu, sustained predominantly by internal problems such as troublesome climatic conditions, difficult geography, less than ideal population dynamics, and disadvantageous external forces, is what initially spawned and has long sustained dependence and underdevelopment. Highly visible negative economic-related values (like corruption)—and their consequences—will diminish in Mexico if and when the country reaches a higher level of economic autonomy and achieves balanced industrial development by sector and by region. Such advances will make it possible to eradicate the vast wealth disparities that have long existed among the Mexican people, with the result that middle-class values will become predominant. In South Korea, for example, before advanced and autonomous industrialization took root, the people commonly used the expression "Korean time" to convey the idea that Koreans had a habit of not arriving on time for appointments. But as the structure of the country's economy changed and industrial development set in, the expression began to fade away. "With the pace of life far more organized and faster," writes Ha Joon Chang, "such behavior has almost disappeared, and with it the expression itself."[19]

I stress again that the causes of Mexico's underdevelopment are multifaceted. Careful examination of foundational factors and how these have made up the overall context and shaped economic activity in the country is mandatory. The common assumption that culture is the all-encompassing or deterministic factor in economic development is simply invalid. On the other hand, the functioning of the state and its institutions is obviously important and requires proper attention. But it must be kept in mind that, since government policy and institutional capacity are not genuine foundational factors (because they are derived from the other foundational building blocks), their role needs to be judiciously assessed. In sum, the task of finding convincing answers regarding development issues in Mexico, the United States, or anywhere else needs to start with examination of authentic foundational factors such as the environment, external relations, natural resources, and population dynamics. It is essential to look at the big picture over a long time span, and that is what this book seeks to do.

Part I consists of Chapter 1, which provides a historical sketch of the U.S. and Mexican economies, and Chapter 2, which addresses social inequalities present in each country. In Part II, Chapters 3 and 4 assess the extraordinary influence of the natural environment on Mexico, Chapter 5 looks at the major contribution of natural resources, and Chapter 6 examines the important role played by population dynamics. Chapters 7, 8, 9, and 10 constitute Part III. These chapters provide a systematic historical analysis of Mexico's relations with the outside world; foremost they consider the enormous impact that relations with the United States have had on Mexico. Discussion of the structure of production and governance and the implementation of public policy is incorporated into each of the chapters as needed. The emphasis throughout the book is on Mexico; information about the United States is included selectively and primarily for comparative purposes.

Notes

1 The term *developing* is used here to indicate that Mexico, like other developing countries, is growing and evolving in the direction of becoming "developed," or traveling on the pathway leading to an advanced state of industrialization and an overall high standard of living. While significantly poor, Mexico of course is much better off than many other developing countries. But in comparison to the "developed" countries of North America, Western Europe, and East Asia, Mexico is significantly behind economically. Throughout this book the terms *developing* and *underdeveloped* are used interchangeably. Admittedly these labels are inadequate not only because of the problem of determining precisely the level of development of any country but also because of the pejorative connotations associated with development-related taxonomy. Despite their limitations, these terms are used in this book because there is a well-established, general understanding among scholars and the general public as to their meaning. The category "Third World country" is used synonymously with "developing country." The term *Third World* was introduced during the Cold War to identify the poorer nation states that were not formally aligned with the "First World"—that is, the advanced capitalistic countries—or with the "Second World"—that is, the industrialized communist countries.
2 Kar (2012), 75.
3 Nominal GDP measures the market value of all goods and services produced in a country in a given year, while GDP-PPP, or real GDP per capita, measures the market value of all goods and services produced in a country in a given year divided by the country's population.
4 Examples of well-known traditional works in the modernization genre include Almond and Powell (1965); Apter (1965); Bauer (1972); Rostow (1966); and Weiner (1966).
5 Rostow (1966).
6 Dependency theory has a voluminous literature. See, for example, Galeano (1997); Baran (1957); Cardoso and Faletto (1979); Frank (1967); Stein and Stein (1970); and Evans (1979). For critiques of dependency theory, see Packenham (1992); and Haber (1997).
7 Criticisms of the neoliberal approach to development are found in Chang (2002, 2008); Klein (2007); and Jeter (2009).
8 On U.S. wealth inequality, see Garitty (2013).
9 Engerman and Sokoloff (2012), xxi, 2–3, 21, 50.

10 The role that U.S. annexationist threats against Mexico played in the formulation of policies favorable to foreign investors are discussed in Chapter 7.
11 Chang (2002), chapter 3.
12 Bernstein (1964), 277.
13 See Theobald (1990), especially 81–88, 113–114, 130–132.
14 This generalization can be confirmed by perusing the vast literature on the economic history of Mexico, both in Spanish and English.
15 Castañeda (2011); Ramos (1938); Paz (1950).
16 Castañeda (2011), 261.
17 See Martínez, "Notes on Appalachia" at www.routledge.com/martinez/mexico/appalachia.
18 Online piracy is a big problem in the United States. In 2011, Columbia University conducted a survey that revealed that 46 percent of adults admitted streaming, copying, or downloading movies, TV shows, or music without authorization. That percentage skyrocketed to 70 percent among eighteen- to twenty-nine-year-olds. Results of the study summarized in an AP article reprinted in the *El Paso Times*, February 19, 2012, 9A.
19 Chang (2008), 196.

PART I
THE MEXICO–U.S. DIVIDE

1
DIVERGENT PATHWAYS

Growing up I frequently heard my father express admiration for the economic power of the United States while he disparaged the Mexican economy. He was particularly incensed with the pitifully low wages paid in Mexico. He blamed the "thieves" who ran the government in Mexico City for the plight of Mexican workers. He was far from alone in that view. Eventually he gave up on his homeland, and that decision changed the fate of our family. From the early 1940s to the mid-1950s my father worked both as a *bracero* (legally contracted worker) and as an undocumented laborer in various parts of the United States, including the Southwest, the Northwest, and the Midwest. He toiled in agricultural fields and orchards, in mines, in railroad yards, and in factories. He was most impressed by the industrial might of Chicago, often referring to that city as a *maravilla*, or a "wonder." When the family immigrated legally to the United States in 1957, we headed to Chicago, where my father landed a factory job.

A high school freshman at the time, I got my first taste of work in a major U.S. metropolis as a newsboy selling the *Chicago Tribune* and the *Sun Times* in downtown Chicago. Like my father, I, too, was awestruck by the "windy city." I was dazzled by the subway and elevated trains, the hustle and bustle on State Street and on Michigan Avenue, the glitzy shops, the swanky theaters, and the gleaming skyscrapers. All that was so different from what I had known before in small towns in both Mexico and the United States, as well as what I had experienced in the rough and tumble, seedy, and largely destitute border city of Ciudad Juárez, where we had lived for about a decade. I understood what my father meant about the economic supremacy of the United States over Mexico. But, I wondered, why was the United States so far ahead of Mexico—and at the forefront of the world?

Many years later I would come to understand that the United States had achieved its global preeminence because it had been able to build a powerful economy that was rooted in many natural advantages that kept multiplying as a result of an expansionist foreign policy that greatly enlarged the country's land endowment. Reading history I learned that when we lived in Chicago in the 1950s, the United States was in the midst of an economic "golden age" because Americans had been able to establish hegemony over world trade following the unprecedented triumphs during World War II. The United States had the advantage of nonexistent or feeble competition from industrially crippled countries in Western Europe and in Asia that were busy rebuilding from the blanket destruction wrought by the war.

Research would reveal to me as well that no other country in the history of the world had ever come into possession of more economically valuable natural assets than the United States. As detailed in Chapters 3 through 6, these assets include a superb geographic location, moderate climates, adjacency to two major oceans and a gulf, first-rate coastlines and harbors, a splendid network of inland navigable waterways, an abundance of fertile lands, and a large storehouse of fuel and nonfuel minerals, as well as, in general, the presence of ecological and demographic conditions that have been ideally suited to support economic activity on a grand scale.[1] Such attributes have also provided the foundation for the building of strong structures of production in agriculture, industry, trade, and commerce. Additionally, the fruits harvested from these dynamic sectors have facilitated the construction and maintenance of strong government institutions.

Mexico's trajectory over the centuries has been different from that of its neighbor to the north. The foundational factors that have molded Mexico's economy have been far less advantageous than those of the United States (as the evidence presented in Chapters 3 through 6 will show). As a result, Mexico's productive prowess and trading capacity have been exceedingly modest by comparison. In 2012, Mexico's GDP amounted to only 7.5 percent of the U.S. GDP. The paramount problem for Mexico has been the persistence over time of two dual structures of production, one fairly well developed and the other predominantly underdeveloped. The developed portion of Mexico is readily evident in modern urban areas such as Mexico City, Monterrey, and Guadalajara, while the underdeveloped segment stands out in many poverty-stricken urban districts and in the severely marginalized countryside. The underdeveloped portion of the country has been excessively large and has spawned many problems. It has given rise to a weak governmental apparatus, deficient institutions, and small internal markets. It has also trapped massive numbers of people in grinding poverty. Although Mexico has made significant advances throughout its history, to this day it has not been able to transcend long-standing obstacles to the realization of balanced development. Balanced development means the attainment of reasonable levels of productivity in the major sectors of the economy accompanied by favorable geographic distribution of that productivity and equitable distribution of its fruits throughout the population. In addition to falling short of achieving balanced development, Mexico has also not been able to overcome the dependency that has long governed its interaction with the United States.

This chapter traces the evolution of the economies of the United States and Mexico with the intent of providing a comparative historical framework in which to place the workings of the foundational forces discussed in Parts II and III. The challenges that Mexico has confronted historically cannot be fully appreciated without understanding the favorable circumstances under which the United States has evolved. To the extent possible I have tried to minimize redundancies between the general overview presented here and the extensive treatment of such topics as foreign investment and trade found in Chapters 7, 8, and 9. But some overlap is unavoidable.

The Construction of the U.S. Economy

Let us begin with a brief summation of the general framework under which the U.S. economy has been shaped before moving on to surveying different historical periods. Within two generations of its independence, the United States possessed a vast, unexploited, richly endowed, and sparsely populated land with much greater economic potential than any other country. The acquisition of such a magnificent territory came at the expense of Native Americans, who were largely removed from their homelands, and Spain and Mexico, which ceded large portions of their domains under the duress of U.S. westward expansionism. Along with its extraordinary endowment, the United States had an exceptional location with direct ocean access to Europe and Asia. These favorable foundational circumstances placed Americans in an ideal position to first build a strong agricultural and trading economy, later a thriving industrial economy, and most recently a flourishing service and mass-information economy. Each of these economies has grown in volume and sophistication over time, yielding lofty productivity rates and a high standard of living for most of the U.S. population. No other country in the world has so successfully capitalized on the four major technological and industrial revolutions that swept the world after 1750 to the degree that the United States has been able to do. The first of these revolutions refers to innovations introduced in the 1760s in textile manufacturing, pottery making, mining, engineering, and the metals industry; the second occurred in the early nineteenth century with advances in the making of iron products and the improvement and utilization of steam power on a large scale, especially in factories and transportation; the third took place in the late nineteenth century and early twentieth century with the development of electricity, assembly-line manufacturing, the internal combustion engine, and radio communication; and the fourth began in the mid- and latter twentieth century with multiple breakthrough inventions, including rockets, jet engines, nuclear power, super highways, jumbo ocean ships, mega seaports, shipping containers, robotics, television, computers, and space-age communication technologies. Understanding the underlying reasons for the great success of the United States in all these areas requires consideration of the overall context in which the country has evolved at each stage in its history, and especially how the natural environment has been so well suited to accommodate the different waves of technological innovations.

England's Thirteen Colonies, 1607–1783: Predominance of Agriculture

The colonial United States, otherwise known as the thirteen colonies, comprised an area of about 360,000 square miles and had a population of nearly 3 million in 1780 on the eve of independence from England. At that time Europeans constituted four-fifths and Africans one-fifth of that population. Historian Gary B. Nash estimates the Native American population at 100,000 or less.[2]

The dominant English immigrants who settled the coastal areas from New Hampshire to Georgia overwhelmingly relied on the magnificence of their surroundings for their livelihood. They were fortunate to have a generally temperate climate largely free of epidemic diseases, sufficient good soil that yielded a wide variety of crops, bountiful timberlands that provided wood for construction and for energy, many streams that supplied water power for mills, many navigable rivers that greatly aided inland transport, excellent harbors that facilitated external trade, and easy access to the generous food resources of the sea. Industry, based largely on household manufacture tied to the processing of raw materials, made up a small but significant part of the U.S. colonial economy. Elemental manufacturing, or "fabrication," revolved around fisheries, textile mills, iron workshops, and glass making. Shipbuilding stood on a higher plane, constituting a bustling and highly profitable activity owing to great advantages that the English colonists enjoyed over competitors in Europe. With timberlands supplying the essential raw material and skilled immigrant artisans contributing the labor to build the wooden sailing ships then in high demand domestically and abroad, shipyards proliferated on the New England coast and on the Delaware River. While the British Crown restrained manufacturing in the thirteen colonies through mercantilist policies, notoriously lax enforcement provided colonists with sufficient latitude to establish incipient manufacturing and to lay the foundation for more advanced industrial development in later years. The colonists also benefited from low taxation on the part of the mother country and from the ability to conduct relatively unhindered surreptitious external trade, including the importation of prohibited technology.

The commercial sector, although employing relatively few people, became increasingly important as the urban population grew and as merchants accumulated wealth and influence. Baltimore, Philadelphia, New York City, Boston, Charleston, and Newport, all seaports with easy access to productive hinterlands, had the largest concentration of city folk. Philadelphia, with a population of

40,000 in 1775, had the distinction of being the largest city and a leader in the basic manufacturing and commerce of the period. In the sphere of foreign trade, these and other urban centers exported ships and agricultural products directly to England and imported manufactures; additionally, colonists supplied foodstuffs and other products to the English West Indies, receiving in return slaves, gold, and agricultural goods.

In 1776, at the time of the Declaration of Independence, the colonies had a "truly advanced" economy that compared favorably with the other leading countries of the period.[3] The progress already achieved set the stage for the building of an even larger and more prosperous economy once colonists won their freedom from British rule.

From Independence to 1860: Industrialization Takes Root

After the war of independence was over in 1783, the new United States of America took advantage of its many domestic assets and timely international opportunities, settling into a pattern of growth that, in a matter of decades, would bring world economic preeminence. The period 1793 to 1807 in particular precipitated great advances fueled by trade in commodities and services provided to foreigners. Americans capitalized on the economic vacuum created by England and France, who were consumed in protracted hostilities for two decades. U.S. ships carried food and other products from tropical areas to Europe and delivered manufactures to many countries. Between 1790 and 1860 the U.S. population rose from 4 million to 31.5 million, and in the four decades from 1820 to 1860 the GDP more than quintupled. By 1840 the rapidly growing U.S. economy was only slightly smaller than the economies of England and France.

Three general developments propelled the extraordinary economic transformation of the United States: First, African slaves provided much of the hard labor required in the large plantation-based economy in the South, an economy that strongly complemented the dynamic commercial and industrial activities in the North. Second, Americans extended the nation's territorial domain through aggressive diplomacy and unabashed military expansionism, pushing the borders to the Gulf of Mexico and the Pacific Ocean. The acquisition of new territories, mostly former possessions of Spain and Mexico, made available massive amounts of fertile land and other valuable resources. Third, because of its prodigious and exceedingly favorable landscape, the United States turned out to be ideally suited to derive great benefits from breakthrough technological inventions and industrial innovations, including improvements in iron production, the mechanization of cloth making, advances in machine work and, probably most importantly, the emergence of the modern steam engine. The latter was used to propel machines, ships, and trains. Steamships encouraged development and expansion of ports located in exceptionally well-situated ocean harbors, which in turn facilitated trade across the Atlantic and Pacific Oceans, in the Gulf of Mexico, and in the

Caribbean Sea. Internally, steamships converted the country's great lakes and large rivers into major shipping corridors and stimulated the building of an extensive network of canals to supplement river and lake transportation. Beyond the waterways, by 1860 the favorable topography, including vast flatlands and mountain ranges with natural passes, allowed for the building of 30,000 miles of railways and a notable expansion of wagon and stagecoach roads in practically all directions. The transportation innovations made it much easier, cheaper, and faster to ship commodities to and from resource-rich areas in the interior of the country, greatly boosting national productivity.[4]

These auspicious conditions spawned a rapid expansion of the domestic market and, with the ongoing international demand for cotton and other raw materials, which the United States could produce in abundance, a rise in foreign trade as well. Annual averages in total foreign trade in the late 1850s surpassed more than three times those of the late 1810s. Although at mid-century the United States was still an exporter of agricultural products and an importer of finished goods, the activity that foreign commerce generated greatly boosted national productivity. Moreover, an extant balance of trade problem was made up with gold from the rich California deposits that fell under U.S. control after the conquest of Mexico's northern frontier, and from capital that flowed in from Europe in the form of investments and loans.

As domestic industrialization gained momentum, the U.S. government responded in a protectionist fashion by imposing high tariffs. Between 1790 and the mid-1820s, duties as a percentage of total imports rose gradually from 10 percent to almost 50 percent. Then the "Tariff of Abominations" in 1828 applied a whopping 62 percent to dutiable imports. However, that exorbitant rate had a very short life and duties dropped into the 40-plus percent range. In the next three decades the downward trend of tariffs on dutiable imports continued, winding up in the 20 percent range by 1860.[5] Such high but not unduly excessive tariffs proved sufficient to protect the fledgling domestic manufacturing sector largely concentrated in the Northeast. Southerners who lived off cotton and tobacco exports consistently opposed high tariffs because the duties effectively made European products artificially more expensive. Apart from the divisive issue of slavery, Southern resentment over the tariffs became an important contributor to the conflict between North and South that led to the U.S. Civil War in the 1860s.

From the Civil War to 1920: Acceleration of Industrialization

In the six decades from 1860 to the post–World War I period, the United States made another giant leap, transforming itself from a largely agricultural to a predominantly industrial society. Americans laid the foundation for the rise of the modern, mass-consumption urban economy that would define the country throughout the twentieth century. On average real national income grew at the remarkable annual rate of 4 percent between 1859 and 1919, while real GNP growth also averaged 4 percent between 1865 and 1908.[6] At the beginning of the period, the Civil War (1861–1865) threatened to split the republic into two separate countries and end the dream of national greatness. But unity prevailed and, although disruptive, the years of internal strife only slowed an economy clearly on an upward trajectory. While the agricultural South suffered serious setbacks during the fighting, the industrial and commercial North actually expanded its production and prospered greatly. For a generation after the Civil War the New England and Middle Atlantic states continued their industrial and commercial dominance, but the South was still able to compete in such manufacturing sectors as textiles, tobacco, lumber, chemicals, and food processing. Midwesterners in particular enjoyed favorable conditions that would in time allow them to build a powerful regional economy based both on agriculture and industry. In the more sparsely settled and arid western states, precious metal mining and other extractive industries predominated for decades. In the early twentieth century the building of dams and irrigation canals made it possible for large-scale commercial agriculture to take root in California and other areas of the Southwest, while food processing and miscellaneous light manufacturing activities sprouted in well-placed western cities. By the late 1910s, the United States had a large, dynamic, well-integrated economy and an extensive common market, with the different sections of the country well connected to one another and strongly complementing each other. The country had reached the status of an advanced, industrialized, and urbanized society, boasting the largest economy in the world.

What specific factors drove the impressive advances of the latter nineteenth century and the early twentieth century? Above all, as explained in detail in Part II, the United States was the best geographically positioned and best endowed country in the world to be able to ride the highest crests of the opportunity waves created by the expanding global economy and the unprecedented world decline in shipping rates. The drop in transport costs resulted from improvements in sailing ships, the advent and quick spread of steamboats, and the timely arrival and swift proliferation of the railroads. Americans had the means to both initiate and capitalize on new inventions, allowing the country to constantly enlarge its productive capacity. After the Civil War five developments in particular propelled the country forward: the extension of the railroad network to the Pacific Coast, greater exploitation of oil for energy and iron ore for making steel, innovations in production technology, the widespread economic use of electricity, and the utilization of immigrant labor on a massive scale.

With a thriving economy and the world correctly perceiving the country as the "land of opportunity," the United States attracted unprecedented numbers of immigrant entrepreneurs, farmers, and workers, predominantly from Europe but also from China, Japan, and Mexico. Between 1865 and 1920, nearly 30 million immigrants entered the United States, with over 80 percent arriving after 1880. Without the human power supplied by the immigrants to exploit the vast natural riches of the country, the U.S. economy would not have grown as spectacularly as it did during the period under discussion.

Expansion of international trade, which was driven by major transportation and communication innovations, also provided a significant boost for the U.S. economy. The acquisition of additional territories during the 1890s (Hawaii, the Philippines, Puerto Rico) gave the United States greater access to the world's natural resources and opened up new markets. Exports nearly always exceeded imports after 1875, giving the United States a perennial favorable balance of payments. Trade with Europe continued at a high level, but a gradual decline in both exports and imports from that part of the world took place after 1880, especially during the World War I period. In its trade with non-European countries, the United States increasingly supplied manufactured and semimanufactured goods to Third World countries in exchange for tropical foods and raw materials such as tin, nickel, copper, and rubber—the latter products were necessary to sustain the rapidly growing U.S. industrial sector. For most of the period, highly protectionist tariffs on dutiable imports averaging in the 40 to 50 plus percent range shielded domestic manufacturing. The Democratic-controlled government lowered duties to the 25 percent range from 1913 until the end of World War I, but afterwards the Republicans reimposed high tariffs again.[7]

The U.S. Economy since 1920: Undisputed World Supremacy

By 1920 the United States had solidified its position as the leading economic power in the world. Remarkably, the country has maintained the top spot since that time, boasting a GDP that in the early 2010s that was twice as large as that of China, the nearest competitor, over 2.5 times larger than Japan's, and over 4.5 times larger than Germany's, the third and fourth ranking economies. Historically, between 1920 and 2000, the GDP of the United States grew from 593 billion U.S. dollars to almost 8 trillion U.S. dollars (measured in 1990 U.S. dollars), reflecting an overall positive climate that facilitated constant expansion over those eight decades.[8] Episodes such as the Great Depression of the 1930s and periodic recessions after World War II interrupted growth, yet such downturns represented only temporary slowdowns for the mighty U.S. economy.

Manufacturing, driven by a robust domestic market and a strong foreign export sector, predominated over all other activities, accounting for approximately 30 percent of the national income between the late 1920s and 1970. New sectors that had an increasing significance nationally include motorized vehicles, aircraft, and the military. To be sure, industry and other sectors of the economy suffered decline during the Great Depression, but with the powerful impulse provided by World War II, manufacturing output soared in the 1950s and 1960s, along with mining activity, wholesale and retail trade, services, and the government sector.

As the world witnessed another industrial revolution in the second half of the twentieth century, the United States, with its vast manufacturing infrastructure, high level of urbanization, and superb research and development capabilities, was the country best equipped to lead the world in technological innovation. And, once again, Americans would be the primary beneficiaries of technology's fruits. Possessing the largest productive capacity, the greatest number of giant corporations, the best and most numerous advanced educational institutions, and a powerful, lavishly funded military-industrial complex constantly in pursuit of new technologies, the United States blazed new trails in scientific discoveries that yielded enormous economic benefits. A generously funded and highly productive research and development program at the service of the military-industrial complex carried over into the mainstream economy. Scientific breakthroughs in weaponry and space exploration, for example, found practical applications in the manufacture of many consumer products, as did the discoveries of scientists employed by corporations and universities. Petrochemicals are a case in point. An array of new products has come out of that industry, including chemicals, plastics, and synthetic rubber and fibers. Machines of all kinds and all sizes were made more powerful, more sophisticated, and more productive. Personal computers, the Internet, cell phones, high-definition televisions, and many other dazzling electronic gadgets dramatically symbolize the great technological breakthroughs of the last generation. And while overseas labor did much of the work required to assemble many of the products invented since the mid-twentieth century, the United States did not relinquish control of design and production decisions. Moreover, American multinational corporations benefited greatly from larger profit margins derived from the offshore location of many factories.

In the transportation sector, a new wave of innovations allowed the U.S. economy to keep growing at a healthy pace. Mass production of automobiles, trucks, and buses has continued since the 1920s. These forms of transportation required surfaced roads and highways, and the U.S. government responded with hefty subsidies to underwrite both regional road networks and the all-important national interstate highway system. Airplanes, which made their first appearance in the early 1900s, evolved into a major and indispensable mode of transportation by the second half of the twentieth century. Together, these various forms of transportation intensified the integration of practically every region and corner of the country with the national economy.

In the sphere of foreign trade, the staunch protectionism of the nineteenth century continued into the 1930s, with the U.S. levy on dutiable imports averaging around 60 percent at the height of the Great Depression. But, as the crisis deepened, protectionism came under heavy scrutiny. Many blamed high tariffs as a prime contributor to the worldwide economic collapse. The criticism leveled at protectionism proved persuasive and, led by the United States, the western democracies moved toward liberalized trade and reduced their tariffs. The stage was set for U.S. domination of the global economy for the next generation.

The timing for opening up trade globally proved favorable to Americans because after World War II the U.S. economy remained unscathed while competitors in Europe and Asia lay in ruins. Convinced that recovery of global commerce had to occur in war-torn allied countries like England and France and in vanquished enemy nations like Japan and Germany, the United States took the lead in promoting globalization via the enactment of the General Agreement on Tariffs and Trade and later through the creation of the World Trade Organization. Lowering tariffs seemed the obvious way to revive international commerce in the capitalist world. But, in addition to tariff reductions, global trade was further enhanced through major improvements in communication and transportation and innovations in production methods. The combined effect of such advancements significantly reduced costs in manufacturing and in shipping via land and water.

Eventually the rise in global trade led to greater competition among nations. Once they recovered from the devastation of World War II, a number of European and Asian countries emerged as serious competitors to the United States, claiming larger shares of trade involving many manufactured products. Gradually the United States lost its former world dominance in the export of steel, technology, machinery, automobiles, electronic products, furniture, and textiles, with the result that, by the 1970s formerly powerful domestic industries began to experience decline. Simultaneously underdeveloped and developing countries took advantage of new opportunities to utilize their cheap labor reserves, attracting assembly industries from the United States and other developed countries.

These changes in the world economic order caused much concern in the United States, prompting many of its citizens to demand a return to greater protectionism as the means to make up lost ground in manufacturing and to reverse trade imbalances that developed with countries like Japan and China. The resurgence in protectionist sentiment is reflected in trade legislation passed in the U.S. Congress after 1970. Responding to chronic protests by domestic farmers, industrialists, and labor unions regarding the rising imports from abroad, policy makers found new ways of shielding the U.S. economy. U.S. presidents acquired new powers to lower imports from countries that conducted unfair trade against the United States. Such authority included adjusting tariffs and imposing nontariff barriers like quotas. At the same time, in an effort to assist poor countries, the United States joined with other advanced nations to reduce or even eliminate tariffs on select imports from the developing world. But protectionism remained alive in the United States, as nontariff restrictions (e.g., quotas, quality controls, etc.) on many products, especially agricultural goods, accompanied the reduction of duties on Third World imports. Protectionist policies directed at both rich and poor nations by the United States created much international friction in the 1980s and 1990s.

Foreign trade became increasingly politicized in the United States at century's end. The 1994 North American Free Trade Agreement (NAFTA) with Canada and Mexico came under particularly heavy fire from U.S. workers who endured job losses resulting from factory closures or relocation abroad, from industries and businesses that struggled to compete with cheap imports, and from politicians who advocated on behalf of domestic producers. In reality, U.S. job losses to other countries and the influx of cheap imports began decades before the enactment of NAFTA, and this agreement did not, contrary to what its name suggests, actually mandate complete free trade because the document included many restrictions. Multinational corporations based in the United States of course have had a far more positive view of the globalization trends that NAFTA represents because they have benefited greatly from the freedom to move capital and manufacturing activities abroad and to outsource many operations to countries with low labor costs.

In sum, after 1980 the United States lost its previously held position as the overwhelmingly dominant manufacturing and trading country in the world as other nations greatly expanded their economies and increased their exports. Yet the United States retained the status of preeminent economic superpower. It did not relinquish the prerogative of imposing greater trade restrictions should it wish to regain some of its previous hegemony. Americans continue to maintain formidable leverage to shape or influence the existing world trade system to gain greater advantage. If desirable or necessary, the United States without much difficulty can bring industries now operating in offshore locations back to U.S. soil. The truth is that, within the context of the international economic system, the United States still has the largest economy and the largest consumer market in the world, and these realities permit Americans to continue to drive hard bargains with other countries from a position of great strength, rather than a position of weakness.

The Mexican Economy

Now when we cross the U.S. southern border and visualize the large physical space that lies between the Rio Grande and Guatemala—the territory known as Mexico—we need to shift our frame of mind to a very different reality. Here is a land acutely dissimilar from the United States and so internally diverse that some have imagined it as not one country, but many countries, or "many Mexicos." Mountain ranges, deserts, and jungles break up the terrain, while difficult arid and wet climates parch some landscapes and deluge others. Mexico can be divided into distinct regions. A basic national problem is that the constraints that block progress in many of those regions has far outnumbered those that facilitate it. Mexico's economy has performed at a lower level than desired largely because there exist natural disadvantages that have undermined development efforts. Considering that Mexico's land mass is smaller than that of the United States, its geography much more challenging, its resources less varied and more limited, its coastal areas physically narrower and less healthy, its good harbors fewer in number and their corresponding hinterlands less fecund, and its favorable urban/industrial and rural/agricultural spaces more scarce and more scattered, it is no surprise that Mexico would encounter greater obstacles in achieving economic development than its northern neighbor.

In addition to having a difficult internal geography, Mexico's drive toward economic progress has as well been frustrated by unfavorable international forces. In the past, Mexicans were subjected to military invasions and political interventions by other countries. Mexico's most significant historical event was the massive loss of prime land and prime natural resources to the United States in 1848 as a result of U.S. expansionism. Those losses severely curtailed Mexico's prospects for becoming an advanced industrial country. Moreover, the redrawn international border, which extended nearly 2,000 miles over easily traversed flat terrain, would facilitate both the legal as well as illegal influx of massive amounts of U.S. manufactured goods into Mexico. Mexico's markets could also be easily penetrated via seaports on both gulfs and the Pacific. Above all, U.S. corporations would encounter little difficulty in penetrating the Mexican economy directly or through alliances with Mexican elites; thus as time passed, foreigners established hegemony over key sectors of the means of production in Mexico. Over generations, that situation has negatively affected the development of Mexico's domestic industries.

Mexico's foreign trade history needs to be seen through the lens of a dependent economy. Reflecting the standard pattern in the underdeveloped world, Mexico has, for most of its history, been predominantly an exporter of crops and minerals and an importer of manufactured products. It is only since the 1980s that manufactured goods have taken over Mexico's exports. But the vast majority of those manufactures rely on low-cost assembly labor, rather than high-cost skilled labor. Within the international community, Mexico has been a "trade-rules follower," rather than a "trade-rules maker." And, significantly, Mexico's trade has been heavily integrated with the U.S. economy, yielding a highly unequal partnership in which Mexico has been the subordinate party.

Despite such inherent disadvantages, however, Mexico is far from being a country of gloom and doom. The Mexican landscape is endowed with significant positive attributes. Mexico has a number of favorable physical spaces that have long sustained large populations and high productivity. Mexico is also better endowed with good land and valuable raw materials than many other nation-states, and those resources have allowed Mexicans to build a large economy. In foreign trade, the global economic climate has worked decidedly in favor of Mexico at various times in history. Proximity and access to U.S. markets, which on the one hand have stifled Mexican industry and commerce, have, on the other hand, been the biggest asset for Mexico's foreign trade.

The Colonial Economy of New Spain: Subservience and Loss of Natural Wealth

For three centuries, from 1521 to 1821, the economy of New Spain, or colonial Mexico, evolved within the framework of the mercantilistic system imposed by

Spain. In practice mercantilism for New Spain meant that, like other Latin American colonies governed and managed from Madrid, Mexico existed primarily to supply wealth to the mother country. Agricultural products and precious metals made up most of the riches extracted from New Spain under the Spanish system of regulation in the New World. With these regulations, Spain exercised control over what could or could not be produced in New Spain and with whom external trade could or could not be conducted. However, to forestall dissent, the Spanish Crown generally administered its colonies using flexibility and pragmatism.

Agriculture and stock-raising constituted the most important sectors of New Spain's economy, surpassing mining production in total value. Of course, among the exports that went to Spain, silver and gold were more valuable than agricultural products, which were mostly consumed in New Spain itself. Major crops grown in Mexico with the blessing of the Spaniards included corn, cotton, chocolate, silk, vanilla, tobacco, indigo, and cochineal. But such commodities as olive oil and wine could not be produced because they competed with exports from the mother country. At one point, the Spanish Crown ordered that cacao production be shifted from New Spain to Venezuela for the purpose of strengthening the latter colony; similarly the mother country on various occasions transferred tobacco growing out of Mexico to other places in the empire.[9]

It is impossible to know the precise structure of economic activity in New Spain toward the end of the colonial period. Nevertheless, using official contemporary data, Mexican historian Fernando Rosenzweig Hernández has calculated that manufacturing constituted perhaps 29 percent of the value of total production, with agriculture and mining making up 55 and 15 percent respectively.[10] Industrial production per capita in Mexico ranked below the levels in Europe but compared well to other peripheral areas in Latin America and Asia. Cotton textile manufacturing, carried on in *obrajes*, or factories, accounted for well over half of all industrial activity in 1800–1801; at the time some 12,000 looms provided jobs for about 90,000 workers.[11] Informal, hard-to-quantify industrial work geared to satisfying the basic needs of the population was commonplace. Cottage activities emphasized the construction of homes, public structures, and churches; the building and maintenance of travel conveyances like stagecoaches, wagons, and wheel carts; and the making of household items, including furniture, clothing, and shoes.

Like colonial masters everywhere, the Spaniards exploited indigenous workers with impunity, using various forms of forced, captive, and low-paid voluntary labor for agricultural, mining, and industrial production, as well as for domestic work. The blatant abuse of Indians eventually prompted the Spanish Crown to do away with oppressive institutions like *encomiendas* and *repartimientos*.[12] But wage exploitation continued in the haciendas, ranchos, obrajes, government organizations, and private homes. Even the Catholic Church took advantage of the indigenous people, extracting unpaid or poorly remunerated labor for the construction of religious and administrative buildings and the tending of fields. African slaves were also utilized in agriculture, mining, and textile mills, as well as in households, where they worked in various domestic roles. By way of comparison, in the territory that made up the thirteen colonies, the British found few Indians willing to supply needed agricultural labor, especially in the plantation economy of the South, where African slaves became the backbone of the workforce.

For most of the colonial period Spain restricted trade in and out of New Spain to only the mother country, with Veracruz and Acapulco serving as the only official ports. Such control of commerce with the outside world limited the ability of New Spain to develop its commercial and industrial sectors and inhibited the possibility of getting on the path toward self-sustaining development. To the Spanish overlords of course that did not matter. From their perspective the significance of the colony lay in the riches it could supply to the mother country.

New Spain's exalted standing as a treasure trove for Spain became more pronounced toward the end of the eighteenth century, when commercial activity greatly increased following trade reforms enacted by Madrid. With liberalization of overseas shipping, including the abolition of the outmoded yearly fleet system, Veracruz became a major trade center, handling hundreds of ships that carried goods exchanged within the Spanish empire. The value of exports, consisting largely of precious metals, far surpassed the value of imports, which were dominated by textiles. The increased economic activity enhanced New Spain's standing within the Spanish empire and drew praise from European visitors who saw great potential for Mexico's future. These travelers focused their attention on the wealth extracted from silver and gold mines, the agricultural output in the fertile central highlands, and the affluence of elites in New Spain's leading urban centers, Mexico City, Guanajuato, and Puebla. Of course, mining, the economy's top performer, yielded riches largely for the few and had minimal links to local industry and commerce. While agriculture thrived in central Mexico, elsewhere farmers confronted serious land and water problems due to scarce rainfall and difficult geography. And Mexico City, Guanajuato, and Puebla, situated in the most climatically attractive and fertile space in New Spain, were hardly representative of cities, towns, and villages located in other much less favorable regions.

The riches of New Spain that were produced by the resource-dependent economy mostly benefitted the Spanish Crown, the Catholic Church, and the elite private sectors both in Mexico and Spain. The indigenous and mestizo masses, which made up about 90 percent of the population, saw little of the wealth trickle down to them. Circumstances for the masses actually deteriorated after 1800 as New Spain experienced serious setbacks. These include famines, crop failures, rising costs for the mining industry, collapse of textile prices caused by increasing foreign competition, and excessive financial burdens imposed on the colony. Such problems created widespread discontent and contributed to the outbreak of the 1810 insurrection against Spanish rule. When Father Miguel Hidalgo y Costilla gave the cry for independence on September 16, 1810, his followers denounced the exploitation of New Spain by the mother country. They bemoaned the fact that massive wealth had flowed to Spain, and that Mexico's internal development had been neglected by the colonial masters.

1810–1876: Crippling Wars, Chronic Instability, and Land Loss

A decade of warfare during the struggle for independence in the 1810s devastated New Spain. The fighting took place in the most productive areas and along the major commercial corridors, affecting all sectors of the economy. The output of silver and the volume of foreign trade experienced great declines.[13] Manufacturing as a whole plunged as the areas hardest hit by the violence were those cities and towns where textile factories were concentrated. By 1812 only four looms operated in Queretaro, compared to 291 ten years earlier. In 1818 some 12,000 textile workers had no jobs. On the eve of independence imports had practically destroyed Guadalajara's cotton textile industry.[14] Agricultural and mining production plummeted as farmers abandoned their fields and mines were left unattended. Internal commerce dwindled as merchants closed their establishments, and external trade practically ceased as fighting interrupted normal operations in the coastal ports. The chaos and misery that prevailed in many cities forced tens of thousands into a struggle for survival. Capital flight made matters worse when wealthy Spaniards, fearing persecution, abandoned Mexico in droves. A British diplomat speculated that the capital taken out of Mexico by fleeing Europeans amounted to 140 million pesos.[15] Thus, when the insurrection stopped and freedom from Spanish subjugation was achieved in 1821, a sobering reality quickly became apparent: making Mexico actually work like a real country would be extremely difficult.

The Chaotic New Republic

Immediately following independence, various political forces fiercely competed for power and for the right to dictate the course to be followed in constructing the new state. Ultra conservatives who favored a monarchical form of government won the initial round with the crowning of Agustín de Iturbide as Mexico's "emperor." But Iturbide was ousted after only ten months in office. Mexico then became a republic. Yet divisions persisted. Some advocated for a strong central government with weak provinces while others preferred a federalist system with strong provinces. In addition, the power of the Catholic Church in the political arena and in Mexican society in general became a deeply divisive issue, as conservatives sought to maintain Church privileges and liberals endeavored to end them. Such polarizing political and religious philosophies triggered endless conflicts and recurring changes of government, and led to the enactment of several constitutions.[16]

Mexico's population, numbering slightly above 6 million at the time of independence, was deeply fragmented by race, ethnicity, class, and physical dispersal.

Spanish-born and Mexican-born whites comprised less than 1 percent of the population, yet they generally ran the country, owned the means of production, and constituted the "active citizenry." While some Euro-mestizos (18 percent of the population), some Indo-mestizos (12 percent), and some Afro-mestizos (10 percent) could also be found at the top of the social pyramid and among the decision-makers, for the most part these three cohorts ranked far below whites in status and power. Indians, the largest component of the population (60 percent), occupied the bottom social and economic rung and generally lived separate lives from the other sectors of society.[17] Institutionalized ethnic discrimination and acute geographic separation contributed significantly to the segregation of the indigenous population. Diverse tribes and bands, many living in remote mountain areas, jungles, and deserts, practiced different cultures and spoke hundreds of different languages and dialects, making it exceedingly difficult for them to be part of the mainstream Spanish-speaking population.

As if the depressed economy and the extant political and social divisions were not unsettling enough, the new republic had to fight a number of wars against powerful countries that coveted all or parts of Mexico's territory. Mexicans repeatedly had to use scarce resources to defend themselves and had to constantly divert their energies away from the work required to build the new society. Between 1822 and 1855 military costs accounted for almost half of the federal government's expenditures.[18] Each war depleted the national treasury, increased the debt, and inflicted more damage on the economy.

Many U.S. historians who have written about the frenzied and confusing first fifty years following Mexico's independence have underestimated the unfavorable circumstances that Mexico faced at the time. Often it is insinuated that Mexicans lacked the will or competence to govern effectively and to do the things necessary to build the economy and stimulate progress. Some writers contrast Mexico's political volatility and economic despair during those years with the stability and prosperity experienced by the United States. The assumption is made that the two countries encountered more or less the same political challenges and that their economies functioned in comparably level playing fields. In reality the United States evolved under generally favorable conditions from its independence to the middle of the nineteenth century, and Mexico's situation was just the opposite. Economic progress came slowly to Mexico not because of any inherent inability on the part of Mexicans to advance, but because of the strong headwinds that the new country encountered.

The Struggle to Industrialize

Mexicans realized early on that the road to industrialization would be difficult in their country because of an extant scarcity of capital, shortages of key raw materials, high production costs linked to difficult internal geography, and the small domestic market. The steady influx of foreign manufacturers, however, constituted the greatest challenge. In order to allow Mexican infant industries to blossom, the government instituted high tariffs and bans on the importation of specific foreign products. Yet those policies yielded far from satisfactory results. Domestic manufacturing would consistently lag well behind manufacturing in the advanced countries, largely because of the powerful U.S. economy, whose higher-quality and lower-cost products flooded Mexico via both legal and illicit channels. Contraband would thrive along the porous 2,000 mile northern border and along the unprotected lengthy coastlines on both Gulfs and the Pacific. In short, whether Mexico practiced open or closed trade, foreign products found their way to the Mexican consumer market, thereby undermining local industries.

To initiate modern industrialization, Mexico also needed to import expensive technology from Europe and it had to involve the state directly in the economy. The capacity to import capital goods, however, depended on the health of the export sector and, unhappily, in that respect Mexico did not perform well for decades following independence. Numbers tell the story. While the value of exports stood at 163 million pesos in the 1800s, it dropped to 84 million in the 1810s and 77 million in the 1820s; thereafter it rose to 102 million and 115 million in the 1830s and 1840s respectively, still significantly below the level of the 1800s. Similarly, the value of imports declined from 304 million pesos in the 1800s to 182 million in the 1840s.[19]

Pro-industry leaders such as Lucas Alamán advocated the use of public resources to supply capital to manufacturers, provide access to modern machinery, and stimulate technical education. But resistance to such policies surfaced among Mexican and British merchants who profited from the importation of foreign consumer goods. They wished to limit domestic manufacturing. Regardless of internal opposition to state promotion of industry, the government-run development bank, known as the Banco de Avio, channeled loans to various industries, especially textile factories located in Mexico City and the surrounding region beginning in 1830. The bank employed foreign technical consultants and placed the emphasis on mechanization, making available over a million pesos in loans intended for the importation of machinery and for investments to improve automated production. Its accomplishments during its twelve-year life span, though modest, nonetheless underlined the importance that national officials assigned to industrial development. It ceased to function, however, in 1842 after president Antonio López de Santa Anna bowed to the desires of special interests tied to the import trade sector. Santa Anna claimed that funds for the bank were no longer available. Still, pro–industry government activity continued through the Dirección General de Industria (DGI). The DGI advocated for the maintenance of a protectionist regime. By the 1840s, the tariff rate on all imports was set at 45 percent, which represented a substantial rise from the 25 percent rate established by Mexico's first tariff law in 1825.[20] The DGI also worked to fight contraband, encouraged the formation of industrial boards at the state level, gathered information on industrial advances in other countries, and published statistical industrial data.

The attention given manufacturing by the government yielded positive results. Dozens of new textile factories that utilized imported modern machinery entered production in the late 1830s and early 1840s, and the output of manta, cloth, and broadcloth increased significantly. Traditional textile centers in the heart of Mexico such as in Queretaro, Puebla, and Guadalajara, as well as peripheral areas in the north and the south, all experienced recovery from the economic downturn that had started in the early 1800s. Mexicans made use of steam engine technology where possible, and advances in mechanized production also took place in the manufacture of such products as iron, porcelain, brick, paper, glass, and chemicals.[21] But the drive toward industrialization slowed down at various points between the late 1840s and late 1860s, during which time Mexico endured a military invasion by the United States, a major civil war, and several years of occupation by French forces. But by the late 1870s stability had returned, and production levels hit new highs in the textile industry, the country's major manufacturing sector. In 1877–1878 nearly 100 textile factories were operating throughout Mexico. Over 258,000 mechanical spindles and more than 9,200 power looms produced greater quantities of cloth than ever before. The amount of raw cotton consumed domestically nearly doubled between 1854 and 1877–1878.[22]

Despite the progress, Mexico lagged far behind the United States and European countries in overall industrial production but performed quite well in comparison to other countries in the poor periphery of Africa, Asia, and Latin America. Impeding the development of a large manufacturing sector was the limited internal demand for finished goods. Several reasons account for this miniscule consumer market. To begin with, perhaps 90 percent of the national population was impoverished and could not afford manufactured goods. Mexicans were also widely scattered, ranging from the highlands and jungles of southern Mexico to the distant desert provinces of the far northern frontier, and the country lacked a transport network capable of effectively tying the many regions together; Mexico did not have navigable rivers to speak of, and its mountainous topography made it very difficult and expensive to build and maintain surfaced roads and railways. The natural obstacles and distances that separated the nation's units of production from centers of consumption kept the costs of conducting internal commerce exceedingly high. Shipping goods from production points like haciendas, farms, or mines to urban markets was challenging because of primitive and expensive transport conveyances that had to traverse uneven and rough terrain on chronically impaired roads, where the risk of banditry was ever-present. By contrast, England and the United States were both well-endowed with navigable rivers and good topography that allowed for the building of a dense network of canals, roads, and railways. Early on, both of these countries developed highly efficient and relatively inexpensive transport systems—and thus sizable internal markets. However, Mexicans at the local and state levels for decades found it necessary to raise revenues through transit fees (known as *alcabalas*) that were applied on goods as they made their way through different jurisdictions around the country.

Typically the alcabala rates ranged from 10 to 15 percent of the value of the products. The central government worried that these alcabalas acted as inhibitors to internal trade and placed more power in provincial hands. Thus national leaders tried on various occasions to eliminate the alcabalas, including banning them in the 1857 Constitution. Despite the prohibition, however, chronic resistance from the financially strapped municipal and state governments kept the alcabalas operational until the 1890s, when the Porfirio Díaz regime did away with them once and for all. Why did it take so long to eliminate the alcabalas? The answer is that federal officials recognized the fund-raising importance of such fees for the provinces, given that the central government itself derived most of its revenues from tariffs on imports and exports.

1876 to 1920: Dictatorship, Growth, and Revolution

Porfirio Díaz, who served as Mexico's president from 1876 to 1880 and 1884 to 1911, inherited better economic conditions when he took the reins of government than any of the presidents before him. The trend toward economic improvement had started when relative peace returned to Mexico following the end of French occupation in 1867. Building on that foundation, Díaz pushed his "progress" agenda by imposing "order" on the citizenry. In strict economic terms, the strategy worked. Forced tranquility and pro-growth policies, including tariff protections for domestic industries, produced significant results. The economy nearly doubled between 1877 and 1895 and almost doubled again between 1895 and 1910, with industrial output growing annually about 12 percent for most of the Porfiriato. The population, meanwhile, grew by only 25 percent during the period between 1887 and 1895 and 17 percent between 1895 and 1910, auguring well for the economy, at least statistically.[23]

While Mexico remained a predominantly agricultural country, manufacturing underwent significant expansion and modernization. Large and medium-sized factories replaced outmoded shops, and family-owned operations gave way to corporations. As always, the Mexico City region dominated industrial production, but other select urban areas such as the northern city of Monterrey emerged as important manufacturing centers. Monterrey's rise as a major industrial center is largely explained by its access to iron ore and coal in Durango and Coahuila, its railway connections to the United States, its business ties with Americans, and its proximity to the port of Tampico. Monterrey became the home of large companies such as Fundidora de Fierro y Acero and Cervecería Cuauhtemoc Moctezuma, both of which included the participation of U.S. investors. The heavy presence of American businesspeople in Monterrey is reflected in the founding of the English-language *The Monterrey News* in 1892. By the early 1900s textile manufacturing made up about 40 percent of all industrial activity nationally, sugar processing 35 percent, mining 15 percent, and others 10 percent. For the first time, Mexico mass-produced such products as cotton textiles, glass, steel, paper, cement, sugar, beer, dynamite, and cigarettes in establishments that resembled those in the advanced countries. Mexican manufacturers were able to claim greater shares of the local market. Textiles producers, for example, controlled nearly 78 percent of the domestic market at the turn of the twentieth century, while iron and steel producers had a 28 percent share and coke producers had a 47 percent share. In general, the period from 1890 to 1911 represents Mexico's first wave of modern industrialization, and it laid the foundation for further progress in later decades. Mexico had become the leading industrial country in Latin America.[24]

While impressive, Mexico's advances could have been greater if geographical constraints had not driven up the cost of industrial activity. Finding sources of water power proved difficult for numerous industries given the country's water scarcity and undependability. Moreover, except in the Monterrey area, the remoteness of coal supplies forced many companies to import U.S. coal. Apart from fuels and other basic natural resources, manufacturing concerns in Mexico also imported machinery, parts, and construction materials, and many employed foreign administrators, managers, engineers, and technicians. Thus Mexico's newfound industrial complex operated within a framework of external dependency.[25]

Notwithstanding the weaknesses of the Mexican economy, the accelerated growth during the Porfiriato boosted Mexico's standing in the world and brought benefits to the Mexican people. Several general factors explain the advances of the era. Political stability and newfound freedom from external threats allowed the government to emphasize growth and to speed up the building of the country's railroad infrastructure. Prior to 1880 only the line between Veracruz and Mexico City and small portions of a few other routes had been completed. With the influx of foreign financing, railway construction took off in the 1880s and continued throughout the Díaz period. By the turn of the twentieth century a modern transportation system was in place that reduced extant geographical barriers and well served the needs of the resource-based economy and the export sector. Mexico's exports also received a boost internationally from significant declines in overland and oceanic freight rates caused by the spread of transportation innovations; both travel times and trade costs dropped appreciably. An auspicious international climate also existed for Mexico's raw materials, as advanced countries entered a period of rapid industrialization. Mexico was able to exploit its natural resources on a larger scale than ever before; for example, the value of Mexico's exports, which were composed largely of silver and other minerals, quadrupled between the mid-1880s and the early 1900s. Additionally, industrialization benefitted from subsidies and tariff protections, while the expansion of the national market, although modest, increased demand for domestic goods.

In 1910, as Mexicans celebrated the centennial anniversary of the commencement of the independence movement, the world marveled at the progress that Mexico had made during the preceding generation. Yet outsiders could not discern the high internal cost of economic growth. For more than three decades the Mexican people had endured an oppressive dictatorship that favored the elite sector of society and gave many generous concessions to foreign investors. Those at the top of Mexican society, including elites who had close ties to foreigners, reaped the fruits of modernization. Those below, especially the workers and landless mestizo peasants and Indians, saw few benefits. Ordinary people experienced food shortages, a drastic drop in real wages, and a general deterioration in living conditions. Data for the period 1898 to 1911 reveal that overall wages plummeted by 23 percent, with agricultural workers enduring an even higher reduction at 27 percent.[26] Thousands of workers lost their jobs as international demand for Mexican metals and other raw materials declined, leading to labor discontent and repression of workers by pro-business lawmen and government officials. Anger and resentment that had been building for years finally exploded into violent insurrection, plunging the country into a long and destructive civil war known as the Mexican Revolution.

The decade-long epic uprising that began in 1910 seriously disrupted Mexico's economy, but it did not destroy it. Agriculture, which had grown slowly during the Porfiriato, was the sector most negatively affected.[27] A comparison of average annual production figures for the period from 1906 to 1910 and 1918 reveals that output of potatoes and barley dropped over 90 percent, sugar over 80 percent, rice and corn over 60 percent, wheat just below 40 percent, and beans over 30 percent. On the other hand, henequen production, which took place in areas such as Yucatán that were largely unaffected by the fighting, rose 86 percent.[28]

The mining industry, which was subjected to repeated interruptions in railroad service, experienced temporary declines, with the production of gold, silver, copper, coal, zinc, and lead falling precipitously by the mid-1910s. Yet the petroleum industry, located on the Gulf Coast, seemed not to be affected, as production of oil surged from almost 4 million barrels in 1910 to over 55 million barrels in 1917. With demand for mining products on the upswing during World War I and a coincidental tapering off of revolutionary violence, mining production as a whole experienced substantial recovery after 1916.[29]

Manufacturing activities in general dropped by 9 percent between 1910 and 1921, but industrial establishments managed to retain most of their physical plants and productive capacity during the years of fighting. In the cotton textile industry, for example, the number of operating mills fell between 1912 and 1917, but productivity still remained high.[30]

The Mexican Economy since 1920: Struggle to Overcome Underdevelopment

In the aftermath of the Revolution, Mexico faced an agenda packed with challenges, and recovery would come slowly. At the broadest level, the country needed to accomplish the following: (1) institute a new system of governance; (2) mend ongoing internal political disputes; (3) resolve disagreements with foreign oil companies; (4) enact land reform for the benefit of landless peasants; (5) ameliorate tensions over state-church relations; and (6) make needed repairs to the damaged economy. These tasks proved overwhelming due to lingering violence, political conflicts, flight of capital out of the country, and an unfavorable international climate that drastically cut the demand for Mexican exports during the latter 1920s and early 1930s. Between 1926 and 1932, export revenues plunged from $334 million dollars to $97 million dollars. Mining output declined by 50 percent between 1929 and 1932, with the all-important oil production experiencing a decline of nearly 20 percent.[31] At the height of the Great Depression, Mexico's national product stood below the level recorded in 1910. To make matters worse, in the early 1930s U.S. authorities pressured hundreds of thousands of destitute Mexican-origin migrants to leave the United States, intensifying the deep social crisis that gripped Mexico. The government responded with initiatives to improve deteriorating living conditions among the masses, including the expropriation and distribution of agricultural land to the peasantry, support for labor unions, and increased expenditures for education and health.

The "Miracle" Years

Welcome relief from the Great Depression began to be felt by the mid-1930s when Mexico sold more of its natural resources to advanced countries as the latter started to work their way out of the global malaise. Then, with the outbreak of World War II and the sudden need for more raw materials in the United States, Mexico's exports rose as never before, and the country's prospects for growth greatly improved. Simultaneously the Mexican government implemented a strategy of import substitution industrialization, or ISI, for the purpose of expanding domestic manufacturing. The protectionist instruments utilized consisted mainly of tariffs and import licensing and to some extent official pricing. By the late 1940s a new surge in industrial growth took hold. At that point manufacturing accounted for 26 percent of the national income, with about one-third of all factory workers concentrated in textile mills. Like other large Latin American countries, Mexico's industries mostly processed raw materials, provided services such as electric power and smelting, and produced basic lower-value consumer goods intended largely for domestic consumption. Most higher-value manufactured goods such as automobiles and appliances were imported from the United States either legally or illegally, or were assembled in Mexico in U.S. subsidiary factories.

Industrial expansion, whether wholly domestic or carried on in partnership with foreign firms, strengthened the economy and made Mexico more self-sufficient at the midpoint of the twentieth century. However, because they lacked technology and enough raw materials, key manufacturing sectors remained heavily dependent on foreign inputs. A number of manufacturers relied totally on imports, while others that utilized Mexican raw materials complained of their erratic availability and high cost. Imports included machinery, chemicals, dyes, lumber, newsprint, and rubber.[32]

Regardless of the abiding external dependence, the rise in industrial production during the post–World War II years ushered in a golden era of impressive national advancements that lasted until the 1970s. Scholars have labeled the progress that took place as Mexico's "economic miracle." Between 1940 and 1970 the national product expanded more than fivefold, with annual rates of growth exceeding over 6 percent most years. On the average manufacturing grew by almost 8 percent annually and agriculture by about 6 percent. By the late 1960s industry made up about a quarter of the national product and employed over 16 percent of all workers. Both agriculture and industry became sources of savings and earners of foreign exchange.[33] Mexico had developed the ability to meet most of its food needs and to export increasing amounts of agricultural commodities such as cotton, coffee, fruits, vegetables, and livestock products. With funding from the Rockefeller Foundation, Nobel Prize winner Norman Borlang, along with the Cooperative Mexican Agricultural Program and later the Maize and Wheat Improvement Program (CIMMYT), conducted research in Mexico that launched the "Green Revolution," which, through crossbreeding and the use of pesticides, substantially expanded yields of wheat, corn, and other crops, successfully increasing food output not only in Mexico but throughout the world.

The Mexican economic "miracle" showered its blessings unevenly, with urban centers in the Central Highlands receiving the greatest share of the benefits. By the mid-1960s well over half the value of the nation's manufactures was concentrated in Mexico City and its environs. Over two-fifths of all industrial workers toiled in the factories of that region, making goods that represented nearly the whole range of the nation's manufactures.[34] In Monterrey, another favored area, tens of thousands of workers in hundreds of factories produced a wide variety of products, including metallurgical goods, textiles, furniture, cement, cigarettes, beer, glass, shoes, and other items. Other important centers like Puebla and Guadalajara trailed significantly behind Mexico City and Monterrey in manufacturing, but they did increase their productivity profile during the period.

In assessing the circumstances that produced the "miracle," five points stand out. First, key political and social changes demanded by revolutionaries during the 1910s were implemented by the 1930s, and that engendered much needed order and stability. Major reforms included the creation of an effective new system of governance, shrinkage of the military as a revenue-consuming national institution, implementation of land reform, and pragmatic accommodation in the long-standing church-state conflict.

Second, the government promoted industrialization and modernization through the practice of state entrepreneurship. It closely managed the nation's economic affairs, took ownership and/or co-ownership of hundreds of enterprises, and protected domestic manufacturing from foreign competition by imposing high tariffs and tough import licensing requirements. The government further fostered domestic industries by steering external investment into high-priority sectors and by limiting foreign investors to minority ownership of

Mexican companies. Officials also carried on campaigns to convince Mexican consumers to buy "Hecho en Mexico" ("Made in Mexico") products instead of foreign goods. By so doing Mexicans could demonstrate support for the industrial development of their country. In 1952, for example, president Miguel Alemán issued a decree requiring that all clothing destined for the domestic market carry the "Hecho en Mexico" label. The decree mandated fines and jail sentences for producers who failed to identify where their wares were manufactured. National industrial leaders strongly criticized *malinchistas* who scorned Mexican products and condemned local merchants who encouraged the consumption of goods made abroad.[35]

Third, with revenues that previously might have gone to the military, the government after 1920 invested heavily in infrastructure projects such as dams, irrigation systems and, most importantly, roads and highways. Paved roadways made it possible for motor vehicles to reach isolated areas of the country not served by railways. Trucks replaced railroads as prime carriers of the country's products within the internal market and also became the major shippers of goods bound for foreign markets. These new transportation venues contributed enormously to lessening, although not completely eliminating, the daunting geographic constraints that traditionally had made it very difficult to build a national economy capable of sustaining disparate regional networks, connecting them to one another, and incorporating all of them into a functional national system. The extant railroad system had previously only partially accomplished that grand objective, falling short because of the high cost and impracticality of building railway lines in the many areas that had difficult terrain. In short, the limits of the transport benefits that railroads could yield in Mexico had for all practical purposes been reached by the 1910s, and cars, buses, and trucks that came along in later decades filled a substantial part of the vacuum.

Fourth, land reform that accommodated both collective farmers and private owners, construction of new water projects that boosted irrigation, and the utilization of "Green Revolution" methods for increasing crop production made a great expansion of agriculture possible, even allowing the country to export food. Inputs of agricultural products stimulated important industrial sectors, including textile, sugar, and coffee manufacturing. And surplus earnings in agriculture benefitted the industrial sector.

Fifth, Mexican exports, including crops, mining products, and basic manufactured goods, found markets abroad, especially in the United States. Earnings from exports rose dramatically from $147 million dollars in 1940 to $850 million in 1956 and over $1 billion in 1964. The composition of exports also changed. From 1940 to 1958 minerals and agricultural products made up around 80 percent of the exports, but as the Mexican economy diversified and the capacity to export industrial goods increased, that percentage dropped to less than 60 by the mid-1960s.[36]

"La Gran Apertura" (The Great Opening)

In the 1970s important changes took place in the structure of the Mexican economy. The economically active population declined from 40 percent to 26 percent in agriculture and from 23 percent to 20 percent in industry, while the services sector grew from 38 percent to 54 percent. The annual rate of growth in manufacturing slowed down to 6 percent per year, compared to 9 percent in the previous decade. Oil production, meanwhile, assumed much greater importance, growing at an annual average rate of 10 percent.[37] One of most vital developments was the rapid expansion of the Border Industrialization Program, which had been created in 1965. The program allowed foreign firms to establish export-oriented assembly factories called *maquiladoras* along the border with the United States and in select areas of Mexico's interior. After a slow start, the maquiladoras mushroomed in the 1970s, employing 76,000 workers by 1974. These plants supplied additional foreign revenues for Mexico and directly benefitted host communities by providing employment opportunities. But maquiladora jobs were concentrated predominantly in the low-wage sector and the plants functioned essentially as foreign enclaves, maintaining few connections with the Mexican national economy. The abundant cheap labor in Mexico and the ease of reimporting finished goods into the U.S. market constituted the primary incentives for foreign multinationals to rush to the Mexican border.

The discovery of new oil deposits in the Gulf of Mexico in the 1970s prompted Mexico to substantially increase petroleum production—and to consequently make the economy more oil-focused and the country more oil-dependent. Whereas in 1977 oil constituted 15.4 percent of the value of Mexico's exports, by 1981 that figure had skyrocketed to 72.5 percent.[38] Increased oil exports supplied the government with additional revenues and elevated Mexico's prestige on the international stage. At the same time, however, petroleum spawned problems familiar to countries whose economies have been negatively affected by the volatility of oil markets. When demand for oil is high, the infusion of sizable amounts of oil revenues from abroad distorts normal economic activity as disproportionate emphasis is placed on the oil industry while other sectors are neglected. In addition, fervent oil economies encourage overborrowing, generate inflation, and breed corruption. When demand and prices plunge, which occurs frequently, oil-dependent economies must then cope with large drops in revenues and the burdensome task of repaying high-interest loans incurred during the "good times." All these problems beset Mexico during the 1980s when an oil glut wreaked havoc on oil-dependent economies around the world. As investors and wealthy Mexicans lost confidence in the direction of the country, they transferred massive amounts of assets abroad. Thus Mexico's national product grew feebly by an average of less than 2 percent during the period of 1980 to 1990, dropping below zero in 1982, 1983, and 1986.[39] Policy mistakes on the part of Mexican leaders undoubtedly contributed to the severity of the debacle of the 1980s, but overreliance on such an unstable commodity as oil to drive the economy and to provide a large share of government revenues lies at the heart of the crisis.

The extraordinary challenges of that period forced Mexico to reassess national economic policies. At the same time the United States, through institutions like the World Bank and the International Monetary Fund, pressured the Mexican government to abandon its traditional role as manager of economic affairs. The Miguel de la Madrid administration (1982–1988) determined that the time had come for Mexico to greatly diminish state activism, instead letting free-market mechanisms more fully determine economic activity. Significantly, the strategy of import substitution industrialization (ISI) was abandoned. As the sun was setting on ISI, its defenders tried to stop the move by pointing out that ISI was not an "exhausted" policy, as critics claimed. The only thing wrong, said ISI supporters, was that Mexico applied ISI policies less fully and less dynamically than East Asian countries, which had used ISI to great advantage to promote homegrown industries.[40] But the Mexican government plunged ahead with structural changes. Apart from scrapping ISI, subsequent reforms in Mexico included reducing government expenditures, cutting social programs, selling public enterprises to private companies, encouraging more foreign investment, and promoting external trade by lowering tariffs and diminishing import controls. President Carlos Salinas de Gortari (1988–1994) enthusiastically embraced the neoliberal agenda started by his predecessor, further reducing the role of government in the economy and opening the door wider to foreign investment and trade by signing the North American Free Trade Agreement (NAFTA) with the United States and Canada, as well as ratifying additional free-trade agreements with other countries. By the end of Salinas's term, Mexico, which only some twelve years before had freely combined socialism and capitalism, now stood as one of the world's foremost practitioners of free market economics.

Mexico's ideological turnabout shifted the national economy from the traditional heavy reliance on commodity exports and the pursuit of import substitution industrialization to an all-out promotion of manufacturing for export under the newly established free-trade system. In practical terms, that essentially translated into modification and expansion of the maquiladora concept that had been implanted along the border with the United States in the mid-1960s. The unprecedented trade and industry external *apertura* has produced striking results. By the 2000s manufactured goods comprised over 80 percent of Mexican products shipped abroad. The reach of that milestone reflected the extraordinary growth of foreign trade and the great infusion of foreign investment (around $20 billion dollars annually) post-NAFTA. In sum, the broad statistical measures related to trade, foreign investment, productivity, wealth creation, and consumption over the past generation have pointed to a Mexico vastly transformed as a more productive and modernized country. The most impressive statistic of all is that Mexico is now ranked one of the largest economies in the world (fourteenth in 2012).

Yet the rosy statistics do not reveal important aspects of the story. While Mexico has received high praise from many quarters for the notable rise in national economic productivity, serious reservations remain regarding what the economic model now in place is actually doing to foster genuine development in Mexico. Without question export-oriented industrialization has added many jobs, increased foreign earnings, and expanded Mexico's expertise in the manufacturing sector. However, the export-processing activities that dominate manufacturing cannot be considered a permanent solution to the development challenge because they are based largely on low-paid, unskilled labor. Mexico's export-manufacturing sector has made little progress in advancing to a higher level of production, one that not only has the capacity to produce plentiful good jobs, but that also contributes significantly to technological progress domestically.

Mexican policy makers and economists of course have understood the limitations of labor-intensive manufacturing industries as these relate to the broader objective of elevating Mexico to First World industrial status. When the Border Industrialization Program was conceived almost half a century ago, the low-wage assembly factories that were established by foreign companies were seen as a necessary first step toward domestic industrial upgrading. Mexican planners optimistically foresaw that in time Mexican firms would be centrally involved not only in low-level maquiladora assembly activities but also in the high-technology industrial production that was projected to develop with the passage of time. Things, however, did not work out as planned. Few domestic firms have been significant players in the maquiladora program—whether on the border or in the interior. The harsh reality of the chronic lack of local capital, technology, and know-how, coupled with the ever-present stiff competition emanating from giant U.S. corporations located on the other side of the Rio Grande, assured that maquiladoras would operate largely as an enclave industry. The vision of nationalistic Mexican policy makers of reducing the dominance of multinational companies and substantially upgrading the status of domestic firms has not materialized.

Mexico's extremely low investment in research and development (R&D) has been a basic problem. In 2011 Mexico's R&D expenditures amounted to about 0.4 percent of GDP, a statistic that had changed little since the 1960s. Mexico consistently ranks last among Organisation for Economic Co-operation and Development (OECD) nations in this important measure. The corresponding R&D figures for South Korea, Japan, and the United States in 2011 were 4 percent, 3.9 percent, and 2.8 percent respectively. Lack of innovation in the Mexican domestic economy is also reflected in patent applications submitted. In 2012 Mexico filed only 191 patents, compared to South Korea's 11,847, Japan's 43,660, and the United States' 51,643.[41] One major problem for Mexico is that multinational companies assume ownership of inventions developed on Mexican soil by Mexican employees and then proceed to sell the patents to clients around the world; for example, the Delphi Mexico Technical Center of Ciudad Juárez recently registered 316 patents in the United States, most of which were developed by creative Mexican engineers.[42]

After the enactment of NAFTA, distinctions between the old and new maquiladoras became miniscule, prompting the Mexican government in 2006 to combine the two sectors under a new national export-specific umbrella program known as IMMEX, or Industria Manufacturera, Maquiladora, y de Servicios de Exportación (Manufacturing, Maquila, and Export Service Industry). The fact that Mexican firms have not become major participants in the IMMEX sector is reflected particularly in the automobile, electronics, and aerospace industries, where U.S., European, and Asian corporations continue to dominate. Thus far the main role of Mexican companies has been to facilitate production and to supply basic *insumos* (inputs or components) to the export-oriented factories. But even in these areas the level of participation of the Mexican firms is, from a development point of view, far from satisfactory: "The most optimistic statistic credits only about 5% of the total value of exports by international firms as sourced from Mexican capital funded companies," states a major maquiladora industry publication.[43] The foremost reason given for this disappointing situation is that U.S. companies in Mexico can easily import most inputs from suppliers in the United States, and thus they have little need to deal with Mexican companies, which, in any case, lack know-how and production capacity, and have a hard time obtaining credit. Volume estimates of insumos from Mexican companies to IMMEX industries have ranged wildly from lows of 2 to 6 percent given by scholars to highs of 20 to 30 percent given by officials. In 2012 Instituto Nacional de Estadística y Geografía (INEGI) figures placed the insumo volume at 30 percent, meaning that 70 percent of all insumos were imported.[44] Even accepting the 30 percent estimate, this is not a particularly impressive figure given that maquiladoras have been present in Mexico for five decades. Further, Mexican insumos are usually peripheral supplies or components. This situation exemplifies the weak connections between the foreign-driven export sector and the Mexican domestic economy. It also underlines the feebleness of the multiplier effect of Mexico's maquiladora exports. In 2010, while in the United States and Brazil each export dollar produced $3.30 and $2.30 respectively, the equivalent figure for Mexico was only $1.80. The "opportunity lost" in Mexico is substantial because the export sector makes up 28 percent of nation's economy, compared to only 11 percent in the case of Brazil.[45]

Another major concern with maquiladoras is that they largely hire low-wage workers. In 2006, INEGI reported that of the 1.2 million persons employed in the IMMEX industries, 78 percent were *obreros* (low-paid ordinary workers), 13 percent were *técnicos* (technical personnel), and 9 percent were *empleados administrativos* (managers and other office employees).[46] Unfortunately starting in 2007 INEGI began combining the data for obreros and técnicos into a single category, making it impossible to determine whether there has been significant employment upgrading in the IMMEX industries since that time. Presumably as more advanced manufacturing operations have been established in Mexico, the percentage of higher-paid técnicos has risen and there has been a corresponding drop in the percentage of employed obreros. But that cannot be established for certain. This is an important issue because Mexico can hardly aspire to become an advanced industrial country with a labor force largely comprised of unskilled, poorly paid workers.

Given the development implications, was it a rational choice for Mexico to privilege foreign-dominated industries with such open access to its economy and its labor force? Why did Mexican leaders not give top priority to promoting and supporting domestic industries? I can only surmise that Mexican policy makers became resigned to the reality that, because of its geographic circumstances, Mexico had few prospects of building a strong domestic industrial and commercial economy in the face of the stiff and ever-present U.S. competition. A new approach to dealing with the giant economy across the border made sense to policy makers. Geographic proximity to the United States offered the possibility of more direct links with the U.S. economy, links that could be used by Mexico for greater benefit. U.S. manufacturing companies could be lured to shift more of their production to Mexico with the assurance of an open border and easy access to low-cost labor, and U.S. commercial firms could be encouraged to set up operations in Mexico as well. But significant costs accompanied this strategy. When the government adopted the cheap labor "comparative advantage" strategy to enhance the country's global "competitiveness," most of the benefits accrued to foreign companies because they were much better equipped than Mexican firms to utilize Mexican workers on a large scale, and their connections with foreign markets were much stronger. Further, with the great influx of foreign consumer goods, Mexican companies were subjected to crushing competition, with the result that many fell by the wayside.

There are other major shortcomings associated with the implementation of the neoliberal model. Balanced national growth has not been achieved. Some sectors of the Mexican economy and some geographic regions have experienced spectacular expansion, but others have stagnated or contracted. The growth of per capita income has been disappointing. Between 1994 and 2005, real GDP per capita growth averaged only 1.3 percent annually, essentially the same yearly rate as during the period 1986 to 1993, before NAFTA went into effect. From 2005 to 2010 the annual rate dropped below 1 percent. These recent numbers are far below those achieved during the period 1950 to 1980, when the Mexican government played a heavy hand in the economy. At that time, GDP per capita grew at an annual average rate of 2.8 percent, or more than double the annual rate recorded in the NAFTA era.[47]

The most distressing years in the first decade of the NAFTA period were in 1995, when the real GDP growth shrank by 6.2 percent, and in 2001, when no growth took place. The minus 6.2 rate recorded in 1995 reveals yet another major economic meltdown in the recent history of Mexico. The crisis that year was generated by a combination of unfortunate developments, including capital and investment flight triggered by concerns over the possibility of serious political instability following the outbreak of the Zapatista rebellion in Chiapas in early 1994 and the assassination of the ruling party's (PRI) presidential candidate later that year. Policy decisions, such as keeping Mexican currency artificially overvalued too long and ill-advised bank lending practices made the crisis worse. The zero growth recorded in 2001 mirrors the impact of cyclical international economic downturns, especially in the United States, with which Mexico had become highly integrated as a result of the implementation of trade measures that intensified cross-border economic interaction.

Mexico experienced another economic downturn when the Wall Street financial debacle of 2008 triggered a severe worldwide recession. But this time recovery came much quicker than in previous crises. While Mexico's real GDP had posted a miniscule 1.3 percent growth in 2008 and a disastrous 6.5 percent negative plunge in 2009, between 2010 and 2012 the annual rate rose to a positive average of 4.4 percent. GDP per capita growth had declined by minus 0.1 and minus 7.1 percent in 2008 and 2009, but then bounced back up in the next four years, averaging an annual growth rate of 2.5 percent.[48]

This latest growth spurt notwithstanding, Mexico's economic expansion over the last generation has actually been quite anemic and has disappointed many people who expected a better performance from the free-trade paradigm established in the 1980s and 1990s. Supporters of that model have blamed the lackluster record on the government's slowness in enacting a litany of long-called-for structural reforms. These include breaking up existing monopolies and oligopolies, curbing the power of entrenched interest groups, changing labor laws, improving infrastructure, allowing private investment in the energy sector, overhauling the tax system and improving tax collection, reducing corruption, improving the judiciary and law enforcement, upgrading education, and removing barriers to credit. In past years the government has had limited success in passing reform legislation or effectively enforcing existing laws to accomplish needed changes. In 2012 and 2013, however, landmark initiatives taken by the government in the education, labor, communications, and media sectors, as well as the tax system, created new optimism. To what extent the most recent reforms will improve national productivity, boost real GDP per-capita growth, and foster greater development in the long run remains to be seen.

Finally, a word on the changing role of oil in the Mexican economy. Dwindling oil reserves and consequent yearly downturns in petroleum output brought more bad news at the turn of the twenty-first century. While in 2004 Mexico produced 3.5 million barrels of oil per day, in 2012 it produced only 2.6 million barrels per day. Yet, because oil currently represents only 6 percent of GDP, Mexico is now in a better position to protect itself from oil production declines and steep price drops than in the past. The drastically lower oil prices recorded in 2014, for example, hurt the country, but not to the degree experienced in the 1980s.

Conclusion

The preceding whirlwind journeys into the economic histories of the United States and Mexico have spotlighted important turning points in the evolution of each country, as well as highlighted key aspects of the overall context that have shaped each economy. Significantly, the sharply dissimilar contexts present in each country spawned inequality early on in the relationship, and that divide grew larger with the passage of time. Inevitably the United States emerged as the stronger and therefore dominant partner in an unavoidable close relationship dictated by close physical proximity. When Americans achieved their independence, they already had one of the most advanced economies in the world owing primarily to the fact that their new republic had a very favorable factor endowment. Just as importantly, the United States had a superb location that facilitated world trade. As time passed, Americans added much more exceptionally productive land to the national domain, thus greatly expanding the nation's natural advantages. By the late nineteenth century the United States demonstrated that it possessed the optimal conditions for the utilization of continuous technological innovations, whether imported from abroad or produced inside the United States. The U.S. economy constantly expanded, rising by the early twentieth century to the very top globally and retaining that rank to the present day.

Mexico's historical trajectory is different. Upon its independence Mexico faced daunting problems and challenges that greatly affected the country's economic well-being for many decades. The task of building the nation became exceedingly difficult because of the destruction left behind by the wars for independence, the persistent shortages of public revenues, acute ethnic fragmentation, continuous conflicts with other countries, and the constant internal power struggles for control of the government. On the northern frontier sparse population and remoteness from central Mexico facilitated the conquest of that valuable region by the United States. Once the national territory shrank by half, Mexico's economic future grew dim. What remained of Mexico still included a noteworthy natural endowment, but the configuration of the restructured national territory had substantial inherent disadvantages that would henceforth constrain economic progress and impede national integration.

Recurring political instability in the postindependence era debilitated Mexico's economy. A long-lasting decline in productivity began in the 1820s, and although some recovery was evident two decades later, Mexico did not reach salutary conditions until after the French Intervention of the 1860s. "Order and Progress," the aphorism propagated by the Porfirio Díaz regime, did in fact ring true during the last quarter of the nineteenth century and the first decade of the twentieth century, when Mexico made impressive gains. But, while the advances of the Porfiriato greatly benefitted the affluent sectors of society, they largely bypassed the masses, sparking popular discontent that brought on the Revolution of 1910. The insurrection seriously disrupted the economy but, after the fighting,

Mexico emerged as a changed nation, boasting a new constitution, a new governmental system, and a new determination for undertaking social and economic reforms. These developments laid the groundwork for bringing modernity to the nation.

After the difficult years of the Great Depression, a favorable international environment during and after World War II made it possible for Mexico to sell more of its raw materials abroad. At the same time, newfound political stability and the influx of foreign capital helped drive an economic "miracle" for several decades after 1945. The government successfully implemented import substitution industrialization (ISI), a popular strategy employed throughout the developing world. It is doubtful that Mexico could have made industrial advances if the government had not played a decisive role in directing economic affairs.

The international economic climate changed radically for the worse in the 1980s, and Mexico, along with many other poor countries, felt compelled to accept the "shock therapy" of neoliberal policies. Mexico could no longer sustain its mixed capitalist-socialist system in the face of powerful international pressures. Global recession, a drastic drop in oil prices, a steep decline in demand for Mexican exports, and an oppressive foreign debt shook the country severely, driving it to adopt the model of a free-market economy. The unprecedented lowering of tariffs in the early 1980s, entry into GATT in 1986, and enactment of NAFTA in 1994 underscored Mexico's embrace of free trade.

While increased interaction with the United States and Canada has enlarged Mexico's economy, neoliberalism has in effect converted Mexico into a geographically convenient, low-cost production country in which multinational corporations, often in alliances with Mexican partners, have established export-oriented assembly manufacturing on a large scale, resulting in sharply elevated foreign dominance and dependence. The external vulnerability of Mexico's economy is revealed particularly in the maquiladora industry, where wild swings of globally driven expansions and contractions have created boom and bust conditions. Dependence is also illustrated in the size Mexico's foreign debt, which stood at $182 billion dollars in 2007, up from $148 billion in 1997.[49] The biggest disappointment of the NAFTA period (1994–2013) is that the annual growth rate of per capita GDP in Mexico has averaged a paltry 0.9 percent, placing the country well below the 1.6 percent average for twenty Latin American nations.[50] The new economy has not diminished poverty, and it has done little to promote balanced development—that is, the kind of development that spreads the benefits of growth equitably to all regions and all sectors of the population.

Recent reforms undertaken by the Mexican government have raised hopes that in the future the economy will perform better. It remains to be seen, however, if changes already made and others contemplated will actually mitigate the structural problems inherent in the current system.

By documenting the divergent economic pathways followed by the United States and Mexico, as well as the different outcomes achieved by each country, this chapter has provided a framework for placing the foundational factors in a broad temporal context. But before taking on the task of assessing the role of such foundational factors in shaping the fate of Mexico and the United States, we must consider how the two differing economic trajectories have shaped the social structures of each country.

Notes

1. For a concise analysis of the meaning of the geographic assets enjoyed by the United States with respect to economic growth and geopolitical issues see STRATFOR (2011).
2. U.S. Bureau of the Census (1975), series Z1–19; Nash (1974), 296.
3. Walton and Shepherd (1979), 4.
4. Taylor (1951), 79 and passim.
5. U.S. Bureau of the Census (2006), 5:510–511.
6. Martin (1939), 6–7; Robertson (1973), 442–443.
7. U.S. Bureau of the Census (2006), 5:511–512.
8. Maddison (2003), 85–86; Holechek (2000), 649.
9. Wolf (1959), 186–188.
10. Rosenzweig Hernández (1963), 491–492.
11. Dobado González et al. (2008), 765, 767, 774.
12. *Encomiendas* refers to lands entrusted to Spanish overlords who could extract labor and tribute from resident Indians. *Repartimientos* refers to obligatory labor provided by Indians for part of the year.
13. Jáuregui (2010), 248.
14. Dobado González et al. (2008), 767–768.
15. Ibarra Bellon (1998), 41.
16. Constitutions were enacted in 1824, 1835, 1845, and 1867.
17. Population figures from Aguirre Beltrán (1946), 236.
18. Jáuregui (2010), 259.
19. Cárdenas Sánchez (2003), 98.
20. At this time the main purpose of maintaining tariffs was to raise revenues for use by the government, and between 1825 and 1845 import duties supplied about half of such revenues. Simultaneously, however, high tariffs played an important role in protecting domestic industries.
21. Thomson (1989), 278–280; King (1970), 3; Cumberland (1968), 169.
22. Thomson (1989), 280.
23. Growth of the Mexican economy measured in terms of national income (Coatsworth 1978, 82). Figure on industrial growth cited in King (1970), 7. Population growth estimates calculated from data in Cumberland (1968), 367.
24. Solís M. (1967), 43, 247; Williamson (2011), 200–205. See also Haber (1989).
25. See Beatty (2001), 153–154, 197–198.
26. Cárdenas Sánchez, (2003), 240–245. Some scholars speculate that real wages in Mexico dropped by perhaps 75 percent between 1810 and 1910. See Rosenzweig (1965), 447; Hansen (1971), 21–23; Cumberland (1968), 224.
27. "Between 1877 and 1907 total agricultural output grew by 21.3%. This annual average rate of increase of 0.7% was scarcely half that of population growth" (Hansen 1971, 27).
28. Jones (1921), 216.

29 Cumberland (1968), 248–251.
30 Haber (1989), 124–125, 140.
31 Haber (1992), 28; Aguilar Camin and Meyer (1993), 106.
32 Horn and Bice (1949), 307; Wythe (1949), 281–286.
33 Alba and Potter (1986), 49; Hansen (1971), 56.
34 West and Augell (1966), 384; Garza (1985), 154, 227.
35 Gauss (2010), 1–3. The term *malinchistas* refers to Mexicans who betray or turn their back on their country and in the process assist foreigners in inflicting damage on Mexico. It derives from "Malinche," the sixteenth-century Indian woman who provided important information and assistance to the Spaniards, thereby making their conquest of the Aztecs easier.
36 Freithaler (1968), 65.
37 México, INEGI (1985), I:251; Gracida (1997), 469.
38 Walker (2013), 78.
39 Capital flight figures from Whiting (1992), 157; GDP figures from Werner et al. (2006), 82.
40 Cypher and Wise (2010), 31–42.
41 Urquidi (1986), 182; OECD (2007), 148; World Intellectual Property Organization (2014); World Bank (2014).
42 *Juárez-El Paso Now* (August 2014), 47.
43 *Juárez-El Paso Now* (June 2014), 12.
44 México, INEGI (2013b), Cuadro 5.
45 *The Economist* (October 30, 2010), 37.
46 México, INEGI (2007a).
47 Haber et al. (2008), 78–79.
48 Weintraub (2010), 12; Banco de México (2008), 123; World Bank (2014).
49 Banco de México (2008), 176.
50 Weisbrot et al. (2014), 1, 6.

2
AFFLUENCE AND POVERTY

La Chaveña, El Segundo Barrio—those were the neighborhoods of my youth when my family lived on the U.S.–Mexico border during the early and mid-1950s. We resided in the tough, working-class *colonia* of La Chaveña in Ciudad Juárez, Chihuahua, during the time that I attended a Catholic school in the heart of El Segundo Barrio, a legendary community in El Paso and in the annals of Chicano/a history in the United States. Both *barrios* were among the poorest and most troubled parts of each city. But I could tell then that the folks of La Chaveña faced greater economic struggles than their counterparts in El Segundo, where the U.S. economy offered better jobs and other opportunities not available on the Mexican side. Regardless of that difference, however, the people of both La Chaveña and El Segundo lived marginalized lives in comparison to the middle and upper classes of Ciudad Juárez and El Paso. At the time I did not comprehend the reasons for the disparities that I observed in both cities, yet I did grasp that great inequalities existed not only between Mexico and the United States but also among groups of people within each country.

Decades later I came to understand the reasons behind such disparities. I learned that asymmetries between nations, as well as wealth inequalities within nations, essentially derive from the kinds of contexts in which both nations and subnational regions develop. Thus the internal social disparities that have existed in both Mexico and the United States are largely rooted in the manner in which different sections of each country and different groups have been impacted by such phenomena as climate, physical geography, natural resources, population dynamics, the means of production, government decision-making, elite greed, and social attitudes. The harsh reality is that contexts everywhere privilege some people and disadvantage others, reinforcing social stratification.

Within Mexico, the northern states and the Central Highlands—the two regions that possess the best contexts on a national level—manifest the highest levels of development, while the southern states, which are saddled with the most adverse contextual constraints, manifest the lowest. The most impoverished group in Mexico is the indigenous population, which is largely concentrated in poor southern states like Guerrero, Oaxaca, and Chiapas. In the United States, generally high levels of development are present in much of the country, especially in urban areas. Nevertheless, pockets of poverty are found in most U.S. cities and also in a number of less developed rural regions such as Appalachia. Whites of European ancestry constitute the most affluent group in the U.S. population, and poverty is most concentrated among indigenous peoples and other dark-skinned minorities. African Americans, Mexican Americans, and Native Americans have historically been the most marginalized large groups.

This chapter points out that wealth disparity and poverty are not recent phenomena for either country. These problems have been around for centuries. Quite apart from differences in living standards spawned by internal geographic features and other foundational factors, the human propensity not to share existing wealth in an equitable manner across population groups has been present in both societies. The depth of inequality, however, has been much more visible in Mexico than in the United States.

Wealth Disparities in the United States

Poverty and Inequality

The United States is a highly developed country, but poverty afflicts a significant percentage of its population. As in any country, U.S. poverty is to a decisive degree rooted in diverse geography, a condition that generates regional inequalities and creates marginalized communities. Even as the United States is awash in extremely well-endowed spaces that generate prosperity, it also has a number of unfavorable spaces that, economically speaking, are practically useless. The country also has "mixed spaces" that mostly yield resource-based wealth linked to agriculture, timbering, or mining. These "mixed spaces" produce little or no genuine development, and the benefits derived from resource exploitation accrue mostly to outside corporations and privileged local entrepreneurs. Examples of "mixed spaces" in the United States include the Mississippi Delta, the Ozarks region, and Appalachia.

In addition to differences in wealth caused by geography, substantial inequalities in U.S. society are rooted in racial and ethnic discrimination. To be sure, discrimination has subsided significantly in the United States in recent decades as a result of the civil rights movement of the 1950s and 1960s, but societal bias has not disappeared. Large numbers of Native Americans, African Americans, and Mexican Americans, as well as other members of Third World immigrant communities remain presently impoverished. Americans of the Muslim faith are also targets of religious and ethnic bias. Numerous states have even attempted to disenfranchise minority-group citizens by passing laws and enacting policies to prevent or discourage them from voting, particularly in national elections.

Despite the belief that the United States is a land of equal opportunity, the structure of U.S. society and the economy has made it difficult for poor people in general to achieve the "American Dream"—that is, to attain a secure middle-class lifestyle. That general pattern was partially interrupted during the period 1940 to 1970, when unprecedented economic growth in the United States spurred significant upward movement of working folks into the ranks of the middle class. Since the 1980s, however, the working and middle classes have lost significant ground in earning capacity and asset accumulation. By contrast, the top sectors of the U.S. population have done spectacularly well in expanding their wealth. These recent dynamics are illustrative of how, over the generations, the brand of capitalism practiced in the United States has worked best for corporations and the elite.[1] In fact, wealth has been concentrated at the top and the incidence of poverty among the masses has been high since the foundation of the country. Rather than having an egalitarian population, as many people have believed, during the early 1770s the thirteen English colonies actually had a highly skewed concentration of income and wealth (assets such as property and stocks) in favor of the rich. In New England the top 10 percent of the population owned 40 percent of the wealth while the bottom 50 percent owned only 11 percent. In the middle Atlantic colonies the top 10 percent owned 32 percent of the wealth while the bottom 50 percent owned only 23 percent.[2] Such disparities continued long after the United States achieved independence. In 1800, 1870, and 1910, the top 10 percent of the U.S. population owned 60 percent, 70 percent, and 80 percent of the wealth respectively and, in 1910 and in the late 1930s the top 10 percent received over 40 percent and nearly 50 percent of the national (earned) income respectively.[3]

Recently the gap between rich and poor has markedly widened in the United States as a result of structural changes in the economy and the enactment of government policies that have favored the rich. Income, asset wealth, and wage data confirm the deteriorating condition of the masses. By 2010, the top 10 percent of the U.S. population owned 60 percent of the wealth, while the remaining 90 percent owned only 40 percent. The top 10 percent received around 45 percent of the national income and the other 90 percent received the remaining 55 percent.[4]

Poverty has been a serious problem for generations. In the early 1900s, for example, between two-fifths and two-thirds of the U.S. population may have lived below the poverty line. Industrial cities with large immigrant populations in particular experienced high levels of deprivation; in New York City in 1904, for example, approximately half the population lived in poverty. While conditions improved in the country in subsequent decades, it is likely that the poverty rate exceeded 50 percent at the height of the Great Depression. Following economic recovery, the U.S. poverty rate had by 1950 dropped to around 35 percent,[5] and between 1960 and 2007 to 2011 the overall poverty rate in the United States declined from 22.2 percent to 14.3 percent, remaining lower among whites but significantly higher among minorities; for example, from 2007 to 2011 whites recorded a poverty rate of 9.9 percent, Mexican Americans 24.9 percent, and African Americans 25.8 percent.[6]

U.S. workers with the least earning power have been especially devastated by the failure of the federal government to raise the minimum wage sufficiently to keep up with inflation. In 1968 the minimum hourly wage stood at $1.60, which at the time represented 94 percent of the official U.S. poverty-level "living wage" of $1.71 for a family of four. By 2009 the federal minimum wage had increased to $7.25 but, with inflation, this figure stood significantly below the extant living wage, with variances depending on location. A number of states have raised the minimum wage a few dollars above the federal standard, but in 2014 even these higher wages continued to trail behind the living wage.

Wealth Disparities in Mexico
Poverty and Inequality

Acute social disparity has, over the centuries, been the most prominent manifestation of Mexico's underdeveloped condition. The high incidence of poverty is the single most important characteristic that defines Mexico as a developing, rather than a developed, country.

Let's begin by glancing backward in time at the social situation in Mexico during the early nineteenth century. The great inequities that separated whites (largely the Spanish population) from *mestizos* (racially mixed population), Indians, and Afro-Mexicans were noted by various contemporary observers. To Alexander von Humboldt, Mexico was a land of extremes: not only was there a great gap separating the rich from the poor, but among the wealthy were many superrich families that had incomes far superior to their affluent counterparts in Venezuela, Peru, and Cuba. At the same time, Capitán José María Quirós of Veracruz speculated that half the population of Mexico was impoverished, and Bishop Manuel Abad y Queipo calculated that, of the goods purchased in Mexico (measured in pesos spent), 45 percent of the population consumed 80 percent and the remaining 55 percent consumed 20 percent.[7] Although hard data are scarce, the extant historical literature suggests that such inequalities did not diminish in the ensuing generations. To the contrary, in periods such as the era of Porfirio Díaz, the gap between rich and poor increased substantially. When the Mexican Revolution broke out in 1910, perhaps 80 percent of all Mexicans were poor.[8] That percentage did not change much for several decades but, beginning in the 1940s, the economic "miracle" brought about significant poverty reduction.

Studies conducted in the 1970s suggest that nearly 60 percent of Mexico's population lived below the poverty line at that time. Some subsequent estimates indicate declining rates of poverty, but calculations vary widely because of the use of different definitions and methodologies, and it is difficult to draw firm conclusions regarding change over time. In general, one can infer from the studies that the poverty level since 1984 has hovered around 50 percent during some years and has risen substantially above that mark during times of economic distress. Reflecting the government's attention to poverty reduction via the enactment of various social programs and cash disbursements, a trend toward change for the better took place in the late 1990s and early 2000s, with the official poverty rate dipping to 42.9 percent by 2006. But deterioration set in after that, with the poverty rate reaching 52.3 percent in 2012.[9] By way of comparison, surveys conducted by the United Nations indicate that the level of poverty in Mexico in 2012 surpassed the average recorded for other Latin American countries by 11 percentage points.[10]

The indigenous population in Mexico has traditionally had the highest levels of deprivation. Apart from discrimination, governmental neglect, and social indifference, physical isolation from the mainstream population has contributed significantly to the marginalization of Indians. In 2000, 85 percent of people who spoke indigenous languages lived below the poverty line; by 2010, that figure had dropped to 79 percent, indicating progress over the intervening years.[11] Map 2.1, which shows the locations of the 1,003 *municipios* that had poverty rates of 75 percent or more in 2010, also reveals the strong correlation between the areas where indigenous peoples reside and the exorbitant levels of poverty in those localities. A high percentage of the destitute Indian towns and villages is concentrated in the remote, mountainous regions of Chiapas, Guerrero, and Oaxaca; the incidence of poverty among the indigenous populations of those states in 2010 was 91 percent, 90 percent, and 84 percent respectively.[12]

The historical pattern of social inequality in Mexico is further demonstrated by income distribution data. In 1950, the top 10 percent of the population received 45.5 percent of the income; in 2000 they received 42.7 percent. The bottom 20 percent, which received only 5.6 percent of the income in 1950, received only 3.2 percent in 2000. The middle 40 percent remained practically in the same position in its share of income from 1950 to 2000, while the middle high 30 percent managed to make some slight gains. By 2008 things looked somewhat better. The share of income that went to the top 10 percent dropped to a new low of 36.3 percent, and the shares received by the bottom 20 percent, middle 40 percent, and middle high 30 percent increased to 4.6 percent, 22.2 percent, and 37.0 percent respectively. The entrenched inequality in the distribution of income in Mexico is also revealed in Gini Coefficients, which stayed in the 50 range between 1950 and 2012.[13] It should be kept in mind that the degree of income inequality is undoubtedly greater than indicated by these data, given that

58 The Mexico–U.S. Divide

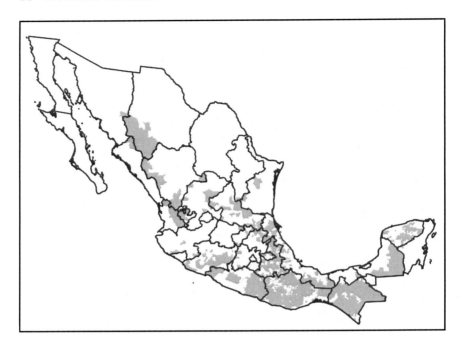

MAP 2.1 Location of municipios with poverty rates of 75 percent or more, 2010
Source: México, CONEVAL (2011), 22.

Mexican billionaires and millionaires underreport their income. It is also worthwhile to point out that many other countries have higher degrees of income inequality than Mexico. For example, circa the mid-2000s, Argentina, Bolivia, Brazil, Chile, Colombia, Costa Rica, and Nicaragua all had higher Gini Indexes than Mexico. On the other hand, European countries such as Denmark, France, Germany, and Sweden had Gini Indexes in the 20s, indicating a degree of income equality substantially above that found in Mexico and other Latin American countries. The United States, with a Gini Index hovering around 47 for recent years, is far less egalitarian than European societies, but still more egalitarian than Mexico and the rest of Latin America.

It is important to underline that despite the long-standing high poverty rates and social inequalities, living conditions in Mexico have improved over time for substantial numbers of people. This is reflected in the infant mortality rate, which declined from 70 deaths per 100,000 births in 1970 to 15 in 2009, and life expectancy, which increased from 56 to 73 years for men and from 60 to 78 years for women during the period 1960 to 2008.[14] With respect to poverty alleviation, the Mexican government has undertaken various notable initiatives, including *Oportunidades* (formerly known as *Progresa*), which since 1997 has provided cash transfers that require families to meet goals like keeping children healthy and in school; *Seguro Social*, or basic health insurance coverage, launched in 2002; and *70 y Más*, which has given financial support to the elderly in rural areas since 2007. Between 2000 and 2010 social spending as a percentage of Mexico's GDP increased from 8.6 percent to 11.3 percent, resulting in the extension of benefits to over half of Mexico's population via these and other programs.[15]

Another indicator of general progress over the long term is the upward social mobility that has taken place within the Mexican population. Estimates indicate that between 1895 and 1996 the percentage of people classified as lower class declined from 90.8 percent to 60.0 percent, while the middle class grew from 7.8 percent to 30.0 percent, and the upper class expanded from 1.4 percent to 10.0 percent. Data based on income and purchasing power suggest that in 2008 approximately 60.8 percent of the population could be considered lower class, 31.9 percent middle class, and 7.2 percent upper class.[16] Estimating the size of the middle class in Mexico has provoked controversy, and we will take up that subject shortly.

History of Substandard Wages, Benefits, and Safety-Net Coverage

While the preceding data indicate general long-term improvement for the Mexican people, wage statistics tell a different tale. It is largely a story of persistent stagnation or decline interrupted by occasional periods of modest upward movement. The fact is that Mexico has long had a reputation of being a low-wage country. One glaring manifestation of that reality is the migration of millions upon millions of Mexicans to the United States from the latter nineteenth century to the early twenty-first century in search of jobs that pay decent wages. Wage deterioration in Mexico was particularly acute during the thirty-five-year rule of the pro-business Porfirio Díaz regime, which ended in 1911, the year insurrectionist peasants and workers and other disaffected sectors of society forced the dictator, Díaz, out of office and into exile. The triumph of the Mexican Revolution of the 1910s would subsequently bring social advances for the masses, including rising wages during the 1920s and early 1930s. However, from the late 1930s to the early 1950s wages mostly declined or remained flat. Then they rose from the late 1950s into the 1970s as a result of the expansion of industrialization during Mexico's economic "miracle."[17]

But when the "miracle" began to fade in the late 1970s and early 1980s, gains made by workers in previous eras eroded as Mexico embarked on a dramatic transformation away from state-directed economics and toward freewheeling capitalism. While well-placed sectors of the population have derived significant benefits from the growth that has taken place under the new paradigm, wages of ordinary workers have fared poorly. In 2009, the average monthly salary in Mexico amounted to $609 U.S. dollars (PPP, or Purchasing Power Parity), well below the average of $1,480 for seventy-two countries surveyed by the International Labor Organization. Mexico ranked fifty-eighth on the list, *below* China, Ukraine, Colombia, Bulgaria, Kazakhstan, Macau, Brazil, Mauritius, and Panama.[18]

The worst income-earning experience in Mexico rests with minimum wage workers, which include about 40 percent of the economically active population. As the official data in Figure 2.1 show, there was a steep deterioration of the real minimum wage from 1982 to the mid-1990s, followed by stagnation and decline from the mid-1990s to 2012. The minimum wage lost more than half its value between 1982 and 1988. By 1995 the minimum wage retained only 62 percent of the worth it had had in 1988, and it continued its downward trajectory into the twenty-first century, dropping in 2012 to 52 percent of the 1988 value. Data assembled by the Organization for Economic Cooperation and Development (OECD) also show that every year from 2000 to 2012 Mexico's hourly minimum wage was the lowest among the twenty-six countries that comprise that organization. Further, within Latin America, Mexico stands out as the only country whose minimum wage is substantially under the poverty line.[19] All the preceding data suggest how far Mexico needs to ascend economically to reach the status of a First World country.

Sustained low wages in Mexico is the most important factor among the attractions that have lured so many assembly oriented multinational corporations to establish maquiladora operations south of the Rio Grande since the mid-1960s. The most intense surges in maquiladora activity in Mexico have coincided with periods of local economic crisis during which there have been sharp devaluations of the Mexican peso (in relation to the dollar) and attendant severe drops

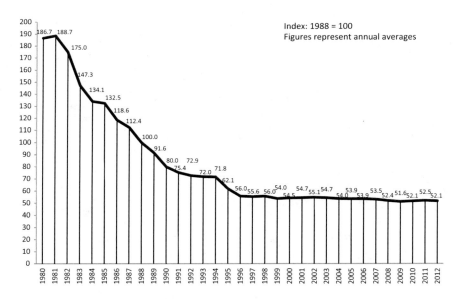

FIGURE 2.1 Evolution of Mexico's Real Minimum Salary, 1980–2012

Source: México, Comisión Nacional de los Salarios Mínimos (2012), 620.

in Mexican wages. The latest manifestation of the power substandard wages have to entice foreign companies to set up manufacturing plants in Mexico surfaced during the period 2010 to 2012. In 2011, the average hourly manufacturing compensation cost in Mexico stood at $6.48 dollars (including benefits), compared to $11.65 in Brazil, $15.91 in Argentina, $22.60 in Singapore, and $35.53 in the United States.[20] *Mexico Now*, the leading maquiladora industry promotional magazine, reported in 2013 that manufacturing firms could expect to hire Mexican engineers for a third the cost of what would be paid in the United States, technicians for one-fifth the cost, and ordinary workers for "up to one-tenth the cost."[21]

In addition to low production costs, Mexico offers foreign companies a compliant workforce and lower transportation costs to U.S. markets than low-wage competitor countries such as China, whose rock-bottom wages during the early 2000s drew manufacturing jobs away from Mexico. However, by the end of that decade Chinese production costs, including wages, began to rise significantly; by April 2013 Chinese wages reportedly topped Mexico's by 20 percent.[22] These changed circumstances prompted many foreign firms to once again favor Mexico over China, thrusting Mexico's manufacturing production into a new boom cycle. Thus Mexico's GDP grew by 5 percent in 2010 and 4 percent both in 2011 and 2012. That dramatic upturn, coupled with simultaneous downturns in the economies of China, India, and Brazil, moved a number of well-placed U.S. journalists, diplomats, and others to heap praise on what they saw as Mexico's new competitive dynamism. But that optimism was based more on illusion than reality because by late 2013 the Mexican economy had slowed down again. Viewed with historical perspective, the recent perceived rapid progress in Mexico is reminiscent of the overstated Mexican economic "leaps" of earlier eras such as during the Porfirio Díaz dictatorship and the oil boom of the late 1970s. Interestingly, in both the Díaz period and the oil-boom years, prosperity was followed by societal upheaval. A revolution erupted at the end of the Díaz regime, and one of the most severe economic downturns in Mexico's history took place following the oil glut of the early 1980s. The lesson is that judgments about swift economic advancements in Mexico must be made with considerable caution.

The 2013 hype in foreign media circles revealed the tendency by some journalists who have little knowledge of Mexico to draw sweeping generalizations based largely on numbers such as rosy GDP data and trade statistics, or based on information gathered in superficial conversations with Mexican and American boosters, promoters, investors, diplomats, or officials. Such media fanfare has shown a profound lack of understanding of the structure of Mexico's economy, which in truth is highly vulnerable to recurring cycles of boom and bust. Mexico, after all, continues to have a foreign-directed, dependent economy, one that as currently structured is unlikely to produce balanced and long-lasting economic development. That is not to deny that the new export-driven manufacturing economy has greatly stimulated growth in Mexico. But, the reality is that the fruits of Mexico's neoliberal paradigm have mostly benefitted the well-positioned portions of the population. The masses remain as marginalized as ever. As previously indicated, historically half—and at times more—of Mexico's population has lived below the poverty line. Further, nearly 60 percent of the employed people in contemporary Mexico (compared to 47 percent in other Latin American and Caribbean countries) eke out a living in the informal sector, which usually means shaky self-employment, low earnings, and lack of access to safety-net programs. In the chronically depressed states of Guerrero, Oaxaca, and Chiapas, between three-quarters and four-fifths of the workers toil in the informal sector. Even in the more developed areas of northern Mexico, where most of the export manufacturing operations are concentrated, two-fifths of all the workers are in the informal economy. In 2010 the same proportion of Mexico's national population totally lacked a safety net; even among salaried workers in the formal sector, 38 percent did not have basic benefits such as health insurance.[23]

The Middle Class

The issue, on the other hand, of how the Mexican middle class has fared under the neoliberal economy since the mid-1990s has drawn increasing attention from the media, academics, and opinion makers. Although lack of uniform criteria for determining the actual size of the middle class makes it difficult to know precisely how this segment of society has been affected by the unprecedented changes that have taken place in Mexico, various well-placed sources offer some clues. The prevailing view is that *medioclaseros* (middle classers), estimated by most credible observers at between 25 and 40 percent of the Mexican population, have had a bumpy ride. For example, a 2002 article in the *New York Times* painted a grim picture of challenges faced by the middle class: "Economic liberalization has done little to close the huge divide between the privileged few and the poor, and left the middle class worse off than before. Battered by a series of severe recessions, teachers and engineers, nurses and small businessmen, all find themselves swinging above and below the poverty line with the rise and fall of the peso, interest rates and the unemployment rate."[24]

But that gloomy assessment is contested by some revisionist analysts who argue the opposite—that the ranks of medioclaseros have expanded substantially. Basing their estimates on individual or family expenditures and general consumption patterns, and citing data from national surveys, these researchers unabashedly claim that Mexico's middle class in fact adds up to 60 percent of the population. This new approach to class analysis follows the methodology of international researchers concerned with the size and characteristics the new "global middle class" in developing countries.[25] Scholar and former diplomat Jorge G. Castañeda accepts the 60 percent estimate and asserts that "the expansion of the Mexican middle class has been simply spectacular since 1994."[26] Castañeda makes reference to various measurements that suggest general improvements in everyday life, including higher income levels, rising home ownership, an increase in the extension of credit for home purchases, higher health insurance coverage, more people sending their children to private schools, a rise in the use of credit cards, and more working people traveling on low-cost airlines, as well as expanded ownership of automobiles, flat-screen televisions, cell phones, and computers. Castañeda credits greater market-driven activity that has enlarged the economic pie and brought down the cost of many consumer goods, and he praises government efforts to control inflation and to reduce poverty. He recognizes that the remittances sent by Mexicans in the United States to their homeland have also played an important role in improving living conditions for a substantial number of Mexicans. Castañeda also takes into account recent major breakthroughs in technology that have made advanced electronic gadgets affordable to lower-income Mexicans and improved their lives. In two recent publications, Shannon K. O'Neill of the U.S. Council on Foreign Relations strongly endorses the notion that the Mexican people now live a predominantly middle- and upper-class lifestyle. In her view, Mexico "has made it." Yet, curiously, she appears to contradict herself as she provides plenty of information regarding Mexico's many challenges in overcoming widespread poverty and fixing other vexing problems that grip the country.[27]

Many recognized experts within as well as outside Mexico dismiss the recent revisionist claims that the preponderant majority of Mexicans now enjoy a middle- or upper-class lifestyle. While the data or reports that Castañeda, O'Neil, and others rely on leave no doubt that the consumption of many commodities and services has increased in Mexico, it does not follow that consumers from the lower end of the income ladder should be counted as members the middle-class ranks just because they own modest homes and possess such products as used cars, flat-screen televisions, or cells phones. A high level of education, a good-paying occupation, strong purchasing power, reliable access to quality health care and, most of all, economic security remain the most important measures for determining who is in the middle class. The revisionists need to explain why unprecedented numbers of Mexicans migrated to the United States between the mid-1990s and 2007, precisely the period during which living conditions supposedly improved so much in Mexico. They also need to explain the impact on both the poor and the middle class of the enormous displacement of rural workers and small farmers brought about by the unprecedented influx of cheap foreign agricultural imports since the enactment of NAFTA. In short, the claims of the middle class-revisionists are grossly exaggerated. What is needed to derive a more accurate estimate of the Mexican middle class is a standard, scientifically based definition of what middle class means in Mexico. The use of differing data and multiple definitions has created confusion and spurred ideological debates that do little to advance knowledge. In 2013 Mexico's official Instituto Nacional de Estadística y Geografía (INEGI) took a welcome step to shed light on the subject by pouring through its massive databases and utilized methodologies related to household income and expenditures, levels of education, home ownership, types of employment, and so on, to conclude that 2.5 percent of Mexico's current households is upper class, 42.4 percent is middle class, and 55.1 percent is lower class.[28] Other official data indicate that a large percentage of the middle class remains vulnerable to economic swings and could quickly join the ranks of the poor. In effect, only a fifth of Mexico's population is definitely not poor and not economically at risk.[29]

Mexico's Contemporary Upper Class

As in the United States, where neoliberalism has thrived since the 1980s and wealth at the top has expanded, many Mexican elites have gotten richer during the same period as a result of the country's economic restructuring and the government's enhanced pro-business policies. According to the U.K.-based research organization Wealthinsight, between 2007 and 2012 the number of wealthy Mexicans grew by nearly a third, with 145,000 individuals having a net worth of over a million U.S. dollars the latter year and sixteen persons worth more than a billion U.S. dollars. What is striking is that the well-to-do in Mexico got significantly wealthier during the global Great Recession—precisely when the number of rich individuals around the world declined by 0.3 percent and at a time in Mexico when a large percentage of people in the middle and lower classes struggled to make ends meet.[30]

Apart from the traditionally wealthy whose fortunes have swelled, newly minted Mexican millionaires and billionaires have emerged from the ranks of those with good connections to Mexican policy makers and ties to multinational corporations, as well as those in a good position to take advantage of fresh opportunities created by the new economy. Privatization of hundreds of state enterprises provided one major avenue for well-situated entrepreneurs to acquire former state firms that had good growth prospects in an expanded market economy. For others, trade liberalization and the growth of the maquiladora industry significantly expanded possibilities to form lucrative partnerships with multinational corporations or to create their own companies designed to render all kinds of services to foreign manufacturing firms. Navigating government regulations, handling import/export transactions, hiring employees, and dealing with labor issues constitute some of the many services offered by typical Mexican broker or shelter companies.[31] Such consultant/service companies actually began to emerge in strategic urban border areas decades before the enactment of NAFTA, when Mexico established the Mexican Border Industrialization Program in 1965. At that time many Mexican property owners also benefitted greatly by providing land for new industrial parks, and Mexican construction companies increased their assets by building the structures for housing maquiladoras. These types of enterprises—and many others—multiplied with the post-NAFTA expansion of foreign-driven export manufacturing throughout Mexico.

The fortunes accumulated by rich Mexicans have understandably drawn much attention in light of the vast gulf that continues to exist between the haves and have-nots. Telecommunications mogul and superbillionaire Carlos Slim Helú has for years commanded the greatest public interest. In 2012 Slim Helú boasted a fortune of $73 billion dollars, allowing him to stay ahead of retired Microsoft entrepreneur Bill Gates (whose worth then amounted to $67 billion dollars) as the world's richest person. Fifteen other Mexicans, having fortunes ranging from $1.3 billion dollars to $18.2 billion dollars, also made the exclusive *Forbes* billionaire list in 2012.[32]

In Mexico, as in many other countries burdened by great wealth inequality, resentment against the rich has run high among the middle and lower classes. Some of the dislike for wealthy Mexicans certainly comes from envy. But, many people believe that fortunes have been made on the backs of exploited workers, or as a result of fraud or corruption, or simply because of business concessions obtained through privileged connections to those in power. The rich are also perceived as not caring much about the general well-being of the country and of being callously indifferent to the plight of the poor, as demonstrated by extremely low charitable giving to nonprofit organizations (not including churches). Further, long-staple behaviors among the rich such as keeping offshore accounts in the United States, the Cayman Islands, or Switzerland, and fiercely opposing the establishment of a fair taxation regime and/or evading taxes, are particularly grating to ordinary Mexicans. In the 1960s, at a time when Mexico's income from taxes as a percentage of GDP ranked among the lowest in the world, an estimated 75 percent of the already lightly taxed high-income groups reportedly practiced tax evasion.[33] Repeated attempts by the government to enact progressive tax reforms in subsequent years met with stiff resistance, resulting in 1980 in the replacement of many taxes with a value-added tax on consumption (IVA). Although everyone was subject to the IVA tax, the new system burdened workers and the middle class much more than wealthy people because the former groups typically spent a higher proportion of their income on basic necessities than the rich. Moreover, the law retained loopholes that continued to allow property owners and investors to easily hide income or to claim sundry exemptions. Tax revenues did rise as a percentage of GNP, but not by much.[34]

Mexico's complicated, unfair, and generally dysfunctional tax system changed relatively little from the 1980s into the early years of the twenty-first century. Exemptions and loopholes still abounded. With rampant tax evasion, public revenues remained low. In 2000, Mexico's tax revenues, at just 15 percent of GDP, ranked below the average for Latin American countries (21 percent) and significantly below the average for the member countries of the Organization for Economic Cooperation and Development (32 percent).[35]

The persistence of Mexico's notoriously inadequate tax system was noted in OECD reports for 2007 and 2013,[36] and in the latter year the Mexican government once again revamped the tax system, imposing higher levies on the wealthy while eliminating robust tax subsidies that had been granted to maquiladoras in 2003 in order to make that sector more competitive with China. The new law also imposed new taxes on junk food and increased the IVA on the northern border from 11 percent to 16 percent to coincide with the rest of the country. The additional revenues expected from the 2013 law has allowed Mexico to spend more on social programs and on infrastructure, but overall it represents reform at a level far below what is needed. Mexico will remain at the bottom of the OECD nations in tax revenues, with its "total tax take . . . [constituting] less than 19 percent of GDP in 2010, compared with nearly 26 percent for Turkey, around 31 percent in Greece, and 36 percent in Germany."[37]

Anti-rich sentiments in Mexico also have throughout history precipitated class warfare. In the 1810s, for example, impoverished peasants and workers who participated in the independence movement capitalized on the chaos to physically attack hated affluent Spaniards and to vandalize their properties. Throughout the nineteenth century, during the age of stagecoach travel, roaming bandits frequently robbed well-to-do travelers on Mexico's principal highways. During the Mexican Revolution of the 1910s insurrectionists from the lower classes routinely sought revenge against landowners who monopolized the good land or who kept the workforce in debt peonage; revolutionists also went after mine owners and other employers who exploited their workers and suppressed labor unions. And, in the latest outbreak of class fury, thousands of impoverished young men (and some women) who form part of the so-called *nini* population (youths who do not go to school or work) have served since the 1980s drug cartels as *sicarios* (hit men) or have joined gangs that are dedicated to such criminal activities as extortion and kidnapping, with people of means, especially business owners, as major targets.[38] Over the last decade the number of kidnappings in Mexico has reached staggering proportions. The most publicized case involved prominent PAN politician Diego Fernández de Ceballos in 2010. Held in captivity for over six months, Fernández de Ceballos was finally released after relatives paid a ransom estimated at $30 million dollars.

Wealthy Mexicans have followed various strategies in response to the violence and threats against them as a class. Commonly they have protected themselves by walling off their homes, controlling access into their exclusive neighborhoods, hiring twenty-four-hour security guards, riding around in bulletproof vehicles, and exercising great caution in their daily routines and travels, making sure they are always accompanied by personal bodyguards. Many affluent families living in the most violent locales have moved to more secure areas of Mexico to escape kidnappings, extortion, or destruction of their businesses (usually by arson). And tens of thousands have migrated to safer pastures in the United States, with most settling in cities in the U.S. borderlands. An untold number of these well-off refugees have moved their businesses from Mexico to the United States or have started new ones. By bringing at least $1 million dollars and creating at least ten jobs, or investing $500,000 in a high-unemployment area, business-oriented migrants easily qualify for entry into the United States under the requirements for an EB-5 visa; thus the United States has reaped significant benefits from the influx of these migrants. In a three-year period from 2010 to 2013, for example, wealthy

Mexicans invested about $45 million dollars in Dallas, Texas, setting up a variety of new businesses.[39] That story has been repeated many times in other cities such as San Antonio, El Paso, Tucson, Phoenix, San Diego, and Los Angeles.

Conclusion

The social inequalities that have long existed in Mexico have drawn much criticism within the country and abroad. Mexicans at the top of the social pyramid have managed to accumulate riches, even vast fortunes, while the bottom half of the population (or more) has historically struggled to make a living. Wealth redistribution initiatives undertaken in the past, such as those of the post-Revolution years, yielded only modest results—and they ran their course long ago. Many Mexicans place the blame for the poverty that continues to afflict the nation squarely on the rich and on corporate exploitation. The elite, it is said, not only monopolize wealth, but they care little about uplifting the masses. Certainly greed and selfishness in Mexican oligarchic circles and in the corporate world constitute important contributors to Mexico's uneven development. In the face of pronounced inequality, three developments more than likely account for the relative absence of serious domestic unrest over the last century: first, migration to the United States by millions of desperate people has provided a major safety valve; second, drastic declines in the rate of growth of the population since the late 1970s have reduced pressures on the economy; and third, recent expansions of the national safety net have made life a bit easier for millions of destitute Mexicans.

In the prosperous United States, poverty has not been as large a problem as in Mexico, and those defined as poor Americans have actually been much better off than poor Mexicans. Still, large segments of the U.S. population, especially dark-skinned minorities, have long been marginalized and have lived below the national poverty line for generations. Additionally, income and wealth concentration has historically been a serious problem in the United States, and the gap between rich and everyone else has grown alarmingly high since the 1980s. The gigantic size of the economic pie in the United States and the safety nets that it produces probably explain why dispossessed Americans have not rebelled.

Notes

1 Extensive historical data on income and wealth inequality in the United States is contained in Picketty (2014).
2 Walton and Shepherd (1979), 146–147, 149.
3 Picketty (2014), 24, 348.
4 Picketty (2014), 34, 348.
5 Patterson (1994), 7, 13, 41–42, 79; Katz and Stern (2001), 6, 13, 34.
6 See www.routledge.com/martínez/mexico/tables/table2.1.
7 Cited in Rosenzweig Hernández (1963), 455–460.
8 De la Calle and Rubio (2012), 31.

9 See www.routledge.com/martínez/mexico/tables/table2.2.
10 Weisbrot et al. (2014), 10.
11 Rhoda and Burton (2010), 62; México, INEGI (2013b).
12 INEGI (2013b).
13 See www.routledge.com/martínez/mexico/tables/table2.3. The Gini Coefficient (or Gini Index) measures income and wealth inequality. A score of 0 means complete equality, whereas a score of 100 indicates complete inequality (one person receives all the income or has all the wealth).
14 De la Calle and Rubio (2012), 40–41.
15 LoPalo and Orrenious (2013), 12.
16 See www.routledge.com/martínez/mexico/tables/table2.4.
17 Bortz and Aguila (2006), 112–138.
18 As reported in *La Jornada* (July 17, 2013).
19 OECD (2013); *The Economist* (2014).
20 U.S. Department of Labor (2012).
21 *Mexico Now* (September–October 2013), 26.
22 Yuk (2013).
23 FNS News (2012); México, INEGI (2010), 73; México, CONEVAL (2012), 35.
24 *New York Times* (September 4, 2002), A3.
25 See, for example, Kharas (2010).
26 Castañeda (2011), 48.
27 O'Neil (2013a, 2013b).
28 México, INEGI (2013a).
29 As reported in *Mexico Now* (November–December, 2014), 22.
30 See Salem-news.com/print/27810, June 30, 2013.
31 Other assistance provided to the maquiladora sector by Mexican shelter firms includes transportation, logistics, warehousing, human resources, medical insurance, environment compliance, language and culture training, legal advice, facilities management, security, utility services, fiscal and tax administration, and cafeteria services.
32 *Forbes Magazine* (2013).
33 González Casanova (1970), 139.
34 Elizondo (1994).
35 Werner et al. (2006), 87–88.
36 OECD (2007, 2013).
37 *New York Times* (November 1, 2013).
38 The word *nini* derives from the saying, "Ni estudian ni trabajan" (They neither study nor work). In 2012, a report from Mexico's Subsecretaría de Educación Superior estimated the total number of ninis in the country at 7.8 million (*La Jornada*, March 12, 2012).
39 World Security Network, Latin America (November 8, 2008); *El Paso Times* (August 7, 2011); *Time Magazine* (January 14, 2013).

PART II
CONTEXT
NATURE AND PEOPLE

3
THE POWER OF GEOGRAPHY

Geography is central to understanding Mexico's uneven development. For starters, Mexico's physical configuration, which is an outcome of war waged by the United States in the nineteenth century, constitutes a space that has major climatic and topographic problems. Had Mexico been able to retain all the territory it possessed at its independence, its future would have been much different—in essence a good deal brighter and significantly more prosperous. Geographical problems would not have been as overwhelming as they have been for the Mexican people. Additional spaces of exceptional worth (such as Texas and California) would have been available to Mexicans to build a much larger economic pie, one that would have provided many more favorable spaces and more opportunities. Much of Mexico's underdevelopment clearly stems from less than ideal environmental conditions, including insufficient rainfall, scarcity of good land, and shortages of key resources, as well as generally unfavorable conditions in the country's ubiquitous mountainous areas, deserts, and jungles.

Contiguity with the United States over a 2,000 mile border has also affected Mexico's economic fate in a decisive manner. As the only developing country sharing a border with the world's superpower, Mexico has been undermined in its efforts to build strong domestic industries in the face of unrelenting competition and pressures from the largest economy on the planet. On the other hand, adjacency to the United States has provided Mexico with convenient access to a lucrative external market.

Geography also explains a great deal of the success achieved by Mexico's neighbor, the United States, which possesses many natural assets that Mexico lacks. Yet the contribution that geography would make to U.S. national greatness was hardly conceivable to those early English immigrants who established a foothold along the eastern seaboard of North America. In the seventeenth century the settlers in the thirteen colonies saw Spain as the big winner in global exploration and colonization because of the Spanish discoveries of vast gold and silver deposits in Mexico and other parts of Latin America. England was disappointed at the relative absence of such natural wealth in those areas of North America settled by its people. Getting rich quickly from mining was not possible in the thirteen colonies. Over the long run, however, opportunities for wealth accumulation would increase significantly for European Americans as the colonies evolved into an independent country whose territory and natural endowment grew immensely. The United States would come to occupy an exceptional space with a superb location between two oceans, one blessed with a temperate climate, abundant fertile lands, plentiful forests, large deposits of minerals, excellent coasts, outstanding harbors, and many inland navigable waterways. These splendid conditions would allow Americans to make full utilization of economic innovations produced during successive industrial revolutions. It is for these reasons that United States became the land of opportunity.

Geographical forces have long been recognized as playing central roles in the fate of nations, yet exaggerated claims by early twentieth-century scholars regarding what they believed to be the deterministic character of climate and physical geography on human behavior subsequently undermined consideration of the environment as a central factor in economic development. "Environmental determinists" were censured for using geography to explain alleged differences in intellectual abilities among the races, and they were further accused of assigning greater significance to geography than to human capabilities. For decades such criticisms discouraged geography-centered studies of economic activity. In recent years, however, a growing number of scholars have rightly argued that one does not need to embrace determinism or minimize human choice to recognize that geography plays an extraordinary role in the creation of uneven economic playing fields among nations.[1]

Environmental Attributes of the United States

The sweeping geographic advantages enjoyed by the United States begin with the physical structure of North America, which, as geographer J. Wreford Watson writes, "provides remarkable balance between central shield, interior lowlands, and marginal mountains. There is not the imbalance which makes Africa mainly shield, which pre-empts the heart of Asia with mountains thrusting the plains to the perimeter, and which breaks up Europe into such highly separable units on the west or puts it under the dominance of one great region in the east. In North America, shield, plain, and mountain are about evenly matched and help to account for a varied and yet even economy."[2] Apart from that natural geological balance, the United States in particular has been also greatly favored by location, benign climates, and many other features of the nation's land mass that in combination with one another have provided unequalled favorable conditions for bounteous economic growth and development.

Country Location and Climate

I became aware of the importance of location in an economic sense when, as a twelve-year-old, I sold newspapers in downtown El Paso. Newsboys with "seniority" were assigned specific spots to set up their makeshift stands and sell their product to passersby. These were usually the best locations, in essence "people magnet" buildings (like the post office) or corners of intersecting busy streets—the most heavily trafficked sites where people inclined to read newspapers congregated or walked by. The boys with the most seniority thus inevitably sold the most newspapers and made the most money. Later in life I was not surprised to learn that the most significant factor one has to consider in purchasing a home or setting up a business is "location, location, location."

The location principle also applies to countries. The geographic location of the United States is unequalled; situated in the middle latitudes of the northern Western Hemisphere, the continental United States is the beneficiary of excellent climatic and soil variability. Moreover, the country sits at the center of the world's major trade routes, has ready accessibility to other continents via two oceans and a gulf, and has easy land connections to two large neighboring countries. It is little wonder that political scientist and geostrategist Nicholas J. Spykman considered the United States "the most favored state in the world from the point of view of location."[3]

The mostly temperate climates in the United States have enabled the growing of a great variety of agricultural crops and have contributed to the relatively healthy environment enjoyed by the country's large population. The annual cycle of warm and cold weather in much of the lower forty-eight states assures that disease-carrying and crop-destroying insects will not live year-round. In the eastern part of the country, the north and central zones have a humid, temperate climate, with cool summers in the north and warm summers in the center, while in the south a humid, subtropical climate predominates. The tip of Florida has a wet/dry tropical climate. The western part of the country is more varied: it includes a semiarid steppe climate over a wide region, a highland alpine climate in the mountain zones, a semiarid and arid climate in the desert areas, a Mediterranean climate in California, and a marine west coast climate in Oregon and Washington. In the far northern state of Alaska, the mid-latitude oceanic and subarctic conditions preclude large-scale population agglomeration and limit agricultural production. On the islands of Hawaii, a warm, humid climate moderated by trade winds allows for the growing of tropical crops and provides generally pleasant living conditions for people.

Upon independence, the United States found itself in a central location that gave its people an advantage in conducting international trade and, as the nation expanded, the advantages multiplied with the incorporation of productive regions favored by superb natural settings, especially agricultural areas. For example, Iowa's great ability to grow corn has been a function of location because the climate, soil conditions, and flat land in the state combined to create ideal farming conditions. In the West, California's latitudinal location on the West Coast translates into a mild climate. The combination of good climatic conditions and vast fertile lands form the basis for the agricultural productivity upon which much of California's economy has depended for generations.

Most of the continental United States has far more spaces suitable for human habitation and economic productivity than either Canada or Mexico. From the beginning European immigrants found the temperate humid climates of the eastern United States quite familiar and comfortable enough since much of Europe has similar conditions. In effect, the favorable environmental circumstances of the Eastern Seaboard substantially increased the economic potential of that region, and it did not take long for it to become the leading economic section within the country. It is true that various parts of the United States are subject to extreme seasonal weather conditions, including severe winters, uncomfortable summers, and the occurrence of seasonal hurricanes and tornadoes. But, generally speaking, the good seasons in the continental United States trump the difficult periods in most places where weather problems exist. Further, the wealth accumulated by Americans long ago allowed them to develop the means to surmount most weather challenges. Such things as paved roads, railways, snow-removal equipment, indoor manufacturing (factories), strong construction materials, central heating, air conditioning, and weather forecasting have made bad weather less worrisome. Chicago is a prime example of a thriving metropolis that has used its excellent location and available technologies to mitigate the harshness of its frequently brutal winters.

Size, Shape, and Topography

Not counting Alaska and Hawaii, the United States ranks fifth in size in the world (third counting those two states), with only Russia, Canada, China, and Brazil having larger areas. But although smaller than those countries, the continental United States has a better location, better climates, and better topographical and other land features, as well as an overall better resource endowment and more numerous and larger habitable areas. If the endowments of Alaska and Hawaii are added, especially their natural resources, the U.S. advantages become even more formidable.

The roughly rectangular shape of the continental United States has yielded major economic benefits to the country. Unlike many nations that have only one or two natural land communication and transportation corridors for the dissemination of information and the flow of people and trade, the United States not only has broad east-west and north-south axes but many diagonal axes as well. Railroads and motorized vehicles have moved efficiently along many modern thoroughfares, and watercraft have carried a high volume of freight via the country's great navigable waterways. Historically the major movement across the United States has been between east and west, where human and commercial traffic travels relatively unobstructed from coast to coast along busy highways and railway corridors, easily connecting regions, cities, and centers of production along the way. Free-flowing traffic between north and south has been equally as intense along excellent transportation corridors on the Atlantic and Pacific Coasts and in the vast region of the Great Plains, but less so in the deserts and mountainous areas west of the Great Plains. The diagonal corridors that join opposite corners of the rectangle complete the extensive web of national linkages in the continental United States—all made possible by the country's large size, convenient shape, and favorable topography.

While significant mountain systems are found in the continental United States, none have presented insurmountable barriers to human and commercial traffic and communication. Certainly the United States has been spared the formidable topographical obstacles present in several South American countries in the Andean region, or in Mexico, where the various Sierra Madre mountain ranges that dominate the landscape impose innumerable impediments. The Appalachian Mountains were initially seen as a serious barrier to migration from the Eastern Seaboard into the U.S. interior, but once exploration yielded a more accurate picture of the topography, that perception changed, and by the early years of the republic, waves upon waves of European Americans traveled around or through the Appalachians via various routes leading to the West. Remarkably, six railroad lines already crossed the Appalachians by 1830, underscoring the fact that the Appalachian Mountains posed few hurdles to modern travel,[4] and eventually many highways were built across the Appalachian region. The other mountain systems in the continental United States underwent similar transportation developments. Some arteries that traversed particularly difficult terrain in areas like the Rocky Mountains, the Cascade Range, the Sierra Nevada, and the Pacific Ranges required significant effort and expense, but natural passes through even imposing mountain terrain made it possible to build extensive roads, highways, and railway lines through them. In short, building modern forms of land transportation in the United States was comparatively easy and inexpensive, at least when compared to Mexico and other mountainous countries.

Coasts, Harbors, and Hinterlands

The continental United States is also favored by excellent coastal areas that border the Atlantic and Pacific Oceans and the Gulf of Mexico. Since the early nineteenth century, favorable conditions have sustained urbanization and economic productivity on a grand scale in these regions, and it is hardly surprising that in 2000 more than half of all Americans lived in the country's coastal areas. Nearly a fourth of the U.S. population resided in the Atlantic coastal region, 13 percent in the Pacific coastal region, 10 percent in the Great Lakes coastal region, and 6 percent in the Gulf of Mexico coastal region.[5] The coastal states (including the Great Lakes states) make up only slightly more than two-fifths of the nation's territory, yet almost four-fifths of the U.S. population resided there in 2010. The coastal states also produced over four-fifths of the country's GDP.[6] Further, the top ten metro areas with proximate ocean access accounted for a third of the nation's GDP, while the top ten inland metro areas accounted for slightly over one-tenth. Seventeen of the twenty largest U.S. urban areas have coastal locations or front navigable lakes or rivers.[7]

Underlying the favorable coastal conditions are the natural indentations of the shorelines. These indentations have bestowed a treasure trove of sheltered inlets and bays that have proved ideal for the building of deepwater ports. Prominent examples include the Boston Bay, Long Island Sound, New Jersey Bay, the Mississippi River Delta, Galveston Bay, Chesapeake Bay, St. Lawrence Seaway, Puget Sound, San Francisco Bay, and San Diego Bay. Having easy accessibility to highly productive hinterlands, numerous well-situated ports on these waterways have served as highly effective funnels for the transfer of products between the interior United States and foreign lands.

The eastern United States stands out as the nation's premiere coastal area. The gently graded and broad slopes stretching from the Appalachian highlands to the Atlantic Ocean created an extensive habitable space ideally suited for diverse economic activity, including dynamic oceangoing trade in the immediate coastal belt, vigorous agriculture in the plains and piedmont regions, and thriving waterpower industries and mining in the highland valleys. Along the 2,069 miles of coastline from Maine to Florida, plenty of excellent bays, inlets, and estuaries have played host to harbors that are favored with unobstructed ties to prosperous hinterlands and with convenient links to the commerce of Europe, Africa, and Latin America. It is noteworthy that more world-class seaports are found along the U.S. Atlantic Coast than along the coasts of Canada and Latin America combined.[8]

The splendid natural endowment of the East Coast was obvious to anyone concerned with economic activity early in the country's history, as evidenced by the following comment from 1810: "The vast extent of seacoast, the number of excellent harbors and sea-port towns, the numerous creeks and immense bays, which indent the coast; and the rivers, lakes, and canals which peninsulate [*sic*] the whole country, added to its agricultural advantages and improvements, give this part of the world superior advantages for trade."[9] Even New England, which was short on agricultural and mineral resources, had other significant assets that propelled it into economic prominence. New England's "deeply embayed coast, the narrowness of the lowland belt, the glaciated soil, the power resources of the plunging streams, the heavy forest growth, and the abundance of fish in the coastal waters were all geographic factors operating to develop maritime life."[10] Fishing, shipbuilding, and commerce became the pillars of New England's seafaring activities, with foreign trade constituting a prime enterprise. Boston, which possessed one of the best harbors in the world and an easily accessible productive hinterland, excelled early on as the trade metropolis of the region. Other smaller ports like Portland, Providence, Portsmouth, New Haven, and Newport also did well in carrying on commercial interchanges with the outside world. In recent decades the volume of trade flowing through the New England ports has not grown as much as in the larger ports in other coastal areas, but maritime activity in New England remains significant.[11]

To the south of Boston, cities like Philadelphia, New York, and Baltimore, having easier access to fecund hinterlands, emerged as important ports by the early years of the republic. Eventually New York City would take the top spot as the preeminent port on the East Coast and rank at or near the top in port activity both in the entire country and in the world. New York City has an exceptional location on a major transatlantic trade route leading to Europe, excellent connections to the rich hinterlands in the Ohio Valley and farther West, and a spacious natural harbor encompassing a waterfront extending hundreds of miles. New York City also received a great commercial boost that competitors could not match following the construction of the Erie Canal in the 1820s. The Erie Canal made it possible for freight to travel inexpensively for hundreds of miles via a water route that linked the Great Lakes to the Hudson River and the Atlantic Ocean, with New York City as the lynchpin in that network. As the railways expanded westward from the East Coast, New York City greatly enhanced its capacity as a commercial and financial center,[12] and later, with the onset of motorized vehicular traffic, New York City enlarged its hegemony over much of the interior of the United States. Apart from having outstanding transportation links, the excellent water depth, lack of strong currents, benign tides, benign silting, a straight entrance channel, and generally ice-free conditions helped make the port at New York City a world-class facility.

Conditions on the coast from Virginia to Florida manifest important differences from those found on the Northern Seaboard. While the harbors in the South Atlantic area are fine, their location is not as favorable. Good hinterlands lie near the harbors, but the productive areas of the Midwest and the northern Great Plains are located far away. Until recent times the South had a predominantly agricultural economy, and much of the South's products were processed in the North and foreign trade was funneled through the large ports in the Northeast. But in the decades following World War II the South became more industrialized, its transportation infrastructure expanded, and its urban centers grew larger. The region experienced a great transformation that led to an economic and population boom. Naturally the coastal areas benefitted from these trends and many southern seaports rose in importance, in particular Savannah, Georgia; Hampton Roads, Virginia; Charleston, South Carolina; and Jacksonville and Miami, Florida.

The U.S. plains adjacent to the Gulf of Mexico, favored by the intersection of numerous rivers and endowed with valuable natural resources both on land and offshore, as well as a climate ideal for the growing of semitropical crops, not surprisingly also developed into a major center of economic activity in the United States. The 1,631 miles of Gulf coastline include many favorable sites that gave rise to dozens of ports that have serviced the region for many generations. The New Orleans and Houston areas have a well-earned reputation as two giant economic engines, providing shipping facilities for sundry agricultural goods and the Gulf's abundant oil, gas, and petrochemical products. New Orleans, at the mouth of the Mississippi River, has been one of the busiest maritime centers since the early nineteenth century, serving as a receptor of imports from throughout the world and as the gateway to a vast and complex U.S. river system encompassing thirty-three U.S. states. In addition, the sprawling Port of South Louisiana offers more than 100 miles of deepwater frontage extending upriver along the Mississippi. In 2006, the Port of South Louisiana ranked first in the United States in total trade and twelfth in the world in cargo handled, while the Port of New Orleans ranked eighth and fiftieth respectively, and the Port of Houston, which extends along a twenty-five-mile-long ship channel, ranked second and fourteenth respectively.[13] Houston's emergence as a world-class port came much later than the rise of New Orleans; it was the discovery of large deposits of oil and gas along the Texas and Louisiana coasts that propelled Houston into commercial prominence beginning in the early twentieth century, and the city has maintained its lofty position to the present. And like Houston, the ports of Galveston, Corpus Christi, and smaller seaside communities in the region draw from the massive productive hinterland of Texas, which is unhindered by natural barriers and supplies agricultural products, cattle, timber, oil, and other raw materials and industrial goods.

The coastal areas of the western continental United States comprise many different landscapes and have a diverse topography; thus they differ significantly from both the Gulf and the Atlantic coasts. Various mountain ranges close to the Pacific Ocean and farther inland break up the terrain in such a way that favorable spaces for human settlement and economic productivity are interspersed throughout the states of Washington, Oregon, and California. Because of the sharp topography, the coastline of these three states (1,293 miles) provides fewer exceptional harbors and hinterlands than is the case on the other two coasts. Nevertheless, the coasts of the far western states are favored with extraordinary natural endowments in select regions, both by the sea and in the interior, allowing for the development of world-class seaports and large population centers. Highly productive spaces have yielded a variety of energy resources, foodstuffs, timber, and industrial products, all of which have figured prominently in the economy of the United States. California's enormous assets have sustained that state's number one economic ranking among the fifty states for decades, while Washington has ranked in the top third and Oregon in the middle of the pack.

A few details pertaining to the California ports further illustrate the importance of the Pacific coastal zone. The contiguous ports at Long Beach and Los

Angeles stand out globally for their level of activity. Together they constitute the biggest mega-port in the Western Hemisphere and rank seventh in the world in handling container traffic.[14] Both are man-made facilities, illustrating that even in the absence of natural harbors, the exceptional physical and climatic conditions that prevail in Southern California have made possible the building of world-class seaports. The massive twenty-four square miles of the Long Beach/Los Angeles port complex has one of the most prosperous hinterlands in the world—the state of California, with its vast natural wealth and huge industrial base. The port facilities have also been favored with terrain that allows easy truck and railroad access directly to the docks, from which cargo can be quickly transferred. Trucks and trains loaded with freight from ships have convenient connections to a vast interstate highway system and a railway network that allow for unobstructed travel on mostly flat land all the way to the East Coast. The clockwork precision and efficiency with which the work is carried out in the ports of both cities is a sight to behold, but without the favorable natural physical conditions that exist onshore and offshore at the Long Beach/Los Angeles port sites, a high level of activity would hardly be possible.

To the north along the California coast are the Ports of San Francisco and Oakland, situated in one of the world's best natural harbors, which combines a magnificent bay and estuary. Such attributes, along with a splendid location vis-à-vis world trade, account for their emergence early on as important gateways to Asia. For generations San Francisco was the more important of the two ports because of its location adjacent to the sea, but in the early twentieth century, San Francisco found it difficult to compete with other Pacific ports, and eventually a lack of space prevented expansion of its facilities to accommodate container shipping on a large scale. As the Port of San Francisco declined in importance, the Port of Oakland took advantage of its excellent location on the inner bay, superior land transportation connections, and superb physical conditions at the port itself to become "a world-class cargo transportation and distribution hub" in the age of containerized shipping. The deepening of the estuary channel and the building of terminal and railway facilities led to a great expansion of operations, eventually elevating Oakland to the country's fourth most important container port.[15]

I first saw the San Francisco Bay and its magnificent harbors when my dad, my brother, and I crossed the Golden Gate Bridge in 1961 on a leisure day trip to San Francisco from Santa Rosa, where we had camped out for a few weeks during one of the summers that we travelled the migrant trail in California. I recall the thrill of crossing the Golden Gate, looking at the San Francisco skyline, gazing at ships entering and leaving the bay, and seeing passenger and commercial ships at the port. That feeling of wonderment always returned to me on many subsequent visits in later years to San Francisco and Oakland, particularly when I lived in Mountain View during my days as a graduate student at Stanford University and U.C. Berkeley, and later when I lived in Palo Alto during a year-long residency at the Center for Advanced Study in the Behavioral Sciences. As I learned more history and gained greater appreciation for the role of coastal areas and harbors in economic development, I frequently reflected on the causes of the immense economic differences between the United States and Mexico, and my thoughts at times gravitated toward history. I could not help but think that Mexicans had lost a great deal when the United States forcibly detached the San Francisco Bay area from Mexico in the mid-nineteenth century. No harbor in the greatly reduced and geographically problematic space that became Mexico after 1848 came close to having the natural advantages of the San Francisco/Oakland area for conducting world trade. The larger point that stayed with me is that the relationship between nature and history matters greatly in understanding a country's fortunes.

Attributes of Mexico's Environment

The contrast in environmental conditions between the United States and Mexico is striking. It is not an exaggeration to say that a rather large percentage of Mexico's territory is not ideal given that mountains, deserts, and jungles dominate the landscape. Mountains have hampered transportation and isolated many parts of the country from each other, deserts have left vast areas uninhabited, and

MAP 3.1 Contemporary Mexico

hot and humid coasts have been difficult to settle. Even in the central plateau, where the climate is generally good, large areas are drought-stricken and therefore uninviting. In short, the number of favorable spaces—that is, those areas most suitable to sustain large-scale economic activity and/or to support population agglomeration—are rather few in Mexico and in many instances remain poorly integrated into the national economy.

Mexican leaders and thinkers have long recognized the reality of Mexico's geographic limitations. In the early twentieth century, for example, the well-known journalist and intellectual Justo Sierra pointed out many of the obstacles that nature posed for Mexico.[16] More recently, Gerardo Esquivel has documented environmental disparities within Mexico's territory and their consequences for wealth distribution. Making it clear that he is not promoting "geographic determinism," Esquivel nonetheless concludes that key "geographic variables explain about two-thirds of the inter-state variation in per-capita income in Mexico."[17] Historians and other scholars have also known that geography has played an important role in constraining Mexico's development. Yet rather than examining Mexico's natural impediments in detail, the usual practice among many scholars has been to merely acknowledge that geographic difficulties exist. That is unfortunate because environmental forces have actually had an enormous impact on Mexico.

Country Location and Climate

A nation's location in relation to other countries matters a great deal. From a geopolitical perspective, Mexico's juxtaposition to the United States historically provided an irresistible temptation for Americans to covet neighboring Mexican lands and eventually to wage war to satisfy that craving. In the absence of natural barriers separating the two countries, Mexicans had great difficulties defending the homeland, especially the wide open northern frontier. Thus the United States and other foreign powers found it relatively easy to mount repeated invasions of Mexico. Such attacks took a heavy toll on Mexico economically and politically, with the most devastating result being the calamitous loss of extremely valuable real estate to the United States. Viewed in global terms, Mexico's geopolitical vulnerabilities fit a historical pattern whereby weak countries situated next to strong countries usually wind up either swallowed up or dismembered by their strong neighbors.[18] In Mexico's case, a practically nonexistent navy and feeble land defenses facilitated foreign intrusions in the nineteenth century. The country lacked a functional navy because of minimal national maritime activity owing to the unhealthy, poorly resource-endowed, and sparsely populated Pacific, Gulf of California, Gulf of Mexico, and Caribbean coastlines. Land forces were largely concentrated in the Central Highlands, where most Mexicans lived. To protect the far-flung northern frontier against U.S. aggression, poorly trained and poorly equipped troops had to travel long distances across vast unpopulated deserts.

Supply lines could not be properly maintained. In short, largely unfavorable geographic factors contributed in a significant way to Mexico's massive loss of land to its expansionist-minded next-door neighbor.

Mexico's location entails other disadvantages. Mexico would be in a much better situation if it were positioned on the main path of world trade routes, rather than on subsidiary and peripheral routes. Additionally, Mexico's trade possibilities would be enhanced if nearby nations in the Caribbean and in Central America had higher levels of economic development. But most importantly, adjacency to the powerful U.S. economy exposed Mexico to the unyielding influx of foreign manufactured products both via legal imports and contraband. That exposure has had the effect of stifling or precluding the development of many Mexican industries; further, the extensive collaboration of Mexican businesspeople and industrialists with powerful U.S. corporations has undermined domestic efforts to build a stronger and more independent Mexican economy.

Of course Mexico's location also has its virtues. Situated in North America and between two oceans, Mexico has enjoyed benefits that many developing countries wish they had. Mexico has had convenient land and water access to the dynamic economy of the United States, and ocean connections to countries in Asia and Europe. These geographic assets have paid significant dividends for Mexico—even if those dividends have been largely tied to the export of raw materials, as was the case in the pre-1980 economy, or linked to the cheap labor supplied by Mexicans to the new export-oriented manufacturing economy.

With respect to climate, the scholarly literature is replete with references to the many difficulties endured by Mexico due to problematic weather conditions (See Map 3.2). These include stifling heat and humidity in tropical areas, scarce moisture in desert zones, and excessive and destructive rainfall in mountain areas. To illustrate the uneven rain distribution: southeast Mexico receives up to 120 inches or more annually, while the arid north receives on average only 16 inches.[19] Given that arid lands comprise over half of Mexico's land surface and an additional third are classified as semiarid, the availability of land for cultivation is rather limited;[20] thus agricultural challenges are considerable.

While deficient moisture has stymied food production, rain that falls in excessive amounts in short periods of time in the vulnerable landscapes of Mexico often brings devastation. Serious flooding, mudslides, and road washouts are frequent occurrences in agricultural zones and in communities located both in low and high altitudes. One of the worst natural disasters of all time happened in 2013 when Tropical Storm Manuel (from the Gulf of Mexico) and Hurricane Ingrid (from the Pacific Ocean) simultaneously struck the relatively narrow landmass of Mexico in the central and southern zones and also battered parts of the northeast and the northwest.[21] Between two-thirds to four-fifths of Mexico's territory was hit by the storms. Torrential rains, raging rivers, flooding, rockslides, and mudslides caused approximately 140 deaths and inflicted immense damage to agriculture. Portions of countless roads and highways were washed out or blocked by enormous mudslides, including the important artery between Mexico City and Acapulco. Guerrero, Oaxaca, and Michoacán were the states that were affected the worst. The government calculated overall damages at $7 billion dollars.[22]

Size, Shape, and Topography

With an area of nearly 0.8 million square miles, Mexico is the world's fourteenth largest country. But the size is misleading. Since mountains, deserts, and jungles overwhelm the landscape, only a relatively small percentage of the land is suitable for habitation or for making a living. The central volcanic axis as a whole stands out as the most hospitable and fertile region of the country. Much smaller but otherwise fertile pockets are found elsewhere.

Mexico is shaped like a cornucopia, or horn of plenty, with the wide end at the border with the United States and the narrowest part at the Isthmus of Tehuantepec. At the Isthmus the land widens, with the continuation of Mexico following an eastward direction into Chiapas and then a northeastward turn into Yucatán. In the past, observers who were mesmerized by the precious metals found in Mexico, and who believed that the country possessed many other riches, indeed referred to Mexico as a cornucopia. They were mistaken in their overly optimistic perception, but such a view influenced the way Mexico was perceived by foreigners and Mexicans alike.

MAP 3.2 Major climates of Mexico (simplified)

Source: INEGI and various reference works. Based on map retrieved on May 19, 2009, from http://mexicochannel.net/maps/climates.gif.

The most overpowering physical feature of Mexico is its mountainous terrain, with about 75 percent of the land situated above 3,300 feet above sea level, compared to some 25 percent for the United States and approximately 12 percent for Canada. Western, eastern, and southern Mexico are dominated by the imposing Sierra Madre Ranges, and rugged topography is also found in the Transverse Volcanic Range of central Mexico and the Baja California Peninsular Ranges. The predominance of high-altitude living in Mexico is further illustrated by the fact that 80 percent of the population lives above 3,300 feet, compared to less than 5 percent of the populations of the United States and Canada. Moreover, twenty of the capitals of Mexico's thirty-two states are situated at over 3,000 feet in altitude, compared to only seven of the state capitals in the fifty U.S. states.[23] Mexico's contorted landscape became known to the King of Spain in the sixteenth century when the conquistador Hernán Cortés gave his first report on what he had found in the land of the Aztecs. Cortés is said to have crumpled a piece of paper, placed it on a table, and stated simply, "This is Mexico."

Geographers, historians, and other writers have long recognized that the ubiquitous mountains have played a decisive role in the evolution of Mexico (See Map 3.3). The Sierra Madre Oriental and the Sierra Madre Occidental run parallel to both coasts and practically become one chain in southern Mexico. There the Sierra Madre del Sur rises in Chiapas and continues southward into Guatemala. The western coast is narrow and in some areas the mountains hug the seashore. Noting the barriers imposed by the Sierra Madre ranges on travel between the interior and the coasts, as well as other problems inherent to Mexico's difficult landscape, Frank Tannenbaum concluded in 1950 that "the physical geography could not have been better designed to isolate Mexico from the world and Mexicans from each other." He observed that travel between Mexico City and Cuernavaca, which are only thirty-six air miles apart, require climbing to nearly 10,000 feet and then trekking down a steep descent to 5,000 feet. He added that in many mountain areas of southern Mexico "the pockets that permit towns and villages to survive are often riven and torn, and man holds onto a steep mountainside for a habitat because no other is available."[24]

The presence of the formidable mountain ranges paralleling the east and west coasts, coupled with the funnel or triangular shape of the country, limit Mexico mostly to one north-south axis from the northern border to the Isthmus of Tehuantepec. From the Isthmus the axis turns eastward-northeastward, ending on the northern coast of Yucatán. Because of this physical configuration and topography, Mexico lacks the ability of the United States to easily establish and maintain communication and transportation corridors in all directions. A glance at any road or railway map of Mexico will quickly reveal that the major routes of travel run north-south along the Baja California Peninsula, the West Coast, the Central Plateau, and the East Coast. East-west connections are few and far between simply because of the powerful constraints imposed by the Sierra Madre Oriental and the Sierra Madre Occidental.

MAP 3.3 Topography of Mexico
Source: Based on map in Cockcroft (1998), 8.

The difficulties of traversing areas of Mexico dominated by mountains are etched in my recollection of two personal trips. Years ago I rode the Chihuahua al Pacífico railroad from Chihuahua City to Los Mochis, Sinaloa, in both directions. I was struck by the immensity of the mountains, the ruggedness of the terrain, and the width and depth of the canyons. I was also amazed by the many switchbacks, high bridges, and tunnels along the route. Only then did I really understand why there was no highway paralleling the railway line and why the Chihuahua al Pacífico was not completed until 1961. My second memorable land journey was the drive I once took from Mexico City to Oaxaca on the old two-lane roadway many years before the construction of the current modern divided highway. I remember a very long, frustrating trip in which I came upon endless mountains that required numerous steep climbs and descents, as well as many dangerous curves. I swore I would never make that maddening drive again, and I never have.

In lectures when I mention the economic impediments that mountains have posed for Mexico, doubters in the audience will often cite Switzerland as an example of a country that has prospered in spite of its ubiquitous mountains. To such skeptics topography is either a nonissue with respect to economic development or they feel that Switzerland has simply dealt with mountainous terrain much better than Mexico. My response is that Mexico and Switzerland are very different from one another and that the effect of topography in each country needs to be assessed in relation to other factors. Mexico, which is forty-eight times larger than Switzerland, is not only dominated by difficult mountains but is also strongly impacted by problematic deserts and jungles. Major consequences for Mexico include severe transportation difficulties, highly uneven population distribution, and the isolation of many regions. Further, Mexico has a large population (115 million in 2012) whose well-being necessitates resources far greater than those required in Switzerland. In contrast to Mexico, Switzerland's small population (less than 8 million in 2012) is conveniently concentrated in a fertile, compact, and highly urbanized plateau. The major Swiss cities, which average less than 1,400 feet in altitude, are separated by short distances, and the transportation connections between them are excellent. The Swiss mountains pose fewer barriers to transportation than those in Mexico because of the presence of natural passes in the Alps. Thus because of these favorable geographic conditions, national integration has been much easier for the people of Switzerland than for Mexicans. I further tell skeptics that Switzerland as a country has other advantages, including a strategic location within Europe, a temperate climate, flatland corridors, and navigable lakes. The Swiss also have access to the sea via the port city of Basel on the Rhine River, and moreover, Switzerland enjoys easy connections to the lucrative markets of France, Italy, Germany, and Austria, the countries that compose the economically advanced "neighborhood" in which the Swiss economy functions.

In his 1938 landmark article on geopolitics, Nicholas J. Spykman concluded that Mexico's physical space, its internal environmental conditions, and its juxtaposition with the powerful United States would severely limit Mexico's future economic prospects. "The shape of the North American continent prevents Mexico from adding significantly to its size by southern expansion, and topography and climate will make it *forever impossible* [emphasis mine] to build on its area a powerful economy."[25] Up to the present, Spykman's observation has been on target. Mexico has been historically unable to build a powerful economy along the lines of the United States or the advanced countries of Europe and East Asia; rather, Mexico's economy remains half-developed and half-underdeveloped. Moreover, before the 1980s the developed part was largely anchored on natural resources, and since then it has rested on the low-cost human labor that drives today's foreign-dominated, export-oriented industrial sector. Mexico's present large economy may be considered "powerful" by some because of the high level of productivity and the nation's lofty GDP ranking, but in truth Mexico is mostly a low-wage assembly country at the service of multinational corporations. Geography has much to do with that reality.

Mexico's Interior: The Preferred Space

Mexico's unique shape, topography, and climatic features long ago produced a great concentration of population and economic activity in the interior territories of the country, rather than in the coastal areas. That anomaly distinguishes Mexico from many other countries where coasts reign supreme. It is not accidental that in the United States, England, Japan, and other economically advanced societies, their littorals, owing to inherent favorable circumstances and the advantage of location by the sea, not only developed first but became the core areas of each country. By contrast, the coasts in Mexico have major disadvantages, beginning with hot and humid climates and the proximity of mountains to the seashore in many locations. Further, the Mexican coastlines are very deficient in good natural harbors, bays, or estuaries, which are all desirable geographic features for the building of ports and the conducting of coastal and overseas trade. The eastern and western coastal lowlands are not only far from ideal as living areas, but physically they narrow substantially going from north to south; eventually the Sierra Madre ranges hug the Pacific Ocean and the Gulf of Mexico for long stretches. The only other major coastal lowland, the Yucatán Peninsula, is burdened by climatic and soil problems as well as isolation, and these conditions limit its economic potential.

With Mexico's littoral traditionally encumbered by serious problems, then, it is not surprising that most Mexicans have always preferred to live in the interior of the country. Even in prehistoric times indigenous peoples largely avoided Mexico's coasts because of the ever-present threat of diseases like malaria and yellow fever and the difficulty of farming in dense jungles, forests, and swamps. As recently as 1955 about 2 million Mexicans had malaria, and nearly 20,000 people died from the disease. At the time malaria ranked third in importance as a cause of death in Mexico, and authorities characterized the problem as the "worst in the hemisphere."[26]

In the mid-twentieth century Mexico still had relatively few people living in the littoral and had limited coastal commerce or long-distance shipping. As a consequence, Mexico's merchant marine and naval forces remained severely underdeveloped. In 1950, Mexico had only 59 registered merchant ships, while Argentina had 369, Brazil had 328, and the United States had over 36,000.[27] Viewed from a global perspective, Mexico was at the time a relatively isolated country, with few external economic ties with other nations apart from the United States, which was (and is) connected to Mexico predominantly via land corridors. Coastal conditions did improve in Mexico in later years, however, as will be pointed out later in this section.

The overwhelming concentration of people in Mexico's interior is illustrated by the fact that only a fifth of the country's population lives in the coastal municipalities.[28] Only three of Mexico's twenty largest metropolitan areas are on the coast. By contrast, seventeen of the twenty largest metropolitan areas in the United States are either on the coast or have water access to the ocean; nine are located directly on the coast and seven have lake or river connections.[29] Tijuana, Acapulco, and Tampico are the only three large coastal metropolitan areas of Mexico; however, Tampico is the only bona-fide large commercial seaport. Although Acapulco has a magnificent bay, it is predominantly a tourist resort, and Tijuana's setting on the coast is meaningless from the perspective of maritime trade because the city is not a seaport. Tijuana is devoid of a natural harbor, lacks a suitable hinterland, and lies in close proximity to San Diego, California, which has a marvelous bay and excellent port facilities. To be sure, though, Tijuana is a large international land port—with an economy that is driven largely by border tourism and cheap-labor industrial assembly operations. Because of their location in the interior, then, Mexico's leading metropolitan areas, as well as many other inland urban centers, have historically functioned at a distance from the ocean and therefore in relative isolation from the rest of the world, with the drawbacks attendant to such a condition.

Not surprisingly, the predominance of economic activity has also been located in Mexico's interior. For example, while they make up only just over two-fifths of the nation's territory, Mexico's noncoastal states produced nearly three-fifths of the country's GDP in 2010. Further, the top ten inland metro areas accounted for half of Mexico's GDP, while the top ten coastal metro areas produced only one-tenth. These data contrast sharply with the situation in the United States, where the economies of states and cities with a seaside location or with inland waterway access are dominant.[30]

Within Mexico's inland territories, numerous intermountain basins and valleys as a whole constitute the most favorable spaces in the country. On the basis

MAP 3.4 Central Mexico

of population size and economic productivity, the territory from Jalisco east to Puebla/Tlaxcala and Morelos/Michoacán north to Zacatécas/San Luis Potosí is considered Mexico's core region. The states in the core region are mostly located in a favorable area of the highlands of central Mexico. There, a moderate climate, relatively adequate rainfall, and level terrain prevail, and a substantial amount of fertile land is available. The Bajío, a fertile plain that incorporates portions of the states of Guanajuato, San Luis Potosí, Querétaro, Michoacán, Jalisco, Aguascalientes, and Zacatecas is a prime agricultural and industrial zone within the broader core region (See Map 3.4).

For centuries the Mexico City area has been the country's most densely populated zone, where economic and political power has been most heavily concentrated. No other area of Mexico, whether in the north, south, east, or west, approaches the combination and scale of natural assets found in the elevated central plateau that once served as the homeland of the Aztecs and other ancient indigenous groups. Within the central highlands, as well as in the country as a whole, the famed Valley of Mexico (i.e., the Federal District and parts of the states of México and Hidalgo) is by far the number one living and economic space in all of Mexico. That has been true historically and is the reason why the Mexico City area continues to be the nation's nucleus and home to over 20 million people, as well as why it accounts for nearly two-fifths of the nation's GDP. The country is governed from Mexico City, and ideas, innovation, and national production are largely concentrated there. Mexico City represents the classic primate city that is so characteristic of metropolises that dominate many countries in Latin America, Africa, and Asia. Urban primacy, however, is not an ideal condition. It usually reflects unbalanced urbanization and uneven economic development. Mexico would surely be better off if it were a multicore country, where the nation's wealth and capabilities were fairly evenly dispersed among many areas, rather than a single-core nation where the national assets are largely monopolized by one region, with the inevitable result that other zones perennially lag behind.

A Closer Look at Mexico's Littorals

This section expands on previous comments regarding Mexico's coastal areas, which overall are about 5,600 miles in length, with the Pacific side extending approximately 3,360 miles and the Gulf and Caribbean side approximately 2,240 miles. A comparison with the United Kingdom, an almost exclusively coastal society, is instructive. Mexico's land area is eight times larger than that of the United Kingdom, but the United Kingdom's coastline is 25 percent longer than that of Mexico's. The United Kingdom's seashore is full of twists and turns and indentations, while Mexico's coastline is mostly smooth and monotonous, with few indentations. For economic purposes the type of coastline that the United Kingdom has, which includes many natural bays, harbors, and estuaries, is far superior to Mexico's coastline, which has few of those attributes. Much of England's economic success historically stems from its favorable coastal conditions and of course its superb location—next to continental Europe and practically in the center of world trade. By contrast Mexico's coastal areas are situated in out-of-the-way spaces in the context of world commerce, although there is good access to U.S. markets.

Despite the natural constraints of Mexico's harbors, capital investments in port infrastructure since the early twentieth century have made it possible for Mexico to participate in world trade at a higher level than many other countries. Yet Mexico's capacity in seaborne shipping is far below that of developed nations. About 80 percent of Mexico's overseas trade is concentrated in five coastal cities: Tampico, Veracruz, Manzanillo, Mazatlán, and Guaymas.[31] As a whole, Mexico's ports rank very low in trade volume in comparison to ports from the major trading countries around the globe. In 2006 not one of Mexico's 107 ports ranked among the top 50 busiest ports in the world in terms of cargo volume. China, reflecting its highly productive coasts, excellent harbors, and massive labor force dedicated to manufacturing, placed nine of its ports in the top fifty. Shanghai came in first overall, while other Chinese ports took spots number four through eight, as well as eleven, fifteen, and sixteen. South Louisiana, the top U.S. port, ranked number twelve; seven other U.S. ports also made the top fifty list.[32] Mexico does much better in the rankings within the sphere of North America. In 2006, Mexico placed six of its ports in the top fifty container ports in North America.[33]

Lacking sufficient natural assets necessary to sustain large seaside urban agglomerations, Mexico cannot hope to compete in maritime trade with countries that have robust coastal regions situated in prime world locations. Mexican ports such as Veracruz, Tampico, Manzanillo, and Lázaro Cárdenas are nationally and regionally important but globally insignificant. Internationally prominent port cities will not blossom on Mexico's coasts because both location and landscape conditions are substandard as compared to what is found in prominent seaside areas in other parts of the world. Mexico would derive great economic benefits if at least one of its coastal areas had the physical configuration and optimal location characteristics of port cities like Seattle, San Francisco, or New Orleans, or some of the advantages enjoyed by the superbly positioned island city-state of Singapore, or a portion of the stunning attributes that distinguish the economically dynamic Pearl River delta in China, where the major metropolises of Hong Kong, Guangzhou (Canton), and Shenzhen are closely linked by both water and land transport. No coast in Mexico can replicate the conditions that favor the above U.S. and Asian cities, and the inevitable result is different economic outcomes in Mexico.

With respect to health conditions, Mexico experienced significant improvements on its coasts and elsewhere as a result of massive antimalaria spraying undertaken during the late 1950s and early 1960s. Malaria ceased to be a problem in urban areas, including in formerly seriously health-challenged cities like Acapulco and Veracruz. Although the intense spraying did not completely eradicate mosquito-borne diseases, deaths from malaria, yellow fever, and dengue declined significantly.[34] The advances in health, along with increased utilization of air conditioning, have certainly made Mexico's coastal areas more habitable. As a result, by 2005 about 20 million people lived in the coastal *municipios*, compared to 15 million in 1990.[35]

Characteristics of Mexico's Gulf Coast

The broad coastal plain that begins at the Rio Grande narrows considerably between southern Tamaulipas and southern Veracruz; the plain then becomes broader in Tabasco and turns into a vast flat area in the Yucatán peninsula. The semiarid climate that is found in Tamaulipas becomes much wetter in Veracruz, Tabasco, and the Yucatán peninsula. Tropical forests predominate in the latter areas. Stifling heat, high humidity, and seasonally strong winds are found all along the Gulf Coast. In the 1820s and 1830s foreign visitors commented frequently on these unfavorable features, with health issues topping the list of concerns. "[The] most dreaded diseases of the coasts are putrid fever and yellow fever, or *vomito prieto*," warned French naturalist and physician Jean Louis Berlandier. "More dangerous than the mephitic gasses of the marshes, these fevers appear in July, August, and September, carrying a large number of individuals to the grave. They are most widespread after a rainy season when a drought evaporates the earth and bares a large part of the swamps."[36]

In some locales of the southern Gulf region, the combination of frequent heavy rainfall, uneven topography, and the narrowness of the coastal plain has long created difficult problems. In Veracruz, for example, the higher altitude of the bordering escarpment produces intense rainstorms that give rise to streams and rivers that break up the coastline. The area is dotted with dense jungle and deep ravines. The difficult terrain of the state of Veracruz goes far in explaining why until the age of paved highways road travel between that seaport and Mexico City was so treacherous, and why it took so long to build the railroad line between those two cities.

The state of Tabasco and the Yucatán peninsula have some of the same problems as Veracruz but also confront other challenges. Tabasco, which is mostly covered with tropical rainforests, is one of the states in Mexico that receives too much rainfall, and serious flooding is a frequent occurrence. Although the land allows for the growing of some standard crops found in tropical areas, excessive wetness has made ordinary agriculture a precarious enterprise, and Tabasco's economy has had to rely heavily on oil and gas production, stock-raising, logging, and fishing. Tabasco's coast is exposed to strong winds and its swampy terrain encourages the growth of dense vegetation that blocks transit into the interior. The mostly flat Yucatán peninsula is a unique region of Mexico. Protuberant rocks, sinkholes known as *cenotes*, and caverns are prominent features of the topography. As a consequence of the ubiquitous soluble limestone terrain, streams do not form at the surface. Instead, there are extensive subterranean streams throughout the peninsula. Rainfall, which is scarce in the chaparral-covered northern part of Yucatán, increases substantially in the center and southern parts of the state, producing jungles and tropical rain forests. Economically, the peninsula in the past depended substantially on henequen production, but in recent decades tourism on the "Mayan Riviera" in nearby Quintana Roo has taken over as the area's predominant activity.

Veracruz and Tampico: Mexico's Major Gulf Ports

The cities of Veracruz and Tampico historically have been the country's most important seaports. Both cities have been anchored to hinterlands in the states of Veracruz and Tamaulipas where, traditionally, basic economic activities such as agriculture, stock-raising, fishing, forestry, mining, and oil production have predominated. The prominence that Veracruz achieved during the colonial period was based on its designation as the lone port on the Gulf authorized by the Spanish government to conduct foreign trade. As a result, enormous amounts of silver and gold flowed to Spain through Veracruz. Since the colonial period, the products that have been exported through Veracruz have consisted largely of sundry natural resources while manufactured goods have made up most of the imports. In recent decades, however, an increasing amount of processed and assembled industrial products have been added to the list of exports.

The much smaller Tampico port maintained a lower profile throughout the long era of Spanish rule and for many decades following Mexico's independence. It was only in the twentieth century that oil exploitation boosted Tampico's economy and elevated the status of its port.

What most caught the attention of early visitors to Tampico was the presence of life-threatening diseases. In 1822, Joel R. Poinsett, the first U.S. Minister in Mexico, referred to the Tampico area as "a land of pestilence."[37] Aside from the sweltering heat and the high humidity, Tampico had to contend with periodic heavy rains, strong winds, and the chronic accumulation of sand at the river's entrance that frequently blocked the access to the port.[38] Ships had to travel about six miles on the Pánuco River to reach the port facilities. Tampico's maritime trade commonly came to a halt during low tide, when even small boats had a hard time making it to and out of the port. Shipping could best be conducted between April and September, when weather conditions improved. Lacking the necessary assets to become a large center of commerce and industry, Tampico remained for decades nothing more than a way station for travelers and a transit point for merchandise, much of it in the form of contraband from Europe and the United States. The economic instability of Tampico is reflected in its fluctuating population: Tampico grew from 2,000 residents in 1829 to 7,000 in 1836, and then regressed back to 2,000 in 1860.[39]

Conditions improved in Tampico when the Mexican government began to eradicate malaria and yellow fever in the country's tropical and semitropical regions at the turn of the twentieth century.[40] Having suffered through devastating epidemics as recently as 1878 to 1879 and 1898, townspeople welcomed the newfound freedom from mosquito-borne diseases. Tampico also benefitted from the government's port modernization projects and transportation improvements. *Tampiqueños* now had railroad connections to San Luis Potosí and Monterrey, and a railway line was under construction that would provide excellent linkage to Mexico City. In addition, the building of a canal through the coastal lagoons to the small but significant oil port of Tuxpan gave Tampico greater access to petroleum, a resource increasingly in demand internationally.[41]

The difficult environmental context under which Tampico struggled in its early development was replicated in Veracruz. At the dawn of the nineteenth century, Alexander von Humboldt recorded his impressions regarding the miseries endured by *veracruzanos* and the fears that terrified visitors who had to disembark or depart by sea from that city. Humboldt called the Veracruz port "one of the most dangerous anchorages" in the world, noting that it was considered a prime center for diseases, especially yellow fever. He commented on the oppressive temperatures and humidity, the bad water that accumulated in putrid swamps, the noxious fumes that emanated from decaying organic matter, the pesky mosquitoes, the hurricanes that periodically devastated the coast, and the strong winds from the north that constantly battered the city and led to the buildup of large sand dunes. The winds Humboldt referred to are the famous storms known as *nortes*, which, between November and March, frequently spawn powerful blustery weather that disrupts shipping in the Gulf and forces the closure of ports. At the time of his visit, the Prussian scientist made note of ongoing discussions among officials in New Spain to possibly raze troubled Veracruz and move its people, as well as the port's customs and immigration operations, to Jalapa (elevation 4,682 feet), a city free of the many health hazards that plagued the coast.[42]

Countless foreigners who entered or left Mexico through Veracruz in later years echoed Humboldt's observations. British traveler William Bullock in 1820 called Veracruz "the most unhealthy spot in the world," a city that "naturally makes the stranger shudder every hour he remains within its walls."[43] Two years later Joel R. Poinsett expressed alarm at the "pestilential diseases . . . the black vomit and bilious fever. . . . All strangers are liable to this infection. No precautions can prevent strangers from this fatal disorder, and many have died in Jalapa who only passed through this city." Poinsett also called the anchorage at the port "very insecure. It is [subjected to] the sudden, frequent, and tremendous northerly gales of winds. . . . The holding ground is so very bad, that no vessel is considered secure, unless made fast to rings fixed for the purpose in the castle wall."[44]

The unattractiveness of Veracruz as a place to live is illustrated in its population history. About 16,000 people lived in Veracruz in 1803. However, that number dropped by more than half by the 1830s as a result of the wars of independence and the political instability that characterized the early years of the Mexican republic. In 1866, Veracruz still only had about 11,000 residents. By way of comparison, owing to their superior location, much better natural harbors, and greater economic and political stability, between 1810 and 1860 New York City grew from 96,000 to 814,000 residents and Philadelphia expanded from 54,000 to 566,000.[45] Despite its many problems, though, Veracruz remained Mexico's leading port throughout the first half of the nineteenth century; about one-half of the country's maritime trade passed through Veracruz in the mid-1850s.[46]

The wretchedness that tormented visitors who had to spend time in Veracruz was matched by the difficult circumstances of traveling from the port to Mexico City, some 7,400 feet above sea level. Although the distance between the two centers was only 261 miles, the rough terrain and rapid rise in elevation presented multiple problems and made the trip a long, uncomfortable, expensive, and risky adventure. The road was often completely covered with sand dunes in the vicinity of Veracruz, was frequently washed out by heavy rains in numerous locations, and devolved into a trail in some areas. In addition, dangers lurked around the steep escarpments and in the areas inhabited by bandits. "Hay que armarse para viajar" (One must be armed to travel), declared one traveler.[47] Apart from the real possibility of getting robbed, sojourners endured discomforts while en route and when stopping in primitive rest stations or overnight shelters. Both ordinary travelers and shippers of freight paid plenty for the services they received. In the 1850s the cost of transporting European imports reportedly often exceeded the original cost of the goods, while in the 1860s a seat on the Mexico City–Veracruz stagecoach cost about ninety times the average daily wage of an agricultural worker.[48] It is a safe bet to say that few who traveled between the central plateau and the Gulf coast looked forward to the experience.

The conditions in Veracruz did not begin to change in a significant way until railroads connected the city with the interior by the 1870s. Land travel at last became easier. Yet the health dangers lingered on for another generation, until medical science confirmed that mosquitoes caused the deadly illnesses, and Veracruz received priority attention in the government's campaign to eradicate the dreaded tropical diseases. Fumigation and constant drainage of swamps and other breeding grounds largely eliminated the mosquito larvae. In 1909 English engineer Reginald Enock reported that Veracruz had successfully overcome its "evil reputation for . . . insalubrity."[49]

The health breakthrough, combined with the government-financed modernization of port facilities and expanded railway service, transformed Veracruz sufficiently to solidify its status as Mexico's most important port. In the early 1910s, even as the Mexican Revolution raged on, "fully half the total foreign maritime trade of the country [passed] through her [Veracruz's] gates, and about a fourth of the total imports and exports."[50]

Mexico's Caribbean Coast

Mexico's Caribbean Coast forms part of the state of Quintana Roo, which composes the eastern portion of the Yucatán peninsula that is situated in Mexican territory. Tropical forests, savannas, mangroves, and reefs are the predominant ecosystems in Quintana Roo and, as in the Gulf zone, torrential storms and hurricanes are frequent occurrences. Isolation and sparse population kept the area a federal territory until 1974, when Quintana Roo became Mexico's thirty-first state. At the time the economy consisted largely of small-scale agriculture, ranching, logging, and fishing. Then, with the planned development of Cancún as a world-class beach resort destination, tourism took over as the dominant industry. Beautiful beaches and Mayan archeological sites have been the main attractions for tourists. Commercial trade with the outside world has not been a significant activity in Quintana Roo. The state's main port, located in the state capital of Chetumal, is mostly a gateway to trade with neighboring Belize.

Mexico's Pacific Coast

Nature is just as challenging in Mexico's western littoral as it is on the Gulf and Caribbean coasts. Before medical breakthroughs reached the Pacific coast, unhealthy conditions in many communities were a constant problem. In addition to a stifling climate, difficult topography along the Pacific shore and on the coastline of the Sea of Cortés, or Gulf of California, has impeded large-scale human agglomeration and economic activity. Southward from Sonora the coastal zones become narrower, disappearing altogether in some places as the formidable Western Sierra Madre Cordilleras meet the ocean. The result is that many areas on the Pacific are cut off from direct communication with Mexico's interior. Deserts predominate in Baja California and Sonora.

Acapulco and Manzanillo: Significant Pacific Ports

Acapulco was Mexico's most important port on the Pacific coast from the 1500s to the dawn of the twentieth century. For much of the Spanish colonial period Acapulco provided an essential link in the long transportation chain that connected the Philippines, Mexico, and Spain commercially. But apart from scheduled stopovers by Spanish galleons and occasional visits by ships from other countries, relatively little maritime activity actually took place in Acapulco over the centuries. Acapulco had the advantage of a deep, well-protected bay, yet, like Veracruz and Tampico, Acapulco had its share of serious limitations, including being wedged between the mountains and the sea, having practically no hinterland, and being burdened by the familiar hot, humid, and unhealthy climate. Alexander von Humboldt referred to Acapulco as a "miserable town" whose climatic conditions seemed worse than those of Veracruz because the mountains surrounding Acapulco kept the air from circulating properly. Only 4,000 people lived in Acapulco at the time of Humboldt's 1803 visit.[51]

After Mexico achieved independence in 1821, Spanish ships completely bypassed Acapulco, sailing from Spain to the Philippines and back via the Cape of Good Hope. For decades the town languished, even losing much of its population.

Then during the California Gold Rush in the mid-nineteenth century a revival occurred as steamers from Panama and Nicaragua on their way to San Francisco made Acapulco a port of call. Enough maritime activity took place after that event to maintain Acapulco's status as Mexico's top port in the Pacific into the twentieth century.

In reality Acapulco remained a backwater town, one seriously constrained by the Western Sierra Madre, which isolated the port from the resources of the interior and made transportation and communication with Mexico City and other urban centers extremely difficult. Acapulco was able to conquer its unhealthy environment with the eradication of mosquito-borne diseases, but it could not overcome the power of the mountains and consequently did not develop into a first-rate commercial port. Lack of railway connections with the interior undermined trade. "As long as there is no adequate railway transportation," noted a government-sponsored study in 1945, "port improvements cannot be justified because the volume of traffic is very low as a consequence of insufficient communications."[52] Plans to build a railroad to Mexico City never materialized because of the overwhelming engineering challenges and prohibitive costs. Construction of a highway to the central plateau was no easy task either, and pavement of that important roadway was not completed until 1936.[53] Highway connections with the interior boosted the city's economy but did little to expand overseas trade or even coastal shipping. Acapulco's future lay in tourism rather than commerce and industry. Tourism indeed thrived after the mid-twentieth century, but it suffered a setback in the early 2000s as drug-related violence escalated in Acapulco and other areas of Guerrero, historically a politically turbulent state in Mexico.

Unlike Acapulco, whose port activities dated to the sixteenth century, the small town of Manzanillo did not achieve port status until 1825. Manzanillo's port took a long time to develop because the area's shallow bay did not offer adequate protection to ships, and the town suffered from the standard stifling heat and sanitary maladies. But Manzanillo had a good location and a better hinterland than Acapulco, making it possible, once modern transportation links were in place, to tap into rich minerals, agricultural products, and livestock in the region. Railway connections from Manzanillo to the interior were completed in 1889, and these were expanded in subsequent years. The multiple favorable factors at Manzanillo prompted the Porfirio Díaz government to finance significant development projects, including deepening the harbor, constructing an artificial port, and eradicating yellow fever. With the passage of time the Manzanillo port expanded its facilities, and by 1960 it had become the fifth busiest port in Mexico in cargo tonnage.[54] A steady increase in trade activity encouraged private and public investments, and by 2002 Manzanillo became the top port in the country in container traffic. In 2006 Manzanillo handled nearly double the number of containers as Veracruz, its nearest competitor.[55]

Mexico's Coasts, Past and Present

Natural disadvantages have clearly constrained economic growth in Mexico's coasts, and that reality has had significant implications for the general development of the country. But there has been change. Since the mid-twentieth century, many of Mexico's coastal areas have become attractive tourist destinations because of their warm weather, sandy beaches, and striking natural beauty. Seaside resorts, along with archeological sites and other attractions, turned Mexico into one of the top ten tourist countries in the world by the turn of the twenty-first century. In 2008 the country generated about $13 million dollars in tourist revenues, which has certainly aided the Mexican economy. Tourism, however, is a fluctuating industry and does not provide a broad-based economic foundation, and ports such as Puerto Vallarta, Mazatlán, Acapulco, and Cancún are largely dependent on that one industry. A high proportion of the inputs in the industry are imported from abroad and much of the profits do not stay in Mexico. Moreover, most of the jobs are low-wage, and tourism-driven land speculation and rising real estate prices hurt the local people.[56]

The reality is that Mexico's coasts will continue to face limitations that will be difficult to overcome. It is unrealistic to expect any of Mexico's port cities to become super metropolises. That said, opportunities to further develop coastal areas do exist, and Mexico has pursued them. In recent years, sizable public and private investments have resulted in the construction of an impressive container-friendly port at Altamira, near Tampico, and significant expansion and improvement of Manzanillo and other ports on the Gulf and the Pacific. The most ambitious but seemingly ill-fated project is the long envisioned container mega-port at Punta Colonet in northern Baja California. After years of planning, the Mexican government in 2008 issued a call for bids to major national and international companies to invest in the building of the port. The selling point was that Punta Colonet would compete with Los Angeles and Long Beach, California, for the lucrative shipping between Asia and the United States. The two Southern California ports have often been overwhelmed by the volume of ships from Asia, and frequently the flow of traffic at these U.S. ports has been stopped or delayed because of congestion or labor strikes. Ships would find it advantageous to drop off cargo at Punta Colonet. That cargo would in turn be moved rapidly between Mexico and the United States via a land route that would connect an express railroad and a highway in Mexico to excellent already existing train and highway corridors in the United States.

The Punta Colonet project has generated much excitement because of the expected economic impact in Baja California, including the projected creation of many jobs and the anticipated emergence of a new city of at least 200,000 people. But the proposed port has encountered many obstacles. Time and again it was given the green light and then put on hold, and finally, in December 2012, the outgoing Felipe Calderón administration cancelled the project, explaining that changing market conditions made the prospects for the long-term success of the port far from certain. Other considerations that surely played major roles in the decision to abandon the Punta Colonet dream include the high cost of building the new port, the planned expansion of competing U.S. ports along the Pacific coast, the expected completion of the widening of the Panama Canal, and the real possibility that the long-contemplated Nicaraguan waterway connecting the Caribbean Sea with the Pacific Ocean will at some point come to fruition.[57] Should the Punta Colonet port ever be built, it would offer little competition to Panama and Nicaragua because at most Punta Colonet would be an isolated way station and transfer point for merchandise making its way largely between East Asia and the United States.

Conclusion

A comparison of major economically significant geographic attributes in Mexico and the continental United States reveals striking differences. Nature plainly has been much kinder to the United States than to Mexico, and this reality has had profound consequences for both countries. The United States has an excellent location on the globe, which has translated into largely favorable temperate climatic conditions and enviable centrality in the world trade system. Most of Mexico, by contrast, is in the problematic tropical and semitropical arid zones and, except for its adjacency to the United States, on the periphery of global commerce. Contiguity with the United States has been a double-edged sword for Mexico—it provides access to U.S. markets on the one hand but great vulnerability to U.S. economic domination on the other. For the United States, large size has meant having abundant resources, plentiful favorable economic and living areas, a rectangular shape that has provided multidirectional transportation corridors, and a favorable topography that has facilitated easy and comprehensive internal travel and movement of products. Mexico's smaller size has meant fewer natural resources and fewer favorable spaces, while the country's funnel-like shape and unique topography have provided good transportation corridors along the north-south axis but not along the east-west axis because formidable mountain ranges have created endless obstructions and hindrances. The United States has superb coasts and hinterlands, and that explains the ubiquitous splendid ports on the Atlantic, Gulf, and Pacific coasts. Mexico's coasts, however, suffer from many limitations, including harsh climatic conditions, limited space between the sea and the mountains, scarcity of good harbors, and deficient hinterlands. As a consequence, only a small portion of Mexico's population historically has settled on the coast, and seaports have developed slowly and modestly. To be sure, advances in the health sector, expansion of national transportation infrastructure, and air conditioning have improved general conditions in Mexico's coastal areas and have stimulated economic activity, including foreign tourism. In the last half century a number of seaside cities emerged as important poles of attraction; nevertheless, coastal Mexico continues to lag significantly behind inland Mexico. The Central Plateau, the county's most favorable region, remains the country's undisputed core area. With respect to economic activity in Mexico's littorals, geography will continue to greatly favor competitors with excellent harbors and superb access to world trade such as China and other East Asian countries, as well as the United States, which has the best collection of natural harbors in the world and continues to be a dominant force in global maritime trade.

Notes

1. See Diamond (1997); Gallup et al. (1998); Gallup et al. (2003); Kaplan (2012).
2. Watson (1967), 3.
3. Spykman (1938a), 43.
4. Semple (1933), 231, 385.
5. The U.S. National Oceanic and Atmospheric Administration defines coastal areas as "counties and equivalent areas with at least 15 percent of their land area in a coastal watershed (drainage area) or in a coastal cataloguing unit (a coastal area between watersheds)" (U.S. Department of Commerce 2012, Tables 25 and 26).
6. See www.routledge.com/martínez/mexico/tables/table3.1.
7. See www.routledge.com/martínez/mexico/tables/table3.2.
8. STRATFOR (2011), 1.
9. Comment attributed to "the geographer Morse" (Brown and Whitaker 1948, 126).
10. Semple (1933), 127.
11. American Association of Port Authorities (2006).
12. Meinig (1993), II:365.
13. American Association of Port Authorities (2006).
14. *National Geographic* (November, 2012), 25–26.
15. Port of Oakland website. www.portofoakland.com.
16. Weiner (2014).
17. Esquivel (2000), 28, 44.
18. Spykman (1938b), 226; STRATFOR (2009).
19. Venezian and Gamble (1969), 3, 5.
20. Bassols Batalla (1980), 101.
21. Mexico's landmass is at its narrowest in Tehuantepec, where the distance between the Gulf of Mexico and the Pacific Ocean is about 125 miles as the crow flies. The distance between Tampico and Puerto Vallarta, both located approximately in the center of the country, is about 500 miles. And the distance from Matamoros to Tijuana, at opposite ends of the border with the United States, is nearly 2,000 miles long.
22. FNS News (September 30, 2013).
23. Esquivel (2000), 10; Rhoda and Burton (2010), 5.
24. Tannenbaum (1950), 3–4.
25. Spykman (1938b), 226.
26. Cueto (2007), 71; *New York Times* (September 7, 1956), 6.
27. Mitchell (2003).
28. Based on data from the 1990, 2000, and 2005 censuses, as cited in México, Comisión Intersectarial para el Manejo Sustentable de Mares y Costas (2011), 10. Using the more

liberal concept of "coastal regions" (as opposed to coastal municipalities), Gustavo Cabrera calculated that in the mid-1990s about a fourth of the country's population lived in the country's 461 "coastal regions." Cabrera defined "coastal regions" as areas that extend from the seashore to points having an altitude of 500 meters or, if 500 meters are not reached, they extend in distance 100 kilometers from the seashore into the interior (Cabrera 2007, 204).

29 See www.routledge/martínez/mexico/tables/table3.2; www.routledge/martínez/mexico/tables/table3.3.
30 See www.routledge/martínez/mexico/tables/table3.1; www.routledge/martínez/mexico/tables/table3.4.
31 Rhoda and Burton (2010), 35.
32 American Association of Port Authorities (2006).
33 American Association of Port Authorities (2006).
34 Cueto (2007), 97.
35 México, Comisión Intersectarial para el Manejo Sustentable de Mares y Costas (2011), 10.
36 Berlandier wrote his memoirs decades before the discovery that mosquitoes caused yellow fever and malaria. As was common at the time, Berlandier believed that unhealthy "gasses" caused disease (Berlandier 1980, I:34; II:434–435).
37 Poinsett (1969), 209.
38 Poinsett (1969), 204–209.
39 Ibarra Bellon (1998), 321–323.
40 Kuecker (2008).
41 MacHugh (1914), 232.
42 Von Humboldt (1966), 31, 180–181, 512–513, 522–523, 536.
43 Quoted in Graebner (1951), 40.
44 Poinsett (1969), 15–17. Other comments by foreign visitors regarding the health dangers in Veracruz are found in Grantz (1982).
45 Siemens (1990), 77; U.S. Bureau of the Census, "Population of the 46 Urban Places, 1810," and "Population of the 100 Largest Urban Places, 1860," www.census.gov.
46 Ibarra Bellon (1998), 306–307.
47 Quote appears in Siemens (1990), 95.
48 Siemens (1990), 103; Calderón (1955), 606; Meyer et al. (2007), 400.
49 Enock (1909), 323–324.
50 MacHugh (1914), 226.
51 Von Humboldt, *Ensayo Político*, 156.
52 Higgins Industries (1954), II:14.
53 Carlson (1936), 532–533; Niblo and Niblo (2008), 35.
54 Tamayo (1962), 563.
55 Goodrich (1913), 252–253; México, Secretaría de Comunicaciones y Transportes website, www.sct.gob.mx.
56 Rhoda and Burton (2010), 130–135.
57 *Journal of Commerce* (January 10, 2005), 19; *San Diego Union-Tribune* (August 14, 2005); *Arizona Daily Star* (October 22, 2006), D6; *El Paso Times* (January 8, 2012), 6E.

4
LANDFORMS, TRANSPORTATION, AND CITIES

From the perspective of working people, is it better to live in a rural community or an urban area? My parents, both of whom grew up in rural Mexico, asked themselves that question numerous times in the 1940s and 1950s when our family bounced back and forth between Mexico and the United States, living in various mining and agricultural towns that provided only low-paying jobs and limited educational opportunities. The countryside experience ended when we arrived at the border city of Ciudad Juárez in the mid-1940s and stayed there for an extended period. Juárez offered more of the kind of economic environment my parents had sought. Both had their sights set on moving to the United States, where they knew opportunities were much better than in Mexico. After a long struggle with the bureaucracy of emigrating legally from Mexico to the United States, my father finally obtained U.S. residency for all of us in 1957. We immediately headed for Chicago. Later we returned to the border to live in El Paso, and then moved to Los Angeles. Living in those U.S. cities, especially in Chicago and Los Angeles, changed our lives. The two latter metropolises were economic powerhouses that provided opportunities unlike anything available in our previous residences.

Cities are central to economic activity because most productivity and innovation takes place in urban spaces. Yet, to achieve high-level economic status, cities need to be situated in favorable surroundings and need to be well connected to the world beyond. Geographic location, the quality of the landscape, and other environmental factors are crucial in determining the level of economic performance of cities. Ease of transport is especially important. In the case of Mexico, the less than ideal geography in much of the country has constrained transportation and made it expensive, and that situation has contributed significantly to urban imbalance. Growth and development have proceeded at a much slower pace in Mexico than in countries whose urban systems have not been impacted by severe geographic hurdles. The geographically advantaged United States is the best example of a large country where the development process has been fostered by convenient terrain on which an exceptional transportation system has been built—that situation in turn has facilitated the emergence and multiplication of cities of all sizes. England, Germany, and France are other examples of countries where, because of favorable geography, transportation development has been relatively easy and cities have flourished.

Transportation and Cities in the United States

Early in its national history the United States could count on natural assets such as excellent coastal plains, abundant navigable rivers and lakes, and plentiful flat terrain on which to build exceptional low-cost transportation that in a relatively short period of time would advance the development of urban centers of varying kinds and sizes. Americans rather easily connected the different regions of the country, established a national market, and promoted societal and political integration. As time passed the impulse to exploit the country's abundant natural riches drove the United States to constantly make improvements in transportation and communication, which in turn translated into greater productivity and prosperity. The rise of cities accompanied that process.

Transportation and Communication

Favorable geography provided the United States with a natural foundation that greatly facilitated wealth creation, which then made possible the building of a highly complex transportation infrastructure. Unlike many other countries limited in their economic potential by a unidirectional growth pattern, the United States has been advantaged by multidirectional growth because the country possesses many attractive coastal and inland regions, and the friendly topography permits easy connections among them. By 2000 the United States had a vast transportation network comprising different venues that carried the nation's passenger and freight traffic in an exceedingly efficient manner. That system incorporated 4 million miles of highways and roadways, 120,000 miles of railways, and 25,000 miles of navigable waterways used for commercial purposes.[1] Without such infrastructure, the United States would not be the economically advanced and highly urbanized country that it became.

Inland Waterways

Apart from excellent coastlines on two oceans and a gulf that make it possible to have exceptional seaports, the United States is endowed with many rivers and lakes in the country's interior. These bodies of water, including the St. Lawrence,

Hudson, Ohio, Mississippi, and Missouri Rivers, as well as the Great Lakes, have facilitated the building of the largest system of commercial waterways found anywhere in the world. In the eastern part of North America, where the major navigable waterways are concentrated, physical obstacles are few, and gentle gradients enable easy descent from higher elevations to the sea. Favorable topography as well has allowed for the building of canals that connect the major waterways. The far-reaching inland waterway transportation networks, then, constitute an integral component of the sophisticated U.S. transportation infrastructure, which in turn is one of the foundations on which the powerful U.S. economy is based (See Map 4.1).

Early on U.S. leaders, having a familiarity with what navigable bodies of water had meant for England's economic takeoff during the industrial revolution of the eighteenth century, understood the great opportunities that waterways represented for the future of the United States. In a letter to the governor of Virginia, George Washington wrote: "Extend the inland navigation of the eastern waters. Communicate them as near as possible with those which run westward; open these to the Ohio; open also such as extend from the Ohio towards Lake Erie; and we shall not only draw the produce of the western settlers, but the peltry and fur trade of the Lakes also to our ports ... binding the people to us by a chain which can never be broken."[2]

Ordinary people of course did not need prodding to use waterways to transport themselves to desirable areas in the U.S. interior. They knew the value of doing so. Utilizing rafts, canoes, barges, and flatboats, the first waves of European American settlers made their way to the western frontier via navigable rivers, man-made canals, and lakes, opening up vast lands known for their bountiful good soil and other valuable resources. Later, with the introduction of the steamboat in the early nineteenth century, the United States entered into a period of accelerated economic growth. The expansion was driven at first by a revolution in waterborne transport and, within a short time, by extensive and speedy construction of railroads.

Between the 1810s and 1860 steamboats multiplied rapidly and penetrated the rich lands between the Appalachian Highlands and the Mississippi River and some areas beyond. They carried passengers and freight back and forth between the agricultural West and the industrial East, precipitating new economic activity on a grand scale and spawning many riverside and lakeside communities in the regions served by the expanding waterway network. By 1848, 2,885 steamboats arrived in Pittsburgh, 4,007 in Cincinnati, 3,159 in St. Louis, and 2,977 in New Orleans, illustrating the growing significance of these river cities.[3] New Orleans had so much water traffic at the time that it ranked as the world's fourth largest port.[4] Steamboats dramatically lowered the price for shipping bulk commodities, especially in an upstream direction. For example, downstream shipping costs between Louisville and New Orleans declined about 68 percent between the 1810s and 1850s, while upstream costs dropped about 95 percent. In 1827 it had taken fifty-two days to ship freight by land and riverboat from Cincinnati to New York; by 1852 that time was cut to only six days.[5]

As many U.S. historians have pointed out, man-made canals greatly augmented the country's natural navigable waterway system. The canals allowed Americans to further exploit the natural resources of the interior, to extend the national market, and to populate the fertile lands to the west. Without a doubt the canal network contributed significantly to the rapid growth of the country's economy. A few canals were built before 1816, but most of the construction came after that date. By 1840 the total canal mileage already exceeded 3,300 miles.[6]

The 364-mile long Erie Canal, which was completed in 1825, overshadowed all other canals in its significance. It connected the Hudson River at Albany with Lake Erie at Buffalo, thus linking New York City with the vast interior via a cheap water route. Rapid population growth took place along the canal as easterners resettled on the lush farmland in the west. The Erie Canal provided the impetus for New York State to become a commercial powerhouse and for New York City to emerge as a world metropolis.

Unlike inland canals, which multiplied rapidly, the Intracoastal Waterway, first proposed in 1808 by U.S. Secretary of the Treasury Albert Gallatin, encountered numerous obstacles that halted development of the grand plan to connect existing bodies of water on the East Coast such as bays, sounds, and rivers with man-made canals across stretches of land.[7] But in the intervening decades coastal projects sprouted in many locales, laying the foundation for realizing the broader national vision. In 1905 the federal government finally began the process of tying the existing coastal channels together, and by the 1930s the Atlantic portion of the waterway was essentially finished. Improvements in the Gulf of Mexico in the 1940s completed the larger network. Since it began functioning, the Intracoastal Waterway has contributed enormously to the economy of the United States by providing a means for bulk commodities to travel at low cost in sheltered waters over long distances. Between 1968 and 1984, on the average 65 million tons of products were transported every year along the Gulf Intracoastal Waterway.[8] Today the 3,000-mile Atlantic and Gulf Intracoastal Waterway system serves a vast region extending from the U.S. Northeast to the U.S.–Mexico border.

Chicago is a good example of the difference that navigable waterways such as these can make for a city already favored with an exceptional location, a superb hinterland, and abundant land transportation advantages. Served by Lake Michigan and the Chicago Sanitary and Ship Canal, the sprawling Port of Chicago has amazing water accessibility to many major U.S. cities near and far away via the Great Lakes, the St. Lawrence Seaway, the Greater Mississippi River network, and the Intracoastal Waterway system. In addition, the five national highways and six major railways that converge in the Windy City provide powerful complements to the waterways. Thus cargo amounting to tens of millions of tons and consisting of both raw materials and finished goods moves annually through Chicago's waterways directly to and from many domestic centers as well as overseas markets.

Landforms, Transportation, and Cities **105**

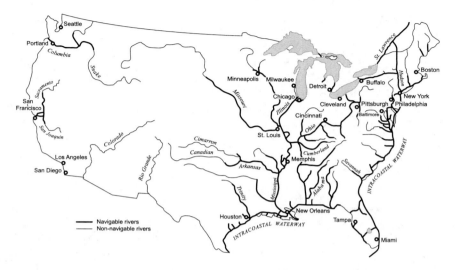

MAP 4.1 Major navigable inland and intracoastal waterways of the United States, 1960s

Source: Based on map in Highsmith and Northam (1968), 426.

Without water connections, Chicago would not have become one of the world's great centers of trade and manufacturing.

Although the railroads and later gasoline-powered vehicles would eventually overshadow river, lake, canal, and intracoastal watercraft, waterborne transportation nonetheless has remained highly significant to the economy of the United States. The simple fact is that the most economical method of shipping bulk commodities has always been water transport. That has not changed with the passage of time. In the mid-nineteenth century river freight rates were about one-sixth those of railroad rates. In the 1940s, the U.S. Office of Defense Transportation calculated that it cost seventy-five times more to ship crude petroleum by truck than by ocean tanker, twenty-one times more by railroad, and four times more by pipeline. A 2008 estimate held that ships used only 10 to 20 percent of the fuel energy required by trucks, while the geopolitical intelligence firm STRATFOR calculated in 2011 that the operating cost per ton per mile was only 1 cent for water transport versus 2.5 cents for railways and 19 cents for trucks.[9]

The enduring cost-effectiveness of water transport is the major reason why U.S. waterways have remained so significant and why the system has been continuously improved and enlarged. For generations billions of tons of cargo such as petroleum, coke, coal, stone, gravel, sand, steel, iron ore, iron, timber, grain, and manufactured goods have been transported on barges and other craft. The Mississippi River and the Great Lakes-St. Lawrence Waterway (or Seaway) systems have stood out as the preeminent commercial waterways of the United States and

Canada.[10] Because of much different geography, natural navigable waterways are scarce in the western part of the United States, with only select portions of the San Joaquin, Sacramento, and Columbia Rivers serving as transportation arteries.[11] These three western rivers provide valuable local and regional services in California and the Pacific Northwest, but their economic importance pales in comparison to the transportation contributions of the Mississippi, Ohio, Missouri, and Hudson Rivers, and of the Great Lakes. In sum, the marvelous inland waterway system forms a basic component of the infrastructure upon which the affluence of the United States is based.

Roads before the Railways

During the English colonial period, land transport in the United States was slow, cumbersome, and expensive, and roads were little more than paths and trails. In the eighteenth century a basic system of roads began to emerge in the thirteen colonies, connecting points along the Eastern Seaboard to each other, and coastal towns to western frontier settlements located less than 100 miles inland. Pack trains of horses carried the freight, and stagecoaches served passengers traveling on the better roads. The high cost of shipping bulk commodities by land limited the use of the primitive highways and kept economic interaction within the colonies locally and regionally based.

Road expansion and improvements ensued once the United States became independent from England and as the economic potential of the western lands became manifest. While the government of the new republic was involved in road construction, much of the impetus came from private entrepreneurs who saw profit possibilities in toll turnpikes. By 1815 a network of turnpikes and other roads connected the settled regions, but problems abounded because the cost of travel remained high as a result of the chronic bad conditions of the roads, including frequent washouts during heavy rainfalls. Only a few well-built roads patterned after the best European highways could withstand the destructive power of the elements. By 1830 the turnpike era ended as a result of the enduring unprofitability of long-distance freighting.[12] Even with refurbishments and enlargement of the road system in subsequent generations, roads remained problematic until the age of motorized transport, when widespread paving of thoroughfares became cost effective and, indeed, a necessity.

It is important to underline that the problems the United States had with its early roads typified the experience of many countries. Road building and maintenance were difficult everywhere, and land travel was universally expensive. However, the challenges confronted by countries with omnipresent mountainous terrain, including Mexico, surpassed the difficulties faced by the United States, which had plentiful flat land and highlands that presented only moderate barriers.

Railways

Just as the ubiquitous waterways in the United States paved the way for steamboats to emerge as prominent players in the nation's economy, the extensive land-transport friendly terrain, including many mountain passes, contributed substantially to the rise of the railroads. The vast stretches of prairie lands and valleys throughout the country made ideal pathways. The Rocky Mountains presented the most formidable barrier to railway construction, yet numerous natural passes made it possible to build several east-west transcontinental lines through that range. Over fifty passes could be utilized for transportation purposes in the state of Colorado alone.[13]

Railroads quickly became an important part of the U.S. transportation infrastructure upon introduction in the 1830s, but the inland waterways remained the principal means of transportation into the 1850s for both passengers and freight. By 1860 the railroads caught up with the waterways, reaching 30,000 miles of track and equaling the volume of cargo carried by steamboats and other vessels that plied the rivers, lakes, and canals. Ten years later the railways counted on nearly 53,000 miles of track, assuring railroad dominance in U.S. transportation for many decades. Railroad construction in the United States proceeded at an astonishing rate in subsequent years, reaching almost 117,000 miles in 1890 (3.4 times more than Germany, then the nearest competitor) and about 250,000 miles in 1910 (6.1 times more than Russia, the new nearest competitor)[14] (See Map 4.2).

The railroads provided more direct connections and faster travel than the waterways. For example, in comparison to river transport, railroads shaved almost half the distance between Pittsburgh and St. Louis and lessened the travel time from Cincinnati to New Orleans by almost two-thirds.[15] Railways established a permanent basis for the continuous exploitation of rich agricultural areas and mineral districts in the interior on a scale heretofore not possible. Railway building and gauge standardization continued at a rapid pace and, by the end of the nineteenth century, the United States had established the basic railroad framework that has served the country since then. Actually, a dense railroad system had already existed in the eastern part of the nation as early as the 1860s, advantaging the large population that lived between the Mississippi River and the Atlantic Ocean. A network of much lower density emerged after 1860 in the western part of the country because of the arid nature of much of the landscape, the large amount of space taken up by mountain ranges, and the lower population in that region.

Once they surpassed waterways in importance, railroads dominated transportation in the United States until the invention of the internal combustion engine ushered in the age of automobiles, trucks, and buses. In the post–World War I years, motorized vehicles became more convenient for personal travel and for the shipping of products, and railroads entered a long period of contraction

108 Context: Nature and People

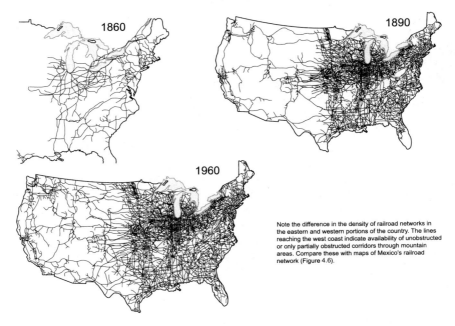

MAP 4.2 Railroad networks of the United States, 1860, 1890, and 1960

Sources: Based on maps in Meinig (1993), vol. 2, 329; and Alexander (1979), 89, 324.

in passenger use and freight shipping. Nevertheless, railroads continued to be extremely significant for the country's economy. Eventually mass motorized transportation and the rapid expansion of inexpensive air travel led to a steep drop in railway use by people. By the late 1970s, railroads accounted for less than 3 percent of passenger traffic, a far cry from 1900, when they had carried most of the country's travelers.[16]

U.S. railroads made an impressive comeback in the last two decades of the twentieth century, at least with respect to freight transport. This turnabout is explained by the expansion of the global economy, which triggered an increased need for cheap transport of cargo containers to and from seaports on the country's three coasts and on the Great Lakes. Railroads continued to work hand in hand with the nation's inland waterways. Perhaps the best example is found in the Great Lakes region, where many railroad lines have for generations met at strategic lakeside ports for the purpose of transferring cargo from one form of transport to another. The convergence of railroads is dramatically illustrated in Duluth, Milwaukee, Chicago, Cleveland, and Buffalo. The enduring pivotal contribution that railways have made to the U.S. economy cannot be underestimated. Presently the iron horse is again in the forefront of the country's freight transportation system as motor highways become more crowded and as the nation pursues the task of becoming independent of foreign oil.

Modern Roads and Highways

When motor vehicles made their appearance in the early twentieth century, the United States had a basic system of rough and unpaved roads. But adaptation to the new form of travel would be swift, and the extant roadways would be transformed into a modern national network within a generation. With the improved highway infrastructure, cars, buses, and trucks not only provided speedy transportation at low cost, but they also penetrated remote or formerly inaccessible places far from the navigable waterways and out of the reach of railroads. Natural passes in the Rocky Mountains and other highland areas in the West enabled the construction of many long-distance highways. Practically every population center and nearly every locale that had exploitable resources was now well incorporated into the national economy. In 1935 the United States was the country with the greatest road mileage, numbering over 3 million miles; that was approximately twice the mileage of second-place U.S.S.R., five times that of third place Japan, six times that of fourth place Australia, and seven times that of fifth place Canada. Many more products were hauled more quickly and more conveniently via U.S. highways. By 1940 trucks carried about a third of all the freight shipped in the country, and by 2007 that figure had risen to more than two-thirds[17] (See Map 4.3).

Meanwhile automobiles became widely affordable to U.S. consumers, and their multiplication, along with the rapid increase of trucks and buses, spurred the government to build the highly acclaimed national interstate highway system in the post–World War II era. Once again, favorable geography allowed the country to take another giant leap in the economic development process. Americans were able to do what most countries in the world could not—carry out the construction of a mammoth modern highway system made to accommodate a vigorous economy as well as human lifestyles that had been fundamentally transformed by motorized vehicles.

Over the years I have gotten well acquainted with numerous U.S. interstate highways and the mostly flat terrain that they traverse. When driving long distances in the United States I am always reminded of the difficulties of land travel in Mexico and other Latin American countries that are seriously burdened by mountainous topography. It is effortless by comparison to travel by automobile in the United States. I give as examples Interstate Highway 5 (I-5) from San Diego to Seattle on the West Coast and Interstate Highway 95 (I-95) from Miami to Maine on the East Coast, and for east-west travel I cite Interstate Highway 90 (I-90) from Boston to Seattle in the Far North and Interstate Highway 10 (I-10) from Jacksonville to Los Angeles in the Far South. I have travelled

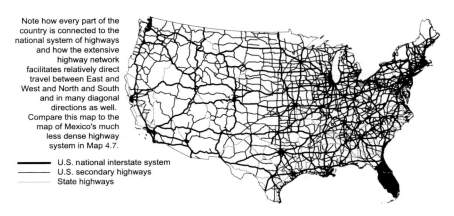

Note how every part of the country is connected to the national system of highways and how the extensive highway network facilitates relatively direct travel between East and West and North and South and in many diagonal directions as well. Compare this map to the map of Mexico's much less dense highway system in Map 4.7.

───── U.S. national interstate system
───── U.S. secondary highways
───── State highways

MAP 4.3 U.S. national highway system, circa 2000

Source: U.S. Department of Transportation (2009); courtesy of Mike Neathary of the Federal Highway Administration.

the length of I-5, I-95, and I-10, and most of I-90. They are all marvelous transportation corridors that carry an enormous volume of traffic and connect the most productive favorable spaces in the United States. The highway I know best is I-10, especially the portion between El Paso and Los Angeles. On the I-10 stretch between Tucson and El Paso, which I drive frequently, I am always struck by the endless stream of trailer-trucks carrying freight and the many long, container-laden trains that rumble on tracks parallel to the highway. Both trucks and trains carry large amounts of freight coming from and going to China via the Long Beach/Los Angeles port complex. In contrast to highways in Mexico, where ubiquitous mountains in huge areas of the country slow down freight carriers and make distances greater, I-10 provides a fairly straight, barrier-free, weather-friendly corridor for thousands of miles from the coast of Florida to the coast of California.

Postal, Wire, and Wireless Communication

Besides facilitating transportation, favorable geography also played a pivotal role in the early development of different forms of modern communications in the United States. Post offices, already numbering more than 28,000 by 1860, eventually reached practically every population center in the country with the spread of railways and motor vehicles. Population centers on the whole could easily be connected, given that towns and cities by definition were located predominantly in the nation's favorable spaces, and extant railway and highway corridors reflected the nation's excellent topography. The rapid growth of the magnetic telegraph network between the 1840s and 1860s has been hailed by U.S. historians as one of the major "revolutions" in the nation's communications history. No longer dependent on people and horses to carry messages, the telegraph used wires to establish a system of instantaneous communication from coast to coast (and also overseas). Geography played a direct role in the telegraph "miracle" because the construction of the lines conveniently paralleled the railroad corridors, which traversed favorable terrain. More than 23,000 miles of telegraph line were in place by 1852 and over 50,000 by 1860. By 1861 the telegraph connected the East and West Coasts.[18] When telephones came along in the early twentieth century they relied on the already established telegraph system, adding a new and far more pervasive form of communication that remains important to the present day. Finally, wireless communications, under continuous development since the mid-twentieth century, have benefited as well from the favorable topography of the United States, which has presented minimal physical obstructions to the signals sent through the air.

U.S. Cities and Urban Networks

The United States became a highly urbanized country as a consequence of three natural advantages. First, Americans possessed plentiful economic and settlement-friendly spaces spread over wide expanses of territory that would lead to population agglomeration in many locations from coast to coast. Second, the powerful U.S. economy attracted millions of immigrants who concentrated in cities because these offered the greatest job opportunities. And third, as a consequence of favorable geography, the country found it relatively easy to develop intercity connecting transportation infrastructure, thereby encouraging further urbanization (See Map 4.4).

The northeastern United States would lead the country in the urbanization process. At the time of independence, Philadelphia, Boston, New York, and Baltimore emerged as the principal centers on the Atlantic coast. These port cities were tied to commerce with Europe and had only minimal links with their interior hinterlands. Smaller communities were scattered on or near the Atlantic coast, with off-coastal sea transportation providing much of the communication among these settlements before the development of an efficient system of roads. Once the population of the coastal region could tap into the resources of the interior through the transportation arteries provided by the rivers, lakes, canals, roads, and railways, the growth potential of the eastern cities expanded appreciably. New York City grew the most rapidly, reaching a population of over 1 million by 1860, assuming supremacy not only in the East but in the entire country. New York City owed its success to having the best location, best harbor, and best accessibility to the largest hinterland in the interior via excellent water and railway transportation. Other eastern cities lagged behind New York City but still

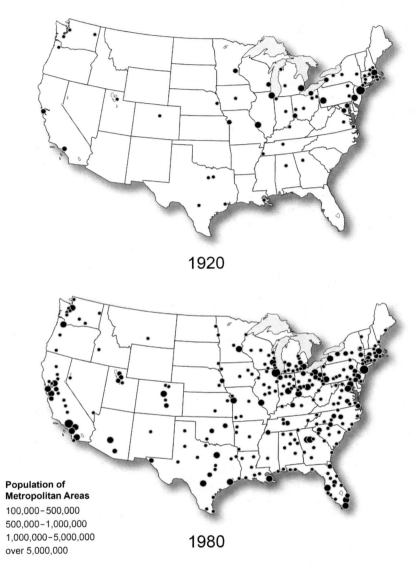

MAP 4.4 Major urban areas, United States, 1920 and 1980

Source: Based on maps in Hammond (1984), U-35.

recorded impressive gains. In 1860 Philadelphia's population numbered 566,000, Boston 208,000, and Baltimore 212,000.

A second set of important cities developed along navigable rivers west of the Appalachian Mountains as steamboats and later railroads provided the means to transport people and products fairly inexpensively over long distances. New

Orleans, St. Louis, Cincinnati, and Pittsburgh, all strategically located in areas with abundant fertile lands and other resources, emerged as the leading urban centers on the Mississippi and Ohio Rivers. Between 1840 and 1860 the population of New Orleans expanded from 102,000 to 175,000, St. Louis from 16,000 to 165,000, Cincinnati from 46,000 to 161,000, and Pittsburgh from 31,000 to 93,000. New Orleans, the leader among the riverside cities, had long been a major port at the mouth of the Mississippi River, and its strategic location would assure its preeminence for generations to come.

A third category of cities blossomed in the Great Lakes region. Vast stretches of fertile land, abundant mineral wealth, and ease of transport by land and water are behind the rise of Chicago, Buffalo, Detroit, Milwaukee, and Cleveland as major urban centers. Chicago emerged as the premier lake city as a consequence of its central location, access to the Eastern Seaboard via the Great Lakes and the St. Lawrence River, and proximity to the Mississippi River and its productive adjacent areas. Chicago's population soared from 4,000 in 1840 to 112,000 by 1860, while other lakeside towns expanded more modestly. Buffalo grew from 18,000 to 81,000, Detroit from 9,000 to 46,000, Milwaukee from 1,700 to 45,000, and Cleveland from 6,000 to 43,000.

The spread of the railroads farther west in the 1870s opened up new agricultural and minerals lands and spurred urbanization. In the north central part of the country many scattered and isolated settlements that had sprouted between the 1840s and 1860s would evolve into small cities once the iron horse connected them to the outside world. In the south central region, namely Louisiana and Texas, towns established during the French and Spanish periods also remained small until arrival of the railroads began to stimulate growth. San Antonio, for example, had 13,000 residents in 1870; by 1900 it had expanded to 53,000 after the railroads had reached Texas. Houston, founded during the days of the Republic of Texas, remained smaller than San Antonio until the oil boom of the early twentieth century. Thereafter Houston developed into a leading port city not only within the United States but internationally as well.

In the northwestern part of the country, roughly from the 100 degree meridian to the Pacific Coast, few European American settlements had been established before 1850 owing to the isolation of much of the territory. But in the two decades after 1850 tens of thousands of migrants from the eastern United States headed west via the famous "Oregon Trail." Many were lured by the well-publicized opportunities present in "Oregon Country," where plentiful land deemed ideal for such crops as cereals, potatoes, fruits, and vegetables could be acquired inexpensively. Some migrants were attracted by the prospect of striking it rich in mining and by job possibilities in the lumbering industry. Soon the newcomers congregated in large numbers in the favorable spaces of the Northwest. The coast offered the best conditions for urbanization, and Portland and Seattle, by virtue of their port functions and access to productive hinterlands, emerged as the cities with the brightest futures.

In the Southwest, San Francisco and Los Angeles, two cities rooted in the Spanish colonial period, were assured great success based on their location on the California coast and because they could easily draw from the great riches found in their hinterlands. San Francisco quickly grew in the post–Gold Rush period, reaching a population of almost 150,000 by 1870, even before the arrival of the railroads. After the iron horse established connections to the rest of the country the local economy and population expanded rapidly and catapulted San Francisco into a major national and international city. Los Angeles, with a population of only 6,000 in 1870, lagged for decades far behind San Francisco in importance. But after the arrival of the railroads in Southern California and the building of the Port of Los Angeles, the "City of the Angels" took off, surpassing San Francisco and all other urban centers in the western United States. With its multiple advantages, eventually Los Angeles became a global city. In Arizona, New Mexico, and West Texas, old Spanish/Mexican settlements like Tucson, Albuquerque, Santa Fe, and El Paso remained small and largely inconsequential until the railroads tied them together and connected them to both the eastern and western parts of the country, as well as to Mexico.

By the latter twentieth century a magnificent network of surface roads, freeways, highways, and superhighways added to the century-old railroad system, providing an easily accessible web of connections for the country's urban centers to almost anywhere. As before, the number of cities, as well as the population that lived in them, was highest in the region between the Atlantic Ocean and the Mississippi River. Between the Mississippi River and the mountain ranges adjacent to the Pacific Coast, urban centers, although numerous, were more scattered, with great distances separating many of them. By 2000, the Pacific Coast itself resembled the Atlantic Coast in its level of urbanization, with cities dotting the favorable spaces of California, Washington, and Oregon.

One of the consequences of urban agglomeration in the United States was the emergence of chains of metropolises, namely corridors in which clusters of cities in close proximity to each other functioned as giant urban economic regions. Such clusters became known as "megalopolises," or "mega regions," of which the United States had ten of the forty identified around the world at the turn of the twenty-first century.[19] The most celebrated U.S. mega region consisted of the urban centers extending from Boston to Washington, D.C., with a population in 2000 of about 54 million people, and possessing one of the world's most powerful industrial, commercial, and service economies. Other major U.S. mega regions included the heavy manufacturing urban corridor from the Chicago area to Pittsburgh, home to about 46 million people, the Charlotte-Atlanta corridor, with a population of more than 22 million, and the economically diverse California urban constellation from Santa Barbara to San Diego (with Los Angeles in between), home to over 21 million people in 2000. These four mega regions contained the most prosperous and most scientifically advanced populations in the world.[20] Other less renowned but still significant mega urban areas include

MAP 4.5 Megalopolises and urban corridors in the United States, circa 2000
Source: Based on map in Pacione (2001), 124.

the bay cities of Northern California, the Florida Peninsula metropolitan belt, the Dallas-Austin-San Antonio urban complex, the Houston-New Orleans corridor, the Denver-Boulder chain, and the Phoenix-Tucson conglomeration (See Map 4.5).

Transportation and Cities in Mexico

Mexico lags far behind the United States in both transportation and urban development. The problem with transport begins with the almost complete absence of inland navigable waterways. Only short stretches of a handful of Mexican rivers can be navigated, and such rivers are located far from the main centers of population. Mountains, which dominate Mexico's landscape, restrict the length of most rivers and cause them to empty quickly into the ocean. Mountains have also imposed formidable barriers to the movement of people and goods by land. Construction of roads and railways in many areas in Mexico has been very difficult and very expensive. Shortening distances between numerous cities separated by mountains is still a major challenge.

Although Mexico's transportation system has significantly expanded and improved over the last century and a half, deficiencies have persisted and costs have remained high. David Hilling's 1990 calculations of the "transportation index" for twenty countries revealed that Mexico had higher transportation costs than other Latin American countries like Chile, Brazil, Venezuela, and Argentina, and substantially higher costs than the U.K., Holland, West Germany, Sweden, France, and Canada.[21] In 2002, *The Economist* reported that it cost three times as much to ship corn by railway from Sinaloa to Mexico City as opposed to shipping it from New Orleans to Veracruz by sea and thence by land to Mexico City.[22] Transportation-related limitations continue to impact Mexico's economic productivity and to sustain the unevenness in the size, distribution, and functions of the country's urban centers.

A "Pernicious Anemia"

Unlike the geography of the United States, which allowed for ease of transportation that encouraged relatively well-balanced urbanization, the problematic geography of Mexico has made transportation very difficult, and that in turn has hampered the development of a system of reasonably spaced cities that interact well in the context of the greater national economy. Only central Mexico has a good spatial distribution of cities. Many writers have recognized Mexico's transportation challenges and their consequences. "If, as it is sometimes said, the lines of transportation form the veins through which flows the blood of commerce," writes historian Charles C. Cumberland, "Mexican economic growth suffered from a form of pernicious anemia until well after 1870."[23]

Geographer J.P. Cole adds, "The longest axis across Mexico is as long as the whole width of the United States (Jacksonville, Florida to Los Angeles, California), some 3,500 kilometers. Mexico is not a compact unit, and movement between the extremities involves great distances. In addition, Mexico is extremely rugged, a feature of the natural environment that affects the life of the country adversely in many ways, and greatly hinders movement over interregional routes."[24] The result of the transportation quandary is that Mexico's ability to integrate many urban and rural subnational economic regions to the national whole has been seriously impaired, and the country's capacity to build its own capital has been greatly undermined.[25] Thus the difficult task of building a modern and efficient transportation system has been at the center of Mexico's historic struggle to develop its economy.

Notwithstanding the fact that advances in land transport technology have diminished numerous impediments presented by mountain ranges, all the obstacles in the country have not and never can be entirely eliminated. As discussed later in this chapter, the first major breakthrough in mitigating topographical disadvantages occurred during the late nineteenth and early twentieth century when, at great expense and effort, the railroad network was put in place. Mexico launched a second wave of transportation modernization after 1920, when the advent of motorized transport spurred the building of a network of paved roads and highways. Many advances ensued during the remainder of the twentieth century, and these made singular contributions to the national economy, as well as to the nation's urban system. Once isolated from each other and from the country's heartland, Mexico's major cities and main rural centers of productivity today are at least connected, even if many are not well integrated, into the national transportation web. However, thousands of remote places in areas not reached by railroads or motor transport continue to have extremely weak links to the rest of the country. These isolated communities remain economically marginalized, much as they have been for centuries.

The Absence of Inland Waterways

Recognizing the economic significance that inland waterways could make for the future of New Spain, Spaniards early on engaged in explorations to determine the navigable possibilities offered by Mexico's rivers. The results were disappointing. In the sixteenth century, for example, Hernán Cortés searched in vain for a water passage between the Gulf and the Pacific at the Isthmus of Tehuantepec. Of course no such water passage existed. Cortés and others urged the King of Spain to finance the construction of a canal that would serve as a communication and transportation corridor in that narrow stretch of land (approximately 125 miles). The idea of building an interoceanic canal through the Isthmus languished during the Spanish colonial period but regained some momentum after Mexico achieved its independence. In the end the project would not materialize because of natural obstacles, prohibitive cost, and politics. Alexander von Humboldt not only endorsed the Isthmus canal idea during his visit to New Spain in 1803 but also speculated on the possibility of building canals in other parts of Mexico, especially from the Valley of Mexico to the Gulf coast. Humboldt, although aware of the dearth of navigable rivers in Mexico and cognizant of the problems that mountains posed for the building of canals, nonetheless naively encouraged such projects.[26] People who thought that canals could be built in Mexico similar to those found in the United States, England, or China simply did not grasp the insurmountable difficulties presented by Mexico's terrain. Mexican historian Francisco R. Calderón has characterized the attempts to build canals in Mexico during the late 1860s and early 1870s as "utopian," citing the frustrated canal projects that had been planned to link Manzanillo with Colima, Lake Tamiahua with the Pánuco River, Lake Chapala with Guadalajara, and Córdoba with the Gulf Coast.[27]

Today Mexico has approximately 1,800 miles of navigable rivers and coastal canals, which is a small fraction of the navigable mileage of the United States. Mexico's great deficiency in this area is a consequence of the unfavorable topography that created short torrential rivers that originate in the highlands and rush quickly to the sea. These rivers have been important for hydroelectric production and for irrigation, but not for transportation. One major problem with respect to navigation is that chronically insufficient rainfall undermines adequate water depths in rivers that otherwise would be more navigable. For example, some rivers that empty into the Gulf, including the Rio Grande and the Pánuco in the North, and the Papaloapan in the South, are navigable from the river mouths into the interior only for short distances because of insufficient water. The Rio Balsas/

Lake Chapala/Rio Santiago complex, which flows from the Valley of Mexico to the Pacific Ocean, can be navigated only in parts and has been useful for transport only in a local context. The Rio Lerma, one of the country's most important waterways, was rendered unnavigable by the chronic presence of obstructions like sand and clay, and also because of many man-made structures like dams and low bridges.[28] None of Mexico's waterways even remotely compares in economic significance to U.S. waterways like the Great Lakes, the St. Lawrence Seaway, the Hudson River/Erie Canal network, the Mississippi River system, and the Intracoastal Waterway. Mexico is not unique in its seriously deficient inland waterway transportation. Most Latin America countries are similarly deprived as a result of highly problematic geography. Colombia, Brazil, Argentina, and Uruguay, however, have benefitted from the navigability of rivers like the Magdalena, Amazon, and Rio de la Plata.

Land Transport before Railways

Prior to the arrival of the railroads in Mexico in the nineteenth century, people and goods moved along footpaths and dirt roads riddled with so many difficulties that travel was very expensive, slow, inconvenient, and even dangerous. Countless roads were little more than well-worn trails that dated back to ancient times. In many places, but especially in the mountains, rains or mudslides frequently washed out or blocked roadbeds, posing a chronic challenge to travelers and to those charged with road maintenance. As if that were not enough, bandits routinely robbed travelers and made off with loot taken from freight shipments. Conveyances like stagecoaches charged high rates, leaving the poor no choice but to journey on foot. Many travelers rode on mules or horses, or on wagons powered by these animals, while the affluent rode on diligences pulled by horses. Freighters packed bulk commodities on the backs of donkeys, mules, horses, and oxen, or used these animals to tow loaded wagons. Low traffic prevailed on the national roads, especially between distant locations such as those from Mexico City to towns on the northern and southern frontiers.

During the colonial period the Spanish crown left the responsibility of building transportation infrastructure to the private sector, which meant that roads and bridges would languish out of neglect. Cumberland characterized the roads of New Spain as "miserable," "ineffectual," and "scarce," pointing out that "more materials moved by pack train rather than by wagon."[29] Only the roadway from Mexico City to Chihuahua City could reasonably handle wheeled vehicles, but even there many freighters preferred not to risk equipment breakdowns and instead kept using mule trains to haul their goods. Long journeys on many roads turned into unpleasant marathon adventures. According to transportation historian Sergio Ortíz Hernán, it took twenty-two days to travel the difficult 261-mile stretch between Mexico City and Veracruz during the dry season and thirty-five days during the rainy season.[30]

Landforms, Transportation, and Cities 119

The wars for independence in the 1810s brought further deterioration to Mexico's roadways. Lucas Alamán, a prominent statesman in the newly established Mexican republic, issued an official report in 1823 in which he criticized the decadent transportation infrastructure. At the time major thoroughfares leading out of Mexico City to other urban centers were interrupted or impassable, including the road to Queretaro, the road to Acapulco, and the two roads to Veracruz.[31] Alamán illustrated his observations by quoting passages from contemporary accounts provided by foreigners who used Mexico's dismal highways. Referencing Alamán's assessment and adding his own perspective, Ortiz Hernán writes that these travelers complained about lengthy travel times, delays, sundry discomforts, and danger from the elements and from highway robbers.[32]

The deplorable condition of the roads in Mexico kept transportation expenses high. In 1842, for example, it cost 17.9 pounds sterling to ship a ton of merchandise from England to Mexico City, with the greatest part of the expense being the difficult land journey from Veracruz to the capital. By contrast, the cost for shipping the same goods entirely by sea to the much more distant South Atlantic port cities of Montevideo and Buenos Aires was only 2 pounds, and the cost to the even farther South Pacific ports of Lima and Santiago was 5.1 and 6.4 pounds sterling respectively. Interestingly, shipments to Caracas, Venezuela, a city on the Atlantic that is significantly closer to England than the other mentioned South American seaports, commanded a rate of 7.8 pounds.[33] The difference is explained by the fact that Caracas is not technically a coastal city. It is located some ten miles from the Caribbean Sea in a narrow valley 3,500 to 4,000 feet above sea level. The valley is part of the Venezuelan Central Range, which climbs to 7,400 feet in altitude. To reach the valley from the coast freighters had to haul their cargo from the port at La Guaira and up the steep mountain, a fifteen-mile trip. The Caracas example is revealing of the high cost of mountain travel and underscores the harsh reality of Mexico's transportation challenges.

Roadways remained woefully inadequate because chronic lack of resources made regular maintenance practically impossible. Internal political struggles and recurring wars against foreign invaders kept draining the national treasury and handicapped road maintenance efforts. The highways that connected the Central Highlands with nearby provincial centers and to the seaports received the most attention and were at least kept semifunctional. But the long-distance roads that linked the core region to frontier areas like Yucatán and the Far North evidenced chronic abandonment. Bandits continued to capitalize on the plentiful opportunities to rob travelers. Stagecoaches on the Mexico City-Veracruz roadway, for example, were held up repeatedly, even several times on particularly bad days. Despite the host of problems, by the mid-1860s useful roads connected Mexico City with cities such as Veracruz, San Blas, Guanajuato, and Oaxaca. But freight rates continued to be prohibitive, reaching as high as $330 dollars per ton for merchandise transported between Veracruz and Mexico City. Government officials made road construction one of their top priorities during the period known as the Restored Republic after the collapse of French-backed Ferdinand Maximilian regime in 1867. Trunk roadways that radiated from the Central Valley were expanded, thus connecting centers of production more effectively with one another and encouraging greater commerce, but the overall quality of the roads remained substandard. According to one estimate, during the 1870s only half of Mexico's federal roads, which amounted to a mere 5,400 miles, could be traversed by wheeled vehicles because of disrepair.[34]

The highly deficient transportation in Mexico before the age of the railroads produced disparate domestic economies largely disconnected from one another. Consumption patterns were determined by the foods and raw materials available locally or in nearby surroundings. Many places only 50 or 100 miles away were functionally inaccessible to local people, thus severely restricting both regional and long-distance exchange. Perishable agricultural goods in particular had no possibilities for sale beyond local markets. At a more general level, Mexican exports abroad "were practically reduced to silver and gold and to a few commodities having small bulk and great value ... [and] only rich people could afford to consume foreign commodities ... on account of transportation charges and high import duties."[35]

Railways: Pipelines for the Export of Raw Materials

The construction of railways in Mexico in the latter nineteenth century significantly mitigated the transportation problems. But the iron horse would have limited reach among the Mexican population because the tracks largely followed the traditional natural traffic corridors permitted by the country's topography. Vast areas of Mexico would not be included in the railroad network since they lacked valuable natural resources or population agglomeration, or simply because difficult terrain blocked the way. Even so, railroads spawned a major transformation in Mexico by reducing the tyranny of isolation and distance, making the raw materials of the interior lands easier to access, and stringing together a functional national market for the first time. Rail transport also greatly improved Mexico's competitiveness internationally because now it was possible to ship minerals in greater quantities, at cheaper cost, and more rapidly from the mines to the country's ports and beyond. In essence, the railroads created the foundation for the modern Mexican economy.

As with road construction, building the railways in Mexico was a daunting task owing to shortages of capital, the high cost of importing expensive equipment and materials, the high cost of hiring foreign engineers and administrators and, most of all, the need to overcome many hurdles posed by constraining geography. These problems slowed the spread of the railroads in Mexico at a time when the United States rapidly increased its track mileage. In 1860 Mexico had only 150 miles of track in service, while the United States already had over 30,000 miles that year and over 74,000 miles by 1875. By 1877, Mexico's track mileage had increased modestly to only 354 miles, whereas in the same year elsewhere in Latin America, Brazil's railway mileage numbered 1,484, Argentina's 1,406, and Chile's 1,009.[36] These numerical differences meant that the United States derived great benefits from railroad transportation decades before Mexico had any significant track mileage. Brazil, Argentina, and Chile, although also lagging far behind the United States, likewise surpassed Mexico in early benefits derived from railways. The three South American countries surged ahead because their favorable spaces were located largely along or close to their coastlines where flat terrain predominated and where, in fact, the railways needed to be built first.

The challenge of railroad construction in Mexico became clear in the effort to build the line between Veracruz, at sea level, and Mexico City, at over 7,500 feet above sea level, with a distance of only 261 miles, or 195 miles "as the crow flies," separating the two cities. At the highest point the line had to reach 8,333 feet in altitude. Construction took thirty-five years, commencing in 1837 and finally reaching completion in 1872. Lack of finances, politics, and the sheer magnitude of the project all figured in endless interruptions and delays. Unavoidable steep climbs, broken slopes, and deep ravines comprised the great impediments that could only be surmounted with many twists and turns in the roadbed and with the construction of many tunnels and bridges. U.S. and British engineers and surveyors, plus an army of domestic workers, participated in the long-lasting and costly project.

Although railroad construction proceeded slowly into the 1870s, the pace picked up considerably in the 1880s and remained at a high level until the end of the Porfirio Díaz regime. The number of miles of railroad track in Mexico increased to 12,268 by 1910, compared to 250,000 in the United States.[37] Three north-south lines stood out, each connecting points along the U.S.–Mexico border with interior population centers and prime agricultural and mining areas of particular interest to the railroad companies and other foreign capitalists. The Mexican Central Railroad Company, owned by investors from Boston, built the line between Mexico City and Ciudad Juárez–El Paso. The Mexican National Railroad Company, which was owned by French and English investors, built the line from Mexico City to Nuevo Laredo–Laredo. On the West Coast, the Sonora Railroad Company, under the direction of Boston railroad magnate Thomas Nickerson, constructed the line from the port of Guaymas to Nogales–Nogales.

Mexico's dependence on foreigners for the financing and construction of the railroads translated into significant loss of control over the planning of route locations. Foreigners were primarily interested in building lines to resource-rich areas and along corridors that would yield significant passenger and freight traffic and, therefore, profits. Critics decried the "helter-skelter" network of trunk lines and branch lines, including roadbeds that led nowhere and were apparently built by the companies merely to receive payment for the construction. First and foremost, the railways constituted a "pipeline" to U.S. markets. Promoting economic development in Mexico or linking disparate regions separated by mountains received secondary consideration. Thus cities close to one another but on opposite sides of mountains remained far apart in railway miles.

Opponents of the Díaz regime pointed out that the benefits brought by the railroads accrued mainly to the rich and powerful, including foreigners. In their view the iron horse (1) encouraged greater concentration of wealth at the top of society as landowners saw their properties rise in value and as entrepreneurs cashed in on alliances with foreign capitalists; (2) strengthened the Díaz dictatorship by putting a rapid means of moving troops to trouble spots around the country at the disposal of the government; (3) allowed foreigners to exploit Mexico's natural resources at higher levels than ever before; and (4) drove many Mexican companies engaged in various forms of transportation out of business and displaced many workers.[38]

Such criticisms had validity, but no one could deny that Mexico badly needed modern transportation to move the country forward. The railroads traveled five to ten times faster than other available transport, diminished the isolation of countless communities, and enhanced greater cohesiveness among the historically fragmented national population. The internal market tripled in size. Just as important, railroads greatly reduced freight costs for both raw materials and finished goods, making it possible for Mexico to subsequently develop a much larger manufacturing and commercial economy: for example, a ton of textiles in 1910 could be shipped from Mexico City to Queretaro on the railroad for a mere three dollars, whereas in the late 1870s the same shipment had cost a prohibitive sixty-one dollars using old-fashioned wagon transport. More generally, railway expansion resulted in an 80 percent decline in freight costs per kilometer between 1878 and 1910.[39]

Despite the progress made in railroad building during and after the Porfiriato, glaring gaps in the network would remain for decades. Construction of new railway lines stagnated, with the result that by the mid-twentieth century many areas remained far removed from the railroad network. The Sierra Madre ranges made it very difficult to build lines from the northern coastlands of the Gulf to those of the Pacific. The western range in particular continued to be a formidable obstacle to communication; since colonial years, towns and cities on the Pacific side had developed independently from settlements in the central plateau. Important northern centers in close geographic proximity to each other such as Guaymas and Chihuahua City, about 275 miles apart, or Mazatlán and Durango, some 135 miles apart, yearned for modern rail or road connections. In order to get to Guaymas by rail, passengers from Chihuahua had to take a tiring roundabout route of over 1,000 miles that went north into the United States to El Paso, then west to Nogales, then south to Guaymas; likewise, to reach Mazatlán from Durango, railroad travelers faced an exhaustive journey of almost 2,000 miles.[40]

The enduring deficiencies in the railroad network were noted in 1945 in a government-commissioned study which pointed out that the extant patchwork of tortuous and circuitous railroad lines continued to significantly increase shipping costs and to slow down productivity:

> With frequency freight is hauled hundreds of kilometers unnecessarily; points that are geographically in close proximity are many days apart by railroad. For example, to reach Mexico City from Tampico, it is necessary to travel 670 kilometers to San Luis Potosí, [a city] that is actually farther from Mexico City than Tampico; to go from Oaxaca to Salina Cruz, 200 kilometers apart, one has to make a four-day trip over a distance of 850 kilometers; to go from Mazatlán to El Salto, Durango, about 100 kilometers in distance, it is necessary to make a circuitous trip of 1,727 kilometers that requires at least four days of arduous travel.[41]

The need for railroad lines through the Sierra Madres had to be weighed against the prohibitive expense that such projects required. And there were no guarantees regarding eventual benefits. The Chihuahua al Pacífico railroad is a case in point. Back in the 1880s, when railway construction began in earnest in the country, the government gave the go-ahead for the construction of the Chihuahua al Pacífico railroad line in order to connect Chihuahua City to the Pacific Coast. It turned out to be a major undertaking of long duration. The project cost over $100 million dollars and took more than eighty years to complete, finally seeing the light of day in 1961. The eventual 418-mile long route across the rugged Copper Canyon region required some thirty-seven bridges and eighty-six tunnels for trains to be able to traverse the Sierra Madre Occidental. In the end the economic outcome of this expensive rail line fell far short of expectations. The western terminus at Los Mochis/Topolobampo did not develop as predicted. Inherent natural disadvantages, including shallow water, isolation, and lack of a good hinterland kept Topolobampo Bay from evolving into a significant port. Los Mochis reached only the status of a regional commercial and distribution center anchored mostly on crop production in the Rio Fuerte irrigation district.[42] On the eastern end of the line, Chihuahua City, also lacking both a prime location and a robust hinterland, did not become a major production center within Mexico on the scale of cities like Monterrey or Guadalajara. Eventually the Chihuahua al Pacífico settled into playing a relatively minor role in freight hauling, although it did make the scenic Copper Canyon region accessible to tourists.

The states of Guerrero and Yucatán provide other examples of never-realized or long-delayed dreams related to railroads. As previously noted, in the port city of Acapulco the mountains proved too powerful a barrier and effectively blocked that city's anticipated railroad pathway to Mexico City and other eastern points. Into the early twentieth century, Acapulco's only link to Mexico City consisted of a very rough road that could not accommodate wheeled vehicles; mule trains carried the freight, as they had for centuries.[43] Acapulco would not be well connected to the country's central plateau by modern land transportation until the

124 Context: Nature and People

age of paved highways. While lack of railroad service severely limited Acapulco's ambitions of becoming an industrial seaport, the natural beauty of the surrounding mountains and the attractive beaches did make it possible for the city to transform itself into a major tourist resort. In southeast Mexico, Yucatán's long-standing isolation from the rest of Mexico finally ended in the 1950s when the railroads reached that distant frontier region. But even with modern transportation, lasting geographical difficulties and sheer physical separation from the heartland would guarantee Yucatán's basic identity as a "world apart" from the rest of Mexico.

Interestingly, the predominantly north-south major trunk lines that were put in place before the Mexican Revolution would hold up over time to constitute the enduring backbone of the national system. The construction that came after the 1910s consisted mostly of secondary trunk corridors and feeder lines meant to incorporate centers of lesser importance into the greater national network. Considering the rather sparse favorable spaces present in Mexico and the problematic terrain encountered throughout the country, the real possibilities for the building of major economically significant railroad lines were largely exhausted by the early twentieth century. The restrictive power of geography that continued to dictate the construction of the country's railroad system is illustrated in Map 4.6.

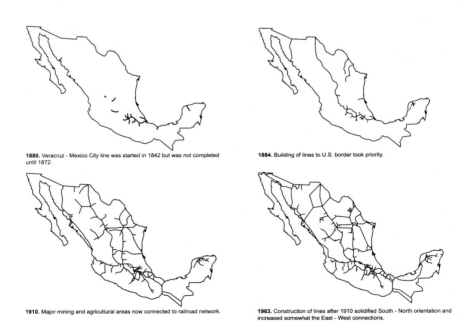

1880. Veracruz - Mexico City line was started in 1842 but was not completed until 1872.

1884. Building of lines to U.S. border took priority.

1910. Major mining and agricultural areas now connected to railroad network.

1963. Construction of lines after 1910 solidified South - North orientation and increased somewhat the East - West connections.

MAP 4.6 Evolution of Mexico's railroad network, 1880–1963

Sources: Nicolau d'Owler (1985), 516a; Hernández Chávez (2006), 167; Guerra (1988), 327; Kelso (1966), 193.

A comparison of Maps 4.6 and 4.2 reveals the much lower density of railroad lines in Mexico than in the United States—especially in the eastern United States, where the U.S. favorable spaces are the most numerous and the most proximate one to another.

During much of the twentieth century, the railroads were a major means of passenger travel and freight shipping in Mexico, but eventually decline occurred in both categories. The downturn resulted from neglect when highway construction achieved a higher priority as Mexico embraced motorized transportation. By mid-century Mexico's railroads suffered from multiple ills arising from inadequate investment in railway modernization and maintenance. The International Bank for Reconstruction and Development noted the deterioration of tracks, erosion of roadbeds, rotten ties, bridges in disrepair, and the preponderance of aging locomotives.[44]

With all their problems, Mexican railroads have provided essential services to the country for over a century and a quarter. Passengers used the railroads extensively for generations until the latter twentieth century, when increased automobile, bus, and air travel precipitated a drop in the quality of railroad service. With respect to freight, the railroads served as the prime movers of bulk products until trucks took over that role. Decline in freight hauling by railway continued into the mid-1980s, but the iron horse made a comeback in the 1990s. Privatization of government-owned railroads, along with increased trade activity spawned by globalization, led to a rise in the freight carried by the railroads, up to 60 million tons by 1996.[45] Interestingly, the historical pattern of ascension, decline, and rebirth of railroads in Mexico is similar to what occurred in the United States.

Modern Roads and Highways

The priority given to railroad building in the nineteenth century kept alive the traditional neglect of roads and highways which, as one Mexican scholar put it, amounted to "agonizing abandonment."[46] Another scholar wrote that on the eve of the Mexican Revolution "the majority of Mexicans still used burros, mules, horses, carts, etc., lacking the option to access more modern transport venues. It is a fact that the most humble sectors of the population continued to carry merchandise on their backs."[47] When civil war engulfed the country during the 1910s, the dismal land transport system deteriorated further. The lack of good supporting roads and highways actually lessened the effectiveness of the railroads, resulting in lower overall economic productivity than might otherwise have been possible with a balanced and well-integrated system of roads and railways.

After the Revolution, enough political stability returned to Mexico and sufficient resources became available to allow the federal government to turn its attention to the building of modern roadways so that the country could capitalize on the recently introduced system of transport based on the internal combustion engine. In 1925, Mexico's newly created National Road Commission formulated an ambitious plan for road construction and improvement.[48] The first phase called for modernizing the roads that connected Mexico City to surrounding towns, to distant cities such as Tampico, Veracruz, Acapulco, Nuevo Laredo, and to the Guatemalan border. The second phase targeted the upgrading of highways to Ciudad Juárez and Nogales and the construction of east-west roads over the Sierra Madre ranges and a thoroughfare to the Yucatán peninsula. Financial constraints and the difficulties of overcoming topographical obstacles would slow the implementation of the commission's plan.

By the mid-1940s more than half the country's roadways still remained unpaved.[49] A government-commissioned study completed in 1945 documented the great concentration of paved highways in central and northeastern Mexico, while large sections of north central, northwestern, and southern Mexico had only short stretches of paved highways, with many roads still unpaved or coated and presumably awaiting paving (see Map 4.7). Lacking both highway and railway service, many parts of the states of Chihuahua, Durango, Nayarit, Jalisco, Zacatecas, Michoacán, Guerrero, Oaxaca, Veracruz, and Campeche, as well as the territories of Baja California and Quintana Roo remained isolated. Some areas rich in natural resources could not be exploited because of the complete absence of roads or their impassability during the rainy season. The 1945 study concluded that Mexico's wide-ranging transportation deficiencies seriously undermined the nation's raw-materials and manufacturing sectors. Costs remained exorbitant not only for transporting natural resources to processing centers but also for shipping goods directly to consumers.[50]

On average about 1,000 miles were added to the road network annually during the 1940s, bringing the total to 15,460 miles by 1951. The Pan American Highway between Ciudad Juárez and Mexico City, which as late as 1949 still included long unpaved stretches, was by 1950 the most celebrated of the completed highways. Many other projects still left much to be desired. For example, the Baja California highway and portions of the Pacific Coast highway remained in dreadful condition. Tropical downpours, wild rivers, jungles, forests, and deserts continued to pose serious problems for both road construction and maintenance in many parts of the country.[51]

Despite the problems, the extension of roads represented significant progress. By the late 1950s, most of the work had been completed on the major trunk lines linking the northern border to central and southern Mexico. An expanding network of roads that radiated from Mexico City now provided improved connections from the Central Valley to the coastal areas, with the highway to Veracruz standing out in the east-west transportation scheme in the nation's heartland. Other transverse routes under development at the time included a new northern road linking Matamoros with Durango, with planned continuation over the

Landforms, Transportation, and Cities 127

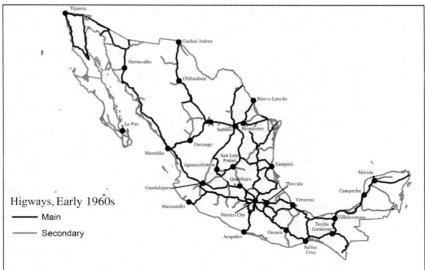

MAP 4.7 Mexican highways, mid-1940s and 1960s

Sources: Adapted from map in Higgins Industries (1954), vol. 2, n.p., and map in Kelso (1966), 192.

mountains to Mazatlán, and a new road across the Isthmus of Tehuantepec. Ongoing projects also included the express highway linking Mexico City to Acapulco and a road intended to connect the northern and southern points of the lengthy Baja California peninsula.[52]

Motorized transport provided a crucial adjunct to the railway system and, in time, motor vehicles surpassed railroads as the country's most important form of moving people and goods around the country. Without automobiles, buses, and trucks, the "economic miracle" experienced by Mexico in the post–World War II period would not have taken place. By incorporating greater numbers of people into the national transportation system, motorized vehicles significantly expanded the national market. Trucks became especially important because they articulated much better than railroads with the nation's centers of production. It cost less to load and unload trucks than railroads; trucks were better able to handle small loads; and trucks could reach many more destinations than railroads. In short, trucks injected new levels of efficiency and flexibility to domestic agriculture, industry, and commerce, and to foreign trade as well.

After nearly a century of continuous work since the commencement of the age of motorized transport, Mexico has made impressive progress in expanding its road and highway infrastructure. By the turn of the twenty-first century, a well-developed network of surfaced roadways worked in tandem with railroads to provide the country with an advanced system of transportation. And construction of new highways continued. In 2007 the Mexican government inaugurated the National Infrastructure Program, an initiative that promised more improvements to the roadway system. Key parts of the planned revamped interstate highway network included modernized corridors linking Mazatlán–Matamoros, Manzanillo–Tampico, and Nuevo Laredo–Mexico City. The most impressive recently completed project (2013) is the new four-lane expressway that crosses the Western Sierra Madre and connects Mazatlán to Durango and other points in north-central Mexico. The new highway required 62 tunnels and 115 bridges, including the Puente Baluarte, the world's tallest suspension bridge—it spans a ravine higher than the Eiffel Tower in Paris and the Empire State Building in New York City. Travel time between Mazatlán and Durango has been reduced by six hours and driving is now much safer than on the old and notoriously precarious highway, appropriately named the "Espinazo del Diablo," or the "Backbone of the Devil," when it was built in the 1950s. The new highway is expected to boost shipping between Mexico's Pacific Coast and U.S. cities in Texas and elsewhere. The most significant economic impact will take place in Mazatlán, as this city expects to increase its port functions and its tourism activities.

On the surface the motorized transportation infrastructure of Mexico now bears some qualitative resemblance that of the United States, but closer examination reveals that Mexico is still in fact far behind its northern neighbor. Mexico's total road and highway mileage adds up to only a small fraction of the total road and highway mileage in the United States, meaning that the density of paved thoroughfares in Mexico is extremely low in comparison to that of the United States; in 2009 about two-thirds of Mexico's long-distance roads (feeder rural and state roads plus free and toll highways) remained unpaved.[53] Although much road upgrading can be done, the Mexican highway network has limited growth potential because of the ubiquitous presence of mountain ranges and because practically all available significant productive areas in the country have already been incorporated into the system. Large areas within Mexico, including thousands of small communities, remain outside the surfaced road system because of their remoteness or lack of economic importance, and chronic shortages of public revenues have meant substandard and erratic road maintenance, which in turn have constantly created interruptions and slowdowns in the flow of traffic. An important consequence of Mexico's continuing deficient road and highway network is that many areas, especially those regions distant from Mexico City, have participated in the country's development only minimally. Finally, the expensive tolls charged in recently built modern highways limit the use of such thoroughfares to affluent people, leaving those of modest means to use the older, slower, and more dangerous roadways. A 2004 official study revealed that Mexican toll highways charged 1.12 pesos per kilometer traveled by automobiles, compared to 1.01 in France, 0.96 in Spain, 0.68 in Portugal, 0.46 in Chile, 0.38 in Russia, 0.17 in Brazil, and 0.07 in Argentina.[54]

Mexican Cities and Urban Networks

The problems that Mexico has had with transportation have placed limitations on the evolution of Mexican cities. Urban development is dependent on accessibility to efficient and cost-effective transport, and Mexico historically has not been the beneficiary of that type of access. As documented in the preceding section, Mexico has succeeded in overcoming significant transportation-related obstacles since the start of railroad construction, but many hurdles still remain. The less than ideal transportation conditions have contributed in a major way to the emergence of far fewer large cities in Mexico than in the United States.

And yet, limitations notwithstanding, city life has been at the heart of the Mexican experience through the centuries. Mexico has indeed utilized those spaces that are suitable for agglomeration to sustain urbanization. At the time of the Spanish conquest in 1519, many indigenous peoples lived in communities of different sizes, including cities with populations under 20,000, cities with several times that number, and in the case of Tenochtilán, Texcoco, and Monte Alban, cities that may have reached populations of 100,000 or more during their zenith.[55] The Spaniards superimposed their own cities on those and other existing indigenous communities and founded new urban centers throughout the Kingdom of New Spain. Not surprisingly, most of the Spanish colonial cities were situated in the Central Highlands, the largest and most favorable space in New Spain. Mexico City, known as Tenochtitlán during Aztec days, assumed the leading position as the largest Spanish city, a distinction it has retained to the present day. Over the course of the colonial period, however, the urban centers of New Spain remained small compared to old European cities like Paris and London, whose populations reached 600,000 and 550,000 respectively by 1700. Around 1750, only about 100,000 people lived in Mexico City.[56]

At the turn of the nineteenth century, the population size of major urban centers in Mexico remained far smaller than those of European metropolises, but they were generally larger than important U.S. cities. Mexico City was more than twice as large as Philadelphia, Puebla was slightly bigger than New York City, Guanajuato surpassed Boston by a few thousand people, and Queretaro and Baltimore had about equal populations. But these comparisons are highly misleading. What really mattered in the long term was the urban growth possibilities that existed in each country. The Mexican cities had far less favorable locations and far less productive forelands and hinterlands than the U.S. cities, and therefore had far fewer possibilities to undertake large-scale commercial and industrial activities. The greater potential of the U.S. cities for fast growth became manifest in short order as the United States developed an advanced transportation infrastructure and, as a result of territorial expansionism, simultaneously added vast amounts of resource-rich lands. The products of those lands greatly benefitted the major U.S. urban centers and fueled their growth. By 1860, New York City had a population of over 1 million, Philadelphia 566,000, Baltimore 212,000, and Boston 208,000. The much less well-endowed Mexican cities recorded far lower growth rates, with Mexico City's population at 210,000 in 1860, Puebla at 75,000, Guadalajara at 71,000, and Queretaro at 27,000 (Queretaro had essentially the same population in 1860 as it had in 1803). The gap between the U.S. and Mexican cities widened significantly in the latter nineteenth century; by 1900 the United States had thirty-eight cities with a population above 100,000, while Mexico had only two—Mexico City and Guadalajara.[57] In the twentieth century, the number and the size of Mexican cities increased significantly, but so did those of the United States. By 2010, Mexico had 56 metropolitan areas while the United States had 343.

Another startling contrast with the United States is that Mexico's urban population has been overwhelmingly concentrated in the interior of the country at a significant distance from the ocean, while the population of the United States has been overwhelmingly located along the Atlantic, Gulf, and Pacific shorelines, and adjacent to the Great Lakes and the major inland rivers. These U.S. areas are prime locations for trade and lend themselves naturally to economic specialization. To be sure, Mexico has important coastal cities. However, apart from serving as commercial ports of modest importance and notable tourist resorts, Mexico's seaside cities historically have been of secondary significance in the national urban configuration. Mexico has been, and continues to be, an inland nation, with its largest and most important urban centers situated in the interior plateaus, plains, basins, and valleys, distant from and totally lacking in direct connection to the ocean via inland waterways. In 2000, eight of the ten largest U.S. cities were situated next to navigable bodies of water, in contrast to only one for Mexico—Tijuana, Baja California, which fronts on the Pacific Ocean. But, significantly, Tijuana is not even a seaport as a consequence of its lack of a natural harbor and its close proximity

Landforms, Transportation, and Cities **131**

MAP 4.8 Location and population of Mexican cities, 1940 and 2000
Source: Based on maps in Garza, (2003), 38, 96.

to San Diego, California, a U.S. urban center that is endowed with a superb bay. With the population of the country's largest seaport, Veracruz, numbering less than 600,000 (in 2010), Mexico does not have a bona-fide seaport metropolis on the scale of even small U.S. ports like Jacksonville, Florida, much less world-class mega ports like Shanghai or Hong Kong. And, unlike the many major riverside or lakeside cities found in the United States, in Europe, or in China, Mexico is totally devoid of large urban centers situated next to inland navigable waterways.

132 Context: Nature and People

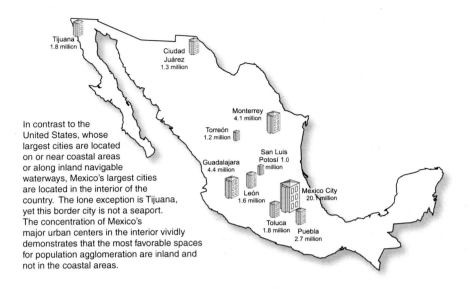

MAP 4.9 Ten largest metro areas in Mexico, 2010

Source: Population figures from Mexico, INEGI (2010).

Reflecting the elevated terrain of much of the country, many of Mexico's cities are located at high altitudes, while few U.S. cities are so situated. For example, twenty of Mexico's thirty-two state capitals/federal entities have altitudes over 3,000 feet, compared to only six of the fifty U.S. state capitals. Just one of the U.S. state capitals is over 7,000 feet (Santa Fe, New Mexico, at 7,200 feet), while the following Mexican state capitals/federal entities surpass 7,000 feet: Toluca (8,793 feet), Zacatecas (8,189 feet), Pachuca (7,959 feet), Mexico City (7,546 feet), Tlaxcala (7,388 feet), and Puebla (7,093 feet). The presence of many high-altitude cities in Mexico has significant economic implications, including greater expense in building and maintaining transportation links with the rest of the country. Cities located in the plains, as is typically the case in the United States, have the great advantage of being more easily connected to each other and to the nation as a whole because highways are more direct and travel times are shorter.

Mexico's elongated, cornucopia-type shape, combined with the high relief found throughout the country, has meant that distances between cities have been greater than would be the case if the country had a rectangular shape, as does the United States, or a circular shape, as does France. The only—and by far the most important—region of Mexico where interurban distances are relatively short is the Central Highlands. Cities in the northern border region, in the southern border region, and in the Yucatán peninsula are located far from the heartland. It has been only since the recent completion of surfaced highways to these far-flung areas that substantive incorporation of the distant cities into the national economy began to take place. In the United States, the West is the only region where substantial distances separate cities; in the eastern third of the country—historically the most populated and most economically dynamic region—the distances are much shorter because of the flat terrain and because the population centers are more concentrated and clustered close to one another.

The fact that the 20 million–plus population of the Mexico City metropolitan area dominates the country so decisively means that the country suffers seriously from population maldistribution and uneven economic development. It should not be surprising that population and economic productivity is so heavily concentrated in the Valley of Mexico, since that region has always been the nation's most favorable space by far. Other favorable regions capable of supporting large cities are few and far between in a country dominated by mountains, jungles, and deserts. In 2010, Guadalajara, Mexico's second ranking metropolitan area, had only slightly more than one-fifth the population of Mexico City; Monterrey, the third ranking city, had one-fifth; and Puebla, at number four, had somewhat more than one-tenth. Tijuana and Ciudad Juárez, ranked at number six and number eight respectively, are two examples of urban centers with a significant shortage of natural attributes that, under normal circumstances, would result in limited growth. But these two cities, both located far from the country's heartland, have the benefit of adjacency to the United States. Their externally oriented economies have been driven primarily by cheap labor industries and tourism. In the United States, large, intermediate, and small cities are found from coast to coast, and no single metropolitan area exerts the overwhelming power and control that is so characteristic of primate cities in the developing world, including in Mexico. The dispersal of multisize urban centers throughout the United States is a function of the widespread presence of favorable geographic sites and advantageous situations that foster and sustain population and economic activity at various levels.

Finally, in Mexico there is a relative absence of "megalopolises," or clusters of sizable cities in close proximity to one another so as to form urban corridors of concentrated productivity and innovation. Mexico City and nearby urban centers such as Queretaro, Pachuca, Puebla, Toluca, and Cuernavaca constitute the only mega region in Mexico. While the highly urbanized Valley of Mexico is comparable to other world megalopolises in terms of population and overall economic activity, it lags far behind in the kind and degree of scientific and technological innovation that characterizes the San Francisco/Palo Alto/San Jose and the Boston/New York/Washington mega regions. Beyond the Valley of Mexico, urban density drops sharply, with many cities outside the core area separated by great distances. Further, in great contrast to the United States and other advanced countries, Mexico lacks urban corridors of closely knit, dynamic cities in its coastal regions. To be sure, a number of coastal cities have recently grown in importance as they have expanded their populations and trading functions, yet significant coastal urban networks have not developed. Low levels of coastal land and water traffic over the generations underscore the low interaction among Mexico's seaports and illustrate the isolation in which coastal communities have functioned historically (See Maps 4.8 and 4.9).[58]

Conclusion

The power of nature in imposing significant constraints on a country's efforts to develop good transportation infrastructure and a well-balanced urban system is clearly revealed in the case of Mexico. Difficult national geography and the limited number of favorable areas conducive to population agglomeration and economic productivity, coupled with chronic shortages of revenues, have much to do with Mexico's struggles to effectively connect and integrate the nation's diverse regions.

Waterborne transportation, the easiest and cheapest form of traffic movement, had monumental limitations from the beginning in Mexico. Although coastal shipping has long connected settlements along Mexico's shorelines, until recent times, coastal cities remained rather small and played only secondary roles in the nation's urban configuration. The almost total absence of navigable rivers, lakes, and canals has been a major disadvantage because Mexico has not had the benefit of inexpensive inland transport and easy flow of traffic between the interior and the coastal regions. A few short stretches of navigable waterways situated in relatively isolated spaces have made some economic contributions to the nation, but overall these have been of relatively minor significance.

Transport on Mexico's roads and highways, as well as railways, have entailed serious difficulties as well. For centuries there were few roads and most remained primitive and in a chronic state of disrepair. Thus the onset of the railroad era was a welcome development, but there was only so much the iron horse could accomplish for Mexico. The impracticality and high cost of building railways through formidable mountainous terrain in the east, west, and south meant that the major trunk lines would have to follow the ancient natural axes of movement, most of which flowed predominantly in a south-north direction. Transverse railroad routes joining population centers along the Pacific and Gulf coasts were the most challenging to build and the most prohibitive in cost, and few lines were actually constructed. Nevertheless, despite the deficiencies of the railroad network, the iron horse immediately made significant contributions to the nation, and those benefits have carried forward to the present. The improved transportation infrastructure created by the railroads received a major boost with the building of an impressive number of surfaced highways during the twentieth century. Modern roadways could penetrate topographically troublesome areas and reach spaces that the railways could not. As a result, cars, buses, and trucks would eventually haul high volumes of passengers and freight to and from practically every significant urban zone and center of production in the country. Nevertheless, difficult topography has constrained the extent and placement of roads and highways, and significant weaknesses can be found in the highway system even today. At the turn of the twenty-first century, transport costs in Mexico remained substantially higher than in many other countries. Still, the combination of motorized transport and railroads provided Mexico with a land transportation infrastructure that has paid dividends. In retrospect, the rapid economic progress experienced by Mexico in two significant eras, 1880–1910 and 1940–1970, cannot be divorced from advances in railroad and highway transportation respectively.

The modernization of transportation has contributed to substantial increases in the population of Mexican cities by boosting urban economic activity and precipitating migration from rural to urban areas. Yet the improved forms of transport have not altered the traditional urban structure of Mexico. Since pre-Spanish days, Mexico's most important population centers have been located in the central plateau, and today Mexico City and its surrounding satellites, which together constitute the lone megalopolis in the country, still occupy the top spot in the national urban hierarchy and far surpass other areas in economic prowess. Outside the Valley of Mexico, urban configurations that fall short of qualifying as megalopolises but that might be classified as secondary urban networks, can be found in only a few other areas. The two best examples are the Guadalajara and Monterrey regions. Large financial, commercial, trading, and industrial cities have yet to emerge in Mexico's coastal regions. As always, economic and political power is still overwhelmingly concentrated in the interior of Mexico, and Mexicans emphatically remain a predominantly inland society.

Notes

1 See nationalatlas.gov, transportation.
2 Date of letter not provided by source; punctuation altered slightly for clarification. From Semple (1933), 267.
3 Hunter (1949), 33, 645.
4 Locklin (1972), 82.
5 Walton and Rockoff (1990), 175.
6 Taylor (1951), 52; Goodrich et al. (1961), 249; Williamson (2011), 15.
7 U.S. Department of the Treasury (1968).
8 The Handbook of Texas Online; see www.tshaonline.org.
9 North (1965), 222; McDowell and Gibbs (1954), 2–3; STRATFOR (2011), 3.
10 Locklin (1972), 722.
11 The Colorado River also served as a busy transportation thoroughfare for three decades in Arizona–Nevada before the arrival of the railroads in the 1870s and 1880s and the subsequent construction of dams. During the navigation years paddle-wheel steamboats plied the Colorado from the Gulf of California northward for distances up to 600 miles (Lingenfelter 1978).

12 Robertson (1973), 139.
13 Lackey (1949), 212.
14 Williamson (2011), 16.
15 North (1965), 222; Hunter (1949), 490.
16 Bamford and Robinson (1978), 205–207.
17 U.S. Department of Commerce (1935), 366; Clough (1953), 111. U.S. Federal Highway Administration (2012), Table 2–1.
18 Taylor (195), 149–152.
19 Florida et al. (2007), 31.
20 Gottman (1961); Haggert (2001), 254.
21 The "index" took into account "surfaced roads per sq.-km., vehicles per 1,000 population, rail travel per person per year, rail tonne-km. freight per 1,000 population, and domestic air km. per person per year" (Hilling 1996, 6–7).
22 *The Economist*, November 30, 2002.
23 Cumberland (1968), 155.
24 Cole (1965), 231.
25 STRATFOR (2009), 7.
26 Von Humboldt (1824), 15, 85–86.
27 Calderón (1955), 530–531.
28 Rivers in Mexico that can be navigated by small ships or barges for fifty kilometers or more are the Bravo (or Rio Grande; 50 km.), Tuxpan (70 km.), Coatzacoalcos (75 km.), Pánuco (100 km.), Tecolutla (100 km.), Tamesí (135 km.), Soto la Marina (150 km.), Papaloapan (250 km.), Mezcalapapa-Grijalva (320 km.), and Alto y Bajo Usumacinta (350 km) (see Cordero Melo 1977, 197). Specific problems undermining the navigability of many rivers in Mexico are discussed in detail in Higgins Industries (1954), I:56–126, and II:2, 39–82.
29 Cumberland (1968), 94.
30 Ortíz Hernán (1994), 48.
31 Cárdenas Sánchez (2003), 72.
32 Ortíz Hernán (1994), 180–181 (my translation).
33 Coatsworth and Williamson (2004), 228–229.
34 Jáuregui (2004), 96–98; Coatsworth (1981), 21–23.
35 Romero (1898) 154. Text slightly rearranged for clarity.
36 Moreno-Brid (2009), 33.
37 México, INEGI (1999), 590; Williamson (2011), 16.
38 Coatsworth (1981), 181–183; Moreno Toscano (1972), 197–184.
39 Cumberland (1968), 221; Moreno-Brid (2009), 50.
40 Rhoda and Burton (2010), 13.
41 Higgins Industries (1954), I:166.
42 Rhoda and Burton (2010), 113.
43 Lee (2003), III:830.
44 Combined Mexican Working Party (1953), 90.
45 México, INEGI (1999), 590–591.
46 Bassols Batalla (1959a), 657 (my translation).
47 Jáuregui (2004), 108 (my translation).
48 Garza (1985), 276–277 (my translation).
49 México, INEGI (2009), Cuadro 13.15.
50 Higgins Industries (1954), I:1, 151, 410, 434, 441; II:103.
51 México, INEGI (2009), Cuadro 13.15; Bassols Batalla (1959a), 674, 677.

52 Combined Mexican Working Party (1953), 94.
53 México, INEGI (2009), Cuadro 13.15; International Road Federation (2012).
54 México, Centro de Estudios Sociales y de Opinion Pública (October 2004), 15.
55 Chandler and Fox (1974), 180–184.
56 Garza (1985), 68.
57 México, INEGI (1985), 24–33; Chandler and Fox (1974), 177–178; U.S. Bureau of the Census, "Population of the 100 Largest Urban Places," 1900.
58 Unikel et al. (1976), 94–95.

5
MEXICO'S FABLED "RICHES"

In 1986, a tumultuous political year in Mexico, ex–Ciudad Juárez mayor Francisco Barrio emerged as a major oppositional force during his campaign for governor of Chihuahua, a race he eventually lost as a result of electoral fraud allegedly perpetrated by the Partido Revolucionario Institucional (PRI), then Mexico's ruling party. While railing against the PRI's dirty electoral tricks, candidate Barrio (of the conservative Partido Acción Nacional, or the PAN) repeatedly lambasted the federal government for "mismanagement" of the economy, claiming that PRI leaders had long "squandered" the country's "rich" natural resource endowment, failing to utilize it to promote progress. Barrio's comments typify long-held beliefs among many Mexicans and foreigners alike regarding Mexico's assumed "bountiful" fertile land and "abundant" mineral and timber wealth. Putting aside the issue of poor governance, the notion that Mexico has an immense amount of natural riches has been exaggerated since the days of the Spanish conquest. In reality, while Mexico's treasure trove of economically useful raw materials is greater than that of many other countries, it is not as ample as commonly believed, and it is certainly far smaller and less varied than what the United States possesses.

At the time of Barrio's emergence as a national political figure and a few years before Mexico's landmark shift to export-oriented manufacturing, resources such as fuel minerals, metals, and agricultural products were, along with tourism, the major sources of foreign exchange. In 1983, basic products constituted 73 percent of Mexico's exports to other countries, with the sale of oil and natural gas providing the federal government with about 30 percent of its revenues (that figure would increase to 40 percent by 2006).[1]

The prominence of raw materials in producing foreign earnings had long fostered the idea that natural resources could provide the foundation upon which Mexico could build national prosperity. But in the minds of many Mexicans, inefficiency and corruption stood in the way of achieving that objective. Once these maladies were eliminated, the reasoning went, the country's economy would grow at a healthier and faster pace and the well-being of the people would improve significantly. Such thinking, however, greatly overestimated the role that natural resources play in the development of national economies. Numerous studies have shown that a country's endowment of good soil, forestlands, minerals, and so forth is not the major determinant for achieving development.[2] Trade, commerce, industry, and technology are more important as drivers of large-scale, lasting development. Still, natural resources must be considered a foundational force in economic activity because they have always played central roles in facilitating growth. Ideally, to derive maximum benefits from the exploitation of raw materials, resource-centered industries need to function in a favorable international context and also need to be well integrated with domestic trade, commerce, and manufacturing. That has generally been the case for the United States—but not for Mexico.

Before the NAFTA age, or prior to the time that manufacturing for export began its rapid rise in Mexico, the country's resource-dependent economy confronted three major problems that have historically afflicted countries in the Third World: First, as already suggested, raw materials industries typically function as enclaves within countries, largely disconnected from other national economic activity. Even though resource exploitation is a stimulant to economic growth, its contribution to broader development is typically minimal. Second, commodity economies are subject to the dreaded "natural resource curse." The "curse" refers to distortions inflicted on resource-dependent economies by international swings in demand and price for raw materials. On one end, high demand and high prices for raw materials lead to overconcentration on the resource sector, with consequent neglect of manufacturing and agriculture. At the other end, drops in demand and price, which often happen unexpectedly, create sudden revenue shortages that bring about serious disruptions. Third, more frequently than not, developing countries conduct trading under international conditions that privilege commodity buyers more than commodity sellers. The more unfavorable the external context is, the worse the effects of the resource curse will be for commodity exporters. Not surprisingly, then, developing countries that are endowed with resources but are disadvantaged in other ways have found it very difficult to embark on a journey leading to self-sustaining development. In the case of Mexico, the "natural resource curse" has severely shaken the country on several occasions, most recently in the early 1980s.

The Natural Resources of the United States

On a visit to Chicago in 2012 I visually surveyed the city and its environs from the 110th floor of the Willis Tower (formerly the Sears Tower) and from the 94th floor of the John Hancock Center. It was a clear, sunny day, and I could see far into the distance from both vantage points. The grandeur projected by the astonishing skyline in the immediate lines of sight and the beautiful cityscapes by Lake Michigan were impressive indeed. But Chicago is far more than the urban splendor that thrills tourists. That day I was particularly interested in identifying landscapes, landmarks, and signposts that revealed the extraordinary economic assets of the greater Chicago area. Transportation advantages of the type discussed in Chapter 4 were readily visible. Directly below was the meandering Chicago River, which had played such a decisive role in the early development of "The City of the Big Shoulders" as a prominent industrial and commercial center in North America. By 1880 Chicago had emerged as the busiest U.S. port, thanks to the connection provided by the Chicago River to Lake Michigan and other important inland bodies of water, especially the Mississippi River. I could see Union Station, from which radiate multiple railway lines that have long transported people and goods to all parts of the country. As I gazed into the distance in my panoramic sightseeing strolls high above ground level, I could make out freeways and roadways fanning out into the vast flatlands that constitute the agriculturally rich Midwestern United States. I could visualize in my mind the timberlands of the deep forests to the north, the vast wheat and corn belts to the west, and the rich coal deposits to the south. I thought of what Lake Michigan meant to Chicago—a source of inexhaustible fresh drinking water and a commercial waterway that since the eighteenth century has linked the city to the Atlantic Ocean. To the south was the Sanitary and Shipping Canal, the waterway that supplanted the Chicago River as an industrial thoroughfare in the early 1900s, and since that time has connected Chicago and northwestern Indiana to the Mississippi River and beyond to the Gulf of Mexico.

Chicago is but one example of numerous U.S. cities made great by their favored locations and easy accessibility to prime raw materials. The vast natural endowment of the United States is most clearly manifested in much of the economic activity concentrated in the country's industrial urban centers. Most of the processing and conversion of raw materials into finished goods, as well as their distribution to national and international markets, have taken place historically in cities.

The record makes it clear that natural resources contributed in a fundamental way to the phenomenal success of the United States. Early on the country's rich natural endowment was noticed by numerous observers. A number of them were so impressed that they described the United States as a country that possessed practically "everything" that nature had to offer for the benefit of humankind. Of course, the United States has never had "everything," but it is a fact that no other country has come close to matching its treasure trove of resources.[3]

In what ways did natural resources contribute to the success of the U.S. economy? First, plentiful good land, forests, water power, and minerals produced strong agricultural, trade, commercial, and manufacturing sectors. Second, the resource sector became well integrated with the rest of the national economy as a result of raw material accessibility and the ready availability of cheap transportation to ship commodities from their point of origin to processing and export centers. And third, the resource industries, along with other sectors of the economy, all developed in a generally auspicious international climate. These circumstances explain why the United States emerged as one of the top economies in the world in a relatively short time after becoming a republic.

Land, Rain, Forests, and Water Power

The natural advantages possessed by the United States begin with the land endowment. A vast amount of fertile soil located on level terrain and on gently rolling plains has been accessible for agricultural production, and an immense expanse of land has been available for pastoral use. According to U.S. Department of Agriculture estimates (made in the 1960s), 44 percent of the continental United States, or 637 million acres, is suitable for regular cultivation, and 12 percent, or 169 million acres, is available for occasional cultivation.[4] And, according to a 1950s calculation by another source, approximately 468 million acres, or 26 percent of the land, can be used for pasture or grazing.[5] The prodigious amount of good land made it possible for croplands and pasturelands to triple in the United States between 1880 and 1945, increasing from 310 million acres to 932 million acres.[6] The United States is so land rich that since the 1930s the government has actually paid many farmers, as well as nonfarmers who own agricultural land, to leave their fields fallow in order to prevent the buildup of large surpluses of crops and the depression of prices.

The stunning success of agriculture in the continental United States stems equally from favorable climates resulting from the country's location in the northern hemisphere's temperate zone. While portions of the United States are subjected to extreme temperatures or acute dryness, advantageous climatic conditions prevail in most of the nation. Unlike Canada, only a small proportion of the United States is subjected to subarctic conditions and, unlike Mexico, where tropical weather overwhelms large areas, only parts of the U.S. South have a bona-fide tropical climate; most of the U.S. southern states has a humid subtropical climate. In most of the northern and southern sections of the continental United States crops can be grown three to six months during the year, and in most of the southeastern and far western parts nine to twelve months.[7] Large and highly productive humid areas are found in farm belts in the Midwestern and Eastern United States, while in the West, arid and semiarid places have thrived by relying on complex irrigation systems. Highly efficient water distribution for agriculture has been carried out for generations throughout the United States via thousands of reservoirs that have been made possible by the building of dams along streams and rivers abundantly and strategically situated across the landscape. Moreover, groundwater sources such as the gigantic Ogallala Aquifer and other subsoil water deposits provide additional water for farming and other uses.

The western United States, being much less favored than the eastern part of the country in available rainfall, has used sophisticated technology to import water from distant sources in order to sustain its dry areas. One of the most interesting stories is how the arid Southwest has been able to meet the water needs of a burgeoning population numbering in the tens of millions. Cities and rural communities in deserts areas of states like California and Arizona have compensated for shortages of locally available water by tapping heavily into the waters of distant streams, valleys, and mountains. That would never have been possible, of course, if such water resources did not exist in the region, and if the technology had not been invented to exploit and transport water over long distances.

Los Angeles (L.A.), which averages only fifteen inches of rainfall per year, is a prime example of a city that has opportunistically harnessed water from remote locations. One might say that L.A. is a water pirate par excellence. Aqueducts have long delivered water to L.A. from various sources in the Owens Valley and from a series of reservoirs that start in the north central part of California and continue southward along the San Joaquin Valley and eventually reach Southern California. A century ago (in 1913) L.A. commenced siphoning water from the Owens River via a 223-mile aqueduct; the city gained control of water in the Owens Valley by secretly buying land and water rights before local farmers realized what was happening. Owens Valley residents put up a feisty and at times violent resistance against the L.A. water snatchers, but to no avail. Then in 1939 L.A. began appropriating water from the Colorado River via the amazing 242-mile Colorado River Aqueduct, whose route includes mountainous terrain.

It is estimated that some 40 million people in the Southwest depend on the Colorado River for most or part of their water, notably the residents of Las Vegas, Phoenix, Tucson, San Diego, and of course L.A. In addition to satisfying human consumption needs, the Colorado River has made available huge quantities of water for irrigation, transforming desert locales into thriving agricultural areas. Two prime farming examples are the Imperial Valley and the Coachella Valley, both in California. The elaborate system of pumping stations, canals, and aqueducts that deliver Colorado River water to places hundreds of miles away are sights to behold. What has made the deepest impression on me, however, is the magnificence of Hoover Dam (completed in 1936) and Glen Canyon Dam (completed in 1966), two of the largest and most important man-made structures in the world. Over many decades these dams have regulated the distribution of immense amounts of water from Lake Mead (at Hoover Dam) and Lake Powell (at Glen Canyon Dam) to many U.S. destinations. Both dams have also generated billions of kilowatt hours of electricity for use near and far away. In short, the contributions of the Colorado River and its mega-dams to human life, to agriculture, and more broadly to the U.S. economy have been enormous.[8]

From Mexico's perspective, the U.S.–Mexico border that was created in the nineteenth century cut off Mexico's direct access to Colorado River water except for the flow from the Arizona–Mexico border to the river's mouth at the Sea of

Cortés, a distance of about fifty miles. Inevitably water controversies between the two countries broke out over the appropriation of water not only from the Colorado River but also from the Tijuana River and the Rio Grande. A treaty signed in 1944 resolved numerous issues. With respect to the Colorado River, that treaty obligated the United States to deliver 1.5 million acre feet of water on a yearly basis to Mexico. But disputes erupted in the 1960s over excessive salinity in the water sent to Mexico by the United States. That problem, as well as other issues, would lead to further negotiations and the signing of another binational water treaty in 1973.

Today many water problems trouble the borderlands, especially on the Mexican side, where the growth potential of many desert communities is rather restricted by water scarcity. When flying over or driving through the California–Baja California and Arizona–Sonora borderlands one is struck by the contrast in the physical appearance of the water-deprived Mexican towns versus the much better watered U.S. towns. That contrast is also starkly apparent in the urbanized coastal area. Beautiful San Diego, California, which receives over half of its water from the Colorado River, is lush with vegetation, while Tijuana, Baja California, which depends on the Colorado River for 95 percent of its water but receives only 13 percent of the amount San Diego gets, is predominantly brown and dusty. The fact that San Diego has a population of 3 million and Tijuana 1.6 million only slightly mitigates the disparity in the water obtained from the Colorado River by each city.[9] Water disparities exist on the Texas–Mexico border as well. For example, El Paso has approximately half the population of its sister city Ciudad Juárez but consumes almost twice as much water per capita, while for decades severe shortages of clean water in Juárez have caused many health problems and led to many deaths, especially among children during the hot summer season.[10]

As I write this in 2014, many parts of the United States are going through the fifth worst drought in the country's history, and there is much talk about severely reduced agricultural output. Droughts of course are cyclical events and constitute aberrations to the normal pattern of rainfall. Unless we have already entered into a permanent change brought about by global warming—which is unclear at this point—recovery should return to the United States in due time. The standard situation in the United States is one of water sufficiency. Under the normal conditions that have existed for most of the country's history, ready availability of water, in combination with abundant fertile land that can be easily worked with farm machinery, have made it possible for Americans to produce a great variety of crops. These crops include grains such as corn, wheat, and rye, semitropical crops like cotton, rice, oranges, and sugar cane, and Mediterranean-type fruits and vegetables such as grapes, strawberries, lettuce, and celery. The United States historically has been able to meet most of its domestic food needs and at the same time has exported large amounts of foodstuffs. Imports of agricultural commodities have been largely limited to tropical products such as spices, bananas, and coffee. By the mid-twentieth century the United States was the top exporter of agricultural goods in the world, not surprising in view of the fact that overall agricultural production in the United States dwarfed that of other countries. At the time Americans produced approximately 25 percent of the crops grown in the world, including "about 61 percent of the corn, 40 percent of the cotton, 35 percent of the oats, 20 percent of the wheat, 21 percent of the flaxseed, 12 percent of the barley, 6 percent of the sugar, and 38 percent of the soybeans."[11]

The United States has remained the world's number one exporter of agricultural goods but has fallen behind China, the European Union, and India in overall output.[12] Given the amount of crops that are routinely wasted and the agricultural land that remains unused in the United States, however, Americans have not lost the capacity to produce much more food if need be and, further, to reclaim the top spot as the planet's number one agricultural producer.

In addition to having plentiful farmland, the United States has also been favored with abundant forests. At the time of initial English colonization in the early seventeenth century, forests covered about half the land surface of what would eventually become the continental United States. With the passage of time many forested areas disappeared as demand for timber grew and as an ever-expanding population sought new spaces to farm and on which to establish towns and cities. The most intense period of forest depletion took place in the second half of the nineteenth century. However, conservation programs initiated after 1900 succeeded in reversing deforestation. By the turn of the twenty-first century the country had about 749 million acres of forestland, 620 million in the lower forty-eight states and 129 million in Alaska and Hawaii.[13]

During the colonial period and for most of the nineteenth century Americans relied heavily on wood, making much greater use of that resource than other countries with smaller forest resources, including England, France, Spain, and Italy. The low cost, abundance, and easy accessibility placed wood in a position parallel to land as a major driver of the U.S. economy. Wood was used for construction, as a fuel for power and heating, and for making chemicals such as turpentine and potash. In 1850, 91 percent of energy consumption came from fuel wood,[14] and the lumber industry ranked second in the creation of market value in 1860, right behind cotton textiles. Wood still retained second place in that category in 1910, immediately behind machinery.[15] As the industrial revolution matured in the United States in the latter nineteenth century, timber became essential in many sectors of the new economy, among them paper manufacturing, modern chemical industries and, as always, construction.

The United States has also derived great benefit from the bountiful waterpower bestowed by nature. At the early stage of U.S. history waterpower was especially important in New England and along the fall line of the Appalachian Mountains as these areas possessed many streams and rivers, including ideal places for building dams. Settlers in colonial days and during the nineteenth century naturally gravitated to the sites where waterpower could be easily accessed and utilized for manufacturing activities. There were many such places. In 1810, one county alone in Pennsylvania boasted "390 water-powered mills, 29 fulling mills, 11 paper mills, 1 gunpowder mill, 12 clover mills, 148 gristmills, and 189 sawmills." By 1840, the United States had approximately 66,000 mills.[16] In New England, energy that originated with naturally moving water remained a preferred cheaper alternative to steam power even as late as the 1860s. At the time less than 30 percent of the energy used by industrial concerns in New England came from steam. This is remarkable in light of the fact that commercial steam engines had been in use and widely available for almost a century.[17]

While waterpower played a major role in the early stage of U.S. industrialization, by the dawn of the twentieth century running water was in decline in the production of power because of the rapidly increasing use of mineral fuels in power plants. Large deposits of oil had been discovered in Texas, California, and other areas, and this resource was ideal for power generation. Nevertheless, in 1926 waterpower still supplied 36 percent of the electricity produced by public-utility facilities the United States, compared to 65 percent supplied by fuel power. Water and fuels, both of which abounded in the United States, complemented each other exceedingly well.[18] But as time passed waterpower kept decreasing in importance in the generation of electricity and, by 2006, hydroelectric power accounted for only 7 percent of the energy consumed nationally. Although hydroelectricity is at present of secondary importance in U.S. energy production, vast hydraulic resources remain unused and are available to the country if necessary. The U.S. Department of Energy has identified nearly 6,000 undeveloped sites with an overall capacity to enlarge the production of hydroelectricity by 38 percent.[19]

Precious Metals: Gold and Silver

Since the mid-nineteenth century, the United States has been one of the top producers of gold and silver in the world, placing Americans in a favorable position for shoring up capital reserves, formulating monetary policy, and utilizing precious metals for manufacturing purposes. The takeover of Mexico's northern frontier in 1848 catapulted the United States into prominence in precious metals mining, with California leading the way in gold production after 1849 and Nevada taking over the top spot generations later. The gold bonanza from these and other states would be long lasting and would contribute many billions of dollars to the U.S. treasury and the national economy. Just four years after the annexation of the mining-rich territories from Mexico, the United States produced a record 104,758 kilograms of gold. By the 1930s only three other countries produced more gold than the United States.[20] U.S. output soared in the last quarter of the twentieth century, averaging over 300,000 kilograms each year during most of the 1990s.[21] Since 1981, Nevada has led the United States in gold production, contributing 83 percent of the national output in 2005. In 2014 the United States ranked fourth in the world in gold production.[22]

Silver production in the United States, which averaged approximately one metric ton per year from the 1830s to the 1850s, increased substantially once large-scale operations took root in California, Nevada, Arizona, and New Mexico, all former Mexican territories. Output soared to over 1,000 metric tons in the 1870s and surpassed 2,000 by 1912. Between 1912 and 2000, annual production levels fluctuated between 1,000 and 1,999 metric tons most years, exceeded 2,000 metric tons sixteen times and dropped below 1,000 metric tons seven times.[23] In 2012 the United States ranked ninth in the world in the production of silver.[24]

Other Minerals

The good fortune of the United States regarding natural resources extends far beyond having plentiful good land, forests, waterpower, and precious metals. Americans have also been the beneficiaries of prodigious industrial minerals. "The United States has prospered greatly from its abundant mineral wealth," wrote geographer William Van Royen in 1952. "It now appears certain that no other segment of the earth's crust of equal area has been so richly endowed with mineral resources. With the probable exception of the [former] USSR, no other important industrialized nation can attain a degree of self-sufficiency equal to that of the United States."[25] The treasure trove of industrial minerals in the United States included vast supplies of conveniently located and easily mined coal, petroleum, and iron ore, as well as "superabundant deposits of sulpher, phosphate, potash, nickel, copper, lead, zinc, gold, silver, helium, natural gas, molybdenum, titanium, salt, magnesium, lower-grade aluminum ores, asbestos, fissionable materials, and a long list of other, less important minerals."[26]

Even after generations of drawing heavily on the extraordinary reserves of mineral resources, in 2006 the United States still ranked second in the world in the production of coal, second in the production of copper, third in the production of oil, and seventh in the production of iron ore.[27] With respect to fuel resources, in recent years the discovery of substantial new deposits of oil and natural gas has brightened energy prospects in the United States. Energy self-sufficiency had become a significant concern for Americans beginning in the early 1970s when U.S. oil production kept declining and the threat of embargos by foreign countries threatened the U.S. economy. But that worrisome trend has been reversed with increased domestic oil and gas production in many parts of the country, especially in the previously little exploited Bakken shale formation in North Dakota. The U.S. energy self-sufficiency level rose to over 80 percent by 2012 and, as domestic output of oil and gas continues to increase, the United States may well take the lead globally in the production of these energy sources by 2020.[28]

Though extremely fortunate in its overall mineral endowment, the United States is certainly not self-sufficient in every commodity and, since the mid-twentieth century, it has found it necessary to import a variety of resources. In 2013 the United States imported between 50 and 100 percent of forty-one select minerals, including bauxite and alumina (100 percent), manganese (100 percent), antimony (87 percent), potash (81 percent), and tin (75 percent).[29] That said, it remains a fact that in volume as well as variety, the United States has had one of the best mineral egg nests in the world. In particular, Americans possess great quantities of key strategic minerals such as coal, copper, iron ore, oil, and natural gas.

The Natural Resources of Mexico

In comparison to the United States, Mexico's resource endowment is quite modest. Mexico, however, ranks far above many other countries in natural wealth; it has been well known historically for large-scale production of silver, oil, and copper, and for cultivation and export of a number of agricultural products. For all its natural wealth, however, Mexico has found it much more difficult than the United States to use the products of the land to stimulate manufacturing on a grand scale and thereby further national development. Apart from chronic capital shortages, other major problems in the full utilization of many of Mexico's natural resources derive from the relative absence of complementary factors; these include the inconvenient location and problematic accessibility of numerous commodities and the lack of cheap transportation to ship raw materials to their destinations. As a consequence of these disadvantages (and others pointed out in Chapters 3 and 4), the extractive industries of Mexico have historically had weak linkages with domestic urban-based industries.

But before going into detail regarding the role that natural resources have played in Mexico's national economy, it is important to provide background on how the notion that Mexico is resource-rich got started and why the idea that Mexico should therefore be a developed country has persisted to our day.

The Legend of Mexico's "Fabulous Natural Riches"

The belief that Mexico is one of the world's treasure troves when it comes to natural resources lives on because Mexico has been a leading producer of silver for centuries, a top producer of various industrial minerals since the late nineteenth century, and a prominent producer of oil since the early twentieth century. But the perception of Mexico's great riches exceeds reality. How did the myth of abundance begin and how has it been perpetuated?

The legend started in the sixteenth century with reports that the conquistador Hernan Cortés submitted to the Spanish King as Cortés sought to convince the monarch of the vast treasures that could be extracted from La Nueva España, or New Spain. The conquistador supplied samples of gold, jewels, and precious stones that he had obtained from the Aztecs, including Emperor Moctezuma. Cortés promoted the idea that gold and other precious metals could be mined in abundance in Mexico once the Indians could be persuaded to reveal the location of supposedly plentiful and fecund mines.[30] As the extraordinary story of the

Spanish conquest of Mexico spread in Europe through word of mouth and as a result of the sensational firsthand account written by Bernal Díaz del Castillo, a soldier in Cortés' army, so did the fable of the colony's "enormous" wealth.[31] Less well-known works written by other Spaniards in the sixteenth and seventeenth centuries added to the mythology. The absence of reliable information did not stop writers from reveling over the perceived mineral abundance and the assumed great fertility of the land.

Baron Alexander von Humboldt's famous *Political Essay on the Kingdom of New Spain*, which narrated the Prussian naturalist's trip to Mexico in the early nineteenth century, reinforced in a powerful way the perception that Mexico was indeed a land of abundance with great economic potential. "This vast empire," he wrote, "under careful cultivation, would alone produce all that commerce collects together from the rest of the globe—sugar, cochineal, cacao, cotton, coffee, wheat, hemp, flax, silk, oils, and wine. It would furnish every metal, without even the exception of mercury."[32] Humboldt's assessment of Mexico's natural endowment was based on direct observation of actually only a small portion of the Spanish colony, and his erroneous conclusions would have been obvious to anyone with scientific knowledge of Mexico's climate, geography, and soil fertility. But at the time no one had such knowledge, and hyperbolized judgments from such a respected authority as Humboldt were widely accepted. Many people even claimed that Mexico was the wealthiest country in the world.

Mexican boosters, yearning for infusion of more capital from abroad, enthusiastically pointed out to foreigners the great advantages bequeathed by nature on their new republic. Intentionally or not, the promoters remained silent about the formidable impediments posed by Mexico's difficult geography. Economist and diplomat Tadeo Ortíz, for example, in 1832 depicted Mexico as having an "extraordinary" climate and "incomparable" soil that created "the most eminent circumstances" to allow the country to produce "everything known on earth."[33]

Not everyone viewed Mexico's natural endowment through such an optimistic lens. Lucas Alamán, a prominent conservative intellectual, writer, and government official at various times from the 1820s to the early 1850s, pointed out that, to succeed economically, Mexico would need to overcome significant natural obstacles. He emphasized the difficult physical configuration of the nation, especially the topographical barriers that impeded good communication and transportation between the interior and the coastal areas, and the irregular rainfall and its severe shortage in many parts of the country. Alamán, being better informed than most of his countrymen, noted that the negative natural factors combined to create serious problems and challenges that would be difficult to transcend. He suggested, however, that Mexico would prevail over such impediments eventually but not in the short term.[34]

Despite admonitions from Alamán and others, the drumbeat extolling Mexico's presumed prodigious riches continued in the latter nineteenth century and into the twentieth century. This is reflected in commentary from foreigners and native sons alike. Traveler Charles Lempriere wrote in 1862 that Mexico was "a magnificent land abounding in resources of all kinds—a land where none ought to be poor, and where misery ought to be unknown—a land whose products and riches of every kind are abundant and as varied as they are rich."[35] In 1881 Albert K. Owen, a railroad enthusiast, remarked in a banquet in Mexico that with adequate transportation infrastructure Mexico would have the capacity to produce more than France, Spain, and Austria combined.[36] Matías Romero, who served in various Mexican government posts from the 1860s to the 1890s, stands out as a major promoter of Mexico, especially in the United States. In 1864 Romero boasted before an audience of U.S. capitalists in New York City: "Mexico is most bountifully blessed by nature. She can produce of the best quality and in large quantities all of the principal agricultural staples of the world—cotton, coffee, sugar, tobacco, vanilla, wheat, and corn. Her mines have yielded the largest portion of all the silver which now circulates throughout the world, and there still remain to her mountains of that precious metal, as well as of gold, which only require labor, skill, and capital to make them available and valuable."[37] For decades Romero hailed the "unlimited" agricultural and mineral potential of his homeland.[38] The message sold well in the United States, as a glowing 1907 article in *National Geographic* entitled "Mexico—The Treasure House of the World" illustrates. The article highlighted Mexico's human labor, its agricultural lands, and particularly its mineral resources.[39]

A growing number of voices sought to counteract the propaganda of the long list of bullish boosters of Mexico. Judicious observers, in particular the distinguished journalist, poet, and politician Justo Sierra, reminded their countrymen of the nation's formidable natural limitations, among them the lack of navigable rivers, the climatic problems caused by location in a tropical and semitropical zone, the unhealthy nature of coastal areas, the problems with soil erosion, the paucity of fertile plains, the shortage of winter snows, the extensive deserts that covered much of the national territory, the ubiquitous and troublesome mountainous terrain, the difficulty and high cost of building transportation and communication infrastructure, and the relative absence of key industrial resources such as coal and iron.[40] But the idea that Mexico should be one of the most prosperous countries in the world because it had "fabulous resources" remained firmly ingrained in the public consciousness throughout the twentieth century. In 1945 the "Mexico is rich" view was expressed forcefully in the two-volume economic study commissioned by the Mexican government.[41] The propagation of the myth by official sources and by Mexicans of all walks of life prompted attempts by eminent scholars of the period such as Daniel Cosío Villegas to set the record straight.[42] But few paid attention and the legend remained alive.

As we will see in the rest of this chapter, Mexico's natural endowment is indeed substantial, but it falls far short of popular expectations. It is true that Mexico has produced precious metals such as gold and silver and industrial minerals such as copper and oil in great quantities. However, the potential of these resources to drive the country's development has been greatly overestimated. Further, the long-held belief that Mexico is a country with unlimited agricultural productive capacity is simply wrong; Mexico's ability to grow crops is actually quite restricted because the country's arable land is in short supply.

Land, Rain, Forests, and Waterpower

Although Mexico is a large country, the ubiquitous difficult terrain, relative scarcity of cultivable soil, and highly uneven rainfall seriously limit the amount of land available for cultivation. Of course substantial productive land is found in various parts of the country, and that is what aroused the interest of legions of U.S. investors and settlers in the late nineteenth and early twentieth centuries. Historian John Mason Hart has documented how huge tracts of Mexico's land, especially in the regions best suited for agricultural production, fell into the hands of Americans during that period.[43] Foreigners joined elite Mexican landowners in monopolizing fertile terrain in the most favorable spaces of states like Chihuahua, Sonora, Durango, Tamaulipas, Coahuila, Baja California, Veracruz, Campeche, Chiapas, Guerrero, and Oaxaca. The freewheeling buying and selling of land, along with the variety of crops produced in the many plantations, farms, and ranches that sprouted in those states, reinforced the fantasy of Mexico's great agricultural capacity.

The harsh reality is that Mexico has long had agricultural problems, with water insufficiency being the major factor. "Mexico is a thirsty land," wrote Tom Gill in 1951. "Half the country has insufficient moisture throughout the year, a third has insufficient moisture in the winter, and less than one-sixth of the country has enough year-long. . . . [T]he rainfall of Mexico conspires against successful agriculture in three ways: in its wide annual variation, in its variation between successive years, and in its deficiency in the regions most important for raising crops."[44]

Recognition that serious agricultural challenges existed in Mexico started in the early twentieth century. In the years before the Revolution, critical assessment of national conditions became the order of the day among critics of the Porfirio Díaz regime. Since then, many works written by Mexicans and foreigners alike have documented the shortage of well-watered land. About 52.3 percent of the national terrain has been classified as very arid and arid, 32.0 as semiarid, 13.4 as humid, and 2.1 as very humid.[45] Thus water deficiency, steep terrain, erosion, bad drainage, and alkali soils conspire to limit Mexico's arable land to an estimated 13 percent of the national territory. To make matters worse, the cultivable land in Mexico is mostly available in scattered and often isolated tracts. Only a few locations in the country boast large concentrations of good soil placed on well-watered and technology-friendly terrain. In 2009 Mexico could count on between 22 and 27 million hectares for agricultural purposes, compared to 176 million for the United States and 68 million for Canada.[46]

Given the limitations of Mexico's land, it is not surprising that before the Green Revolution the country's agricultural productivity per acre was exceedingly low.

Canada produced five times the amount of corn and nearly double the amount of wheat as Mexico, Iowa produced almost nine times the amount of corn, and Kansas produced thirteen times the amount of wheat.[47] Mexico's productivity improved with the Green Revolution, but change came slowly. In 1960 Mexico still harvested less land than Iowa, and the total amount of irrigated land in Mexico was less than the land irrigated in California.[48]

Efforts to improve Mexico's agricultural capacity on a large scale date back to 1926, when the government began to invest significant resources to increase the amount of arable land. Numerous large dams and dozens of reservoirs were built, and an extensive canal infrastructure was put in place. Millions of hectares of land were improved or brought under irrigation cultivation for the first time. The irrigation projects, in combination with significant improvements in crop yields through the use of hybrid seeds, fertilizers, and pesticides eventually allowed Mexico to produce enough food for its population and even to export crops. Between 1943 and 1964 Mexico doubled the yield of corn per hectare and quadrupled overall corn production. Additionally, Mexicans exported 500,000 tons of wheat on a yearly basis, while two decades earlier they had imported half that wheat.[49] Mexico seemed to have achieved food self-sufficiency, and its "agricultural miracle" received wide praise.

But the food miracle faded quickly. Since the late 1960s Mexico has experienced serious problems in agricultural production, and in recent years Mexicans have become disturbingly dependent on foreign food. Between 1940 and 1980 the percentage of the country's cultivated land devoted to corn, beans, wheat, oats, and other basic foods dropped from almost 80 percent to only 57 percent. By the early 1980s the insufficiency of domestically grown cereal crops contributed in a significant way to malnourishment among at least 21 million Mexicans.[50] Imports of large amounts of basic foods became a necessity, rising from 7.2 million metric tons during the period 1983 to 1990 to 16.2 million metric tons during the period 1994 to 2001.[51]

Multiple reasons explain the dramatic transformation from food self-sufficiency to food dependence. To begin with, Mexico's population grew from 38 million people in 1960 to 97 million by 2000 and 115 million by 2012, requiring much greater food output to meet national needs. Additionally, commercial growers, especially foreign companies, converted more and more of the best irrigated land exclusively for the winter fruits and vegetables export market, and in the early 1990s the government eliminated landownership protections long extended to small communal farmers and reduced agricultural subsidies, precipitating a drastic decline of farming activity in the poorest areas of Mexico. Post-1994 NAFTA-mandated reduction of tariffs for food imports also led to a massive influx of cheap grains from the United States, further decimating small farmers, especially corn growers. By the dawn of the twenty-first century Mexico relied heavily on the United States and other countries to feed its population. In 2008, imports supplied an estimated 40 percent of Mexico's food needs, including all its soy, half its wheat, 23 percent of its corn, and 60 percent of its rice,[52] and the ability of Mexican farmers to grow corn and other basic crops remained significantly below that of U.S. farmers due to insufficient agricultural modernization.[53] Moreover, prolonged drought conditions over the last two decades have rendered useless many millions of acres of cultivable land. The estimate in 2011 for lost agricultural land was 7.5 million acres, while some 60,000 head of cattle perished for lack of water during the winter of 2011–2012. In Chihuahua, the Tarahumara Indians could not harvest their crops, requiring emergency assistance to prevent starvation.[54]

The recent agricultural problems have also taken a heavy toll on Mexico's forested areas as pressure has risen to clear more land for crop cultivation and livestock grazing. These land demands have added to the long-standing problem of overexploitation of wooded zones for lumbering operations and domestic needs. According to official estimates Mexico has lost 37 percent of its verdant lands, with deforestation taking 155,000 hectáres of forests annually between 2005 and 2010. Environmentalists, however, believe the amount of lost forest lands is much higher, perhaps reaching 500,000 hectáres annually.[55]

The last subject addressed in this section is the role of waterpower in supplying Mexico's energy needs. Before the invention of the steam engine and prior to the age of electricity, running water in streams and rivers provided power around the world for basic activities such as grain and textile milling. In various parts of Mexico, but especially in the central highlands, available water sources were utilized to build a thriving textile industry during the colonial period and for much of the nineteenth century. The industrial corridor along the Atoyac River in the states of Puebla and Tlaxcala is one example. Here many waterpowered obrajes were established to manufacture yarn, cloth, and other products. But shortages of cotton and technology limited the production of such factories. In reality waterpower played but a small role in Mexico in the production of energy to sustain manufacturing. Human and animal labor drove most economic activity. In short, Mexico's situation differed significantly from that of other countries where greater availability of waterpower and machinery played decisive roles in the rapid growth of industry.

With the onset of the age of electricity, Mexico put many of its rivers to work generating energy, resulting in the enhancement of the country's manufacturing capacity and improvement of living conditions. But power-generation conditions in Mexico were far from ideal. Because of climatic and topographical problems, harnessing waterpower to produce electricity required extra expenditures. Hydroelectric plants, whose construction began in the 1890s, faced challenges like unpredictable rainfall, deforested watersheds that produced "thin ribbons of water or raging torrents," excessive seepage of rainfall into the ground as a result of soil porousness, and the real possibility of earthquake damage to dams in many locations.[56] Yet engineers found ways of overcoming multiple hurdles. By 1910, Mexico had more than forty hydroelectric plants engaged in the production of electricity.[57] Most of the capital for the building of the plants came from the

United States, England, and Canada. In the 1920s, as Mexico began to recover from the instability of the revolutionary years, the government again took up the task of increasing the country's capacity for generating hydroelectric power. An ambitious program of plant construction began during the Plutarco Elías Calles administration. Many new dams were built and for years running water supplied the bulk of the power to produce the country's electricity.

By the mid-twentieth century coal, petroleum, and natural gas took over the running of most of Mexico's power plants, but hydroelectricity still supplied about 45 percent of the nation's electricity. In 1960 the government purchased several foreign power companies that operated in Mexico, enabling Mexico to become more energy-independent. Mexicans living in cities became the principal beneficiaries of the electrical expansion, while large numbers of people who lived in isolated areas, especially in mountain regions, remained without access to electricity because of insufficient power line infrastructure. But significant advances took place in the latter twentieth century and the early twenty-first century. By 2009, 98 percent of Mexico's population reportedly had access to electricity, compared to only 40 percent back in the 1970s. In 2009, water power produced 22 percent of Mexico's electricity, natural gas 35 percent, oil 35 percent, coal 9 percent, nuclear 2.6 percent, and renewable sources 2.4 percent.[58] Mexico had become largely self-sufficient in power generation and even exported some electricity to Guatemala and the United States.

Precious Metals: Silver and Gold

After the Spanish conquest, Mexico became a major producer of precious metals, with Mexican mines yielding 60 percent of the output of specie extracted from the New World from 1521 to 1810. Silver, the top metal mined in New Spain, was highly valued around the world because of its purity and quality. Thus many countries used the Mexican peso as their hard currency, including the United States, China, the Philippines, and other parts of the Far East. In the United States the peso continued in circulation until the mid-nineteenth century.[59]

After 1810 silver production continued to be Mexico's major economic activity. Unfortunately, the disruption of the mining industry during the wars for independence, the post-1821 political power struggles, and repeated conflicts with other countries resulted in major losses for Mexico. Silver output fell below that of the colonial period. As the country achieved greater stability in the latter nineteenth century, the production of silver steadily increased, with significant expansion taking place after 1880. By 1910, annual silver production stood at 2.4 million kilograms. Decline ensued during the early years of the Mexican Revolution, but recovery began in 1917, resulting in production going well beyond the 1910 level by the early 1920s. During the late 1920s the average yearly production surpassed 3 million kilograms, but another decline set in during subsequent years. From 1945 to 1954 the annual average silver production sank below the 2 million kilogram standard.[60] In the late twentieth century, silver production rose once again, fluctuating between two and three million kilograms from 1985 to 2008. In 2012, Mexico ranked first in the world in silver output.[61]

While silver production has been a big plus for Mexico generally, the industry has been fraught with uncertainty because of price volatility. In the late nineteenth century, for example, the value of silver dropped precipitously as the world moved away from the silver standard to the gold standard. The price of an ounce of silver in U.S. dollars plunged from $2.94 dollars in 1864 to $.49 in 1902, with the largest declines taking place in the 1890s. Prices ebbed and flowed after 1902 generally in a modest upward direction, but disaster struck again during the Great Depression, when a low of $.25 per ounce was recorded in 1932. In 1942 a long-term pattern of gradual price increases began anew, culminating in an all-time high of $21.80 per ounce in 1979. But in 1992 the price was down again to $3.71, only to bounce up to $5.22 in 1999, $9.00 in 2005, and $18.50 in 2010.[62]

The extraction of gold in Mexico has been predominantly a byproduct of silver mining, and gold production has been much less than that of silver. Between 1821 and 1840 Mexico produced 18,400 kilograms of gold, which represents a drop in production of 35 percent compared to the previous twenty years. By the mid-nineteenth century production steadily increased, with significant expansion taking place during the 1880s, 1890s, and 1900s. In 1910 production reached 41,420 kilograms but declined drastically to less than 10,000 in 1914 and 1915. Then output gradually rose again, but it would take decades for activity in Mexico's gold mines to come close to the levels recorded during the early twentieth century. Using 1910 as a benchmark year, average annual declines were on the order of roughly one-third from the 1920s to the 1940s and four-fifths from the 1950s through the 1980s. In the 1990s and 2000s gold production rose again, reaching an all-time high of 50,365 kilograms in 2008. In 2012 Mexico ranked eleventh in the world in gold production.[63]

For a century, from 1833 to 1930, the price of gold remained remarkably stable at an average of about $20.68 dollars per ounce. In 1931 that figure dropped to $17.06, but within three years it went upward into the $30-plus range, where it remained until the late 1960s, when a new upsurge began that upped the price into the hundreds of dollars, reaching a remarkable $612 in 1980. The price then went in a downward direction, falling to $317 in 1985, rising to $384 in 1990, falling again to $279 in 1999, and skyrocketing to $1,696 in 2012.[64]

To be sure Mexico has derived significant revenues from being a major producer of silver and a minor producer of gold. Yet these precious metals have not played a significant role in promoting general economic development. As is common in mining industries throughout the developing world, linkages between the precious metals industry and agriculture, manufacturing, and commerce have been weak in Mexico. In reality the precious mining sector has been largely disconnected from the mainstream economic activities that constitute the foundations of long-term, sustainable development. And the wealth that silver and gold has produced has gone mostly to mine owners, middlemen traders, and investors. Mine workers have gained little except wage income, while the population at large has only witnessed the flow of the valued metals to privileged elites in the country and abroad. Mexico of course is not unique. In many places, precious metals industries have feeble linkages to domestic economies, and the masses get few benefits.

Volatility in demand and price has created a disruptive roller coaster. The draconian downward spiral in the price of silver in the late nineteenth century, for example, led to a serious drop in revenues and resulted in an overall deterioration of Mexico's terms of trade. Since silver made up over half the value of the country's exports at that time, the negative impact on the economy is not hard to imagine. The shock caused disarray in various economic and government sectors. Other problems encountered in the precious metals industry have been unlawful mining and illegal flow of silver and gold out of the country. For example, in the nineteenth century British operatives surreptitiously exported Mexican gold and silver without paying applicable export taxes. Further, historian John Mason Hart cites instances of unauthorized extraction of silver as well as contraband silver shipments to the United States by American mine owners from the fabulously rich Batopilas, Chihuahua, mining district from the 1870s to the 1910s. These activities amounted to outright theft, depriving the Mexican government of revenues needed to undertake projects beneficial to the country.[65] Other acts of dishonesty such as illegal mining in public lands and corruption of officials by both foreign and domestic companies have long been a reality in Mexico's silver and gold mining industries. Of late even some drug cartels have taken over operation of mines.

Oil

While silver production propped up Mexico's exalted image as a "resource-rich" country for centuries, since 1900 another important mineral—petroleum—has continued to bolster that reputation. For much of the twentieth century and continuing to the present, revenues from oil have been of fundamental importance to the government. Even with the rise of export-oriented manufacturing, in 2010 the oil sector still accounted for 14 percent of Mexico's export earnings and provided a third of the government's revenues. Production of oil started slowly in Mexico at the turn of the twentieth century, but by the early 1920s Mexico supplied 25 percent of the world's total. With demand for petroleum on the increase because of the expanding automobile industry, in 1921 Mexico produced a record high of 193 million barrels of crude oil. Subsequently, however, production dropped as a result of greater international competition and political problems with the foreign oil companies that owned and operated the Mexican fields. By 1933, in the midst of the Great Depression, production plunged to 31 million barrels. In 1938 the Mexican government nationalized the oil industry following the refusal of U.S. and British companies to obey a pro-labor ruling issued by the Mexican Supreme Court. Understandably production fell after the expropriation. Mexico needed time to set up a new institutional framework and to fully develop the technical and business expertise necessary to run the industry. Mexico also had to contend with efforts on the part of the expropriated companies to sabotage production and undermine sales of Mexican oil on the international market. Production, which stood at 47 million barrels in 1937, went down from there in subsequent years. By 1946, however, production reached 49 million barrels and steadily climbed after that. The biggest oil boom in Mexican history began in the late 1970s with the discovery of large deposits in the Gulf of Mexico, which allowed the country to emerge as one of the top ten oil producers in the world. In 1982, production reached over 1 billion barrels, a new record. But the good times ended abruptly during the oil bust of the 1980s. After years of struggle to make up lost ground, an upward surge in the industry ensued the following decade. In 1996 oil production surpassed 1 billion barrels anew.[66]

Recently Mexico's oil industry has been confronted with daunting new challenges. Numbers tell the story. Proven reserves fell from over 48 billion barrels in 1998 to just over 10 billion barrels in 2013, while the country's largest field, Cantarell, yielded 74 percent less in 2010 than in 2004; during those years the Cantarell contribution to Mexico's total crude oil production plummeted from 63 percent to 22 percent. Overall production in Mexico fell from 3.8 million barrels a day in 2004 to 2.9 million in 2013. Whereas in 1990 Mexico was the fourth largest oil producer globally, by 2013 it had slipped to ninth place.[67] Although large deposits of untapped oil were believed to lie in the deep waters of the Gulf of Mexico, the state company PEMEX (Petroleos Mexicanos) had neither the money nor the expertise to explore or exploit those fields, so in 2013 the Mexican government overcame decades of nationalistic resistance to allowing private companies to participate in the oil industry, and a new law permitted contracting with foreign companies to do necessary explorations. This turn of events, as well as the prospect of exploiting untapped shale fields, have created optimism about the future of the oil and gas industry. Yet daunting challenges remain, including the increasing theft of oil by drug cartels. In 2013 criminals stole some 7.5 million barrels of oil worth over a billion dollars.[68]

The volatility that has characterized silver and gold prices is replicated in the oil industry as well. During the roller-coaster twentieth century price fluctuations occurred as follows: significant peaks and valleys in the 1910s, 1920s, and 1930s; mild rises and falls in the post–World War II period; fairly flat movement but tending slightly downward in the 1950s and 1960s; gigantic upsurge in the late 1970s followed by steep drops into the early 1980s; moderate peaks and valleys from the mid-1980s to the end of the century; and a historic ascent that started in 1999 and continued for years, only to fall again by late 2014.[69] For Mexico and other countries with large oil sectors, such price fluctuations are a double-edged sword. While high prices mean more revenues and greater economic activity, low prices have the opposite effect.

Mexico is well acquainted with the shocks triggered by sharp drops in oil prices. In the early 1980s, the economy faced an extraordinary crisis following the decline in the average price of Mexican crude from $36 dollars a barrel to under $20. The price nosedive aggravated an already existing serious situation that had arisen from a general drop in demand for Mexican products on the international market because of a worldwide recession. At the time Mexico also faced a bloated foreign debt caused by a substantial increase in the cost of borrowing money from foreign banks. Finding it exceedingly difficult to repay the external debts, which amounted to about $96 billion dollars by 1986, Mexico turned to international lending organizations for emergency loans. These institutions required Mexico to undertake fundamental structural reforms as a condition for making the loans. Mexico complied with the stipulations and abandoned its mixed capitalistic/socialistic system in favor of a predominantly free-market economy, but the government still retained control of the oil industry as mandated by the Mexican constitution. Despite the fact that oil exports as a percentage of all exports have now dropped to less than 15 percent, Mexico's dependence on oil is still too high. Because PEMEX provides revenues to cover about a third of the federal government's budget, drops in oil production in effect translates into a major reduction of programs that benefit the Mexican people.

Other Minerals

Besides producing precious metals and oil, Mexico historically has been a significant supplier of other minerals useful for industry. These minerals include copper, lead, coal, zinc, antimony, arsenic, graphite, iron, manganese, molybdenum, and tungsten. By the 1980s, Mexico produced more than forty different minerals and exported twelve non-fuel commodities. In 2006, Mexico "was the world's second ranked producer of bismuth, fluorspar, and silver; and the third ranked producer of strontium (celestite). Mexico also was the fourth ranked producer of fuller's earth; the fifth ranked producer of arsenic and lead ore; the sixth ranked producer of bentonite, cadmium, and zinc ore; the seventh ranked producer of diatomite, gypsum, and salt; the eight ranked producer of kaolin, manganese, and molybdenum; and the tenth ranked producer of cement."[70]

As notable as Mexico's production of industrial minerals has been historically, several caveats are in order. The prominence of minerals in the economy has misled many into believing that Mexico has no equal among mineral-rich countries. The folly in such thinking is revealed in data gathered by the British Geological Survey, which indicated that of sixty-four key minerals produced by nations around the world during the period 2004 to 2008, Mexico produced thirty-one, while the United States produced forty-five. Japan, commonly thought of as a mineral-poor country, in actuality produced twenty-five key minerals.[71] Mexico historically has also had to turn to foreign sources to obtain key minerals either unavailable or not conveniently accessible in the country. Although the manufacturing sector in 1940 overall derived 77 percent of needed raw materials domestically, select major industries obtained only a small portion of their raw materials from inside the country, including paper manufacturers (30 percent), ceramics manufacturers (33 percent), and metal-working industries (39 percent). By 2010 non-fuel mineral imports into Mexico amounted to 52 billion pesos.[72] Strategic resources like coal and iron ore have also been difficult and expensive to mine because of their location in remote areas, and the shipping of these materials to processing centers has likewise been costly, and as indicated earlier, conditions in Mexico have been far from ideal for integrating the mining industry with other sectors of the economy. This was especially significant in the days when minerals made up the lion's share of the Mexican export economy.

Conclusion

This chapter has shown that contrary to popular thinking, Mexico comes nowhere close to living up to its mythical reputation as a land of "great natural riches." While Mexico is much better off in its resource endowment than many other countries, it ranks significantly below the United States, which is in a league of its own in the world in terms of its endowment of good land, valuable minerals, and other resources. On the whole, Mexico's legendary "treasure house" has actually ranged from abundance of some prime commodities to acute shortages of other significant resources.

Mexico's agricultural land is seriously deficient in both quantity and quality, and the same can be said for rain, which falls excessively in some places and scarcely at all in many areas where it is badly needed. As a consequence of these crop-growing disadvantages, large segments of Mexico's population have historically struggled to meet food requirements and other basic needs. Poverty, especially in the countryside, has been widespread over many generations.

In one area, that of mineral productivity, Mexico's reputation is well founded. Mexico indeed has one of the largest endowments of minerals in the world, and that fact alone places it on a higher plane than many other countries classified as "underdeveloped" or "developing." Besides silver and oil, which top the list of Mexico's resources, other minerals have contributed to the building of the Mexican economy and have produced robust revenues for the national treasury, though in recent decades, with the dramatic rise of export-oriented manufacturing, natural resources have become a much smaller part of the economy. Prior to 1980, however, when minerals played a prominent role in trade, Mexico was subjected to constant fluctuations and volatility in prices and demand for commodities in the international market. As a result the Mexican people lived with a high degree of vulnerability to forces far beyond their control. The history of both silver and oil illustrate how frequently good times were followed by bad times because of ever-changing global conditions. The devastating shocks to the Mexican economy spawned by drastic drops in the oil price in the 1980s are illustrative of the "resource curse" frequently experienced by countries that rely too heavily on natural commodities. It is well established that oil not only seriously distorts and undermines traditional sectors of the economy such as manufacturing, but it also tends to concentrate wealth, breeds corruption, and exacerbates external dependence.

Mexico's historical experience and that of other resource-abundant developing countries make it clear that industrialized economies capable of providing a high standard of living cannot be constructed solely or predominantly on the exploitation of raw materials. The record of developed countries demonstrates that, in the long run, healthy manufacturing and technological, commercial, trading, and financial sectors are far more important than natural resources for generating prosperity. And yet the significance of the Mexico's natural endowment cannot be underestimated both in the distant and recent pasts. Minerals in particular were largely responsible for keeping the Mexican economy afloat over many generations. Without natural resources, conditions in Mexico would have been much worse. But being a resource-abundant but at the same time dependent country was not a healthy situation for Mexico. Recognition of that reality contributed in a significant way to shaping the government's landmark decision in the 1980s to steer the country in the direction of export-oriented manufacturing.

And yet, while Mexico successfully pulled itself away from raw materials dependency, in reality natural resource dependence has remained a fact of life. Mexico now relies heavily on its ultimate natural resource—human labor. It is the sizable low-wage labor sector that largely sustains the country's predominant economic sector—manufacturing, which overwhelmingly uses low-skilled workers in maquiladora-type assembly operations. Workers make salaries and wages that are significantly below those in the United States and other developed countries. Moreover, manufacturing in Mexico is heavily dominated by foreign-owned corporations, underscoring the continued external dependence of the national economy.

Notes

1 *Current History* (March 1987), 126; Rudolph (1985), 186; *Review of the Economic Situation of Mexico* (October 2007), 310–311.
2 Sachs and Warner (1999), 43–76; Rodríguez (1999), 277–303; Sachs and Warner (2001), 827–838.
3 Potter (1954), 78–80, and passim; Wright and Czelusta (2004), 9.
4 Data cited in Highsmith, Jr., and Northham (1968), 65.
5 Miller et al. (1954), 62.
6 Van Royen (1952), I:13.
7 Atwood (1940), 8.
8 But trouble lies ahead as expected increases in population will place greater pressures on an already overutilized Colorado River whose flow may well decline as a result of climate

change. A 2012 study by the U.S. Bureau of Reclamation predicts that by 2060 between 50 million and 75 million people will depend on the Colorado River for their water, yet the river flow may decline by as much as 9 percent (*El Paso Times*, July 23, 2012, 3B).

9. Cohen (June 2011), 19–21, 33–35.
10. Martínez (2006), chapter 6; data supplied by officials in El Paso and Ciudad Juárez.
11. Miller et al. (1954), 40.
12. U.S. Department of Agriculture, Foreign Agricultural Service (May 2011); Investopedia.com (July 12, 2012).
13. Lubowski et al. (2002), 25; Weigert (1957), 575; McIlwraith and Muller (2001), 319–320.
14. As mineral fuels became important for generating energy, the percentage for fuel woods dropped to 73 percent in 1870, 36 percent in 1890, and 21 percent in 1900 (Rosenberg 1972, 159).
15. Hughes and Cain (2003), 206, 333.
16. Hindle and Lubar (1986), 157.
17. Rosenberg (1972), 66.
18. Stabler (1927), 434–435, 446.
19. Weigert (1957), 578–580; Rosenberg (1972), 159; U.S. Energy Information Administration (2006).
20. Van Royen (1952), 127–128.
21. U.S. Bureau of the Census (2006), IV:315–317.
22. U.S. Geological Survey (2005), Nevada, 30.1; USAgold.com, www.usagold.com.
23. U.S. Bureau of the Census (1960), 371; U.S. Bureau of the Census (2006), IV, 315–316; Coatsworth in Lier (1989), 31.
24. U.S. Geological Survey (2007); The Silver Institute, www.silverinstitute.org.
25. Van Royen (1952), II:6.
26. Murphey (1966), 645–646, 662 (map).
27. U.S. Geological Survey (2007); U.S. Energy Information Administration: "World Coal Production, 1997–2006" and "World Crude Oil Production, 1960–2000."
28. Bloomberg News (2012); U.S. Geological Survey (2007).
29. U.S. Geological Survey (2013), 6.
30. Cortés wrote five letters to the king of Spain between 1519 and 1524 (see Cortés 1986, iii, 3, 5, 29, 40–41, 47, 92–93, 99–100, 160).
31. The Díaz del Castillo eyewitness account was first published in 1632, well over a century after the Spanish conquest of Mexico (Díaz del Castillo 1955).
32. Alexander Von Humboldt's *Political Essay on the Kingdom of New Spain* was first published in 1811 (see Von Humboldt 1824, 2–3, 25).
33. Cited in Martín Echeverría (1954), 269 (my translation).
34. Alamán's view are summarized in Martín Echeverría (1954), 271–272.
35. Lempriere (1862), B.
36. González Navarro (1984), 135.
37. Romero (1898), I:385.
38. Romero (1898), I:393–394.
39. *National Geographic* (August 1907).
40. González Navarro (1974), 139–140; Esquivel (2000), 28, 44. See also Martín Echeverría (1954), 275–280.
41. Higgins Industries (1954) I:1.
42. Cosío Villegas (1949), 81–112.
43. Hart (2002), chapters 3–8.

44 Gill (1951), 58–60. Text slightly rearranged for clarity.
45 Bassols Batalla (1980), 101.
46 One hectare is equal to 2.5 acres. De Grammont (2003), 354; Rhoda and Burton (2010), 37, 93.
47 Tannenbaum (1950), 183.
48 Cumberland (1968), 11, 14.
49 México, INEGI (2009); Sonnenfield (1992), 28; Rhoda and Burton (2010), 219.
50 Sanderson (1983), 4–8.
51 Data from the United Nations Food and Agriculture Organization (cited by Yúnez-Naude and Barceinas Paredes in Randall 2006, 230).
52 Vigna (March 14, 2008).
53 Schwartzman (2012), 142.
54 *Reuters* (March 21, 2012).
55 México, Secretaría de Medio Ambiente y Recursos Naturales (2007), 14; *La Jornada* (December 27, 2013), 33.
56 Wythe (1949), 286.
57 MacHugh (1914), 197; Wionczek (1965), 527–528.
58 Cline, (1962), 284; Bassols Batalla (1980), 256, 258; U.S. Energy Information Administration, (2009); Rhoda and Burton (2010), 104–105.
59 Cline (1962), 271; Cumberland (1968), 86; Pletcher (1958), 35–36.
60 González Reyna (1956), appendix table.
61 México, INEGI (2009), Cuadro 9.1; Mexican Mining Industry, www.promexico.gob.mx; The Silver Institute, www.silverinstitute.org.
62 Kitco, www.kitco.com/charts/historicalsilver.html.
63 Data between 1521 and 1910 drawn from González Reyna (1956), Appendix table, and between 1911 and 2008 from México, INEGI (2009), Cuadro 9.1. There are minor discrepancies between these two sources.
64 Kitco Bullion Dealers. http://66.38.218.33/scripts/hist_charts/yearly_graphs.plx; Goldprice, www.goldprice.org.
65 Hart (2008), 8, 85, 89–90, 143, 168–170.
66 Grunwald (1970), 250; México, INEGI (1999), Cuadro 11.1.
67 U.S. Energy Information Administration (2014); Banco de México (2008), 123.
68 *El Paso Times* (September 26, 2014), 2.
69 Grunwald (1970), 250–251; Mayer-Serra (2006), 143.
70 Rudolph (1985), 196; quote from U.S. Geological Survey (2006).
71 British Geological Survey (2010).
72 Wythe (1949), 281; British Geological Survey (2010); México, INEGI (2011), Cuadro 3.2.1.

6
PEOPLE AND THE ECONOMIC PIE

As I look back on my childhood in Mexico during the 1950s, one of the things I remember most vividly is the kids who populated the different *colonias* (neighborhoods) where we lived. There were lots of children then. It was easy to belong to a "gang" and just "hang out" or "do stuff." With little effort we could start up soccer or baseball games on the street as scores of *muchachos* (boys) were always within sight or earshot. My parents did their part to build up Mexico's youthful population. They had six children, which seemed typical. Years later, after moving to the United States, I often visited my old colonias in Mexico and noticed that the number of children who congregated or played in the streets kept declining as time passed. Life had become more tranquil for the younger generation—as well as for the adults. Families had gotten smaller, and fewer youngsters ran around as freely as my friends and I had done many years before.

What I witnessed in the neighborhoods where I grew up was a reflection of what occurred throughout Mexico beginning in the last quarter of the twentieth century: a demographic revolution. By 2012, the average number of children per family had dropped to 2.3, compared to 7.3 in 1960. That remarkable demographic transformation resulted from Mexico's determination to prevent population pressures from undoing major economic advances that had taken place in the decades after World War II. It took some time for Mexico to respond in an organized fashion to the problem of overpopulation, but the family planning initiatives enacted in the 1970s did not take long to yield results. Significantly lower population growth rates were noticeable as early as the mid-1980s.

The rapid population growth and related strains that Mexico has experienced have spared the United States. Both underpopulation and overpopulation have posed serious problems for Mexico, but not for its wealthy neighbor. Mexico's population has been acutely maldistributed as a consequence of burdensome geography, while the population of the continental United States has been relatively well dispersed from coast to coast. Mexico has been far less successful than the United States in attracting immigrants from Europe, and geographic encumbrances have hindered Mexico's capacity to integrate indigenous peoples to a greater extent than is the case with the United States.

People in the United States

Population Size

With the great expansion of its territorial possessions in the nineteenth century, the United States created the large space and large resource base necessary to support one of the great agglomerations of people in the world. The U.S. population grew from 4 million in 1790 to 23 million in 1850, 76 million in 1900, 151 million in 1950, 281 million in 2000, and 314 million by 2012. Such numbers have provided the United States with a substantial supply of labor to drive a continuously expanding economy and a vast consumer market. Immigrants and their descendants are largely responsible for the spectacular growth of the U.S. population, underscoring the fact that the United States has long been the land of opportunity for people throughout the world. The ability of the United States to absorb wave upon wave of immigration from abroad is demonstrated by the historical record. Between 1820 and 2000 an astounding 66 million legal immigrants entered the United States, with the years 1880 to 1920 and 1960 to 2000 constituting the two periods of greatest influx.[1] More than 23 million immigrants arrived during the period 1880 to 1920 and over 24 million immigrants arrived during the period 1960 to 2000.

The size of the U.S. population has harmonized well with the nation's economic and social needs, assuring continuous growth and rising prosperity over the generations.

Physical Distribution

The generally favorable physical distribution of the population in the different geographic areas that make up the United States is a testament to the many attractive areas in the country that are capable of supporting sizeable numbers of people and large-scale economic activity. In 1870, before the spread of the railroads to the western continental United States, more than 82 percent of the population lived between the Mississippi River and the Atlantic Ocean. Once the railroads reached the West Coast, the states of California, Oregon, and Washington took off economically and attracted large numbers of settlers. Those three states, as well as others within the inland West, have been growing ever since at higher rates than other regions. By 2010 the West (as defined by the U.S. Census) had caught up with the other regions, strengthening the equilibrium relative to the Northeast, South, and

164 Context: Nature and People

Midwest. The current population balance among the various sections is reflected in the figures given in Table 6.1 and in Map 6.1. In terms of GDP, the Northeast stands out in its contribution of over a fifth of the national output although it makes up less than 5 percent of the national territory. The West accounts for less

TABLE 6.1 Regional Distribution of U.S. Population and GDP, 1900-2010[1]

	Percent of Territory	Percent of Population			Percent of GDP
		1900	1950	2010	2009
Northeast	4.7	27.6	26.1	17.9	20.6
South	24.5	32.2	31.2	37.1	34.3
Midwest	21.2	34.6	29.4	21.7	20.5
West	49.5	5.7	13.3	23.4	24.2

[1] I have followed the U.S. Census Bureau regional classification scheme, which groups the states into four regions, as follows: **Northeast**—Connecticut, Maine, Massachusetts, New Hampshire, New Jersey, New York, Pennsylvania, Rhode Island, and Vermont. **South**—Alabama, Arkansas, Delaware, District of Columbia, Florida, Georgia, Kentucky, Louisiana, Maryland, Mississippi, North Carolina, Oklahoma, South Carolina, Tennessee, Texas, Virginia, and West Virginia. **Midwest**—Illinois, Indiana, Iowa, Kansas, Michigan, Minnesota, Missouri, Nebraska, North Dakota, Ohio, South Dakota, and Wisconsin. **West**—Alaska, Arizona, California, Colorado, Hawaii, Idaho, Montana, Nevada, New Mexico, Oregon, Utah, Washington, and Wyoming.

Sources: My calculations, based on population and economic data in U.S. Census Bureau, *Censuses of Population* (1900, 1950, 2010), and U.S. Bureau of Economic Analysis (2011).

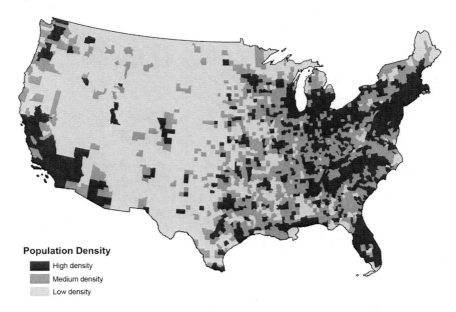

MAP 6.1 Population density of the United States, 2010

Source: Adapted from U.S. Bureau of the Census (2010).

than a fourth of the GDP, yet it constitutes almost half of the national territory. This is explained by the vast desert and mountainous spaces in the West where the population is sparse and where there is relatively little economic activity.

Demographic Trends

Owing to several factors, the United States historically has not experienced population pressures of the kind present in Mexico. A spacious territory has yielded a relatively low population density. Even though U.S. density tripled during the twentieth century, it still remained relatively low at 80 persons per square mile in 2000, compared to the overall world density of 120 persons per square mile.[2] Resource abundance and steady economic growth have also shielded the United States from stresses associated with an oversupply of workers, and trends in U.S. fertility and mortality rates, coupled with immigration, have worked for the country instead of against it. Contrary to the standard pattern in the classic demographic transition model, the decline in fertility in the United States preceded the decline in mortality, preventing overpopulation when the country was still physically small. Fertility moved generally in a downward direction from 1800 to 1940, rose during the "Baby Boom" period of the 1940s and 1950s, and then dropped anew in subsequent decades.[3]

In Europe during the nineteenth and early twentieth centuries, declining death rates and stable or rising birth rates produced excess people whose employment needs could not be satisfactorily met in their homelands. As a consequence tens of millions of Europeans migrated to the United States, which had emerged as the biggest country in the world in need of large numbers of working people. During the second third of the twentieth century, population pressures eventually dissipated in Europe as a result of drastic declines in birth rates and the stabilization of death rates. Once European countries reached zero or negative population growth rates, the historical pattern of exporting population was reversed. A new trend took hold, that of importing population, in particular immigrants of working age.

With few Europeans needing to migrate abroad, the United States began to rely primarily on Mexico and other parts of Latin America, as well as Asia, for its immigration needs. The upsurge in immigration from the Third World contributed to a temporary rise in the fertility rate in the United States, which during the 1990s stood at 2.1 (children per woman), compared to the European rate of 1.4. By 2010 the U.S. fertility rate had dropped to 1.9, with white European Americans having a rate of 1.8, Hispanics 2.4, African Americans 2.0, and Asian/Pacific Islanders 1.7.[4]

Population Composition and Assimilation

Racial and ethnic diversity has characterized the U.S. population since the first days of the republic. In 1790, people of English extraction comprised 47.5 percent of the population; people of Welsh, Scottish, Scot-Irish, and Irish together made up 20 percent; other Europeans 12.5 percent; African Americans 19 percent; and Native Americans 1 percent. As immigrants from all the continents made their way to the United States throughout the nineteenth and twentieth centuries, the heterogeneity of the population increased, but people of European background greatly outnumbered newcomers from other continents through the 1960s, assuring a European American numerical majority and overwhelming cultural dominance up to that point. But with the subsequent immigration shift that took place in the latter twentieth century, the number of people of Latin American and Asian origin swelled, and the overall racial and ethnic composition of the U.S. population changed significantly. Of the 24 million legal immigrants who settled in the United States between 1960 and 2000, 44.4 percent originated from Latin America, 27.0 percent from Asia, and only 17.0 percent from Europe; the remaing 11.6 percent hailed from other parts of the world. As a result, the share of white European Americans in the overall population dropped from 83 percent in 1970 to 64 percent in 2010, while the percentage of African Americans rose from 11 to 13 percent, the percentage of Latin Americans, or Hispanics, rose from 5 to 16 percent, and that of Asians from 1 to 5 percent. The continuing diversification of the U.S. population is assured well into the future with the arrival of approximately a million legal immigrants from some 200 countries every year during the 2000s.[5]

In many countries racial and ethnic diversity has posed serious problems, but in the United States, the extraordinarily favorable geography and large economy have given the country a great capacity to successfully assimilate or acculturate people from all over the world. That does not mean the celebrated U.S. "melting pot" phenomenon has been problem-free. Racism and class divisions have significantly slowed down the integration of people of African, Asian, and Hispanic descent. Immigration, especially from Asia in earlier generations and more recently from Latin America, has spawned intermittent dissenting protests from mostly white European Americans who have charged that multiculturalism has been costly and has posed a threat to national unity. Although the historical record does not support such alarmist claims, there have been continuous tensions over the integration of immigrants and ethnic minorities into the mainstream U.S. population. In reality material costs associated with the assimilation of foreigners or minorities have been more than offset by the economic contributions made by immigrants, and the political or cultural integrity of the United States has never been threatened by the multiracial and multiethnic makeup of society. U.S. history textbooks are replete with information regarding the overwhelming positive role that immigration, whatever its source, has made to the growth and welfare of the United States.

People in Mexico

As with so many other things, Mexico's population dynamics are much different than those of the United States. Mexico's population is much smaller, much less well distributed, and much poorer. Population pressures have been felt more strongly in Mexico, and the demographic transition in Mexico started later and has played out differently than in the United States. With respect to race and ethnicity, Mexico's population is not as ethnically heterogeneous as the population of the United States. Still, diversity has been an important factor in Mexican society, and it has posed challenges.

Population Size

When the Spanish conquest took place in 1519, the indigenous population of Mexico may have been as high as 25 or 30 million, but a precipitous decline subsequently occurred as Indians died in massive numbers from smallpox and other deadly diseases introduced by the Europeans. By the middle of the seventeenth century Mexico's population may have shrunk as low as 1.4 million. Thereafter demographic recovery slowly ensued and, by 1810, 6.1 million people lived in Mexico. That number increased to 15.1 million by 1910. During the chaotic years of the Mexican Revolution, the population decreased by about a million people as a result of war-related deaths, decease, and outmigration. In the 1920s growth resumed anew with the restoration of political stability, and by 1930 the population stood at 16.6 million. At that point the onset of declining death rates and rising birth rates ushered an explosion of the population, which reached 25.8 million in 1950 and 48.2 million in 1970. A new population policy implemented by the government in the 1970s slowed the growth, but the population still had significant momentum and rose to 97.5 million by 2000 and 112.3 million by 2010. These numbers do not include millions of Mexicans who have resided abroad or their (foreign-born) offspring. In 2010 an estimated 11.9 million people of Mexican birth lived permanently in the United States. If these 11.9 million Mexicans are taken into account, the size of Mexico's population (broadly defined) was theoretically 124.2 million in 2010[6] (see Table 6.2).

Population Distribution

If optimal circumstances prevailed in Mexico, the country's population would be distributed evenly between the coasts and the interior and among the northern, central, and southern sections of the country. But those ideal physical conditions have never existed in Mexico. Mexicans have overwhelmingly congregated in the most favorable spaces of the nation, with the harsh environments in the mountains, deserts, jungles, and unhealthy coastal areas constituting far less attractive choices. That distribution has made economic development more difficult and national integration a greater challenge. Showing precisely how geography has determined settlement patterns in Mexico is difficult, however, because the collection and organization of population data have been determined by the political boundaries of states and municipalities, and such boundaries are seldom drawn on the basis of natural divisions that differentiate ecological regions.

TABLE 6.2 Population of Mexico, by Ethnicity (for Select Years), 1500–2010

	Total in Millions	Percent of Total Population[1] Indians (Unofficial)	Indians (by Language/Self ID)	Mestizo (Unofficial)	White (Unofficial)	Other
1500	25 to 30	100.0	—	—	—	—
1646	1.4	74.1	—	25.1	0.8	—
1810	6.1	60.0	—	39.8	0.2	—
1910	15.1	39.5	12.9 (language)	53.0	7.5	—
1930	16.6	—	16.0 (language)	—	—	—
1950	25.8	—	11.2 (language)	—	—	—
1970	48.2	—	7.8 (language)	—	—	—
2000	97.5	30.0	7.1 (language)	60.0	9.0	1.0
2010	112.3	30.0	5.9 (language) 14.9 (self ID)	60.0	9.0	1.0

[1] Figures for 1500, 1646, and 1810 are derived from the monographs cited below. Total population figures from 1910 to 2010, as well as figures for the percentage of Indians based on language or self-identification are derived from official census data. Unofficial ethnic breakdowns for 2000 and 2010 are based on CIA estimates.

Sources: Borah and Cook (1963); Iturriaga (1987), 90; Carlson (1936), 474; CIA (1981–2000); Mexico, Comisión Nacional para el Desarrollo de los Pueblos Indígenas; México, *Censos Generales de Población, 1910–2010*; México, INEGI (2010); México, INEGI (2004).

Based on a classification scheme that divides Mexico into six regions, Table 6.3 shows how the acutely unequal distribution of Mexico's population in 1900 continued largely unaltered throughout the twentieth century and into the twenty-first century (see also Map 6.2).[7] The domination of the Central Highlands, which makes up less than 14 percent of the national territory but constitutes the most advantaged space in the country, is readily apparent. Slightly more than half of the Mexican population lived in the Central Highlands in 1900, and close to the same percentage lived there in 2010. Moreover, almost half Mexico's GDP was concentrated in that region in 2010. Within the Central Highlands, Mexico City (or the Federal District) has traditionally had the largest population and the biggest economy. As recently as 1970 nearly half the nation's industry was concentrated in Mexico City and, in 2006, Mexico City still accounted for one-fifth of the national GDP.[8] The Meseta Central has historically ranked a distant second to the Central Highlands in the size of its population and the size of its GDP. Southern Mexico, the Gulf Slope, Southeast Mexico, and Northwest Mexico have trailed behind.

As pointed out in Chapter 3, the less than ideal distribution of Mexico's population is also evident in the number of people who live in the interior versus those who live on the coast. Mexico's interior lands, especially the Central Highlands, for centuries have sustained the greatest number of residents because they have

TABLE 6.3 Regional Distribution of the Population and GDP in Mexico, 1900–2010

	Percent of Territory[1]	Percent of Population				Percent of GDP	
		1900	1950	2000	2010	1999	2010
Central Highlands[2]	13.7	50.1	47.5	49.1	48.5	54.4	47.6
Meseta Central[3]	37.0	18.1	18.0	15.6	15.8	19.3	18.8
Southern Mexico[4]	12.1	13.6	13.0	11.3	11.3	5.5	5.5
Gulf Slope[5]	7.7	8.8	10.7	9.9	9.7	7.3	7.8
Southeast Mexico[6]	8.4	4.1	4.0	5.2	5.6	4.9	11.7
Northwest Mexico[7]	21.0	5.3	6.7	8.8	9.2	9.0	8.6

[1] Continental Mexico. Excludes offshore territories. Regional divisions follow classification scheme by Henderson (1966), 122.

[2] Includes the Federal District and states of Jalisco, Puebla, México, Michoacán, Guanajuato, Hidalgo, Morelos, Querétaro, and Tlaxcala.

[3] Includes states of Chihuahua, Nuevo León, San Luis Potosí, Coahuila, Zacatecas, Durango, and Aguascalientes.

[4] Includes states of Oaxaca, Chiapas, Guerrero, and Colima.

[5] Includes states of Veracruz and Tamaulipas.

[6] Includes states of Yucatán, Tabasco, Campeche, and Quintano Roo.

[7] Includes states of Sinaloa, Sonora, Baja California, Baja California Sur, and Nayarit.

Sources: Population calculations based on data from México, *Censos Generales de Población* (1900, 1950, 2000, 2010); México, INEGI (2010). GDP calculations based on data from México, INEGI (2012); Garza (2003), 490.

the best climates and possess the best soils and other resources. Mexico's coastal areas had relatively small populations prior to the medical breakthroughs that diminished the threats posed by malaria and yellow fever. Eventually health and other improvements in living conditions coupled with the expansion of modern transportation made coastal spaces more habitable. Nevertheless, the coastal areas have continued to significantly trail the interior regions in their ability to support large populations.

Another long-standing challenge for Mexico is the people who live in small towns and villages, given that many of those places are located in remote, resource-poor areas. In 2010, 23.2 percent of the Mexican population resided in communities that had fewer than 2,500 people, and 14.3 percent lived in municipalities numbering between 2,500 and 14,999 inhabitants.[9] Indigenous people are mostly concentrated in those smaller rural locales. The highest numbers of Native Mexicans are found in Oaxaca and Guerrero in the South; Yucatán and Quintana Roo in the Southeast; Veracruz on the Gulf Slope; Puebla, Mexico state, and Hidalgo in the Central Highlands; and San Luis Potosí in the Meseta Central. In the 2000s over 800,000 Indians lived in the Federal District, most of them concentrated

170 Context: Nature and People

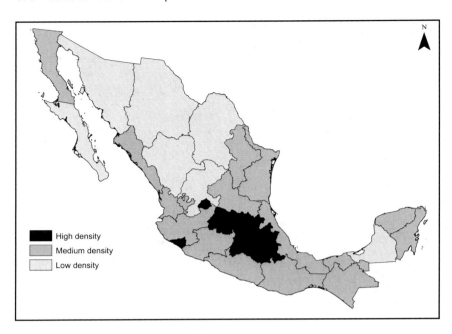

MAP 6.2 Population density of Mexico, 2005
Source: Based on Mexico, INEGI (2005).

in the marginalized zones of the Mexico City metropolis.[10] Physical isolation is a basic reality for large numbers of Indians who long ago were driven from the fertile plains and valleys into less desirable desert areas, jungles, and mountain regions. The case of the approximately 50,000 Tarahumaras of Chihuahua, although extreme, is illustrative. Beginning in the Spanish colonial period and lasting for centuries, the Tarahumaras migrated from their ancestral homelands into exceedingly inhospitable mountainous terrain in order to get away from the whites and mestizos who encroached on their way of life. Waves of Spanish, Mexican, and U.S. farmers, miners, and loggers, and most recently drug traffickers, drove the Tarahumaras deep into the rugged high country in the Copper Canyon region, where good land is extremely scarce. For generations the Tarahumaras have lived in caves and dirt-poor villages that are located far from Mexican towns and can only be reached by foot or horseback. Exposed to the elements and victims of long-lasting droughts, the Tarahumaras currently manifest the highest level of deprivation of any large indigenous group in Mexico. But isolation is not unique to the Tarahumaras. Large numbers of Indians in states such as Oaxaca, Guerrero, Veracruz, Chiapas, and Yucatán likewise are physically separated from the mainstream Mexican population, with attendant unfavorable economic and social consequences.

Demographic Trends

In general, Mexico has followed the typical demographic transition model evident throughout the world. But the time frame in which the transition has progressed in Mexico fits the pattern of developing countries, which means that the phenomenon commenced rather recently in Mexico. Advanced countries began transitioning much earlier, undergoing significant drops in mortality rates during the nineteenth century and experiencing declines in fertility between the 1870s and early 1900s. Such trends started even before for a few developed countries, most notably France and the United States.[11] Mexico initiated its transition at a much later time because improvements in sanitation and health required to spur downward changes in mortality rates commenced later, and because it took proactive government and societal intervention to bring about significant declines in fertility rates. Additionally, Mexico's transition has taken place in a shorter time period than is the case with the advanced nations, where demographic-related health advances evolved over longer time spans.

For most of the nineteenth century Mexico's population grew at less than 1 percent a year, increasing to 1.6 percent in the late 1870s as modernization and urbanization began to be felt with the arrival of the railroads and the expansion of the economy. In the 1920s and 1930s the mortality rate started to drop significantly, providing the foundation for the rapid population expansion that would take place in later decades. The annual growth rate averaged 1.7 percent in the 1930s, but then it jumped to 2.9 percent by the 1950s. In the 1960s it reached 3.5 percent, a highly disturbing rate that brought on the unprecedented national campaign to drastically reduce fertility. The government-led birth control program launched in the 1970s succeeded, and the average annual growth rate fell to 1.8 in the 1990s and 1.1 in the early 2010s. The fertility rate itself plummeted from an average of 7.3 children per woman in 1960 to 5.0 in 1980 and 2.3 by 2012.[12]

Prior to the mid-twentieth century, pressures associated with overpopulation were not a major concern in Mexico. Throughout the colonial period and during the 150 years after independence, Mexicans generally thought that the country had too few people. A prevailing view in Mexico, as elsewhere in the world, was that a large population was necessary for national security. "The belief that population numbers are directly related to national power is one of the most persistent themes in the history of population theory and policy," writes C. Alison McIntosh. "The larger the nation, the more soldiers it could mobilize for its armies; the more densely populated the land, the better it could resist the incursions of its neighbors; the more rapid the growth of population, the more easily could men be spared to found colonies, engage in international trade, and carry abroad the national language and culture."[13] Many Mexicans believed that a modest national population (7 million in 1840) had been largely responsible for the massive loss of territory to the United States in the 1830s and 1840s, given that the military had had a diminutive pool of men from which to draw recruits and that the small number of Mexicans who lived in the northern frontier could hardly have been expected to effectively defend their vulnerable lands against a powerful expansionist neighbor.

Nationalism and the desire to promote economic growth also drove the Mexican government to embrace the pro-population stance embodied in the dictum "to govern is to populate," made famous by the nineteenth-century Argentine intellectual Juan Bautista Alberdi. Like Alberdi, who advocated the colonization of the interior of Argentina, particularly with European immigrants, officials of the Porfirio Díaz regime sought to lure Europeans to Mexico with the aim of "uplifting" the overall "quality" of Mexico's people and augmenting settlement in sparsely populated spaces. In reality, Mexico had few opportunities to offer immigrants and therefore was far less successful than countries like Argentina, Brazil, Uruguay, Chile, and of course the United States, in attracting Europeans during the age of mass migration from the Old World to the Western Hemisphere. That is not to say that the Díaz government failed completely in its quest to lure foreigners to Mexico. Small numbers of immigrants from a variety of European countries, including Spain, England, Ireland, Germany, France, and Italy, as well from the Middle East, Asia and the United States, did settle in Mexico. Yet in 1910 immigrants made up less than 1 percent of Mexico's population, and most of them originated not in northern Europe, but rather in Spain, Mexico's former colonial master, and in Mexico's neighboring countries, the United States and Guatemala. Disappointed, Mexicans concluded that any significant expansion of the population would necessarily have to be the result of natural increase and not immigration because Mexico simply lacked the agricultural, industrial, and commercial prospects that enticed immigrants to permanently leave their homelands for greener pastures elsewhere.

The Revolution of the 1910s triggered renewed concerns over the size of Mexico's population as the fighting caused an unprecedented number of deaths, slowed down the birth rate, and precipitated the exodus of hundreds of thousands of Mexicans to the United States. In addition, the "Spanish influenza" epidemic of 1918 drove up the death count. The prevailing view during the period still held that Mexico needed a large population for security reasons and to recover economically from the devastation wrought by the civil war. Nationalism and patriotism demanded pronatalist policies, a position strongly endorsed by the Catholic Church. Although some leftist leaders opposed the enactment of pronatalist policies and instead advocated for women's reproduction rights, most influential citizens followed the official line and supported unhindered population growth. President Alvaro Obregón, for example, expressed the belief that Mexico could feed 100 million people, or seven times the population Mexico had in 1920. The Secretary of Health stated in 1927 that "the destiny of a nation is fundamentally linked to its demographic potential," adding that a country with a small population "can never become, despite the idealism of its superior intelligences, a great nation."[14] In 1936, two years into the Lázaro Cárdenas administration

(1934–1940), Mexico passed the first General Population Law, which encouraged natural growth and the repatriation of Mexicans who lived abroad. The government forbade the sale of contraceptives, and some states imposed taxes on adults who did not procreate. Large families received monetary awards and public recognition for their efforts to help Mexico become a great country. A second Population Law in 1947 amended the 1936 law by promoting higher immigration from other lands but, as in the past, the results proved disappointing. Only small numbers of foreigners moved to Mexico, with the exception being the approximately 30,000 Spanish refugees who fled Franco's dictatorship between 1937 and 1942.[15] Support for population growth continued in the late 1940s and early 1950s at the presidential level, as Manuel Ávila Camacho (1940–1946) and Miguel Alemán (1946–1952) expressed delight when census data confirmed the rapidly expanding number of people in the country. These presidents felt that population growth reflected well on their administrations.[16]

Intellectuals like Antonio Caso and Gilberto Loyo shared the pro-population views propagated by political leaders and members of the clergy. Caso argued that fears of a Malthusian calamity made sense in countries with limited resources, but not in big nations like Mexico that, in his view, had sufficient resources and the human potential to overcome the challenges of a larger population. Loyo reasoned that the expansion of the population would lead to economic growth and social integration. Apart from advocating for reduced emigration of Mexicans to the United States and stepped-up immigration of skilled workers to strengthen Mexico economically, Loyo opposed birth control initiatives and urged fiscal policies favorable to large families.[17]

Mexico's obsession with increasing its population must be understood in the context of the beliefs that had existed for centuries that the country had more than sufficient space and good land to accommodate large numbers of people. Further, in the 1950s and 1960s the future looked bright because the economy was expanding rapidly and food production was increasing as a result of the Green Revolution. Of course, as many contemporary experts and leaders recognized, Mexico did not actually have the abundant natural endowment necessary to sustain a large population. But pointing out such shortcomings in the euphoric climate of growth was not popular.

Another strong impetus for promoting demographic expansion in Mexico came from the efforts of other countries to substantially raise their populations for economic reasons or for the purpose of maintaining or increasing their power on the international stage. The United States, for example, had boosted its population from 40 million in 1870 to 123 million by 1930, while Mexico's population during that period grew feebly from a diminutive 9 million to only 16 million. Lingering apprehensions among nationalistic Mexicans who feared losses of more territory only intensified as they observed the rapid growth of the "Colossus of the North." After all, on various occasions during the 1910s the United States had intervened in Mexico's political affairs and had militarily invaded and occupied

Mexican soil; in addition, a number of U.S. leaders and influential entrepreneurs had repeatedly called for the annexation of Baja California. Those leaders who were suspicious of the United States felt that, with a small population, Mexico could not hope to properly settle vulnerable spaces or put up any meaningful defense against an antagonistic neighbor perceived as determined to obtain more Mexican land at any cost.

Mexicans were also influenced by events in Western Europe where, during the 1920s and 1930s, population growth became an urgent concern because of the ongoing decline in fecundity, the losses of people incurred during World War I, and the uncertain political climate that followed that conflict. Thus a number of European governments sought to boost fertility by rewarding motherhood, outlawing abortion, limiting birth control information, and restricting access to contraceptives. Authoritarian regimes in Nazi Germany and Italy aggressively used pronatalist propaganda and implemented repressive measures to convince people that procreation amounted to diligent patriotism expected of the citizenry. In France, the fear of depopulation had been a long-standing preoccupation because in the late eighteenth century a decline in the fertility rate had set in and the population had grown very slowly. By the second half of the nineteenth century worried French leaders and intellectuals constantly raised the alarm regarding their country's economic, political, and military vulnerability. Demographic issues were frequently discussed among local groups and learned societies, leading to the creation of pronatalist regional associations as well as the National Alliance for the Growth of Population, which was founded in 1896. In the early 1920s the French government passed repressive antiabortion and anticontraceptive laws that remained in force for more than four decades. But such "harsh" measures were accompanied by "positive" policies. During World War I the nation embraced the practice among many French employers of giving family allowances to employees and granting other protections to families. In subsequent decades, and especially following the shock of World War II, the French government assumed greater responsibility for financing a wide variety of benefits and services to mothers and children, eventually developing the most comprehensive and generous family-centered welfare system in Europe.[18]

Given the international climate, it is hardly surprising that in Mexico pronatalism held strong sway over the state and society. Nevertheless, by the 1930s and 1940s antinatalist voices became louder. Some of the strongest criticism directed at the pronatalists originated with foreign observers who were familiar with Mexico's shortages of good land and other resources. Nathanial and Sylvia Weyl, for example, painted Gilberto Loyo as a "fascist" for thinking that Mexico's problems were rooted in a small population, and they denounced the government's 1935–1940 pronatalist six-year plan, calling it "romantic nationalism." Clarence Senior blasted policies such as giving awards to women who had many children, pointing out that the expanding population undermined the advances made by Mexico in the years following the Revolution. Tom Gill felt that the notion that large numbers of people could be settled in empty lands was seriously flawed because aridity rendered so much of Mexico's land unproductive. Promoting increased population in Mexico was akin to inviting guests into a home that did not have enough food and other basic resources to meet their needs. "The cause of human happiness would best be served if a decent standard of living would first be achieved for the population currently here before inviting guests yet to be born to share in a miserable life," wrote Gill in 1951.[19]

Bad economic news on occasion shook the confidence of pronatalist policy makers. For example, upon taking office in the midst of a recession in 1952, president Adolfo Ruiz Cortines expressed concern over the failure of agricultural production and real income to keep up with population growth, which by then surpassed 3 percent annually. But when the national rate of economic growth reached twice the population growth rate during the mid-1950s with the "economic miracle" well under way, Ruiz Cortines once again spoke with optimism about Mexico's expanding population. The continued high rates of economic growth in subsequent years likewise gave the next president, Adolfo López Mateos, the rationale needed to adhere to the conventional thinking. López Mateos characterized population issues "as a challenge to the creative capacity and the enterprising spirit of Mexicans." The federal government's pronatalist position had plenty of support among many state officials, who typically expressed confidence that Mexico could successfully address any population-related pressures linked to basic things such as food, water, health, education, housing, and jobs. Intellectuals generally also went along, revealing overwhelming opposition to birth control in a survey in 1960, while labeling family planning as defeatist and immoral. The issue was not "fewer children, but more production and less injustice," said Gilberto Loyo. Some state and local officials who were confronted with providing basic services to exploding populations at the municipal level could hardly agree with such thinking since many communities did not have sufficient resources to meet the growing demands. Such officials became increasingly pessimistic as they projected rapid population growth in their areas into the future.[20]

The antinatalist position gained momentum as unemployment and underemployment rose and reports of shortages of land, water, electricity, sewage systems, housing, and especially schools became more frequent throughout the country. Various participants in a 1959 conference on the impact of population growth on natural resources warned that Mexico would face serious problems if nothing were done about population. "One does need to be a seer to quickly reach the conclusion that at some point we will need to control fertility," stated Ingeniero Emilio Fernández Lira. "It is evident—not today or tomorrow—but in the not too distant future, there will need to put in place controls for a specific number of inhabitants, because we will not be able to produce more [in an economic sense]."[21] In 1964 newly elected president Gustavo Díaz Ordaz suggested that the rapid growth of the population was unsustainable without the investment of more capital, of which Mexico had very little, and without the creation of 400,000 new jobs per year, which posed a major challenge for the country. In 1968 governor Eduardo E. Elizondo of Nuevo Leon lamented the belief that Mexico "was a horn of plenty," pointing out that such a poetic notion only produced "anguish among a population that grows at a rate with which no type of economic growth can keep pace." Feeling pessimistic about Mexico's ability to defeat the "threatening demography," Elizondo expressed frustration that the rising cost of providing education to the state's growing population necessitated reducing expenditures for such basic needs as infrastructure, security, administration of justice, and general welfare.[22] As the discussion over population issues got louder, a number of nonprofit organizations and agencies emerged to provide family planning services, including the Association for Maternal Health (1959), the Mexican Foundation for Family Planning (1964), and the Foundation for Population Studies (1965).[23] In addition, some academic institutions established research programs that tracked demographic trends. In the absence of national data, it is difficult to know the thinking of ordinary people regarding population controversies during those critical years, but some localized surveys suggest that by the end of the 1960s most Mexicans understood the urgent need to reduce fertility and supported family planning, including the use of contraceptives.[24]

In the 1970s, Mexico finally confronted the demographic explosion that threatened to undermine a significant part of the hard-earned economic progress of the "miracle" years. Mexicans could hardly ignore that the population had trebled in only four decades, with the result that cities grew too rapidly, social problems overwhelmed many communities, and record numbers of migrants left for the United States. Government officials and society at large reluctantly acknowledged that Mexico was headed for disaster if nothing were done about the excessively high fertility rates. The spirited debate that ensued eventually led to the embrace of unprecedented antigrowth policies by the government. Meanwhile, a generally resigned Catholic Church adopted a remarkably tolerant stance to the drive to slow the population expansion. In 1974, an amendment to the Mexican Constitution granted the right to all persons "to decide freely, responsibly, and with knowledge the number and spacing of children," while a new Population Law called for policies to reduce population growth, with an emphasis on raising the demographic consciousness among the Mexican people, especially among women, through the dissemination of information via education channels and the mass media. A new agency, the Consejo Nacional de Población (National Population Council, or CONAPO), was charged with creating specific mechanisms and designing new tools to carry out the overall policy. A decade later state governments set up their own Population Councils. Active coordination and cooperation among the government, the business sector, the academic community, and civil society in the implementation of a variety of programs succeeded in rapidly increasing awareness among all sectors of Mexican society, and demographic behavior changed in an impressive manner. By the mid-1980s

Mexico began getting international recognition for its efforts, including receiving the United Nations award for population policy in 1986.[25]

Notable drops in fertility rates after the mid-1970s effectively slowed down growth, leaving Mexico in a much better situation at the turn of the twenty-first century than would otherwise have been the case had the country not acted aggressively. With the current fertility rate at just about the replacement level and an annual growth rate of 1.2 percent, the future looks more manageable. Mexico is already benefiting from a "demographic bonus" linked to the lower dependency ratio. In 2010, the combined dependent cohort of Mexicans under age fourteen and over sixty-five numbered 55 individuals for every 100 persons. This represents a significant improvement from the 74/100 ratio in 1990. The demographic bonus is expected to last some thirty years, during which the country is expected to achieve greater domestic savings and more evenly spread economic growth.[26] Of course the demographic landscape of the future also includes the inevitable continuing aging of the population, and Mexico, like other countries that now have high percentages of elderly people, will see a return to an unfavorable dependency ratio. Additionally, migration to the United States and other countries will continue, although the volume may drop with the passage of time.

Population Composition and Assimilation

Mexico's population is overwhelmingly mestizo, meaning a mixture of Indians with Europeans of predominantly Spanish origin and, to a far lesser degree, with Africans, Asians, and sundry peoples from the Americas. As is the case in other Latin American countries such as Guatemala, Bolivia, and Peru, Indians constitute the ethnic foundation of Mexico's population, and the integration of indigenous peoples into national life has been a major historical theme. No one knows how many Indians lived in Mexico before the arrival of the Spaniards in the New World in 1492, but the native population must have been sizable given that hundreds of indigenous languages are thought to have been spoken and that large concentrations of Indians lived in urban centers in the Central Valley. Two respected U.S. scholars have estimated that right before the Spanish conquest Mexico's Indian population numbered between 25 and 30 million.[27] The exact number is, of course, impossible to calculate, and that estimate may be too high. What is clear, however, is that the Indian population declined precipitously in Mexico after 1500. That occurred largely because of lack of immunity to diseases that were introduced by the Europeans. The data in Table 6.2 show the declining percentage of the Indian population and the corresponding expansion of the mestizo population in Mexican society over the course of several centuries. According to the official 2010 census, only 15 percent of the national population self-identified as indigenous, and just 6 percent reportedly spoke an indigenous language. Unofficial estimates, however, have put the Indian population at 30 percent, mestizos at 60 percent, whites at 9 percent, and others at 1 percent.

Racial discrimination and ethnic bias among whites and mestizos and class divisions rooted in economic inequalities have long been recognized as major inhibitors to the social integration of Indians. Geography, however, has been an equally powerful force. Rugged mountainous terrain has perpetuated the traditional physical isolation of many Indian groups and has reinforced the heterogeneity of the indigenous population. Continuing Indian diversity is illustrated by the large number of indigenous languages and dialects that have survived. Today the Mexican government recognizes sixty-two indigenous languages spoken by over 6 million Indians. Some linguists, however, believe that the actual number of indigenous languages may be 100 or more.[28] Whatever their number, these languages confirm the perpetuation of a multitude of distinct cultures and unique identities. The descendants of well-known groups such as the Aztecs, Mayas, Zapotecs, Mixtecs, and Yaquis, as well as many others not so well-known, are largely concentrated in their traditional homelands, assuring diversity and fragmentation.

Indian heterogeneity has made it necessary for the government to carry out different strategies to introduce the Spanish language and national culture to the widely dispersed Indian populations. The use of many languages is needed to take censuses and to provide services like education and health care to countless Indian communities, including some 13,000 villages where over 70 percent of the people speak an indigenous language and another 4,000 villages where between 30 and 70 percent speak an indigenous language. Most of these communities have populations numbering a few hundred people and are located in remote areas.[29]

An important subject regarding the composition of the population of many countries is the racial and ethnic backgrounds of immigrants. Since Mexico has been a people exporter rather than a people importer, the rather small number of immigrants arriving in the country has not altered the makeup of the population. As previously noted, the limited economic opportunities available in Mexico have significantly restricted the influx of immigrants. In the Americas, the United States has attracted the most immigrants by far, with Argentina, Canada, and Brazil also drawing significant numbers. Most immigrants arrived in those countries from Europe between 1880 and 1914. Few Europeans made their way to Mexico. In 1921, immigrants comprised 0.7 percent of the total population of 14.3 million, with Spaniards, Chinese, and Americans the three top groups. By 2010, some 961,000 persons of foreign birth lived in Mexico, still constituting a miniscule 0.9 percent of the total population. Americans made up 77 percent of the 961,000 foreigners, Guatemalans 4 percent, and Spaniards 2 percent.[30] The current presence of significant numbers of Americans in Mexico reflects the rising economic integration with the United States.

Conclusion

This chapter has examined population issues that have had important economic consequences for Mexico historically. Pressures related to underpopulation on the one hand, and to overpopulation on the other, top the list of challenges confronted by Mexicans. Severe drops in the number of people in the early Spanish colonial period took place as many millions of indigenous peoples perished from new diseases introduced into Mexico by Europeans, as well as other misfortunes caused by the chaos of the Spanish conquest. Eventually the Indian population stabilized and growth resumed, but Mexico remained an underpopulated country for centuries. Lack of sufficient people significantly weakened Mexico's ability to adequately populate and properly defend its far-flung northern territories, leading to the loss of half the national patrimony to U.S. expansionist aggression during the 1830s and 1840s. The trauma of those years and the desire to develop economically drove Mexico to promote pronatalistic polices over the next several generations. Mexicans were not alone in pursuing robust population growth. Other countries, especially in Europe, also sought to expand their populations for security reasons and to achieve higher rates of economic productivity.

Mexico's pro-population policies worked only too well, and by the mid-twentieth century overpopulation replaced underpopulation as the major problem facing the country. Even with the national economy averaging a healthy 6 percent annual growth between the 1940s and early 1970s, the country could not keep up with the explosive demand for new jobs, and governments at all levels were hard-pressed to satisfy rapidly rising needs in housing, education, health, and other services. Large numbers of destitute, unemployed, and underemployed Mexicans migrated permanently to the United States during the period of rapid population expansion, joining several million compatriots who had left the homeland in previous eras. Such strains eventually forced a complete reversal of demographic policies, and in 1974 Mexico launched a population control program that achieved spectacular outcomes. Since the 1980s Mexican fertility rates have plummeted, with the result that at the beginning of the second decade of the twenty-first century, Mexico drew nearer to zero population growth.

But even as the population growth rate has declined, economic expansion has remained insufficient to provide enough good employment opportunities for people in the lower half of the social order. Mexicans continue to move to the United States in the familiar quest to improve their living conditions. Out-migration, coupled with chronic job shortages and persistent widespread poverty throughout the country, are clear manifestations of an imbalance between the number of people who live in Mexico and the ability of the country's economy to support them. It should not be surprising that this long-standing problem continues unabated because the unfavorable foundational forces and structures that have undermined the country have not gone away and cannot be expected to disappear because they are rooted in an environment that is extremely difficult to alter. The negative power of nature in Mexico is well illustrated in the unfavorable distribution of the population, with some spaces inhabited by too many people and others by too few.

Notes

1. Calculations based on data from U.S. Department of Homeland Security, Office of Immigration Statistics (2002), Table 1.
2. U.S. Bureau of the Census (2002), 15.
3. Coale and Zelnik (1963), Table 2; Population Reference Bureau (2003); Klein (2004), 79, 157, 177–179, 258.
4. Population Reference Bureau (2000), 6; Pew Research Center (2012b); Population Reference Bureau (2012).
5. U.S. Department of Homeland Security (2002), Table 1; U.S. Department of Homeland Security (2008), Table 3; Population Reference Bureau (2000), 16; Population Reference Bureau (2006), 17; Pew Research Center, (2012), Table 1.
6. Calculation based on data from Pew Research Center (2012a).
7. The classification scheme, which appears in Table 8.4, is borrowed from geographer David A. Henderson (see Henderson in Ewing 1966, 122).
8. Garza (1985), 154; México, Cámara de Diputados (2009), Table 2.
9. México, INEGI (2010), 5.
10. Navarrete Linares (2008), 22.
11. Chesnais (1992).
12. If Mexicans living abroad had been counted as part of Mexico's population the overall growth rates would have been higher during the stated periods, but more than likely fertility rates would be slightly lower (CONAPO 2004, *Review of the Economic Situation of Mexico* (2007a), 107–109; Levy et al. 2001, 21–22).
13. McIntosh (1983), 28.
14. González Navarro (1974), I:121 (my translation).
15. González Navarro (1974), II:Cuadro 30.
16. González Navarro (1974), I:124–125; Cabrera (1994), 109.
17. González Navarro (1974). I:122–124.
18. McIntosh (1983), 38, 43–57.
19. Quotes (my translations) of the authors cited here are found in González Navarro (1974), I:125–126.
20. González Navarro (1974), I:126–129, 132–133.
21. Mexico, Instituto Mexicano de Recursos Naturales Renovables (1960), 228–229.
22. González Navarro (1974), I:130, 133–137.
23. Cabrera (1994), 111.
24. González Navarro (1974), I:138–140.
25. *Current History* (March 1987), 114.
26. *New York Times* (June 8, 1999); INEGI (2010), 8.
27. Cook and Borah (1960).
28. Navarrete Linares (2008), 69–72; Geo-Mexico website, post #448 (April 23, 2010) and post #4050 (May 3, 2011).
29. Rhoda and Burton (2010), 62, 63.
30. Mexico, INEGI (2009), Cuadro 1.15, 1a. parte; Mexico, INEGI, Informativo oportuno, "Los nacidos en otro país" 1:2 (May 2011).

PART III
CONTEXT
EXTERNAL RELATIONS

7
SO FAR, SO CLOSE

A comment attributed to the dictator Porfirio Díaz (1876–1880 and 1884–1911) exemplifies Mexicans' memory of unpleasant events linked to relations with the United States. One day Díaz is believed to have said, "Poor Mexico, so far from God and so close to the United States." More than likely Díaz had in mind Mexico's devastating land loss to its northern neighbor in the 1840s and repeated U.S. interventions in Mexican affairs. But perhaps Díaz also mulled over the full meaning for Mexico of sharing a border with an economic powerhouse. Whatever material benefits Mexico derived from the United States, Díaz may have reasoned, these had to be weighed against the substantial control that American capitalists had established over Mexican mining, transportation, agriculture, commerce, and industry. The smothering effect of the U.S. economy over Mexico's manufacturing sector must have also worried Díaz. U.S.-made machinery, consumer goods, and other finished products gushed like a torrent into Mexico both legally and illegally via the porous 2,000-mile northern land border and the unguarded seaports on the two gulfs and the Pacific. Conceivably Díaz and other leaders agonized over the development consequences of that trade for Mexico.

But Mexico's troubles with other countries were not confined to the United States. In the nineteenth century serious conflicts broke out with various European nations as well. As a result of these encounters, the very survival of Mexico as a nation-state was called into question on various occasions. Throughout the twentieth century Mexico's foreign relations proved far less tumultuous than during the previous century—with the exception of the 1910s, the decade of the chaotic Mexican Revolution. The Revolution seriously disrupted U.S.–Mexico relations, but after the violence subsided, interaction between the two neighbors improved. Nevertheless, since 1920 disagreements and confrontations have surfaced with regularity between the two neighbors up until the present day.

Without a doubt foreign relations constitute a foundational force of great significance for Mexico and for that reason the topic requires detailed analysis. Our central concern in this chapter is with assessing the political impact on Mexico of dealing with a powerful and dominant neighbor. Succeeding chapters delve into the details of binational economic interaction, with a focus on capital flows, legal and illegal trade, and migration.

To provide context to Mexico's subordinate status vis-à-vis its northern neighbor, we begin with a sketch of the extraordinary transformation of the United States from a small collection of peripheral English colonies to the world's most powerful country.

The Formation of a Global Superpower

In 1783, when Americans achieved independence from England, the national territory of the newly formed United States of America stretched from the Atlantic Ocean in the east to the Mississippi River in the west, and from the Canadian border in the north to the Florida border in the south. About 3 million whites of European background and 800,000 blacks of African origin shared that space with a few thousand indigenous people. Competing European powers controlled adjoining territories, with England having dominion in Canada and Spain having jurisdiction over Florida and most of the terrain from the Mississippi River westward to the Pacific Ocean. Within four generations after 1783, an aggressive U.S. foreign policy would result in drastic alterations in the political geography of North America, with an attendant extraordinary growth of the U.S. national domain.

By the early nineteenth century, the ideology of manifest destiny had become influential among the U.S. population and in government circles. That doctrine held that the Almighty wished for the United States to become a powerful nation by pursuing territorial expansionism toward the west and south. Thus, utilizing various strategies—including clandestine infiltration, illegal occupation, purchase, aggressive diplomacy, insurrection, and military aggression—the United States would proceed to acquire Louisiana from France in 1803 (after France obtained it from Spain in 1800), Florida from Spain in 1819, Texas from Mexico in 1845, and New Mexico, Arizona, California, Nevada, Utah, Colorado, and parts of Wyoming, Kansas, and Oklahoma from Mexico in 1848 and 1853. Oregon and Washington became parts of the U.S. national domain through a treaty settlement with England in 1846 and Alaska was purchased from Russia in 1867. The territories acquired from France and Spain added 968,046 square miles to the nation, the land acquired from Mexico brought in 947,898 square miles, and Oregon and Washington added 286,541 square miles. In seven decades—between the birth of the country in 1783 and the signing of the Gadsden Treaty with Mexico in 1853, the United States more than tripled in size, from an initial 888,811 square miles to 3,022,387 square miles. The purchase of Alaska from Russia in 1867 added

586,400 square miles and boosted the country's total square mileage to 3,608,787 (see Maps 7.1 and 7.2).[1]

Opportunities to further augment the already sizable U.S. possessions presented themselves at the end of the nineteenth century, a period referred to in U.S. history as the "age of imperialism." In the 1890s the United States increased its presence in the Pacific by adding more land to its overseas "portfolio," which already included several small but strategically situated islands that had been obtained in the 1850s and 1860s. Hawaii fell into U.S. hands in 1898 through annexation following the overthrow of the Kingdom of Hawaii, in which U.S.

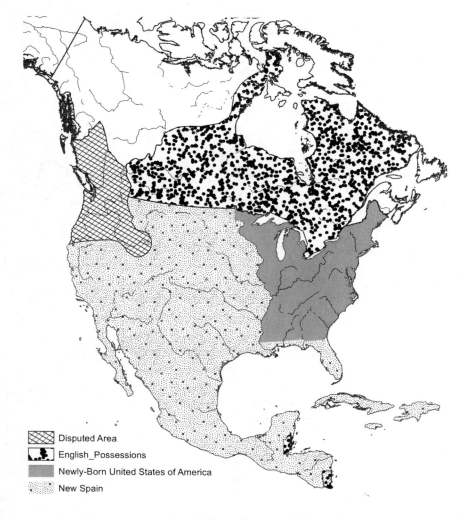

MAP 7.1 The political geography of North America in 1783

MAP 7.2 Territorial expansion of the United States and the absorption of Spanish and Mexican territories, 1795–1853

Source: Based on map in Martínez (2006), 12.

diplomats and business interests played a leading role. That same year, the United States acquired the Philippines, Guam, and Puerto Rico after defeating Spain in the Spanish–American War, which had broken out during the Cuban struggle for independence. Cuba went on to achieve its freedom from Spain, but the United States took possession of the southern tip of the island for the purpose of maintaining a military base at Guantanamo. In the Pacific, Filipinos were subjected to U.S. colonial rule from 1898 until 1935, when their country became a commonwealth of the United States. Full independence finally arrived for the Philippines in 1946. Puerto Rico has been a U.S. dependency since 1898, with commonwealth status conferred in 1952.

In Central America, the United States gained "perpetual" control of the Panama Canal Zone in 1903. That small but militarily strategic and commercially valuable transportation corridor became U.S. real estate after a faction of Panamanians, who enjoyed decisive U.S. support, led a successful insurgency that resulted in independence from Colombia. In return for U.S. assistance, the fledgling Panamanian government granted Americans de facto sovereignty over the tract of land on which the all-important Panama Canal was built. Foreign control over the canal, however, generated considerable discontent among Panamanians after it opened in 1914. Six decades later the United States gave in to the long-standing Panamanian nationalist sentiment that called for establishment of local sovereignty over the Canal Zone. In 1977 Panama and the United States agreed to a treaty that provided for the transfer of the Canal Zone to Panama in 1999.

Clearly territorial expansionism and control of foreign lands significantly enhanced the might of the United States on the world stage. At the same time, such an aggressive foreign policy produced confrontations and armed collisions; ideological power struggles, security issues, and economic rivalries have embroiled the United States in international conflict for generations. This is illustrated in the western hemisphere by the many U.S. interventions in Mexico, the Caribbean region, and in Central America at various points during the twentieth century. In Europe and Asia, the United States played central roles in the epic global struggles represented by World War I and World War II and, in the 1950s and 1960s, the United States battled Communism directly in Korea and Vietnam. Most recently, concerns over accessibility to oil resources and worries about terrorism drove the United States to fight the Persian Gulf War of 1991 and to invade Iraq and Afghanistan in 2003, followed by extended occupations of those two countries. At this writing the United States and its allies are engaged in a bombing campaign to prevent Muslim jehadists from establishing an "Islamic State" in portions of Iraq and Syria.

The Formation of Mexico, U.S. Expansionism, and Land Cessions

The emergence of Mexico as a state contrasts sharply with that of the United States, starting with the roots of Mexican nationhood. Up until 1521 Mexico functioned as a fragmented collection of autonomous indigenous communities. After that date it became a Spanish colony known as the Viceroyalty of New Spain. The Spaniards thus began dispossessing the indigenous peoples of their lands and started building the foundation for a New World society controlled from Europe. Mexico City served as the capital of New Spain and as a key base of operations for expanding Spanish territorial control in North America. By 1783, New Spain consisted of vast territories, including present-day Mexico, the terrain between the Mississippi River to the Pacific Ocean, Florida, Central America, and much of the Caribbean zone (see Map 7.1).

As the United States began its nation-building trajectory, Americans and European immigrants traveled westward and southward toward Spanish lands in ever-increasing numbers. U.S. expansionists dreamed of the day when Spain would be driven out of North America and the western border of the United States would be the Pacific Ocean. The acquisition of the Louisiana Territory in 1803 by the United States from France ushered in a long period of conflict with Spain over the amount of territory that had actually changed hands. The confusion began in 1800 when Napoleon pressured Spain to return Louisiana to France in exchange for certain Italian lands. Three years later, Napoleon, unable to effectively occupy Louisiana and fearing that it might fall into English hands, sold it to the United States. Spain considered that transaction illegal because by prior agreement France could not dispose of Louisiana without Spain's approval. Though Spain was in no position to stop the United States from acquiring Louisiana, it did contest the amount of territory involved.

Significantly, neither the Spain–France exchange in 1800 nor the France–U.S. transfer in 1803 specified the precise limits of Louisiana. Spain argued that the land in question consisted of only a small tract adjacent to the Mississippi River. The United States countered that Louisiana included all lands in the west that drained into the Mississippi River as well as other lands east and north of the Rio Grande. Under this interpretation, old Spanish settlements such as Santa Fe, New Mexico, and San Antonio, Texas, which France had never governed, had suddenly become American cities. Spain rejected the U.S. interpretation.

The dispute over Louisiana was finally settled in 1819, when the Adams-Onis Treaty fixed the border between the United States and New Spain along an irregular line beginning at the Sabine River, proceeding north to the forty-second parallel and from there to the Pacific. Texas remained a Spanish province. In turn, Spain acknowledged U.S. ownership of Florida and gave up claims on the Pacific north of the forty-second parallel. A firm border now seemed to be in place, but that would turn out to be illusory.

In 1821 Mexico won its independence from Spain after a decade of warfare. At that point Mexico was larger in size than the United States, extending from Costa Rica in the south to the forty-second parallel in the north. California and Texas constituted the far northwestern and far northeastern provinces respectively. In 1823 Mexico lost Central America when Guatemala, Honduras, El Salvador, Nicaragua, and Costa Rica created the Federal Republic of Central America. But Mexico retained western Chiapas, formerly a province of Guatemala during Spanish days. Mexico capitalized on the confusing political climate in the Guatemalan borderlands to further increase the size of Chiapas by annexing more land claimed by Guatemala. Mexicans justified these annexations on the grounds that the people of Chiapas preferred to be aligned with Mexico rather than Guatemala. Guatemala rejected these claims and for years sought to reincorporate the lost lands. At times armed conflict erupted in the disputed territories. The matter was finally resolved by a treaty in 1882 that favored Mexico, and the delimitation of the permanent Mexico–Guatemala border was completed in 1902 (see Map 7.3).[2]

MAP 7.3 Republic of Mexico, 1824

But let's return to the dawn of Mexico's independence from Spain, when Mexico's major preoccupation became to maintain its freedom and territorial integrity. In 1829 the Spanish attempted to recapture their former colony. About 3,000 Spanish troops sailed from Cuba and landed in the port city of Tampico with the intent of marching to central Mexico and taking control of the country. Barely eight years old as a nation-state and suffering from deep political divisions, an empty treasury, a feeble economy, and an ethnically splintered population, Mexico still managed to repel the Spaniards. Mexican troops under the command of Antonio López de Santa Anna surrounded Tampico and deprived the invaders of supplies and medical help for soldiers stricken with yellow fever. The Spaniards surrendered and Mexico retained its independence. Two other European powers, France and England, cast their eyes on California, but neither would ever go beyond expressions of interest. Russians, on the other hand, established a small but temporary agricultural and sea otter hunting outpost just north of San Francisco.

But the biggest threat to Mexico's sovereignty and territorial integrity turned out to be the neighbor to the north. American leaders determined early on that the United States must take possession by peace or by force of the Mexican far northern frontier, a sparsely populated area weakly governed from distant Mexico City. In less than a generation, half of post-1823 Mexico—the part with the greatest economic potential—would wind up in the United States.

The story of Mexico's immense land loss began when U.S. expansionists recognized Mexico's tenuous hold on Texas and escalated their efforts to acquire that province. By the early nineteenth century U.S. leaders knew enough about Texas to appreciate its tremendous agricultural, ranching, commercial, and trading potential, leading some to advocate aggressive action to capture it. Rather than attempting to acquire Texas by force, however, the United States in the 1820s and early 1830s adopted a policy of seeking to persuade Mexico to sell that province along with adjacent territories. But Mexico proved unreceptive.

Meanwhile, during the years that the U.S. government tried to purchase Texas, tens of thousands of American and European immigrants found their way to that province, some entering legally and others without authorization. Legal immigration consisted of invited colonists brought in by land agents such as Stephen Austin, who received generous land grants from the Mexican government. Recognizing the need to populate it but lacking enough domestic migrants willing to move to the northern frontier Mexico, following a precedent set by Spain, allowed foreigners to settle in Texas. The American migration started as a trickle but became a flood when reports circulated widely in the United States and in Europe regarding great land opportunities in Texas. By 1831 Americans and their slaves outnumbered the Mexican Texans, 23,700 to 4,000. The vast majority of the foreigners had entered Texas illegally.

Mexico soon grew weary of the presence of so many Americans in Texas. In the early 1820s permitting foreign colonization of sparsely populated and weakly protected frontier territories had made good sense, but Mexican officials then had no way of knowing that the first flow of American immigrants would trigger other migration waves. In effect Texas became a major outlet for the continuous westward movement of the United States. Swelling numbers of restless American farmers, ranchers, entrepreneurs, laborers, adventurers, wanderers, and fugitives from the law saw Texas as an ideal place to start anew, obtain cheap land, conduct lucrative trade and commerce and, for some, engage in profitable schemes outside the law. An alarmed Mexico could do little to stop the invasion from the east because Mexicans lacked the military manpower and resources to effectively secure the Texas–United States border.

Americans and European immigrants who entered Texas in the 1820s and 1830s had heard plenty about the extraordinary natural riches in that province. Travelers, settlers, writers, reporters, and land speculators wrote innumerable letters, newspaper articles, promotional leaflets, and even books intended to encourage migrants to head to Texas. Many observers characterized Texas as a vast "paradise" and "the garden of Eden," a beautiful land blessed with great fertility, a wonderful climate, abundant resources of all kinds, and an exceedingly favorable geography. Texas, they said, possessed unlimited potential and industrious immigrants could expect to prosper. The fact that numerous Texas land speculation companies emerged throughout the United States illustrates the widespread American belief in the richness of Texan land resources. In 1829 U.S. senator Thomas H. Benton compared Texas to northern Italy and Southern France, also considered paradise-like areas. Benton described Texas as "a most delicious country; [blessed with] fertile, bountiful prairies covered with grass and flowers; vast meadows and most delightful champaign country; dry, pure, elastic air; springs of sweet waters; clear and rapid streams; no swamps; abundance of buffalo, horses, and deer."[3]

The writings of early U.S. enthusiasts and speculators understandably contained exaggerations, yet there is no question that Texas had the necessary attributes to become an economic powerhouse. That, plus geopolitical considerations, drove Mexico to do all it could to retain ownership. Over the centuries Spaniards and Mexicans had known about the attractiveness and potential of Texas through reports submitted by explorers, missionaries, and officials. Mexico's Committee on Foreign Relations described the province in 1821 as "so fertile, of such benign climate, so rich in metals and natural resources that when descriptions of it by geographers were read out, instantly one came to believe that they were talking of Paradise."[4] Colonel Juan Nepoceno Almonte ascertained the vast natural resources of that province and commented on Texas' great economic potential as part of a fact-finding mission to Texas in 1835:

> Texas is soon destined to be the most flourishing section of this republic.... The geographic position of Texas is extremely advantageous for commerce.... Above all, the abundance of navigable rivers and of good ports that are found in Texas . . . give it an immense advantage over the rest of the states in the Mexican federation, which unfortunately do not possess the same facilities for the exportation of their products, and whose foreign commerce can not but be unimportant for many years to come.... Texas is the most valuable possession of the republic and may God grant that our negligence may not be the cause for the loss of so precious a portion of our territory.[5]

Knowing the value of Texas, repeatedly Mexican government officials and others expressed concern about the intense interest in that province on the part of the United States and emphasized the need to strengthen Texas defenses.[6]

But Mexico could not stop the slow invasion of Texas by Americans, nor could it prevent the subsequent insurgency that broke out and the eventual creation of the renegade Republic of Texas in 1836. The de facto independence of Texas from

Mexico after that year led to greater numbers of Americans making their way to "paradise." In 1836 Texas counted among its settlers an estimated 30,000 Americans, 14,000 Indians, 5,000 Blacks (mostly slaves), and only 3,500 Mexican-origin people. By the time Texas had become part of the United States through annexation in 1845, the population had more than quadrupled to 125,000, with recently arrived Americans making up the predominant majority.[7]

The unilateral incorporation of Texas by the United States precipitated outrage among Mexicans, who still considered that province a part of the national patrimony. Yet, although Mexico did not recognize the U.S. annexation of the treasured province, the chances of ever recovering Texas faded quickly because Mexico lacked the capacity to confront the United States militarily. Friction with the United States escalated to new heights as the U.S. government pressured Mexico not only to accept the loss of Texas but to consider selling California and other northern lands. Unrelenting attempts by the United States to alter the border, ongoing disputes over extant claims for property damages by U.S. citizens against Mexico, and Mexico's rejection of aggressive U.S. diplomatic efforts to force Mexico to act created a major crisis. In April 1846 President James Polk found the pretext to declare war on Mexico following a U.S.-provoked skirmish along the Rio Grande. Polk justified the declaration of war by claiming that "American blood had been shed on American soil." It did not matter that the skirmish actually took place within Mexican territory. Despite condemnation of the war declaration from U.S. political leaders such as John Quincy Adams, Henry Clay, and Abraham Lincoln, and opposition from prominent intellectuals like Henry David Thoreau and Ralph Waldo Emerson, Polk and the U.S. Congress proceeded to carry out the war. In December 1847 Abraham Lincoln in a series of eight congressional resolutions harshly attacked Polk for taking the country to war, branding the president a liar and a coward. Lincoln focused his criticism on the sham claim that the encounter between Mexican and U.S. troops had occurred on U.S. soil.[8]

The war was a lopsided contest. At that point in time the United States was already a world power, while Mexico continued to be a frail and fragmented society engaged in the initial stages of nation-building. Much better trained and equipped U.S. soldiers invaded Mexico by land and sea. General Zachary Taylor's troops advanced into Tamaulipas and Nuevo Leon; another army traveled the Santa Fe Trail and penetrated New Mexico, California, and other northern Mexican states; U.S. naval forces joined land soldiers in the invasion of California; finally, in the most important operation of the war, combined U.S. naval and land forces took the port city of Veracruz and then advanced to Mexico City. Control of the capital by the Yankee army gave the U.S. government the upper hand in dictating the terms for bringing hostilities to a close.

After the Treaty of Guadalupe Hidalgo ended the war in February 1848, Mexico's territorial domain had shrunk by half in comparison to what it had been prior to the Texas insurrection in 1836. The United States compelled Mexico to formally accept the 1845 U.S. annexation of Texas and also forced it to cede California, Arizona, New Mexico, Colorado, Nevada, Utah, and parts of Wyoming, Kansas, and Oklahoma (see Map 7.2). Years later General Ulysses Grant, who had served as a junior officer with the forces that had invaded Mexico and who occupied the U.S. presidency from 1869 to 1877, characterized the war with Mexico as "wicked" and "the most unjust and most unholy war ever waged by a stronger nation against a weaker one . . . an instance of a republic following the bad example of European monarchies, in not considering justice in their desire to acquire additional territory."[9]

U.S. Obsession with California and Eventual Conquest

For the United States, Texas and California had stood out as the big prizes that needed to be plucked from Mexico, and by 1848 both of those provinces, in addition to other lands, were under the U.S. flag. California was actually considered a larger plum than Texas, and its acquisition brought joy to President James Polk and his fellow expansionists; they had long thought of California as "must have" territory for the United States. A brief narrative of that long-held interest follows.

In the early nineteenth century, as Yankee clippers began to conduct trade with Mexican settlements on the California coast and as American traders and fur trappers penetrated California by land from the east, word dribbled back to the United States that California was a land of great promise. That caught the attention of land-hungry American settlers who set their sights westward beyond the boundaries of the United States. Meanwhile, U.S. government officials and prominent merchants took great interest in the harbor of San Francisco for its potential in facilitating lucrative trade with Asia. The Russian hunting and trade colony at Fort Ross, which was established in 1812 to serve the needs of the far-flung Russian American Fur Company, had been of concern to both the Spanish and Mexican governments, as well as to the United States, but sale of the outpost by the company in 1838 ended the threat of Russian incursion into California. The possible colonization of California by France or England remained a larger concern for both Mexico and the United States. Although aware of the Monroe Doctrine, which had been enacted by U.S. President James Monroe in 1823 as a warning that the United States would oppose efforts by European powers to colonize any territories in the Americas, France and England nonetheless made no secret of their interest in California. U.S. leaders determined that if Mexico were to cede California to another country, it must be the United States and no one else. The U.S. policy became one of trying to entice Mexico to sell California to the United States while at the same time encouraging Americans already living in that province to actively promote a favorable U.S. view among local Mexicans. In the 1830s and early 1840s the United States offered to buy the San Francisco Bay from Mexico, without success.[10]

England dreamed of the possibility of acquiring California if not by conquest then perhaps in exchange for cancellation of Mexico's debts. English merchant Alexander Forbes went to considerable lengths to collect data on California, publishing a glowing, detailed report in 1839. He believed California was destined to become one of the preeminent economies in the world and hoped that England would colonize it. Forbes emphasized California's benign climate, great agricultural potential, locational advantages for trade, and the superiority of the San Francisco Bay.[11]

The information about California's magnificence that spread via Forbes's book was complemented by other works, including a similar volume by French diplomat Eugene Duflot de Mofras,[12] and a very popular memoir/travelogue written by Harvard student/sailor Richard Henry Dana Jr. "If California ever becomes a prosperous country," wrote Dana Jr. in 1835, "[the Bay of San Francisco] will be the center of its prosperity. The abundance of wood and water; the extreme fertility of its shores; the excellence of its climate, which is as near to being perfect as any in the world; and its facilities for navigation, affording the best anchoring-grounds in the whole western coast of America,—all fit in for a place of great importance."[13] The "secret" about California's great worth—and vulnerability—was out, and that triggered much anxiety among Americans concerned about the possible "loss" of California to a competing power.

By 1842 plenty of auspicious reports about California, including speculations regarding gold deposits, circulated in the United States to further excite expansionists and prospective settlers.[14] That year U.S. Secretary of State Daniel Webster's interest in California soared upon receiving a dispatch from Waddy Thompson, the U.S. minister to Mexico, who stated that Mexico might be willing to give up its continuing claim to Texas and also part with California if the United States forgave Mexico's debts. Thompson added that California was "destined to be the granary of the Pacific." In reality Mexico had no intention of doing what Thompson suggested.[15]

The heightened U.S. apprehension about the fate of California reached new heights in October 1842, when a U.S. fleet under the command of Commodore Thomas Ap Catesby Jones captured the capital city of Monterey. Jones, reportedly convinced that England was about to invade California, and also believing that war had erupted between Mexico and the United States over the conflict in Texas, declared California under U.S. rule. When neither premise proved true, Jones apologized to the local Mexican authorities and quickly sailed away.[16] The incident confirmed Mexican officials' suspicions of the U.S. determination to take military action if necessary to establish ownership of California. And indeed that is what would eventually transpire.

In March 1845, newly inaugurated U.S. President James Polk remarked that he considered the acquisition of California a top priority for his administration. Newspapers across the United States stepped up their calls for Americans to annex California before the British seized it. In November, Secretary of State James

Buchanan instructed envoy John Slidell to negotiate disagreements with Mexico over the Texas annexation and to press for the purchase of California. "The possession of the bay and harbor of San Francisco is all important to the United States," wrote Buchanan. "The advantages to us of its acquisition are ... striking."[17]

Meanwhile, businessman Thomas O. Larkin had secretly assumed the role of Polk's "confidential agent" in California. He was charged with promoting the peaceful secession of the province from Mexico and subsequent voluntary annexation to the United States. But Larkin's mission was upstaged by the outbreak of the war between the two countries in April 1846 and by the "Bear Flag" rebellion that broke out in California during the early summer of that year. The central figure in the Bear Flag insurrection was John C. Fremont, the famous western explorer, military officer, and U.S. presidential candidate. Fremont had led a "surveying" party into California in December 1845, but in March 1846, Mexican authorities, suspicious of their motives, forced them to leave. As Fremont and his fellow "scientists" traveled toward Oregon, an agent of Polk and Larkin delivered a secret message to them, whereupon they quickly turned southward. Many historians believe that Fremont received instructions from Polk to assist in the impending U.S. conquest of California, but lack of conclusive documentation makes it difficult to know if that was indeed the case. Upon his return to California Fremont, under official orders or acting on his own, took charge of an armed movement started by U.S. settlers in June 1846. At Sonoma the rebels proclaimed the "California Republic," with a "bear flag" as their standard. Fighting Mexican Californians along the way, the rebels marched to San Francisco, where Fremont took command of the newly organized California Battalion of American Volunteers. On July 7, however, Fremont's "republic" dissolved as Commodore John D. Sloat officially invaded California on behalf of the United States as part of the ongoing war with Mexico.

The war ended following the U.S. invasion of central Mexico in 1847 and the signing of the Treaty of Guadalupe Hidalgo in 1848. In a message to the U.S. Congress in July 1848, President Polk reflected on the value of the territories acquired from Mexico. He spoke about the great natural wealth of California, including its ideal climate, fertile land, mineral resources, and superb harbors. "The possession of the ports of San Diego and Monterey and the bay of San Francisco," said Polk, "will enable the United States to command the already valuable and rapidly increasing commerce of the Pacific.... By a direct voyage in steamers we will be in less than thirty days of Canton and other ports of China."[18] President Ulysses S. Grant would later characterize the territory obtained from Mexico as "an empire of incalculable value."[19]

Under the terms of the Treaty of Guadalupe Hidalgo, the United States paid Mexico $18 million dollars for California and the rest of the ceded lands, including $15 million in cash and $3 million in assumed debts that Mexico owed U.S. citizens. The extraordinary value of the territories obtained by the United States dwarfed the compensation received by Mexico. More importantly, the war had monumental consequences over the long term. It significantly changed the destiny of the United States for the better economically and radically altered the fate of Mexico for the worse.

What Mexico Lost and What the United States Gained

History books in Mexico have long lamented the enormous land cession forced upon Mexico by the United States as a consequence of the Texas rebellion of the 1830s and the War of 1846–1848. Manuel Medina Castro, for example, points out that the United States despoiled Mexico of 51 percent of its territory, an area as large as Germany, Italy, Portugal, Spain, France, Scotland, Ireland, and England combined. Agustín Cue Canovas condemns the "greed" that drove U.S. expansionism and led to the detachment of Mexico's valuable northern frontier. He particularly bemoans the loss of valuable coastlines, ports, and minerals, as well as agricultural and ranching land.[20]

The transfer of ownership of extremely productive areas like Texas and California into foreign hands severely diminished the development prospects of Mexico and constricted economic opportunities for future generations. Moreover, the border change meant that the powerful U.S. economy was able to physically draw much closer to Mexico, with the result that, in a rather short amount of time, Americans established hegemony over their neighbor to the south. The proximity of U.S. industry and commerce, coupled with an easily breached 2,000-mile land border and easily penetrated Mexican coastlines, would have the effect of undermining the development of domestically controlled industrial and commercial sectors in Mexico. Mexican industrialists, merchants, and entrepreneurs would find it very difficult to compete with their U.S. counterparts. American corporations would capitalize on that situation by enticing generations of Mexican elites into accepting partnerships and joint ventures. Such alliances proved lucrative for those involved but not for Mexico's homegrown industries. The end result would be pronounced Mexican dependence on the United States.

American annexation of Mexico's northern frontier added 792,000 square miles to the U.S. national domain and along with it a treasure trove of natural riches. Over the last century and a half, the vast resources in the former Mexican lands have contributed enormously to the economic growth and enduring prosperity of the United States. Minerals illustrate that point dramatically: the ceded Mexican territories accounted for 42 percent of the total value of the nonfuel mineral production in the United States in 2008, and seven of the top U.S. nonfuel mineral-producing states had once been part of Mexico's patrimony. These states include Arizona, which ranked first in the United States with production valued at $7.8 billion dollars; Nevada, second at $6.3 billion; California, third at $4.2 billion; Utah, fourth at $4.1 billion; Texas, sixth at $3.4 billion; and Colorado, ninth at $2.0 billion.[21] For Mexico, the loss of those nonfuel minerals, coupled with the additional loss of fuel minerals, vast fertile lands, fecund forests, and exceptional harbors on the Pacific and Gulf Coasts, represent an incalculable economic setback.

Further insights regarding the magnitude of Mexico's gigantic losses can be gleaned from a cursory assessment of the economic productive capacity of the two most valuable areas in the territories the United States acquired from Mexico—Texas and California. Had Mexico retained these two states, it unquestionably would have become a much more prosperous country. This is not to say, however, that Texas and California would have developed in exactly the same way as they have under the United States given all the advantages the two states have had as integral parts of a highly advanced economy anchored in the Midwestern and eastern parts of the country. But with Texas and California, Mexico as a nation would have had much more natural assets with which to work to enhance the nation's development capabilities. I have heard it said that retention of the northern territories would not have made much difference for Mexico because Mexican leaders would have followed their "usual misguided policies" and kept areas like Texas and California underdeveloped, but this is a cynical and racist view. The fact is that, historically, those parts of Mexico (such as the Mexico City area) with favorable circumstances have achieved high levels of development.

The Value of Texas

Texas added 267,339 square miles to the U.S. national domain, or about 7.4 percent of the land mass of the continental United States. Texas was rich in natural resources, including a great variety of fertile soils, vast grasslands, nearly 4,000 miles of rivers and other streams, productive coastal areas, a variable climate, dense forests in the eastern part of the state, and a treasure-trove of minerals, most prominently oil and natural gas.

Only 213,000 people lived in Texas in 1850; thereafter the population exploded as a result of continuous economic growth largely driven by exploitation of the state's resources. Texas had 3 million people in 1900, 8 million in 1950, and 25 million in 2012. These numbers demonstrate the capacity of Texas to sustain a large economy and a population that surpassed those of many countries around the world.

During the nineteenth century agriculture and ranching dominated the Texas economy, with the exportation of cotton and beef constituting the principal activities that generated most of the wealth. Products shipped to other parts of the United States or abroad could easily make their way over the plains by road or via the railways, or by way of the ports on the Gulf.

A long period of petroleum-induced prosperity began in 1901 with the discovery of large deposits of oil in the Houston area and subsequent significant finds in other parts of the state. As the oil boom unfolded, Texas supplied about 15 percent of the world's "black gold" by the mid-1920s and about 25 percent by the early 1930s. In 1929 Texas received almost $6 million dollars in revenues from oil production taxes; such revenues would increase into the hundreds of millions of dollars in subsequent decades, reaching almost $376 million in 1996. Output of large quantities of fuel minerals has been accompanied by significant production of nonfuel minerals as well, including iron, uranium, magnesium, sodium, graphite, and sulfur. In time Texas achieved the distinction of being the top producer of minerals in the United States.[22]

Agriculture and ranching as well as oil and natural gas production drove the Texas economy for several generations, providing the foundation for manufacturing and service industries that developed following the decline of the oil industry that began in the 1980s. Texas added high-tech industries and the production of a wide variety of goods to its traditional manufacturing that rested on the processing of minerals and agricultural products. The continuous expansion of the economy led to the emergence of nationally and internationally prominent cities such as Houston, Dallas, Fort Worth, and San Antonio. Urban agglomeration in turn stimulated monumental activity in trade, commerce, and technological innovation.

In the early 2010s Texas ranked second both in population (25 million) and in the size of its economy ($1.1 trillion dollars GDP) among the U.S. states. Texans retained the number one ranking in crude oil production, a position they have held for many decades. The Texas economy was nearly the size of the entire Mexican economy. At that point Texas would have ranked fifteenth in the world if it were a country.

The Value of California

The observations made by President James Polk and other U.S. commentators during the 1840s concerning California's enormous potential for economic growth proved highly accurate. The richly endowed Golden State, as California came to be called, added 158,698 square miles to the national domain (4.4 percent of the continental United States), and quickly attracted large numbers of Americans and immigrants from other countries following the discovery of sizable gold deposits in the foothills of the Sierra Nevada. Gold production remained significant for decades, with mines in the Mother Lode gold belt leading the way. For example, the Idaho Maryland Gold Mine alone yielded $70 million dollars in gold between 1862 and 1956. In recent times gold production in California has declined, yet the value of gold output in the state still amounted to $138.5 million dollars in 2009.[23]

Mining activity has stimulated other industries in the state, including agriculture and stock raising, long mainstays of the economy. Once the railroads connected California with the rest of the country in the 1880s, the Golden State acquired the means to inexpensively ship its many natural products to the major population centers in the U.S. Midwest and East. By the early twentieth century California positioned itself to become a leading agricultural state in the United

States and a major source of food for export abroad. Agriculture thrived in a number of ideal natural settings throughout the state that reflected the variety of good climates, abundant fertile land, and plentiful water, much of it distributed to the ubiquitous fields and orchards through irrigation. As more and more land came into cultivation in the twentieth century, the state, in cooperation with the federal government, constructed one of the world's biggest and most elaborate systems of water delivery, both for agriculture and human consumption. The state's two major rivers, the Sacramento and San Joaquin, played key roles in supplying the needed water, but many other smaller streams, especially those that originate in the Sierra Nevada, contributed as well. In addition, for over 100 years the state has withdrawn massive amounts of water from the Colorado River, which makes up the boundary between California and Arizona. With such abundant supplies of water on hand, California's green areas, including the Central Valley, Sacramento Valley, Salinas Valley, San Joaquin Valley, Napa Valley, Imperial Valley, and the Oxnard Plain have been able to produce an extraordinary diversity of crops, many on a year-round basis. Not surprisingly, California has been the top producer of agricultural products in the United States since the middle of the twentieth century. In 2007, revenues from farming in California were nearly twice as much as in Texas, the state that ranked second in agricultural output.

Oil production is yet another basic industry that started early and has yielded tremendous wealth in California for generations. Oil drilling began in the 1860s, with various fields in Southern California in operation by the 1880s. By 1900 production had risen to over 4 million barrels, but this was only a preview of what would follow. In the 1920s California experienced an oil boom as oil discoveries took place in many areas, including Los Angeles, Orange, Ventura, Santa Barbara, Kern, and Fresno counties, and California temporarily assumed the position of leading oil producer in the United States. Between 1851 and 1951 California produced 13 billion barrels of oil, second in the world only to Texas, which produced 30 billion barrels.[24] At the turn of the twenty-first century California ranked fourth among the leading oil producing states in the country.

As in Texas, agricultural products, oil, and other natural resources have long constituted the foundation for California's other major industries, including manufacturing, trade, and commerce. The state's diverse resource base supplied the impetus for the growth of major cities and gave rise to processing and distribution centers of national and international importance. Favorable location and a mild climate contributed to the emergence of defense and aerospace industries, and natural beauty spawned a booming tourist economy. In the latter twentieth century the wealth generated by the California economy facilitated the establishment of the most advanced system of higher education in the world, permitting innovative research that led to major technological breakthroughs and the creation of high-tech industries.

In sum, without all the natural advantages enjoyed by California, the building of one of the world's great regional economies and the advent of unprecedented human productivity and agglomeration would have been impossible. With the population growing from 10 million in 1950 to 37 million in 2012, California became the most populous state in the United States. Urban areas in California, led by San Diego and Los Angeles in the south and San Francisco-Oakland-San Jose in the north, are major centers of trade, industry, and innovation in the global economy. In the early years of the twenty-first century California enjoyed high national rankings in various economic categories, including state domestic product (first), manufacturing (first), market value of agricultural products (first), crude oil production (third), and nonfuel mineral production (sixth). If California had been a country in 2011, its economy would have been 40 percent larger than Mexico's economy, and it would have ranked as the twelfth largest economy in the world.

Mexico's External Relations, 1848 to 1920

The Treaty of Guadalupe Hidalgo, which officially ended the U.S.–Mexico War in February 1848, expressed the commitment of both nations "to establish upon a solid basis relations of peace and friendship, which shall confer reciprocal benefits upon the citizens of both, and assure the concord, harmony and mutual confidence wherein two Peoples should live as good Neighbors." Lamentably, it would take generations to bring about the "harmony and mutual confidence" required to carry on the stable and cooperative relationship called for by the treaty. Instead, bitterness and distrust lingered for many years, and Mexico continued to feel threatened by the seemingly never-ending U.S. appetite for more land, the tendency of Americans to intervene continuously in Mexican affairs, and the increasing U.S. dominance over Mexico's economy.

In 1853, five years after the signing of the Treaty of Guadalupe Hidalgo, President Antonio López de Santa Anna faced considerable U.S. pressure to alter the northern border once again. A dispute had arisen after 1848 over the location of a portion of the boundary dictated by the Treaty of Guadalupe Hidalgo, and the United States capitalized on that issue to present four new proposals to Santa Anna for the purchase of different parts of northern Mexico, ranging from large areas to small ones. In need of money to keep his teetering government afloat but cognizant of the political storm that would erupt in Mexico if he ceded a sizable portion of the national patrimony to the United States, Santa Anna agreed to sell "only" the Mesilla Valley and other areas of Chihuahua and Sonora in exchange for $10 million dollars. The deal was consummated in El Tratado de Mesilla, or the Gadsden Treaty. Thus the United States secured more land and mineral resources, plus an important weather- and terrain-friendly southern railroad route to the Pacific Ocean.

The border treaties of 1848 and 1853 marked the end of the tumultuous relationship that had been driven by U.S. expansionist policies since Mexico's independence in 1821. But conflict did not disappear. Serious controversies broke out periodically long after the permanent boundary was settled. For most of the latter nineteenth century, the greatest sources of strife sprang from recurring transboundary Indian raids; problems with slave hunters, smugglers, bandits, and cattle rustlers; and the actions of desperate characters that congregated in the borderlands from California to Texas and Baja California to Tamaulipas. Many American adventurers added to the friction by engaging in repeated filibustering expeditions into various northern Mexican states; in the 1850s, the "Golden Age" of filibustering, greedy and predatory men seeking fortune or power cast their eyes on the thinly populated northern tier of Mexican states, launching numerous invasions into Baja California and Sonora. Some of the invaders sought to detach portions of Mexico and convert them into "independent republics." While the U.S. government officially disapproved of such attacks on Mexico, it did little to stop them.

Besides the United States, which posed a continuing threat to Mexico's territorial integrity, Mexicans also had to be concerned with imperialist France. Serious trouble with the French first surfaced in 1838 when a mini-war broke out over unpaid claims related to French properties that had been damaged during civil disturbances in Mexico. The French military blockaded, bombarded, and landed soldiers in Veracruz after Mexico refused to pay an inflated sum of money demanded by France. But the invaders were repelled by Mexican troops, and the skirmish came to a quick end when Mexico agreed to pay 75 percent of the compensation proposed by France. Two decades later Mexico still had problems paying its debts, prompting France to join England and Spain in 1862 in a punitive campaign to collect money from Mexico. The three European powers landed troops in Veracruz and took control of the customs house, confiscating tariff revenues to cover the debts owed the three countries. But imperialist France had more sinister plans than its two European partners. Instead of remaining on the coast the French launched a full-scale military invasion and captured Mexico City, the seat of the government, and they installed Austrian archduke Ferdinand Maximilian as ruler of Mexico in 1864. Maximilian served as surrogate emperor of the French for almost two years, during which time the forces of Benito Juárez carried on a guerrilla war against the foreign usurper. In May 1867 the Maximilian regime collapsed, and Mexico's government reverted to Benito Juárez. During the French occupation, the United States and Mexico actually drew closer together, as Americans protested the French presence in Mexico and U.S. volunteers and arms flowed to the Benito Juárez forces to help the cause of liberation of the country. A month after being deposed, Maximilian perished before a firing squad, an event that served as a warning to other foreigners who might have imperialist designs on Mexico.

After the expulsion of the French, the United States took center stage once again in Mexico's foreign relations. Two issues provoked tensions: troubles along the U.S.–Mexico border and further expansionist sentiments among influential sectors of U.S. society. After the signing of the Treaty of Guadalupe Hidalgo, cross-border Indian raiding and banditry continued to inflame passions in northern Mexico and in Texas and Arizona. Cries for direct intervention into Mexico grew louder in the United States, and another war between the two neighbors seemed a possibility by the 1870s; however, diplomatic compromise averted a military clash. With the arrival of the railroads in the U.S. Southwest and in northern Mexico, and the attendant influx and expansion of law-abiding citizenry, as well as the imposition of greater governmental control over the region, instability at the border declined.

The second source of friction stemmed from recurring proposals for annexation of Mexican lands by U.S. investors and their supporters in the U.S. Congress and the American media. Mining and land interests in particular advocated for the purchase or outright seizure of parts or the whole of Mexico by the United States. In 1877, the *San Francisco Chronicle* reported that high government officials in Washington were seeking to convince Mexico to part with much of its land adjacent to the United States in exchange for settling damage claims against the Mexican government. Subsequent research has not determined if the White House considered this a serious proposal, but it is clear that support for the idea existed in the U.S. Congress. On the other side of the issue, the *New York Times* in 1878 lambasted annexation advocates, arguing that "intelligent men" should not seek to bring into American society "mongrel" Mexicans or "willingly annex the smallpox or the yellow fever."[25]

In the 1880s annexation sentiments grew stronger as some members of the U.S. Congress proposed the purchase of portions of northern Mexico, in particular Baja California. Irritated, Mexican President Porfirio Díaz warned that any attempt to annex Mexican lands would be resisted militarily, while Mexican foreign minister Matías Romero took the unusual step of making the case against U.S. annexation of Mexico in an article in *The North American Review* in 1889. Romero admonished American expansionists to consider the consequences of pursuing annexation, warning that the Mexican people would "fight to the last extremity to preserve [the integrity of the country]" and that "a war with Mexico now would be quite a different affair from the one of 1846 and 1847." At the same time, Romero took pains to persuade readers that annexation of Mexican territories would create many racial problems for the United States because of the challenges of assimilating millions of Mexican Indians. Romero added that as members of U.S. society Mexicans would become voters and upset the political balance in the United States, and that the sudden influx of Mexican workers into the U.S. labor force would bring down wages and disrupt the U.S. economy. Americans needed to understand, wrote Romero, that annexation was unnecessary because U.S. economic interests had already received the concessions from Mexico that they had always desired. He pointed out that the Mexican government adhered to the belief "that the best way to prevent annexation is to open the country to the United States and to grant them [Americans] all reasonable advantages, so as to make annexation useless and even dangerous. In pursuance of that policy, the old Mexican land laws have been recently modified, and the most liberal railroad, mineral, and other grants have been freely given to its [U.S.] citizens."[26]

Despite the pleas from Romero and other Mexican officials, as well as censure from many U.S. political leaders, annexationist-minded Americans were not ready to give up. In 1891 U.S. Senator Matthew Quay of Pennsylvania attempted unsuccessfully to get approval from the U.S. Congress for a proposal to pursue the purchase of much of Mexico's northern borderlands. Quay's plan was soundly rejected by many newspapers across the United States.[27] But annexation reared its head again in 1897 when President William McKinley asked the U.S. Senate to create a committee to look into the possibility of purchasing Mexican lands. As with previous efforts to change the existing border between the United States and Mexico via dollar diplomacy, the McKinley initiative did not yield fruit, and U.S. initiatives to purchase or appropriate Mexican lands came to halt in 1898 just before the outbreak of the Spanish–American War. Wishing to assure that Mexico remained neutral in that conflict, and mindful of the need to repair U.S.–Mexico relations, McKinley informed Congress that his office would no longer consider any proposals to acquire additional territory from Mexico. For its part, the Porfirio Díaz government remained neutral during the war, despite stiff opposition to such a policy among various sectors of Mexican society sympathetic to Spain.[28]

While annexation fever went on for years in the halls of the U.S. Congress and among U.S. investors and many newspaper publishers, Mexico and the United States for the most part carried on a business-like relationship in a spirit of guarded coexistence. U.S. financial interests and corporations invested substantial amounts of money in railroad, mining, ranching, agricultural, and industrial operations in Mexico. Yet latent discontent with the increased presence of foreigners south of the border began to build among Mexicans. While many government leaders and domestic elites welcomed U.S. investors, others, including Mexican peasants, workers, and intellectuals, resented the power and influence of foreigners in their country's affairs. Nationalistic Mexicans particularly abhorred the constant threat of U.S. intervention, the racial discrimination practiced by foreigners, and the unequal wages paid by American employers (Mexicans were paid usually half the wages paid to Americans). Thus anti-American sentiment contributed significantly to the explosive discontent that surfaced in Mexico in the early twentieth century.

In 1910 widespread Mexican opposition to the dictator Porfirio Díaz incited a popular insurrection and plunged the country into a civil war that became known as the Mexican Revolution. This internal conflict introduced a new era of serious disputes with the United States and, as in previous years, the border region stood out as a zone of intense friction. Anti-Americanism intensified in Mexico as the United States intervened repeatedly to protect its economic and political interests south of the border. Such interventions include the participation in 1913 of U.S. Ambassador Henry Lane Wilson in the overthrow of President Francisco Madero, the U.S. military invasion of Veracruz in 1914, the entry in 1916 of 10,000 U.S. soldiers into Chihuahua seeking to capture the famous revolutionary Pancho Villa, and numerous incursions of U.S. troops into Mexico's border areas. The Villa hunt of 1916–1917, which was prompted by an attack conducted by Villa's troops on Columbus, New Mexico, in March 1916, came close to provoking another war between the two countries. Bandit and insurgent activity in the South Texas border region, as well as U.S. suspicion that Mexico intended to become an ally of Germany during World War I, aggravated the tense climate that developed during 1916. But diplomacy prevailed and the crises eventually passed.

During the last years of the 1910s an uneasy peace settled along the border as the violent phase of the Mexican Revolution waned and the United States turned its attention toward World War I. Yet repeated calls for the U.S. annexation of Baja California among some Californians, the introduction of a resolution by U.S. Senator Harry F. Ashurst in 1919 proposing the U.S. purchase of that peninsula, and the incursion of U.S. troops into Ciudad Juárez that same year during Villa's last attack on that border city kept Mexico on edge regarding U.S. intentions.

Mexico–U.S. Relations since 1920

After the Mexican Revolution the relationship between Mexico and the United States underwent significant change. Bilateral conflict continued but, unlike in previous generations, disagreements would never again deteriorate into armed confrontation. The thorny issues that had previously generated the most strife—border delimitation and territorial sovereignty—faded into historical memory, and cross-border interaction advanced toward a state of normalcy. Henceforth disagreements would derive instead from ever-increasing cross-border economic interdependence and integration. For example, discord over foreign ownership of Mexican agricultural land and oil deposits created headaches in the 1920s and 1930s. Die-hard interventionist factions in the United States called for the use of force to curb growing Mexican nationalism and assertiveness in recapturing land and resources under the control of foreigners, but the response from Washington was confined to temporarily withholding recognition of Mexico's central government and to applying diplomatic and economic pressures. Moreover, U.S. leaders did not pursue sporadic, isolated suggestions to acquire more land from Mexico, and Washington resisted pressures to intervene directly on behalf of U.S. oil companies in the landmark Mexican expropriation of the oil industry in 1938.

In 1940 Mexico's efforts to establish closer commercial ties with Japan and Germany raised concerns in the United States. But after Japan's attack on Pearl Harbor on December 7, 1941, and following the sinking of two of Mexico's oil tankers by German submarines, Mexico unequivocally allied itself with the United States during World War II. The Mexican government took strong actions against Germany, Japan, and Italy, confiscating properties of citizens of those countries, arresting suspected enemy agents, and relocating Japanese settlers in Baja California and Sonora to the country's interior. Mexico also agreed not to sell raw materials to the Axis countries and to make its resources available to the United States at market prices. In the military sphere, a Mexican air force squadron served in the Pacific in support of the Allied cause, and Mexico also agreed to supply guest workers to the United States to meet labor-emergency needs during the war years under an arrangement known as the Bracero Program.

As the United States confronted global warfare in the 1940s and the Cold War with the Soviet Union in subsequent decades, it made good sense for Americans to maintain a close alliance with Mexico. While still disapproving of many Mexican policies, the United States abandoned the use of military aggression, stopped intervening directly on behalf of U.S. investors, and no longer engaged in the nonrecognition of Mexican governments considered less than accommodating to U.S. interests. The two countries actually moved toward greater bilateral cooperation.

Friendships, of course, are constantly tested, and interaction between the two neighbors since 1940 has on many occasions become distant and discordant. In the arena of global affairs, there has been friction since the 1960s over Mexico's opposition to U.S. interventionist policies toward Latin America and other parts of the world, including recent U.S. actions in the Middle East. But most disagreements between Mexico and the United States have arisen from ever-increasing cross-border interaction; dividing the waters of the Rio Grande and the Colorado River, for example, created friction for decades and finally resulted in various water treaties enacted in the 1940s and 1970s. Trade, foreign investment, drug trafficking, and human migration are the major subjects that have taken center stage in the modern U.S.–Mexico relationship. These issues are discussed in detail in Chapters 8, 9, and 10.

Conclusion

The early histories of the Republic of Mexico and the United States of America differ drastically, with alterations in the size of each country constituting the greatest contrast. In 1821 Mexico had twice the territory of its northern neighbor. After repeated foreign relations disasters during the first four decades of its existence as an independent republic, however, Mexico emerged as a much smaller country, about one-fifth the size of the United States. Americans significantly enlarged their physical space—much at Mexico's expense. The loss of half of its territory to the United States constituted a colossal setback for Mexico because Texas, California, and other lost provinces had enormous economic value. The U.S. takeover of Mexico's northern frontier greatly reduced Mexico's chances of achieving a level of development capable of providing a high standard of living for most Mexicans. After 1848, Mexico was left with a landscape dominated by mountains, deserts, and jungles, and would confront formidable constraints for developing its agriculture, industry, commerce, and trade. Mexicans would live in a landscape with erratic climates, a serious shortage of good land, narrow and unhealthy coastal areas, few good harbors, and a limited number of "favorable spaces" suitable for human settlement and for large-scale economic activity. By contrast, the United States acquired a land mass from Mexico that had great agricultural, industrial, and trade potential. It is not an exaggeration to say that the patrimony ceded by Mexico assured that the United States would become the preeminent superpower on planet Earth.

After the mid-nineteenth century the extant economic divergence between the two countries intensified. The vast natural endowment now in American hands would play a major role in promoting rapid U.S. domestic progress and making possible unprecedented global hegemony. Mexico, by contrast, would assume its place in the world as an underdeveloped and dependent country, with its internal progress and external influence seriously restricted by the shrunken and problematic territory. While Mexico would contract no further, it had no choice but to accommodate to or, when circumstances permitted it, contest the subordination that would dictate the relationship with the United States. Still, it should be said that, as disadvantaged as Mexico has been in comparison to the United States, it has been significantly better off than most other Latin American countries, especially those popularly known as "banana republics."

Notes

1. U.S. Bureau of the Census (2006), III:3, 345–46.
2. Benjamin (1996), 6–12.
3. Benton's description is found in Barker (1928), 14–15.
4. Quoted in Benson (1987), 225.
5. Almonte (1925), 178, 180–181.
6. Benson (1989), 276–279, 284, 291, 297.
7. Handbook of Texas Online: https://tshaonline.org/handbook/online.
8. The U.S. Congress took no action on Lincoln's resolutions (see Greenberg 2012, 248–251).
9. Grant (1885–1886), I:53. Greenberg (2012), 274.
10. U.S. government interest in acquiring California is detailed in Pletcher (1973), 94–101.
11. Forbes (1973), 89, 102–106, 193–195, 206.
12. Duflot de Mofras (1937).
13. Dana (1911), 290.
14. Smith (1919), I:323.
15. Pletcher (1973), 98–100.
16. Harlow (1982), chapter 1.
17. U.S. Senate Executive Document 52 (1845), 79. (Buchanan to Slidell, November 10, 1845.)
18. U.S. Senate, 30th Congress, 1st Session, July 8, 1848 (Message from the President of the United States).
19. Grant (1885–1886), I:56.
20. Medina Castro (1974), 89; Cue Canovas (1970), 39.

21 U.S. Geological Survey, (2008), Table 4.
22 Pool (1975), 162; *Texas Almanac* (2008).
23 U.S. Geological Survey (2009).
24 Federal Writers' Project (1939), 83–84; Nash (1977), 101; Miller (1954), 72.
25 Jayes (2011), 27, 69, 72.
26 Romero (1889), 532, 535.
27 Editorials written against Senator Quay's proposal appeared in a document published circa 1892 ("Public Opinion in the United States on the Annexation of Mexico").
28 Menchaca (2011), 151, 164–165.

8
CHASING CAPITAL

In the early 1980s Mexico experienced one of the worst economic crises in its history. Unsustainable indebtedness, sharp drops in international oil prices and in the influx of foreign investment, plus reduced external trade, all played large roles in that epic catastrophe. I witnessed the desperation of Mexicans who had lost their jobs as a result of the depression-like conditions that engulfed Mexico. Large numbers of displaced people from the working class and the professional ranks from south of the border sought jobs in the United States. At the time I directed a research center at the University of Texas at El Paso (UTEP), and a number of Mexican educators inquired about the possibility of getting research or teaching positions at UTEP. They bitterly referred to "la crisis" in Mexico and recounted how their lives had dramatically changed for the worse. I expressed my sympathy and told them that I would see if there was anything I could do to help them in their efforts to secure positions in the United States. But there really was nothing I could do, and that was frustrating for me.

The 1980s collapse is a dramatic example of Mexico's external dependence, and how the practice of betting heavily on future oil earnings, of securing burdensome loans from foreign creditors, and of over-relying on foreign investment can create deep vulnerabilities. Such vulnerabilities invite disasters. Since Mexico became a republic, it has repeatedly turned to other countries or to foreigners residing in Mexico to supply capital. Borrowed money has been used to keep the government afloat, to cover defense or security needs, to pay indemnities, and to stimulate economic growth. Immediately after independence the newly formed Mexican government sought the aid of British moneylenders, and loan-seeking would be repeated often in subsequent generations, especially during moments of financial exigency. Investment capital also flowed into Mexico early on from Great Britain and from France, Spain, and the United States. Toward the end of the nineteenth century, the United States became Mexico's principal source of foreign investment and has maintained that position ever since.

Mexico's Need for Foreign Capital

Mexico's traditional need to seek money from foreigners is rooted in its limited capacity to generate sufficient internal capital to fuel the economy and provide revenues for government operations. Problematic geography has been a major contributor in this respect. Before the onset of the railroad age, highly inefficient transportation seriously undermined the exploitation of mineral resources, the country's major natural asset. Since Mexico lacked navigable inland waterways, land travel was the only option to move bulk commodities within the country and to the major coastal ports. Yet travel on primitive, ill-kept, and generally dreadful roadways was not only difficult but exceedingly costly because of the ubiquitous mountainous terrain. Agricultural land, Mexico's other natural asset, also offered limited possibilities for capital formation not only because of the transportation problem, but more fundamentally because the overall endowment of fertile soil was small in size and the best farming areas were confined to the Central Highlands and otherwise scattered locales around the country, rather than being concentrated in contiguous sizable tracts such as was the case in the rich agricultural regions of the Midwestern United States. Unlike Mexico, the geographically advantaged United States was able to generate vast amounts of capital as a result of its ability to tap its magnificent land and mineral endowments without major difficulty. Industrial production also came much more easily to the United States. Resource-rich areas there were not only more accessible, they were overlaid by inland navigable waterways, roadways, and railways that greatly facilitated the inexpensive movement of products internally as well as to other countries via the nation's world-class seaports.[1]

As for public revenues, Mexico historically has had a low tax base and the cost of collecting taxes has been high; moreover, massive tax evasion has posed a major problem for the state. Over time the government has imposed many types of taxes, including service fees and levies on imports and exports, and taxes on business, industry, property, rents, personal income, and sale transactions. But the revenues gathered by the Mexican government have traditionally fallen short of meeting expenditures; thus Mexico's limited capacity to produce capital internally and myriad problems in raising sufficient tax revenues early on compelled the government to turn to foreigners repeatedly to meet the nation's financial needs.

Borrowing—and Its Curses

Borrowing money abroad is especially risky for poor countries because they often find it difficult to repay their loans. That creates pressures to use scarce revenues to make loan payments while slashing government spending and imposing austerity measures. The least desirable outcome from failure to repay loans on a timely basis—or worse, from default—is armed external intervention on behalf of creditors. Less severe intervention might involve the exertion of pressure to compel borrowers to make significant changes in governmental or economic policies, changes that borrowers might not consider beneficial to them. Even if unpaid foreign loans do not lead to drastic scenarios, or if loans are actually repaid in a timely fashion, in the end borrowing may result in net monetary losses rather than net gains if eventual repayments substantially surpass the value of the loans, or if the expected benefits from the loans do not materialize. Whatever the case, inevitably money borrowing deepens a country's dependence on others and creates vulnerabilities. During certain periods in nineteenth- and twentieth-century Mexico, loan dependency reached very high levels, and frequently it had catastrophic consequences.

Let us turn to the conditions that led Mexico to seek foreign loans following the consummation of independence from Spain in 1821. At the time Mexico faced a debt of 76 million pesos as well as monumental economic problems owing to the warfare that had taken place during the struggle for independence. Agriculture and mining were in tatters, trade with Spain had come to a halt, old Spanish debts needed to be paid, capital flight had slowed growth, and an empty public treasury now had to support the army and a new bureaucracy. Beginning with the ten-month Agustín de Iturbide imperial regime during 1822–1823, the new government sought loans from assorted moneylenders, including creditors in other countries, foreigners living in Mexico, rich Mexican citizens, and the Catholic Church. In 1824 and 1825 British firms issued two loans to Mexico totaling 32 million pesos with rates of 5 and 6 percent annual interest respectively. The British loans, plus additional high-cost borrowing from other sources, placed the newly formed and cash-strapped Mexican government in a highly unfavorable position for many years. In 1827 Mexico defaulted on the British loans following a European banking and commercial crash that triggered a sharp drop in foreign trade in Latin America. Countries in Central and South America defaulted as well. In subsequent years the Mexican government and British investors agreed to several restructuring and rescheduling plans that only yielded unsatisfactory results. The default on the British loans would make it very difficult for Mexico to obtain money abroad, and thereafter the government relied largely on local moneylenders known as *agiotistas*.

A disturbing pattern took hold. As the Mexican economy limped along, government revenues languished and budgets remained unbalanced, driving desperate regime after desperate regime to get expensive loans from agiotistas. Sometimes the annual interest rate on the loans exceeded 200 and 300 percent, and one loan in 1828 reportedly topped 500 percent. By 1837 the internal public debt stood at 82 million pesos and the external debt at 46 million pesos. In the early 1840s the Mexican government levied new taxes that affected almost everyone in the country, but the returns were greatly diminished by the high costs of collecting money and operating the treasury department. In 1843, for example, the taxes collected amounted to 73 percent of total operating costs. Mexico simply did not have—and could not afford—the administrative infrastructure required for efficient tax collection. The unfavorable economic situation in Mexico made it very difficult for the government to meet its financial obligations and, on at least seven occasions between 1823 and 1861, it reluctantly declared seven moratoriums on loan repayments. Significant portions of the monetary compensation received from the United States in conjunction with the border-altering treaties of 1848 and 1853 were used to make loan payments. In addition, desperation drove the government to commit tariff revenues to creditors in lieu of cash payments. In 1861, for example, 91 percent of the import levies collected in Veracruz, the country's main port, were designated to pay the foreign debt. Yet the foreign debt kept rising, reaching 80.5 million pesos in 1870.[2]

The oppressive external debt, coupled with accumulated unpaid claims filed by foreigners for losses of property, brought devastating consequences for Mexico. An early example of trouble linked to money is the mini-war that France waged against Mexico in 1838 over unpaid claims submitted by French citizens whose properties had been damaged during political disturbances. In the 1840s Mexico's overdue payment of loans tempted England to seize California, but the English plans were thwarted by the possibility that the United States would forcefully prevent such an annexation. In 1846, the United States used the issue of outstanding property loss claims of its citizens against Mexico as part of the justification for waging war against Mexico and annexing half its territories two years later. And in 1862, appeals from Mexico-based foreign agiotistas to their home governments for help in collecting payment for loans gave France, England, and Spain a pretext to capture the port city of Veracruz and to collect tariff revenues otherwise intended for the Mexican treasury. The 1862 action by the three European countries foreshadowed France's imperialistic takeover of Mexico in 1863 and the subsequent installment of Austrian Archduke Ferdinand Maximilian as emperor, a position Maximillian held until his ouster and execution in 1867 by the loyalist forces of Benito Juárez.

During the French occupation, the fledgling Juárez government took great risks to secure money from foreigners, many of whom expected that the growing presence of American capital would eventually lead to the annexation of portions of Mexico to the United States. In its desperation to remain viable, the Juárez regime in effect jeopardized the nation's sovereignty by increasing the power of foreign financiers and businesspeople in Mexico. The Juárez government sold bonds backed by guarantees of Mexican land and natural resources and also granted generous business concessions. Mexican agents worked with U.S. firms in New York and other financial centers to sell many of the bonds. In the two-year period from 1865 to 1867, Mexican agents sold between $16 million and $18 million dollars worth of bonds. But later, the fragile governments of the Restored Republic could not deliver on many of the high returns attached to those investments. Delayed loan payments and cancellation of many questionable bonds inevitably drew threats of retribution by foreigners. By 1875 about thirty claims against Mexico had been filed with the U.S. government by disaffected American underwriters.[3]

Mexico could not get past the disputes with foreign creditors until the Porfirio Díaz regime issued land grants to old bondholders during the late 1870s. Then in the 1880s an economic upsurge produced new revenues that allowed Mexico to liquidate long-standing financial obligations. In 1887 Mexico finally paid off the remainder of the old English debt from the loans obtained in London back in the 1820s. Because of the accumulation of dividend arrears over many years, Mexico wound up paying 75 million pesos on the original 32 million peso London loans.[4] The newspaper *El Siglo Diez y Nueve* called the long-lasting problem of the British loans "one of the great economic disasters of the century" for Mexico.[5] But the long-delayed restoration of Mexico's credit allowed Mexicans to begin a new chapter in external borrowing. By the end of the Porfiriato the foreign debt would rise to around 250 million pesos.[6]

Foreign Investment

The influx of foreign investment capital during the decades following independence turned out to be less perilous politically than the externally obtained loans or the outstanding claims for property losses constantly submitted by foreigners. Nonetheless, like loans, investment capital that entered Mexico contributed to Mexico's risky exposure and subordination to outside interests.

Foreign capital flowed rapidly into Mexico's interior after 1821. For years Europeans, especially the British, had looked forward to the day when Spain's colonies in the Americas would break free and permit greater trade and exploitation of their raw materials by foreign interests. Mexico, seen as having the richest deposits of natural resources of all the Latin American countries, attracted $65 million dollars in foreign investment by 1825 from England, Germany, France, and the United States. Over the next several decades, however, many investors in Mexico's mining industry would experience much frustration and see dreams vanish as a result of the high cost of extracting minerals in the country's mountainous areas, as well as the constant disruptions in the production process caused by unstable political conditions.

In Mexico's far north, especially in Texas, New Mexico, and California, the influx of American entrepreneurs accelerated when Mexico allowed increased land and sea trade and immigration from the United States. Commerce involving U.S. merchants flourished on the Santa Fe and Chihuahua trails, while coastal California became a magnet for Yankee clipper ships that conducted a brisk trade with Mexican *Californios*.[7] The lower Rio Grande region in particular attracted U.S. investors who acquired vast amounts of local land and conducted lucrative business on both sides of the border. Charles Stillman is one example.

A prominent capitalist with ties to old wealth in New England, Stillman built a transnational empire in Texas, Nuevo Leon, and Tamaulipas that consisted of commercial, transportation, mining, and real estate holdings. When Union forces blockaded Confederate ports during the U.S. Civil War in the 1860s, Stillman and other American capitalists profited greatly from the shipping of Texas cotton and other Southern products out of Bagdad, Mexico, a bustling makeshift seaport on the Tamaulipas coast.

In 1876, after years of frustration over the resistance of the Sebastian Lerdo de Tejada government to grant foreigners desired concessions in Mexico, powerful Texas businessmen used their wealth and connections in the United States to help Porfirio Díaz wage his "Revolution of Tuxtepec." Díaz received substantial cash contributions from his American friends, including grants amounting to $174,000 dollars from the Texans and $320,000 dollars from New York financiers who held Mexican bonds. The Remington Arms Company supplied hundreds of rifles and large amounts of ammunition.[8] Díaz's rebellion succeeded and, following a coup, he got himself elected president. The U.S. government was slow in accepting Díaz as Mexico's legitimate president, but American magnates lobbied successfully for recognition. All the assistance rendered by foreigners to Díaz paid off because, once in office, he enacted policies favorable to American bankers, railroad companies, merchants, and landowners. Obviously the backing that Díaz received from U.S. supporters gave the president a good reason to help them with their business ventures in Mexico. However, as previously noted, it seems likely as well that the Díaz government extended privileges to foreigners as a way of thwarting possible annexation of Mexico by the United States. At the time American speculators constantly pressured the U.S. government to acquire more land from Mexico, either by purchase or by force.

Anxious to exploit Mexico's natural riches, foreign investors arrived in unprecedented numbers. British, French, and American capital poured in during the 1880s, 1890s, and 1900s as the Díaz government provided property protection and kept militant labor unions in check. Foreign railroad companies received vast tracts of land in exchange for the construction of track lines, many of which connected the areas with the richest natural resources to U.S. destinations. One railway company received 3.5 million acres, another 2.2 million acres, and another 819,000 acres. Foreign surveying companies likewise obtained massive amounts of real estate both as payment for their services and via purchase of land at reduced prices. By the 1880s and 1890s scores of major U.S. corporations and thousands of medium and small American property owners controlled plantations, farms, and ranches in the most favorable areas of Mexico. Enjoying a great deal of freedom to run their estates as they wished, Americans produced a wide variety of products mostly for export to the United States, including timber, livestock, guayule, chicle, sugar, coffee, and sundry tropical fruits and vegetables.[9]

By 1910 foreigners owned over a third of the land in Mexico, with Americans holding some 130 million acres. Much of the land under American control was on or near the coasts and along the northern border, both highly strategic national spaces that were by law officially off-limits to foreigners. Some examples of foreign individual and corporate land monopoly in Mexico include 7 million acres held by William Randolph Hearst, 5.5 million acres by Edwin Jessup Marshall, 4.7 million acres by Texaco, 3.8 million acres by the Continental Rubber Company, and 3.5 million acres by the Mengel Company. Much of the land that wound up in U.S. hands was sold in small- or medium-sized holdings to individual American colonists; these colonists numbered at least 9,000, and perhaps as many as 12,000, by 1910.[10] A significant percentage of the land controlled by foreigners had once belonged to Mexican peasants and rural communities that lacked the power to effectively contest the pro-elite and pro-foreign land policies promulgated by the Díaz government. "I really don't see what is to prevent us [Americans] from owning all of Mexico and running it to suit ourselves," remarked a contented William Randolph Hearst.[11] Hearst's belief in the inevitability of U.S. annexation of Mexico was widely shared among fellow Americans who had settled into comfortable lives in Mexico.

As with the land, Mexico's mines and oil fields fell into foreign hands when the Díaz government abandoned a long-observed principle of state control over natural resources. First, a new mining code enacted in 1884 allowed foreign ownership of subsoil minerals. Then Mexico's tax law was altered in 1887 to exempt mercury, iron, coal, and sulfur from mining taxes. Finally, the mining law of 1892 gave foreign companies permanent control of the ores under their stewardship. Such concessions spurred an upsurge in foreign investment. Copper and oil became increasingly attractive to foreigners owing to the rising demand for these resources as industrialization spread across the globe. Between 1884 and 1892 American companies increased their mining holdings from just 40 sites to nearly 2,400, and by 1896 they controlled the majority of the 7,000 active mines in Mexico. Toward the end of the Díaz regime, American investors supplied about 81 percent of the mining capital.[12]

The Guggenheim American Smelting and Refining Company (ASARCO), the Anaconda Amalgamated Copper Mining Company, and the Cananea Consolidated Copper Company stood out among the American concerns involved in Mexican mining operations. In the oil industry, major U.S. interests were led by Mexican Petroleum and Standard Oil, and the British by El Aguila Company. The oil companies concentrated their drilling along the Gulf Coast from Tampico to Veracruz, historically the region having the greatest petroleum deposits.

The overwhelming foreign control of Mexico's economy by 1910 is indicated by the fact that foreign capital composed 78 percent of the capital invested in the country's 170 largest companies, including 100 percent of the capital in oil, 98 percent in mining, 96 percent in agriculture, 87 percent in electricity, 84 percent in industry, 77 percent in banking, and 62 percent in commerce and communications.[13] It is hardly surprising, then, that many Mexicans became deeply antagonistic toward foreigners—and toward the numerous Mexican government officials and other elites who had lucrative ties to foreign companies. When the Mexican Revolution finally erupted, the U.S. government reacted with alarm at threats against U.S. interests, making it clear to Mexican leaders that, if necessary, U.S. military force would be used to secure American investments in Mexico. Indeed, the United States made good on its threats, repeatedly intervening in Mexican affairs.

Taking Back the Country

Despite the aggressive actions taken by the United States to protect American interests during the Revolution, Mexican radical and progressive elements proceeded in 1917 to write a new national constitution that reinstated the principle of state ownership of subsoil resources and affirmed the right of the government to carry out agrarian reform for the benefit of the landless peasantry. Hence, many properties held by Mexican *hacendados*, U.S. corporations, and sundry foreign colonists became targets for expropriation. Mexican reformers who wrote the new constitution were driven both by revolutionary ideology and by the knowledge that many property owners who controlled Mexico's mineral resources or monopolized the land had engaged in fraud or had received favored treatment by the government. However, lingering unsettled conditions in many parts of Mexico and the hostile reaction of property owners would delay implementation of these reforms for years.

After the enactment of the Constitution of 1917, Mexican leaders proceeded cautiously against American interests to avoid direct intervention by the U.S. government. When President Venustiano Carranza cancelled the land concessions of the powerful Campeche-Laguna Corporation in 1919, U.S. bankers and other corporate interests threw their support to Alvaro Obregón, who had risen in opposition to Carranza. But once Obregón took office following Carranza's ouster and assassination, he faced the dilemma of implementing the constitution in the face of U.S. government opposition to the expropriation of foreign-owned properties. Washington made its position clear by withholding recognition of the Alvaro Obregón government until the expropriation threat was removed. U.S. officials urged Obregón to repeal new agrarian laws passed by the Congress because of their perceived unfairness to American landowners. Washington also vigorously opposed initiatives to expropriate oil fields owned by American petroleum companies. Facing an internal political rebellion and fearing that the United States would support rivals of his government, Obregón entered into a compromise known as the Bucareli Agreements in 1923. That pact, which was subsequently legitimized by several rulings of the Mexican Supreme Court, held that titles to oil obtained by foreigners before 1917 would remain secure. In return for his cooperation, Obregón received official U.S. recognition.

Obregón's successor, Plutarco Elías Calles, also felt the pressure of the United States when Mexico nationalized some rural properties owned by Americans and when the Mexican Congress began debating new nationalistic oil and land legislation. In 1925 U.S. Secretary of State Frank Kellogg, while suggesting that Washington would not support Calles in case an internal revolt might break out against him, demanded restoration of the expropriated lands and called for the Mexican Congress to stop considering laws that would result in further Mexican takeover of U.S. properties. The Mexican government ignored the threats and passed the Law of Colonization in 1926 and the Alien Land Act in 1927. The first law dictated terms for Mexican peasants to acquire land declared available for colonization, and the second instructed foreigners on the correct procedures to sell their land or, in the case of corporations, on how to enter into partnerships so that Mexicans would henceforth own majority shares of the properties. A new petroleum law required that oil companies exchange their property titles for fifty-year leases. These new laws, coupled with the expropriation of 35,000 acres of land belonging to William Randolph Hearst, outraged the United States and created a diplomatic crisis.

Talk of possible war ensued when some U.S. documents that suggested an impending American military attack on Mexico surfaced.[14] In the early days of the Mexican Revolution, the U.S. government had formulated official War Contingency Plans to invade Mexico in order to secure mining resources and land belonging to Americans should diplomatic efforts fail to resolve disputes. The plans were periodically revised as circumstances required. Historian W. Dirk Raat writes that, in case the United States saw no other way to obtain relief, one of the plans called for "U.S. forces seizing oil and coal fields in Mexico, blockading Mexican seaports and sealing the U.S. border, cutting the railway lines from Guatemala, advancing into Mexico City, and eventually replacing U.S. troops with a Mexican constabulary under U.S. direction and control."[15] It is uncertain whether the United States really intended to use force against Mexico in 1926–1927, but the threat of military action apparently prompted a change in Mexican policy. The crisis dissipated following a 1927 Mexican Supreme Court ruling that declared key portions of the new petroleum law unconstitutional. Within months of that decision the Mexican Congress made appropriate adjustments to the petroleum law, which greatly pleased U.S. oilmen. Over the next six years the Mexican government kept Washington at bay by taking fewer actions that might be interpreted as threats by Americans who owned land or had oil interests. That approach produced the most amicable climate between Mexico and the United States since the days of Porfirio Díaz.[16]

Apart from facing U.S. aggressive actions linked to American investments, Mexico also encountered pressures from foreign creditors over its external debt. In default of its debt since 1914 and with a liability of $700 million dollars in 1922, Mexico's shaky economic circumstances necessitated a series of agreements that made it easier on the Mexican treasury. Mexico met its obligations until 1928, when it cancelled a scheduled payment following revenue shortfalls linked to drops in the value of oil and silver. Creditor banks reacted by pressuring Mexico to drastically reduce public expenditures in order to free up revenues for debt repayment. The government refused to do that. At the time Mexico faced a difficult situation because it had already committed substantial resources for major irrigation projects and highway building programs, both critical to the nation's development, and also had to finance military operations to suppress an ongoing rebellion by ultraconservative Catholics who resisted state policies directed at the Catholic Church. With the outbreak of the Great Depression and attendant reduced revenues from foreign trade, Mexico continued to withhold loan payments into 1929 and 1930. Further renegotiations followed, leading to the cancellation of $211 million dollars in interest that had accumulated since 1914, but still left Mexico with a restructured foreign debt of $318 million dollars in 1930.[17]

At the same time resentment against Americans still ran high in the mid and late 1930s because of the enduring dominance that foreigners exercised over key sectors of the Mexican economy. According to Mexican economist Emilio Alanís Patiño, in 1930 foreigners possessed 40 percent of Mexico's total wealth, and by 1935 foreign companies controlled 100 percent of Mexico's electricity industry, 99 percent of the oil industry, 98 percent of the mining industry, 79 percent of the railroads and streetcars, and 54 percent of manufacturing.[18] In a climate of intense nationalism and populism, President Cárdenas expropriated almost 50 million acres of real estate owned by both Mexicans and foreigners, including agricultural lands, mines, and forests. If land officially declared open for colonization prior to Cárdenas is included, between 1927 and 1940 the Mexican government expropriated about 6.2 million acres of American-held rural properties. In addition, an unknown amount of acreage involved foreign-owned land taken outright by squatters, for which owners received no compensation.[19]

The Los Angeles–based Colorado River Land Company (CRLC), which owned about 850,000 acres of Baja California land adjacent to the Colorado River, was one of the largest foreign concerns that had to give up part of its Mexican holdings as a result of expropriation. When organized in 1902, the CRLC had registered as a Mexican company, committing itself to following Mexican laws and holding yearly stockholder meetings in Mexico. The company had also implicitly given up rights to U.S. protection against expropriation. On the surface the CRLC functioned as any other Mexican company. But there was no question that the CRLC was a U.S. corporation; it was a mere extension of the American CRLC, with all the stockholders based in the United States. CRLC officials wined and dined Mexican bureaucrats with the aim of securing favorable leases, low-interest loans, and reduction of property taxes. The company kept about 88 percent of its Baja California holdings fallow, which contrasted significantly with the much more widely cultivated land owned by CRLC on the U.S. side of the border. Further, the cotton produced on the cultivated portion of the Mexican tract was exported to the United States, underscoring the lack of interest on the part of the company in establishing linkages with Mexican markets. Although the CRLC operated within Mexican law and performed good works such as assisting with flood control projects in the Mexicali Valley, many Mexicans had long questioned the wisdom of having large amounts of land in the border region under foreign ownership. They worried particularly about the possible U.S. takeover of the Mexicali Valley because of easy American access to the area and its almost complete isolation from the rest of Mexico. In 1906 American farmers in the Imperial Valley had in fact demanded U.S. annexation of the Mexicali Valley following great flooding from a failed diversion project involving an irrigation canal that carried Colorado River water to the Imperial Valley. (The flooding led to the creation of the Salton Sea.) Part of the irrigation canal was located in Mexico due to terrain considerations; U.S. farmers focused on the fact that the breach had occurred on the Mexican side, and their frustration grew during the sixteen long months it took to finally fix the problem. Some ignored the fact it was an American engineer under the employ of the California Development Company who not only erred in the building of the diversion scheme but apparently failed to inform Mexican authorities of the project. In any case, the CRLC did not support U.S. annexation, but that did not allay Mexican suspicions about American intentions. The Mexican military commander in the region warned that the vulnerable Mexicali Valley could be lost to the United States should Mexico City fail to secure it. Thus, in accordance with the post-Revolution top-priority policy of regaining control of the country's coasts and border areas, the Cárdenas government in 1937 expropriated half of CRLC's holdings. Cárdenas also proceeded to quickly build badly needed infrastructure, thus establishing the foundation for economic and population growth in the area and de facto incorporation to the rest of Mexico. Newly constructed irrigation canals delivered much-needed water to the valley, and brand new public highways and railroads finally connected the heretofore isolated region to other parts of the country. Such government support precipitated a great influx of Mexican settlers who substantially expanded agricultural productivity and brought prosperity to a previously largely undeveloped region.[20]

Meanwhile, many American property holders called on the U.S. government to forcefully stop the expropriations carried out by the Mexican government. Yet President Franklin Delano Roosevelt recognized the right of Mexico to recover the land, asking only that fair compensation be given landowners. Roosevelt followed that same policy of recognition of Mexico's rights and insistence for fair compensation when the landmark oil expropriations took place in 1938. Roosevelt's unprecedented favorable stance toward Mexico stemmed from an ideological affinity with the efforts of President Cárdenas to improve conditions among the Mexican masses, a resolve to leave behind the U.S. imperialistic policies of the past, and a desire to build a "neighborly" alliance in the years prior to U.S. entry into World War II. The United States, however, did send a message of displeasure to Mexico after the oil expropriation by ending the silver-purchase agreement that had been in operation since 1934. For his part, Cárdenas kept Washington well informed of planned land expropriations and, once accomplished, promised fair compensation packages to former landowners whose ownership claims were certified by Mexico's Agrarian Claims Commission.

Mexico's support for the allied cause in the early stages of World War II improved its bargaining position with the United States, resulting in a closer bilateral economic relationship. In 1941, an agreement provided for the resolution of the agrarian controversy, and in 1942, Mexico successfully renegotiated most of its debt obligations by having foreign holders of Mexican government securities and shareholders in railway companies each accept $50 million dollars in payments instead of the actual amounts owed to each, which were calculated at ten times that figure. American landowners who had lost land began receiving compensation checks in 1943. Resolution of these matters prompted the United States to resume purchasing Mexican silver, sign a new bilateral trade pact, facilitate loans, and assist with the stabilization of the Mexican peso.[21]

The dispute over oil proved more difficult to resolve than the land controversies, as American and British oil firms fought to undo the expropriation of their properties by every means at their disposal. "The affected companies unleashed ... a ferocious international propaganda campaign against Mexico, proposing, at the same time, to close down international markets to PEMEX [Petroleos Mexicanos, the newly established Mexican state company], drowning 'Mexico in its own oil' and denying it access to production machinery needed to maintain the rhythm of production," historians Héctor Aguilar Camin and Lorenzo Meyer write.[22] Lacking the support of the U.S. government for reversal of the Cárdenas decision, the U.S. companies turned to making extravagant demands for compensation, which the Mexican government rejected. The British exaggerated their claims with equal fervor. Heated negotiations eventually produced settlements and ended the impasse. In 1942 Mexico agreed to pay $29 million dollars to various American oil firms, and in 1947 it settled with the British petroleum companies for payment of $130 million dollars.[23]

The land and oil expropriations were direct outcomes of the nationalism stirred up by the Mexican Revolution. Exploitative, illegal, and discriminatory practices carried on by foreign companies provoked the sensibilities of Mexicans, as did the feeling that their country had been subjected to colonialism. Mexican leaders felt that real progress could only occur if Mexico regained ownership of the nation's resources. Indeed, motivated by profits, foreigners had run their operations in Mexico as enclaves largely disconnected from the domestic economy. They had also exploited Mexican workers. Rarely did foreigners consider Mexico's development needs or the urgency of improving conditions among the masses. The Mexican nationalization agenda had been difficult to implement, but by the early 1940s the government had succeeded in ridding the country of the overwhelming control that foreigners had exercised over Mexico since the days of Porfirio Díaz.

New Rules for Foreign Investors

Mexico's nationalistic surge, coupled with the economic downturn spawned by the Great Depression, led to a drop in direct U.S. investment from $683 million dollars in 1929 to $287 million dollars by 1943. Nevertheless, as World War II awakened demand once again for Mexican raw materials, the economy picked up and so did foreign investment. Thus in 1944 Mexico issued new rules designed to prevent a possible postwar economic downturn should foreign investors suddenly shift their capital to other countries after the war. Foreigners would now need advance approval from the Mexican government in order to invest and would be required to form partnerships with Mexicans such that Mexicans would be majority owners of new companies. The government also prohibited private investment, both foreign and domestic, in the publicly owned oil industry, and restricted investment to Mexican citizens in sensitive sectors such as banking.[24] In later years the government expanded the list of industries subject to the Mexicanization rules and also established requirements for increasing local inputs in industries that used imported components. In 1962 a new law aimed at the foreign-dominated automobile industry required local content amounting to 60 percent and mandated that the making of auto parts be reserved for firms (whether foreign or domestic) operating in Mexico. Although foreigners found these and other policies inconvenient, external capital did not stop flowing into Mexico. The multinational companies satisfied many requirements through the creation of subsidiary companies, many of which bore Mexican names. Foreigners also determined that Mexican officials did not fully enforce the rules. Moreover, the Mexican government subsequently lifted many of the restrictions.[25]

As the "economic miracle" of the post–World War II period unfolded in Mexico, a new wave of foreign capital made its way into the country. By 1964 U.S. capital totaled $1.3 billion dollars,[26] by far the largest sum among investors from other countries. Once again, large portions of the Mexican economy were falling into the hands of multinational corporations. Studies by prominent Mexican economist José Luis Ceceña showed that foreign firms controlled or had significant influence over 58 percent of the largest 400 companies in Mexico, either through full ownership or through affiliation with Mexicans. Ceceña expressed alarm over the growing disappearance of Mexican companies whose inferior resources and lack of technology placed them at a great disadvantage vis-à-vis the much stronger foreign firms. "Every day the number of Mexican companies and businesses that come under the control of Yanqui monopolies grows in our country, displacing Mexican citizens from all activity.... The list of Mexican companies that have been absorbed by foreign firms is a long one.... The problem is very serious." Ceceña strongly criticized self-serving Mexicans who joined forces with foreign companies at the expense of the local firms and urged the Mexican government to intervene more forcefully to diminish the trend toward greater external dependency.[27]

The prospect of a much higher rate of return in Mexico than in the United States kept luring U.S. companies south of the border, notwithstanding the nationalistic mandates and regulations imposed by the Mexican government. In the 1960s, new laws required Mexican majority ownership in mining enterprises, the automobile industry, and banking. The government also threatened to nationalize such key sectors as the aluminum, cement, steel, and paper industries.[28] Foreigners learned soon enough, however, that corruption-prone Mexican officials could be "flexible" and could be "persuaded" to allow circumvention of the regulations. It was common knowledge that foreigners paid Mexican citizens to front as "owners" of foreign-financed businesses and that foreigners maintained de facto control of companies by keeping large blocks of stock in a few hands while dispersing the majority shares among many individual Mexican partners. Such U.S. companies as Chrysler, Ford, Anderson Clayton, and General Electric took full advantage of the government's "flexibility" and continued to operate in Mexico without having to subject themselves to majority Mexican ownership.[29]

As foreign firms increased their participation in Mexico's economy, the cost of importing technology rose, causing balance-of-payment problems. The Mexican government found it increasingly difficult to regulate technology transfers, trademarks, and patents, which, given Mexico's acute underdevelopment in science, technology, and innovation, presented a major challenge. Calculated in terms of number of researchers per each 10,000 inhabitants, in the late 1960s the ratio of Italian researchers to Mexican researchers was nearly 7:1, West German researchers to Mexican researchers more than 18:1, Japanese researchers to Mexican researchers 25:1, and U.S. researchers to Mexican researchers more than 43:1. In 1969 foreigners received 93 percent of the patents awarded in Mexico, compared to 51 percent in Brazil, 28 percent in West Germany, and 25 percent in the United States.[30] These figures illustrate one of the most significant aspects of Mexico's excessive external dependence. Having limited capacity to innovate and develop their own technologies, Mexicans relied on foreigners to carry out research and development. Under such circumstances Mexico's domestic industries had little chance of competing with foreign corporations.

In 1965 multinational corporations involved in assembly manufacturing began setting up maquiladora operations in Mexico's northern border cities under the newly created Border Industrialization Program. Mexico enticed foreign companies to relocate with guarantees of 100 percent ownership of their firms and duty-free importation of machinery and inputs used in the maquiladoras. Mexico's northern frontier proved highly attractive for multinationals because the border economy was closely linked with that of the United States and because cheap local labor was readily available. Between 1970 and 1984 the number of maquiladoras in Mexico mushroomed from 120 to 680, with most plants located directly on the border. In later years, the maquiladora industry grew in an even more impressive manner as real wages in Mexico declined due to currency devaluations, as factories expanded beyond the border, and as the Mexican government continued to extend concessions to foreign investors. By 2001, 3,735 maquiladoras employed about 1.3 million workers. To be sure, these factories became an important contributor to industrial job creation in Mexico, but they functioned as enclaves, drawing almost all their inputs from abroad while providing only limited stimulation to local manufacturing sectors. In the early years of the program only 1 to 2 percent of the inputs originated with Mexican firms; by the 1990s that figure had expanded to perhaps 6 percent.[31]

Foreign capital destined for areas that did not qualify for the maquiladora program had to abide by different rules. Mexico made such rules more stringent in 1973 with the enactment of the Law to Promote Mexican Investment and to Regulate Foreign Investment. The new regimen alarmed many foreign investors. Mexico passed this law in response to worsening balance of payments problems and the competitive advantage that multinational corporations had been accumulating for years in the domestic market by acquiring existing Mexican companies rather than establishing new firms. From 1966 to 1973, between two-thirds to three-quarters of all foreign subsidiaries consisted of acquisitions in some sectors of the Mexican economy. One of the government's prime worries was that transnational enterprises "were likely to be producers in concentrated, oligopolistic product markets in which their sales accounted for a significant proportion of total sales in the market," a situation that "represented a threat to Mexican domestic business."[32] In addition to addressing these concerns, the 1973 law restricted foreign ownership to less than 50 percent in new manufacturing ventures; sought to channel capital and technology into heavy industry, mining, and tourism; and specified the industries exclusively reserved for the state (energy, communications, and transportation). The strong U.S. reaction to the law died down within eighteen months of its passage as foreigners learned that it was not as onerous as first imagined, that companies that invested in favored sectors such as mining qualified for tax and tariff concessions, and that the traditional ways of circumventing investment laws remained undisturbed. The government assured foreign companies that they could retain majority control if they demonstrated that their operations were making a significant difference alleviating unemployment among Mexicans or contributing to Mexico's trade deficit reduction efforts.[33]

In the export-oriented agricultural sector, partnerships between Mexican and American investors did not always work out according the principle of co-ownership. U.S. corporations often found ways to retain almost complete control over operations and managed to place domestic competitors at a disadvantage. For example, a study conducted by Ernest Feder in the 1970s on the strawberry export industry revealed that U.S. companies made most of the important decisions pertaining to inputs, production, labor, prices, marketing, exportation, and return on investments. "Mexican firms and merchants cannot act on their own," wrote Feder. "[Business] relations established by U.S. brokers are so tightly knit that they form an insurmountable obstacle for Mexican businessmen."[34] A study by David R. Mares, on the other hand, indicated that Mexican growers of fresh winter vegetables for export had the upper hand in managing that industry. Mexicans "wrestled control of much of the processing and distribution network [involving their industry and] also built alliances in the United States that gave them [Mexicans] substantial leverage in Washington, D.C."[35] The contrasting conclusions reached by these two scholars suggest a spectrum of arrangements regarding the degree of U.S. control or influence in Mexico's export-oriented agricultural sector. Much depended on the types of crops grown, where they were produced, and who owned what.

Economic Crisis and the Onset of Neoliberalism

In the early 1980s, as Mexico faced severe economic distress as an outcome of international recessions and a drastic drop in demand for oil and other raw materials, the government increased its borrowing abroad to weather the crisis. By 1981, Mexico's foreign debt reached $75 billion dollars, placing extraordinary pressure on the country. As the debt kept rising and default and bankruptcy seemed imminent, Mexico turned to foreign organizations such as the World Bank and the International Monetary Fund for emergency loans. The lending organizations demanded that, in exchange for bailout packages, Mexico must abandon state-directed development economics in favor of a free-market paradigm. With the economy in shambles and its political position greatly weakened, Mexico made the momentous decision to cast aside state management of the economy. Instead, Mexico adopted a system of relatively unrestrained capitalism. A new export-oriented model replaced import-substitution industrialization (ISI), with attendant liberalization of foreign trade and foreign investment regulations. Several dramatic actions taken by Mexico City underlined the country's transformation. In 1986 Mexico joined GATT (General Agreement on Tariffs and Trade); in 1994 the Mexican government entered into a new trade and foreign investment partnership with the United States and Canada under NAFTA (North American Free Trade Agreement); and in the 1990s and 2000s Mexico signed free-trade agreements with many other countries. Regulations adopted in 1989 and 1993 streamlined approval procedures for new foreign investments, relaxed export-related local content requirements, opened up sectors of the Mexican economy previously closed to foreigners, allowed 100 percent external ownership in many industries, and made it easier for foreigners to acquire properties along the coasts and in border areas.[36] What happened in Mexico after 1980 is reminiscent of what had occurred one century earlier, when Porfirio Díaz allowed non-Mexicans to take control of the country's economy.

NAFTA stimulated a sharp increase in new foreign direct investment (FDI) in Mexico as the Mexican government agreed to extend new protections to private property, including guarantees against expropriation. Incoming FDI averaged about $5 billion per year in the early 1990s but skyrocketed beyond $20 billion annually after 2000, with U.S. capital composing about 70 percent of the total. Since export-oriented production drew most of the FDI, Mexico's exports recorded spectacular growth in a short period of time, tripling in value between 1994 and 2002. Manufactures became the predominant exports by far, reaching nearly 85 percent of Mexico's exports by 2010. Advocates of free markets heaped praise on Mexico for reinventing itself into one of the most open economies in the world and becoming a haven for external capital. They cited the remarkable growth in manufacturing exports as evidence of the success of the open borders, free markets strategy.

Yet, while overall numbers are impressive, the increases in FDI and manufactured exports have not translated into the life-improving development that most Mexicans hoped for when the country adopted neoliberalism as the national economic model. Observing that Mexico needs FDI, former Minister of Foreign Relations Jorge G. Castañeda nonetheless has acknowledged that the "drawbacks" to FDI are both real and significant: "This 'foreign' investment is generally financed with local resources, rarely benefitting the balance of payments; the technology it introduces tends to be both antiquated and expensive; it caters more often to headquarters' needs and sensibilities than to those of the local economy; it is rarely in for the long haul."[37] A major problem is that global uncertainties have resulted in considerable fluctuations in the influx of FDI into Mexico, creating uncertainty. For example, inflows of new FDI declined from $27.1 billion dollars in 2007 to $14.4 billion in 2009 with the intensification of the Wall Street–instigated Great Recession.[38]

Since the 1990s, FDI has done little to create manufacturing jobs that are firmly rooted in Mexico's domestic economy or that pay high wages. Official statistics show that over three-fourths of IMMEX industry (export manufacturing) employees are *obreros*, or ordinary, low-paid workers. Further, products assembled in maquiladoras make up over half of Mexico's celebrated industrial exports.[39] From 1994, when NAFTA took effect, through the latter 2000s the export sector failed to produce enough jobs to reduce unemployment or to diminish the steady migration of Mexican workers to the United States. Migration only slowed down when the Great Recession stunted growth and job opportunities in the United States after 2007. Further, the greater presence of foreign firms in Mexico has not led to high levels of substantive linkages with local producers, either via inputs or spillovers. To a significant degree, the maquiladora assembly sector remains disconnected from the domestic economy, much as it was a generation ago. More troubling, FDI has led to domestic deindustrialization in key areas such as the information technology (IT) sector. In their study of high-tech industries in Guadalajara at the turn of the twenty-first century, Kevin Gallagher and Lyuba Zarsky found that "the FDI-led strategy has had limited success in stimulating the growth of Mexican firms either as competitors or suppliers to the multinationals. Instead, Mexican industry is being hollowed out and the economy as a whole has been bifurcated into a foreign 'enclave economy' and a domestic economy. Within the IT sector, a once thriving domestic industry was largely wiped out and replaced by a foreign IT enclave."[40] To remain competitive during China's aggressive global expansion in the early 2000s, the foreign-dominated IT sector of Guadalajara shifted to more advanced production requiring sophisticated processes and services, many of which were developed outside Mexico. Having much less capacity than foreign companies, local firms could not make the necessary rapid upgrading and therefore became less competitive or went out of business.[41] In the automobile sector, foreign-owned companies depend on many parts made in hundreds of Mexican factories, but most such companies are U.S. subsidiaries or are jointly owned and operated with Mexicans. That said, whether foreign-owned or jointly owned, such companies do impact the Mexican economy by engaging in such activities as buying local electricity, leasing land, paying rents, and consuming a variety of Mexican-made products and services rendered by Mexicans.

However the overwhelming presence of external capital in Mexico is rationalized, the reality is that the Mexican economy is dominated by foreign corporations. One major sector is finance. In 2005 foreigners owned 83 percent of all assets held by Mexico's banks.[42] The automobile industry is another foreign-controlled sector. By 2000, General Motors, Nissan, and Volkswagen produced two-thirds of the automobiles made in Mexico; Ford, Chrysler, Honda, and Toyota accounted for the remainder.[43] The question arises as to why there is not at least one wholly owned Mexican automobile company that makes a Mexican-brand car. Why is that possible in Japan and in South Korea but not in Mexico? In the broadest of terms, the contiguity of Mexico to the United States has been the factor that best explains why Mexican firms, whether in the automobile industry or in other sectors, have not produced high-end Mexican brand durable goods. Mexican companies have found it exceedingly difficult to engage in head-to-head competition with powerful U.S. corporations. The alternative has been to form alliances with foreign firms that control production from their home bases but allow for assembly operations and the manufacture of select low-end inputs in Mexico. Much the same phenomenon has occurred in Canada, the other country that abuts the United States. While more developed than Mexico (owing to a generally more favorable context, including having a much smaller population), Canada has also experienced the stifling of its domestic industries as a consequence of the overwhelming presence of U.S.-controlled subsidiaries, or branch plants. Canadian scholars and other analysts have produced a voluminous literature documenting the high degree of dependence on the United States of Canada's manufacturing sector, the concentration of Canadian trade with the United States, the relatively low level of research and development carried out in Canada, and the "invasion" of U.S. brands ranging from automobiles to home appliances and fast-food chains.[44] Mexico, it turns out, has much in common with Canada.

In Mexico, even retailing has fallen largely into U.S. hands. That is exemplified by the incredibly rapid expansion of Walmart after 1991. That year the giant U.S. retailer entered into a joint arrangement with the Mexican firm Cifra, which owned chains of Mexican stores and restaurants. In 1997 Walmart became majority owner of Cifra, giving birth to Walmart de México, or Walmex. By the early 2000s, Walmex had become Mexico's largest retailer as well as the top private-sector employer; it operated more than 2,000 retail outlets in Mexico in 2012, including Superstores, Sam's Clubs, Superamas, Suburbias, Bodega Aurreras, and sundry other department stores and restaurants. Critics have accused Walmart of undermining Mexico's sovereignty and have denounced it for flooding the Mexican market with cheap foreign goods that cause serious damage to domestic industries. Walmart has also come under heavy fire for engaging in widespread corruptive practices to obtain permits and concessions in order to expand its operations in Mexico. In the grocery sector, the invasion of foreign-owned supermarkets has contributed significantly to the gradual disappearance or deterioration of traditional *mercados* (city markets) and neighborhood stores operated by Mexicans. In Mexico City, the domestic food sector controlled only 30 percent of grocery sales in 2011, compared to 80 percent in the 1960s; during the first decade of the twenty-first century alone, neighborhood store sales dropped by almost 60 percent.[45]

The wisdom of Mexico's overreliance on FDI to bring about growth has been questioned by skeptics of neoliberal economics. Contrary to the manner in which China and other Asian countries have successfully used the state to promote development, Mexico has placed the nation's fortunes on the shoulders of markets mostly controlled by sectors tied to foreign capital. The problem is that foreign capital has little if any interest in bringing about genuine, long-lasting development to Mexico.

Until recent years, FDI moved essentially in one direction, from the United States and other advanced countries into Mexico. Mexicans themselves invested relatively small amounts of money abroad. But that changed in the 1980s, 1990s, and early 2000s, when substantial flows of Mexican capital left the country because of domestic economic uncertainties, new NAFTA-related investment possibilities in the United States and Canada, new investment opportunities in other countries, especially in Latin America, and escalating drug-related violence throughout Mexico. By 2007, Mexican FDI in the United States amounted to $6 billion dollars, with additional billions invested in other countries. Destinations included private banks accounts abroad, as well as direct investments in a variety of foreign enterprises. Mexican multinationals such as Grupo Carso, Cemex, Alfa, Grupo Mexico, Famsa, Modelo, Gruma, Bimbo, Lala, Grupo Salinas, and Cinepolis channeled capital into such sectors as telecommunications, cement, auto parts, mining, beverages, foodstuffs, financial services, media, and entertainment. The U.S. border states, and in particular U.S. border cities, became favorite destinations for Mexican businessmen seeking new opportunities. In 2010 alone, Mexicans invested about $16 million dollars in Texas in the creation of new businesses.[46]

Conclusion

Mexico's far-reaching dependence on and vulnerability to external forces is illustrated in the long-established reliance on borrowed foreign money and capital from foreign investors. This practice is not much different from that of many other Third World countries that have secured revenues from abroad.

As we have seen, Mexico has often placed itself at the mercy of the more powerful nations from whence the borrowed capital derives. Mexican history demonstrates that the most precarious times for indebted nations and recipients of external investment are when disputes break out with foreigners who blame the host country for losses and aggressively pursue compensation, or when foreign creditors request immediate payment for outstanding loans, or when foreign investors whose properties are threatened by expropriation demand armed intervention by their home governments.

The other external source of funds—foreign investment—has been beneficial to Mexico in many ways. At the same time, it has also meant loss of sovereignty and diminished control over natural resources, and it has provoked conflict. For example, the takeover by foreigners of most of Mexico's prime lands and mineral resources during the Porfirio Díaz era incited outrage and contributed to the outbreak of the 1910 Mexican Revolution. After the Revolution, Mexico used the Constitution of 1917 as its legal justification for expropriating foreign-owned properties and for placing limits on the influx of foreign capital into the country. On several occasions during the nationalization era, strong opposition from the United States compelled Mexico to moderate its actions and to make concessions to foreign interests.

In the 1980s and 1990s, financial crises drove Mexico to reverse the policies toward foreign investment that had been adopted for several decades after 1940. Mexico once again allowed capital from abroad to enter the country with few restrictions. The results have been mixed. On one hand, unprecedented flows of foreign investment have increased industrial production, expanded business activity, and created jobs (though mostly low-paying). On the other hand, reliance on foreign capital has seriously undercut the government's ability to implement an economic agenda that serves the interests of Mexico first. Lobbying on behalf of multinational corporations has been strengthened significantly by the omnipresent alliances between Mexican elites and foreigners in the form of partnerships and joint ventures, through brokerage and legal services extended to foreign firms, and by Mexicans serving as board members or shareholders of transnational corporations. In short, although necessary, foreign investment has not provided the kind of capital required to build a robust domestic economy in Mexico.

Notes

1 STRATFOR (2011).
2 Figures regarding the size of the debt from Bazant (1995), 107. Other data cited from Zaragoza (1996), 15–16, 70, and Tenenbaum (1986), 51.
3 Hart (2002), 10–16, 27–32, 41–42, 48.
4 Costeloe (2003), 326.

5 Quoted in Salvucci (2009), 2.
6 Cecena (1970), 98.
7 Boyle (1997).
8 Hart (2002), 66.
9 Hart (1987), 131–132; Hart (2002), Parts I and II, Appendix 1.
10 Hart (2002), 160; Hart (1987), 159–160.
11 Quote appears in Hart (2002), 167.
12 Hart (1987), 142; Hart (2002), 152; Raat (1992), 90–91.
13 Caseña (1970), 54, 81–84.
14 Dwyer (2008), 38–42.
15 The War Contingency Plans evolved into "Special Green Plans" that were continuously updated until 1946, when they were declared obsolete (Raat 1992, 132).
16 Dwyer (2008) 38–42.
17 Aguilar Camin and Meyer (1993), 103–104.
18 Alanís Patiño (1943), 101, 113.
19 Dwyer (2008), 269.
20 Kerig (2001); Dwyer (2008) 46.
21 Dwyer (2008), 269; Marichal (1989), 227–228.
22 Aguilar Camin and Meyer (1993), 155.
23 Dwyer (2008), 141–148, 159–163, 188–192, 231, 258–261; U.S. Department of State, Office of the Historian, www.state.gov/milestones/1937–1945/mexican-oil.
24 *New York Times* (November 17, 1944), 8.
25 Whiting, Jr. (1992), 71–76.
26 Raat (1992), 154.
27 Cecena (2007), 87–88, 110; quotes from 123, 126–127 (my translation).
28 Haber et al. (2008), 46–47.
29 Ruíz (2010), 162.
30 Whiting, Jr. (1992), 117–119.
31 Whiting, Jr (1992), 147.
32 Whiting, Jr. (1992), 86.
33 *New York Times* (December 26, 1974), 65–66.
34 Feder (1977), 7, 34.
35 Mares (1987), 4.
36 Haber et al. (2008), 73–74.
37 Castañeda (2011), 168.
38 Banco de México (2008), Cuadro A63; U.S. Department of State, Bureau of Western Hemispheric Affairs (2010).
39 México, INEGI (2007b); Haber (2008), 92.
40 Gallagher and Zarsky (2007), 3. Mexico's IT manufacturing activities date back to the 1940s and 1950s, when the country began to produce radios and televisions, as well as component parts. In Guadalajara, by the mid-1990s, during the IT boom, national firms worked alongside multinationals, and both sectors prospered. But when the multinationals retrenched or pulled out of Guadalajara after 2000, the Mexican firms practically disappeared.
41 Sturgeon and Kawakami (2010).
42 Haber et al. (2008), chapter 4; Weintraub (2010), chapter 3.
43 Rhoda and Burton (2010), 103.
44 See, for example, Laxer (1989); Hurtig (1991); Clarkson and Mildenberger (2011).

45 Geo-Mexico website, post #6455 (May 5, 2012); Tilly (2005), 196–2007; *Arizona Daily Star* (September 6, 2011), A15; *New York Times*, (April 21, 2012), (April 24, 2012), (May 17, 2012).
46 *Christian Science Monitor* (July 15, 1996); *Latin American Business Chronicle* (March 11, 2010); Office of the United States Trade Representative, www.ustr.gov; *Latin American Herald Tribune* (Caracas, Venezuela) (November 1, 2010).

9
LEGAL AND ILLEGAL TRADE

Trade is built on the principle of comparative advantage—meaning that, in order to participate efficaciously in trade, nations need to have an edge on supplying products that others want or need to buy. But having comparative advantage is far from enough to guarantee equitable returns from trade because of asymmetries in global interaction. Conducting profitable trade is dependent on whether sufficient opportunities are in fact available for exchanging products, and whether the right conditions truly exist for engaging in fair trade. Historical evidence shows that a level international playing field has not existed in world trade. The terms that have governed global trade have favored advanced countries and disadvantaged poor nations. Another issue for trading nations is the accessibility to other countries that can afford to buy foreign goods. The farther the distance separating trading partners the higher the cost of traded goods and the lower the returns. Thus remote countries, especially those that lack access to the sea, are at a great disadvantage when it comes to trade.

In the case of Mexico, a mixed picture emerges when foreign trade is examined from a development perspective. Mexico's comparative advantage historically has been in the exportation of raw materials and manufactured products assembled by low-wage workers. Imports have always been dominated by industrial goods requiring advanced manufacturing and complex technologies. Mexico's trade paradigm has not only placed Mexico in a subordinate position vis-à-vis the advanced countries with which it has conducted trade, but that model has not produced balanced development at home. That is not to say that trade, especially with the prosperous and physically proximate United States, has not brought benefits to Mexico. Indeed trade with the United States has generated substantial wealth in Mexico. The problem is that the bulk of the riches derived from trade have always gone to select sectors—namely, foreign and domestic corporations and well-placed Mexican merchants, industrialists, and owners of "shelter" companies. In assessing the significance of trade for Mexico, it is important to not lose sight of the reality that even though Mexico's situation for conducting trade has been better than that of many other developing countries, the overall context that has governed Mexico's interaction with the outside world has been far from ideal. Mexico's bargaining position has been weaker than that of its main trading partners, especially the United States. Foreign trade illustrates Mexico's high degree of external dependence more than any other form of external interaction.

This chapter surveys the history of Mexico's foreign trade, with an emphasis on interaction with the United States. For convenience sake, I will refer to legal trade as *conventional trade*, and to illicit trade as *contraband trade*. The contraband examined here consists of everyday consumer goods whose importation has been prohibited by Mexico or goods that Mexico has permitted for legal importation but that have entered the national territory without paying requisite duties.

Mexico's Foreign Trade in the Postindependence Period

Conventional Trade

One of the major challenges faced by Mexico upon independence in 1821 was intense foreign competition faced by the most important domestic manufacturing sector—the textile industry. The liberalized trading system established by Spain during the late colonial period had included a new policy in 1802 that allowed neutral countries to trade directly with New Spain. That decision opened the door to foreign textile traders who did great damage to the Mexican cotton and wool industries, especially during the chaotic wars of independence from 1810 to 1821. Major textile centers such as Mexico City, Puebla, and Guadalajara lost tens of thousands of jobs. After years of struggle against the foreign onslaught, sufficient recovery took root by the 1830s to once again allow domestic textiles to reclaim their preeminent place in Mexican industry.[1]

Structurally, the export-import paradigm that had functioned during the colonial period remained essentially the same in the postindependence years: precious metals and raw materials made up the products sent abroad, while manufactures made up most of the imported goods. Exports consisted mostly of silver, gold, copper, tin, cochineal, indigo, hides, vanilla, wood, and sugar, while imports consisted largely of textiles, yarn, clothing, tools, machinery, paper, iron, steel, wines, liquor, olive oil, spices, silk, and luxury items.

Like other nations at the time, Mexico imposed ad valorem tariffs on imports both to raise revenues for government operations and to protect domestic industries. Normally tariffs supplied between a third and a half of the government's revenues. The first tariff law in Mexico set an ad valorem tax of 25 percent on all imports and prohibited the importation of nine foreign products. The tariff increased sharply after 1823 and the number of prohibited imports rose as well. On the list of prohibited goods were products that competed with domestic goods, such as select manufactures, metals, textiles, cotton and woolen cloth, and timber, as well as a variety of foodstuffs. By the 1840s the ad valorem rate reached 45 percent and the number of prohibitions rose to about sixty items. The tariffs did not go unchallenged by those who advocated for open trade with the rest of the world, and a debate about trade ensued that often became quite contentious. On one side were those who wanted protectionism or prohibitionism; their ranks included industrialists, artisans, commercial interests, and cotton growers. Those who favored free trade included merchants who desired easier access to foreign goods in order to expand their merchandise offerings, and select industrialists who needed foreign inputs such as U.S. cotton for the manufacture of cloth.[2] In government circles, conservatives by and large favored higher tariffs and prohibitions, while liberals supported fewer trade restrictions.

Friction between Mexico and the United States over trade-related matters surfaced early on and has been a constant irritant to the present day. Mexico's protectionist and prohibitionist policies, as reflected in the nation's 1837 and 1842 tariff laws, frustrated U.S. officials and merchants, who felt that U.S. products had an inherent right to enter Mexican markets with minimum interference. Some Americans advocated aggressive diplomacy to pry open Mexican markets. Thus in 1847, at the time that war with Mexico raged on, U.S. Secretary of the Treasury R.J. Walker advised U.S. President James Polk that "[Mexico's commercial prohibitions] should not be permitted to continue." During the U.S. occupation of Mexico, the U.S. military in fact imposed de facto free trade, ignoring extant Mexican tariffs and allowing foreign products, especially from the United States, to flow into the country without restrictions. Enormous amounts of U.S. goods entered Mexico freely and merchandise moved within the country exempt from the *alcabalas* (taxes or transit fees) normally paid to municipalities or states. While the Mexican federal government lamented the loss of tariff revenues during the U.S. occupation, both Mexican and European merchants protested loudly over the damages done to their businesses.[3]

Contraband Trade

Toward the end of the Spanish colonial period, contraband was a paramount problem for New Spain at a time when foreign trade flowed more freely into Latin America than had been the case before. Illicit European textiles and other unauthorized products that entered New Spain in the early 1800s reportedly exceeded the production of the colony's *obrajes* by three or four times. In the 1810s, during Mexico's war of independence, French diplomats speculated that the value of illegal trade surpassed the value of legal trade by substantial amounts. Much of the prohibited merchandise that found its way into Mexico was manufactured in England, then transported to Jamaica, and finally distributed surreptitiously throughout Latin America.[4] Testimony rendered by many sources indicates that little changed with the passage of time.

After Mexico became a republic, government officials, intellectuals, industrialists, and businesspeople expressed alarm at the harm that contraband inflicted on the state in the form of unpaid customs duties and the damage done to vulnerable domestic industries that could not compete with cheap imports. In 1823 Mexico's Minister of Finance referred to contraband as "scandalous," "disastrous," and "punitive," and called smugglers "villains" and "traitors." Well-placed sources calculated that Mexico lost between 25 and 75 percent of all tariff revenues due to smuggling. In the latter 1820s, various industrialists concurred that the value of illicitly imported goods probably exceeded exports by two to one. Henry G. Ward, the British charge d'affaires, expressed his belief that contraband was "infinitely greater" than legal commerce. The U.S. minister to Mexico, Joel R. Poinsett, not only recognized the prevalence of the illicit trade but admitted significant complicity among Americans. "I regret to state that the organized system of smuggling, carried on by American vessels . . . justifies the officers of this [Mexico's] government in regarding with suspicion every vessel sailing under our flag," Poinsett wrote to U.S. Secretary of State Henry Clay in 1826.[5] Perhaps two-thirds of all imports from the United States between 1821 and 1845 entered Mexico illegally. Mexico's customs duties, which increased from an average of 25 percent in 1821 to 45 percent by the 1840s, provided a major incentive for smuggling.[6]

Contraband activities flourished not only on Mexico's coasts but on the northern land frontier as well. Starting in the late eighteenth century, when Spain still governed Mexico, illicit merchandise from the United States dribbled steadily into Texas, New Mexico, and California. By the time Mexico achieved its independence, legions of American traders and merchants, as well as Hispano entrepreneurs from New Mexico, utilized well-established routes such as the Santa Fe Trail to introduce a variety of bootleg manufactures into Mexican soil.[7] In the late 1820s a European American trader commented that in an eighteen-month period U.S. merchants had smuggled furs worth over 100,000 pesos into Mexico. Consumers in San Luis Potosí could buy illicit British goods at half the legal price and, in the mining town of Catorce, they could purchase such foreign products as "French and English manufactures, Spanish wines, Havana and Virginia tobacco, Catalan paper, mantas and furniture from the United States—all articles smuggled in through the port of [Matamoros]."[8]

Smuggling into Mexico increased substantially after 1837 with the passage of laws that prohibited the importation of cotton textiles and other consumer products. Unscrupulous businesspeople stepped up their contraband operations, while honest Mexican industrialists complained bitterly of their inability to sell their products. Interestingly, numerous businesses run by large foreign concerns kept expanding, suggesting deep involvement in unauthorized commerce on the part of Europeans and Americans based in Mexico. The British stood out in the conduct of smuggling transactions, especially those involving cotton and cotton cloths. For example, a brisk trade in cotton blankets manufactured in Manchester, England, sprouted in Yucatán. The contraband blankets traveled through the jungles of British Honduras into Mexican territory, and once in Yucatán they sold at 40 percent below the normal price. Other products originating in England that wound up in Mexico included iron and steel goods, stoneware, and crockery, while Spain supplied condiments, wines, and paper, and France introduced products similar to those of Spain in addition to textiles.[9]

The difficulty of controlling contraband intensified during and after the U.S.–Mexico War of 1846–1848. The free-flowing trade imposed by the U.S. occupation forces became institutionalized as American and Mexican merchants capitalized on lucrative opportunities and Mexican consumers became accustomed to acquiring foreign products at reduced prices.

The Altered Border and Trade Patterns, 1848 to 1880

Conventional Trade

After the war, Mexico's renewed effort to collect tariffs on imports provoked opposition from American interests. In 1855 James Gadsden, the negotiator of the Gadsden Purchase, called on the U.S. government "to kill [Mexican barriers to trade] outright and to secure guarantees against their resurrection."[10] U.S. advocates for low tariffs in Mexico ignored the protectionist policies of their own government; in fact, the United States maintained high tariffs during most of the nineteenth century. In late 1820s, for example, U.S. tariffs had averaged over 50 percent. Although significant declines took place in subsequent years, by the late 1860s U.S. tariffs would rise once again to the 50 percent range, generally staying at or near that level for decades afterward.[11]

In reality, Mexican tariffs could be evaded rather easily. Foreign merchants could introduce their products into Mexico without paying duties simply by bribing customs officials or getting duty "exemptions" from the government. Referring to President's Santa Anna's practice of granting such exemptions, the U.S. consul in Veracruz wrote in 1854 that "[the] Tariff is not a rigid law in the Republic . . . His Most Serene Highness violates it constantly by selling exclusive privileges."[12] With the ascension of the liberals into power after Santa Anna vacated the presidency, Mexico moved in the direction of trade liberalization. That policy change precipitated a significant rise in imports of cotton manufactures from the United States and pleased American merchants who had longed desired to have convenient access to Mexican markets.[13]

After the defeat of Emperor Ferdinand Maximilian by Benito Juárez's forces and the restoration of the republic in 1867, Mexico's foreign trade began to increase in a significant way. Various developments explain the favorable turn of events: Domestic political conditions stabilized, and Mexican commodities became more attractive abroad as industrialization speeded up in Europe and North America. Land freight costs dropped dramatically with the construction of railroads in many countries, including in Mexico itself, and finally overseas shipping became much less expensive with the emergence of faster, more efficient, and cheaper sailing vessels and steamboats.

Between 1872 and 1876, the overall value of Mexico's exports averaged $27 million dollars annually, with Mexico's products mostly going to the United States, England, and France. Precious metals made up 81 percent of Mexico's exports; other products included cochineal, wood, hides, skins, coffee, and fibers. Imports consisted largely of manufactured consumer goods and technology. Textiles, most of which originated in England, made up 54 percent of Mexico's imports. Iron and steel also came from England and hardware from Germany. France supplied wines and spirits and Spain sent olives and olive oil. The United States provided railway engines and cars, agricultural machinery, and various types of processed foodstuffs, including flour and canned goods.[14] Mexico sought to protect its fledgling industries with import duties that averaged about 50 percent, but of course many products were smuggled into the country and evaded the tariffs.

In the latter 1870s, the long-standing debate between Mexican free traders and protectionists (including prohibitionists) reached a crescendo.[15] Two basic questions dominated the discussion, just as they had as far back as the 1820s: How high should tariffs be? And what products should be prohibited from entering Mexico? Both sides forcefully presented their cases in the press and in the chambers of Congress. Free traders argued that protectionism encouraged inefficient production, led to monopolies, and fostered contraband. The higher the tariffs, they maintained, the more contraband entered the country and the more revenues the government lost. Protectionists countered that high tariffs and the prohibition of select imports were necessary to allow infant industries to develop and flourish in Mexico, thus safeguarding the nation's manufacturing sector and securing desirable jobs for Mexican workers. Protectionists also pointed out that, without high tariffs, government revenues would fall. One Mexican advocate of protectionism dismissed free trade as inappropriate for a struggling country like Mexico, declaring, "There are utopias that dazzle as much as they injure; the free-trade doctrine . . . is not only unrealistic but absurd and even ignoble. Free-trade fantasies have been dreamed by well to do economists in productive and rich countries."[16] The 1880 tariff law, which favored domestic industries, indicates that protectionists emerged as the victors of the debate.[17]

Contraband Trade

Reestablishment of Mexican tariffs after the U.S.–Mexico War only increased the attractiveness of illegitimate commerce, raising the stakes for a frail federal government and for weakened domestic manufacturers. Smugglers had a decided advantage because of the practical impossibility of controlling the flow of goods along the sparsely populated 2,000-mile new border between Mexico and the United States and along the equally isolated and weakly protected lengthy Mexican coastlines on the Pacific, the Gulf of California, and the Gulf of Mexico. Such conditions facilitated the further institutionalization and strengthening of armies of unscrupulous merchants and scores of dishonest officials eager to profit from smuggling operations. Reacting to the rise in illicit trade, Mexico's Department of Colonization and Industry in 1849 warned of the impending ruin not only of Mexican industry but of the government itself, given that revenues from customs duties, on which Mexico City depended heavily to run the country and to maintain the public order, had declined so drastically.[18] The following year Finance Minister Manuel Payno underlined the point that contraband activity had spread throughout Mexico, citing the plentiful availability of prohibited goods on the northern frontier and in central Mexico. "There is not one legislator or government official who does not know where they are sold."[19]

Mexican officials sought to mitigate smuggling by implementing various policy measures, including banning foreign vessels from coastal shipping, strengthening port inspections, tightening customs administrative procedures, adding customs personnel, and replacing corrupt revenue agents with honest ones. The government also periodically dispatched roaming patrols to the northern frontier, charging them with detecting smuggling operations and intercepting contraband shipments. Plans also existed to patrol coastal waters with a fleet of customs boats, but a lack of resources doomed the project.[20]

Besides the challenge of stopping smuggling at the largely unguarded land borders and coastlines, Mexico had to contend with U.S. merchants who felt entitled to openly take their merchandise into Mexico without paying duties. If challenged by Mexican authorities, the merchants would request intervention from the U.S. government. U.S. merchant Samuel A. Belden asked for such intercession in his effort to recover 565 bales of tobacco confiscated by Mexican authorities, pointing out that he and others had been "induced to engage in a very extensive business in Mexico" by U.S. officials at the time of the 1847–1848 occupation and had been "promised protection." Belden, who valued his loss at $500,000 dollars, was ultimately awarded $128,000 but also fined $26,000 by a magistrate in Nuevo León.[21] A dozen other U.S. merchants submitted similar claims, presumably ending with comparable outcomes as Belden.

For the Mexican government, the urgency of curbing smuggling derived from the need to collect tariffs. In the 1850s, more than three-fifths of the central government's revenues came from tariffs.[22] Mexico's heavy reliance on tariff revenues was not out of the ordinary. Other countries, including the United States, likewise followed the practice of financing governmental operations largely from the collection of customs duties. But Mexico, unable to secure its northern border and its coastlines, could collect only a fraction of the duties to which it was entitled.

At the Rio Grande, the unique economic conditions that unfolded after the war gave rise to highly organized contraband operations that kept getting more sophisticated as time passed. The designation of that river as the international border in 1848 disadvantaged the Mexican border communities in relation to counterpart U.S. border towns, whose commercial establishments were now directly connected to the powerful U.S. economy. Mexican *fronterizos* (borderlanders) immediately saw their cost of living rise dramatically because they now had to pay Mexican tariffs on goods imported from the U.S. side. They, as well as people who resided farther south within the states of Chihuahua, Coahuila, Nuevo León, and Tamaulipas, historically had been dependent on many basic necessities produced in Texas when that province belonged to Spain and then to Mexico. In response to the drastically changed economic circumstances after the war, exporters, importers, shopkeepers, store owners, and consumers on both side of the border found myriad ways to avoid Mexico's tariffs. U.S. communities like Rio Grande City, Roma, Eagle Pass, Laredo, and Brownsville, and Mexican towns like Nuevo Laredo, Mier, Camargo, Roma, and Matamoros became centers for the large-scale distribution of contraband to local markets and to the interior of Mexico.

Reacting to complaints from borderlanders regarding the high cost of living on the border and wishing to help honest local merchants stay in business, for a time the Mexican government lowered the tariffs for select basic products. The new policy, however, proved insufficient to bring the desired level of relief. Many local people felt the best solution would be for Mexico City to allow goods from the United States to enter their communities tariff-free, or at least subject to nominal duties. The central government, however, rejected that idea and attempted instead to force compliance to the treasury laws. Free trade on the border would not become a reality for a few more years.

In 1850 Mexican federal officials created the Contraresguardo de Gendarmería Fiscal with the intent of eradicating the contraband trade that flourished throughout northeastern Mexico. This initiative was reminiscent of the 1830s, when Mexico City had used the military to block trade between *norteños* (northerners) and the insurgent Republic of Texas. Contraresguardo agents intercepted and inspected trade caravans and searched businesses and residences suspected of being part of the vast contraband network. Such actions provoked a hostile reaction among a population long accustomed to importing, selling, and buying extralegal merchandise. Numerous confrontations broke out between the federal agents and townspeople in various communities in Nuevo Leon, requiring the intervention of state and local officials, whose sympathies were with the people and not the federal government.[23] The assumption of power in Mexico City by the liberals in the mid-1850s led to less protectionist trade policies and less aggressive efforts to curtail smuggling, reducing some of the tensions in the borderlands.

On the largely wide open Pacific and Gulf of California coasts, contraband activity went on as it had for generations. Smuggling played a prominent if not decisive role in the economies of port cities such as Guaymas, Mazatlán, San Blas, and Acapulco. "Contraband was a fact of life on the west coast," historian John Mayo writes. "Trade was based upon it, merchants regarded it as an everyday matter, and officials depended upon it: whether they accepted bribes, or had their salaries paid from advances made to government by the merchants/contrabandists, their everyday needs were indirectly supplied by the working of the system."[24]

The Mexican government was particularly concerned about the unsanctioned and untaxed exportation of gold and silver. With perhaps 30 to 40 percent of all exported precious metals bypassing Mexican customs controls, the Mexican treasury lost millions of pesos every year in uncollected levies. The heavy involvement of the British in the illicit exportation of precious metals was well known. "All the English merchants gain enormously from the immense contraband trade which is carried on along the whole of our coast," commented Minister of Foreign Relations José Fernando Ramírez in 1852. "This contraband traffic continues on a large scale and to the incalculable injury of the [Mexican] government, and also of the English creditors, on account of the fraudulent exportations of silver which are constantly made in the harbours of the Pacific under the protection of the British flag."[25]

In Mexico's far northwestern frontier, the influx of smuggled goods steadily increased with the arrival of more Americans in Arizona following the signing of the Gadsden Treaty in 1853. The remoteness of Sonora and Baja California made it easy for both American and Mexican merchants with unscrupulous leanings to use the borderlands for contraband trafficking. In the 1860s Americans audaciously established a town, Puerto Isabel, at the mouth of the Colorado River, clearly in Mexican territory and in defiance of Mexican authorities. The Mexican government's attempts to take control of the port were thwarted by Americans who acted as if the town were on U.S. soil, even expelling the Mexican customs official and executing three of his employees in 1870. U.S. troops based in Yuma freely patrolled the area and kept watch over the Americans living in Puerto Isabel. The port served as a depot for the shipment of goods both into the United States and into the interior of Mexico for about a decade, but eventually decline set in with the arrival of the railroad in the region in 1877. Because of the distances, the desert terrain, and the dangers from bandits and hostile Indians, most likely most of the contraband that flowed into Sonora originated not on the northern border but in the Pacific and Gulf of California coastal towns, where, as pointed out above, smuggling operations were well institutionalized. Textiles and clothing made up most of the contraband. As time went by, a wide variety of foodstuffs such as rice, sugar, nuts, chocolate, canned fish, meat, and fruits became increasingly popular.[26] As elsewhere, the illicit traffic in northwestern Mexico deprived the Mexican government of needed revenues and undermined legitimate commerce and industry, yet it kept the underground economy humming and brought benefits to consumers.

In the Lower Rio Grande Valley, a new challenge in the fight against contraband emerged in the late 1850s when the state of Tamaulipas responded to renewed pressures from the citizenry to allow the importation of foreign products into the border region without the payment of duties. At the time, Mexican states enjoyed greater autonomy to make such decisions, and governor Ramon Guerra in 1858 declared the Tamaulipas border area a free-trade zone, or a Zona Libre. Keenly aware of the potential that the Zona Libre would create opportunities for increased smuggling, Governor Guerra appealed to his countrymen to prevent that from happening. In article 8 of the Zona Libre decree, he admonished that "it is the duty of the inhabitants of the frontier to prevent, by all the means in their power, this privilege from being converted into a shameful smuggling traffic; it is, therefore the duty of every inhabitant of the frontier voluntarily to become a sentinel, constantly on the watch to prevent smuggling; otherwise, the Government will be under the painful necessity of withdrawing this privilege, by revoking the present decree."[27] As things would turn out, most borderlanders would neither consider it their "duty" to assist the authorities in preventing smuggling nor become "sentinels" for the government. First and foremost, borderlanders would look out for their own interests and seek the best deals available in purchasing consumer goods, having few scruples should such products be of illegal origin. Contrary to Governor Guerra's warning that smuggling would bring about an end to the Zona Libre, borderland free trade went on for years.

Under the Zona Libre products from the United States, Europe, and Asia could be imported duty-free into the Tamaulipas border communities, with the proviso that such goods must only be consumed locally. Predictably, much of the untaxed foreign merchandise wound up in Mexico's interior because it could now be warehoused at the border indefinitely, allowing smugglers to pick the most convenient time to send goods illegally to contacts in Saltillo, Monterrey, and other interior cities. But some of the merchandise that entered the Zona Libre, especially goods from Europe, also made its way into the United States without incurring U.S. duties. The amount of foreign goods that entered Tamaulipas increased substantially during the U.S. Civil War when, as a result of the Union blockade of Southern ports, merchants from the Confederacy used Matamoros and other Mexican towns to export their cotton and other products abroad. Both honest and dishonest merchants made fortunes during this period of commercial boom on the border.

In the 1870s, the Mexican government increased the number of border guards and tightened up bureaucratic procedures for handling the flow of merchandise into and beyond the Zona Libre. Anyone introducing contraband into Mexico faced stricter regulations, more paperwork, and stiffer penalties. Even mistakes in the documentation pertaining to goods traveling to the interior could result in a doubling of the established tariffs.[28] But the government's efforts had little effect and smuggling continued to thrive.

Protectionism and the Drive to Industrialize, 1880 to 1920

Conventional Trade

Economic growth accelerated in Mexico during the last two decades of the nineteenth century with the simultaneous international rise in demand for raw materials and Mexico's own efforts to expand railway infrastructure in order to increase capacity to exploit the nation's resources. By 1898, Mexico had 8,000 miles of railroad tracks in place, compared to only 670 in 1880.[29] On the industrialization front, the government implemented a policy of import substitution based on selective protectionism. For example, in the period 1889 to 1990 the average tariff for all imports was 43 percent, but it was much higher for specific items, including crystal and china (111 percent), cotton goods (106 percent), wool and silk fabrics (99 percent), paper products (85 percent), groceries and foodstuffs (78 percent), iron and steel (74 percent), and drugs and chemicals (60 percent).[30] In subsequent years the government included additional industrial sectors under the umbrella of protectionism, favoring especially newly launched manufacturing ventures. José Y. Limantour, the head of the Hacienda (Finance) Ministry from 1893 to 1911, maintained that pragmatic development, rather than trade ideology, should drive Mexico's policies. Although inclined toward free trade, Limantour felt that fledgling industries in a country like Mexico needed long-term protection carried out with "correct measure and good judgment." Protectionism would enable Mexico "to supply itself by producing its own sugar, most of the cotton consumed, different types of cloth, articles made from steel and many other objects, at the same time providing jobs to many thousands of women and men, with salaries three or four times higher than those in the countryside."[31]

The protectionist policies of the Porfirio Díaz regime led to advances in domestic manufacturing as the import-substitution strategy paid dividends. Foreign consumer goods dropped from 75 percent of all imports when Díaz first assumed office in 1876 to only 43 percent when he vacated the presidency in 1911.[32] Yet for all its successes, Mexican industry at the turn of the twentieth century consisted mostly of handcrafted goods and processed foodstuffs, and manifested weaknesses typical of manufacturing in emerging economies, including inefficiencies, high production costs, lack of access to capital, and low labor productivity. A major problem was that, apart from select products like hats and processed tobacco, most Mexican industrial goods were not competitive beyond the Mexican market.

The reality of noncompetitiveness unsettled a commission of export-minded Mexican textile manufacturers and merchants representing thirty companies who traveled to South America in 1902 with the intent of finding new markets for their products. Their first challenge was getting to South America. Since Mexico lacked a merchant marine, they had to depend on foreign ships, which first took them to the United States, then to England, and finally to Brazil, where they began their tour. They discovered that intense competition existed in Latin America for textiles and, that just like Mexicans, Brazilians and other Latin Americans protected their own industries with high tariffs, which of course drove up the cost of Mexican goods, which were high to begin with because of the elevated costs of production in Mexico and because of the high cost of shipping. The commissioners returned home disappointed but better informed about Mexico's dim prospects of tapping into international markets.[33] In short, it was unrealistic to expect that an industrially challenged country like Mexico could successfully sell its manufactured goods abroad, with a few minor exceptions. Mexico's consumer-oriented industries by necessity concentrated on satisfying domestic needs.

The boom in foreign trade that Mexico experienced from 1880 to 1910 rested on the expanded exportation of agricultural products and minerals and the increased capacity to import needed capital goods and other products.[34] In comparison to earlier trends, significant diversification took place during the Porfiriato in both the export and import sectors. By the early 1900s the export of precious metals dropped below 50 percent of all exports as the price of silver, traditionally Mexico's most important export, declined drastically in the international market. Increasingly products such as henequen, coffee, rubber, vanilla, chicle, sisal, tobacco, peas, and garbanzos assumed greater prominence among Mexico's exports, and on the eve of the Mexican Revolution, trade with the United States dramatically illustrated Mexico's dependence on its northern neighbor. Between 1877 and 1910, the percentage of all exports destined for the United States had risen from 42 to 76 percent. Like exports, imports also expanded appreciably, and the United States became Mexico's major supplier, accounting for 55 percent of all imports by 1910. Some important changes in the composition of imports took place as well. Because of Mexico's ability to manufacture more goods, such products as textiles, vegetable materials, alcoholic beverages, paper, arms, and explosives declined as a proportion of overall imports. Materials needed to sustain the country's expanding industrialization increased as a percentage of total imports; processed iron and copper, coal, coke, tin, chemicals, electrical goods, vehicles, and machinery are examples of imports meant to support domestic factories and the transportation sector. Select consumer imports such as yarns, woolens, leather goods, and preserved meats also rose in importance as Mexico's middle and elite sectors purchased more foreign goods.[35]

As indicated earlier, the building of the railroads in Mexico from the 1870s to the 1900s had an enormous impact on foreign trade. Reliable, inexpensive, and speedy transportation finally connected many resource-rich districts, processing zones, production centers, and consumer markets directly with each other and with the United States. Thus the new railroad infrastructure precipitated a great surge in the volume of raw materials and agricultural products that flowed between Mexico and its northern neighbor. Interestingly, the fact that mining exports made up such a large percentage of commodities transported by the railroads underlines the reality that mine owners, who tended to be foreigners, appropriated the lion's share of the benefits generated by railroad construction.[36]

Along Mexico's northern border the local economy functioned largely as an appendage of the U.S. economy, with communities such as Matamoros, Nuevo Laredo, and Ciudad Juárez heavily dependent on American goods. Responding favorably to petitions from borderlanders for elimination of tariffs on the border because of isolation from Mexico's centers of production, in 1858 the state of Tamaulipas had established a border free-trade zone known as the Zona Libre. Chihuahua had done the same. Then in 1885 the Porfirio Díaz government decreed the entire northern border a federal Zona Libre. As detailed in the next section, the return of free trade would increase both legal and illegal commerce and, at the same time, precipitate binational friction.

The violence unleashed by the Mexican Revolution after 1910 inevitably hurt foreign trade, but some sectors were affected more than others. For example, the value of imports dropped by 22 percent between 1910–1911 and 1918, but the value of exports actually rose 18 percent from 1912–1913 to 1918. The export of silver fluctuated wildly as a result of production interruptions and price declines. Output of silver averaged about 70 million troy ounces between 1907 and 1914 but dropped precipitously to only 23 million troy ounces in 1916. Although silver production bounced back to 63 million troy ounces in 1918, it remained below the level recorded a decade earlier. The top five exports to the United States from July 1918 to January 1919 included silver, copper, lead, gold, and cotton.[37] With respect to oil, by 1921 Mexico had become the third largest producer in the world, generating over 193 million barrels that year.[38]

Contraband Trade

With the federal Zona Libre in full swing after 1885, the duty-free importation of foreign goods into the Mexican border region boosted smuggling into the interiors of both Mexico and the United States and sparked a new round of acrimonious debates. Mexican merchants complained bitterly that contraband was ruining their businesses, while American merchants demanded an end to the Zona Libre because illicit merchandise inevitably made its way into U.S. soil. In his 1892 article published in *The North American Review*, Matías Romero addressed the concerns of Americans who considered the Zona Libre a Mexican act of hostility against the United States. Romero, who actually advocated for the abolition of the Zona Libre, acknowledged the damage the institution inflicted on U.S. merchants who conducted their businesses in a lawful fashion. Nevertheless, he informed U.S. readers that the injury to Mexico was ten times greater than that done to the United States because smuggling could be conducted much easier in Mexico, and the costs to the Mexican government of trying to prevent it far surpassed those in the United States. Romero also reminded Americans of advantages that the Zona Libre bestowed on U.S. commerce: "It practically makes a portion of Mexico a free market for all products and manufactures of the United

States, since [U.S.] merchandise of all kinds . . . may be imported into and consumed on Mexican territory duty free, and be warehoused in the region of the zone for an unlimited time."[39]

Eventually opponents of the Zona Libre prevailed. The Díaz government gradually raised duties at the border, imposed numerous restrictions on trade transactions, and finally eliminated the controversial institution entirely in 1905. These developments inconvenienced the contraband community, but its members quickly adjusted to the new circumstances and kept illicit goods flowing into Mexico.

An unprecedented development in border smuggling took place during World War I when the United States prohibited the exportation of sugar and other foods, strategic materials, and many manufactured goods. Inevitably that policy precipitated trafficking of the forbidden products into Mexico. "Smuggling has suddenly become an avocation of thousands of Mexicans of the lower class upon both sides of the Rio Grande," reported the *Los Angeles Times* in 1918. "It is stated by United States customs officials and government river guards that never before in the history of the border was there such activity in crossing contraband goods and commodities into Mexico as at this time. While the actual smuggling is done chiefly by the peon element of Mexicans, they are known to be in the employ of merchants and other business interests."[40]

The most profitable contraband activity throughout the 1910s was arms smuggling, as the demand for weapons skyrocketed in Mexico during the era of the Mexican Revolution. Illicit arms trafficking from the United States into Mexico of course was nothing new; it had gone on for generations, with arms sales rising and falling in accordance with the fluctuating political climate of Mexico. Such cities as San Antonio and El Paso had long hosted the black market transnational arms trade and, during the Revolution, U.S. businesspeople based in those two communities supplied revolutionaries with enormous quantities of rifles, machine guns, ammunition, and other war materiel. In El Paso, the Shelton-Payne Arms Company and the firm of Krakauer, Zork, and Moye distinguished themselves as premier "merchants of death," as two border historians have characterized these establishments.[41] Frequently arms dealers played a direct role in arranging for the smuggling of the deadly payloads into Mexico, all despite U.S. neutrality laws and arms embargoes imposed by the U.S. government against different Mexican revolutionary factions, as well as efforts by Mexican authorities to thwart the smuggling operations. With the help of crooked merchants and sundry supporters and sympathizers, Pancho Villa and other rebels easily circumvented the restrictions and secured their prized merchandise. Thus, while American arms dealers cashed in on booming sales, while middlemen made handsome commissions, and while Mexican insurgents carried on their struggles for power in Mexico, hundreds of thousands of Mexicans perished from warfare sustained by arms contraband predominantly originating in the United States.

U.S.–Mexico Trade Relations, 1920 to 1980
Conventional Trade

While the political situation in Mexico improved significantly after the Mexican Revolution, economic conditions fluctuated in accordance with international circumstances. In 1920 Mexico seemed on its way to recovery when the value of exports far surpassed the value of imports. In subsequent years, however, international demand for the country's exports dropped substantially, causing export revenues to decline from $344 million in 1926 to only $97 million by 1932, at the height of the Great Depression. Oil in particular was hard hit as rising petroleum output in Texas, California, and Venezuela seriously cut into Mexico's exports. Oil production in Mexico plunged from 193 million barrels in 1921 to 33 million in 1932. While in 1932 Mexico still retained a positive trade balance, the value of both exports and imports was substantially below that of a decade earlier. Recovery from the Great Depression eventually set in by the mid-1930s as demand for Mexico's natural resources picked up once again. By 1938, minerals made up about 80 percent of Mexico's exports, agricultural goods 15 percent, and manufactured products 5 percent. As World War II got underway, exports rose dramatically. In 1944, Mexico once again recorded a positive trade balance.[42]

In the post–World War II period Mexico faced an unfavorable situation as the value of imports skyrocketed, surpassing the value of exports. That necessitated revision of a 1942 reciprocal treaty with the United States that had given both countries relatively open access to each other's markets. The imbalance developed in Mexico because of a postwar reduction in the demand for natural resources in the United States, while U.S. finished goods entered Mexico in ever-rising quantities. Negative trade balances were recorded by Mexico in 1946, 1947, and 1950.[43] Mexico sought to impose new tariffs on imports to correct the problem, hoping the United States would not object. However, the United States, which by then had become the prime proponent of global free trade, resisted Mexico's proposal. Frustrated and anxious to balance its trade and to push along its domestic industrialization agenda, Mexico proceeded to impose what it felt were necessary restrictions on imports. In 1947, Mexico set an average tariff of 50 percent on about 5,000 foreign consumer goods and completely prohibited the importation of many items. On the other hand, needed foreign products such as raw materials and capital goods commanded low tariffs, ranging from 5 to 15 percent.[44] To further reduce imports, Mexico required importers to obtain licenses. In 1956, 28 percent of total imports were subjected to licensing, and that figure escalated to 65 percent by 1965.[45]

Meanwhile, Mexico's exports to the United States encountered barriers. Despite its free-trade advocacy, the United States maintained some tariff and nontariff restrictions that adversely affected Mexico and other Latin American countries. U.S. import duties averaged 11 to 25 percent for products like wool, wheat, and corn, and exceeded 25 percent on cotton, some vegetables and fruits, flaxseed, sugar, cigars, zinc, and lead. The United States further restricted imports by using devices such as excise taxes, sanitary regulations, quotas, and licensing requirements. "Probably many of the Latin-American countries would benefit by a removal of [U.S.] duties on their exports," wrote Paul V. Horn and Hubert E. Bice in 1949. "Some export advantages might very readily accrue to Mexico if we removed restrictions on the importation of live cattle, zinc, lead, copper, and petroleum."[46]

In 1951, Mexico and the United States amicably agreed to let the 1942 trade treaty expire. The lack of a formal agreement, however, had minimal impact on bilateral trade, with products flowing across the border in ever-increasing amounts. By the late 1950s the United States received about three-quarters of all Mexican exports. Overall, metals and other raw materials made up 24 percent of Mexico's exports, agricultural and livestock products 64 percent, and manufactures and semimanufactures 12 percent. Because the value of imports surpassed that of exports every year during the 1950s and 1960s, Mexico normally would have had a balance of payments problem. However, revenues earned from foreign tourism, border transactions, and remittances from Mexicans working in the United States offset the imbalance.[47] During the period, internal economic diversification made it possible for the Mexican government to expand the domestic sources of revenue collection, relying less and less on import duties to support state expenditures. In 1965, only 16 percent of government revenues came from tariffs, significantly down from 44 percent in 1910. Mexico now used tariffs to protect domestic industries and only secondarily for channeling funds into the public coffers.[48]

By the mid-1970s, with the discovery of new oil deposits in Mexico's Gulf region, petroleum exports rose substantially, and by the end of the decade extractive materials comprised about 68 percent of Mexico's exports. With oil as the driving force behind the country's expanded trade, the value of Mexican exports to the United States rose fivefold between 1975 and 1980, while the value of imports went up threefold.[49]

But controversy broke out between the two neighbors during the late 1970s over the price of petroleum and natural gas. The United States, wishing to become less dependent on Middle Eastern oil, sought to increase imports of energy resources from Mexico, but Mexico demanded higher prices than the United States was willing to pay. A series of missteps and misunderstandings in delicate negotiations led to mutual accusations of lack of good faith in arriving at a suitable compromise. Mexican leaders concluded that the only thing that arrogant U.S. officials desired was to buy Mexico's oil and gas as cheaply as possible, while the United States felt that Mexican officials let exaggerated nationalistic ideology cloud their decision-making. In the end, the feuding neighbors reached an understanding, and president José López Portillo ordered increased exports of natural gas to the United States. Mexico felt compelled to put aside nationalistic sentiments given the need for U.S. cooperation on other issues such as migration, credit, investment and, in particular, trade. The fact that in the mid-1970s the value of Mexico's imports from the United States was more than twice the value of Mexican exports to that country underscored the depths of Mexico's external dependence. This episode is a classic example of the atmosphere of distrust and suspicion that has historically characterized the U.S.–Mexico relationship, as well as the traditional weak bargaining position of Mexico in dealing with the United States.[50]

Apart from differences over oil and natural gas prices, other disagreements emerged when Mexico reduced its imports and at the same time expanded its exports, creating an unwelcome imbalance for the United States. Several factors created that imbalance. In the early 1980s Mexico's ability to buy imports plunged as a full-scale economic crisis shook the country. Currency devaluation made Mexico's exports cheaper and more attractive, and the volume of products destined for the United States increased. The expanded exports from Mexico predictably met resistance from American competitors, who accused Mexican exporters of unfair competition. Farmers in Florida and California constantly challenged the quality and suitability of Mexican fruits and vegetables and forced the U.S. government to institute quotas and to conduct periodic investigations of alleged Mexican "dumping."[51] Such U.S. tactics were not new. Over several decades U.S. growers had "succeeded in establishing, and then altering, tariffs, health and sanitary restrictions, pesticide and herbicide level restrictions, size and grade requirements, and other protectionist barriers in order to insulate their industry from Mexican agricultural imports."[52] And U.S. agricultural exporters themselves had a history of "dumping" goods on Mexico and other countries. The aggressive effort of U.S. growers to limit the amount of fruits and vegetables imported from Mexico into the United Sates was, and remains, a source of resentment among Mexicans.

From Mexico's point of view, the support given by Washington to domestic agricultural interests exemplified the indifference in the United States for fair trade. Mexicans felt that U.S. leaders did not sufficiently appreciate the generally unfavorable trade climate faced by developing countries, especially the harsh reality that prices for primary commodities usually rose at a lower rate than the cost of technology and finished goods. Mexico joined other developing nations in insisting that asymmetries in global trade justified concessions from the industrialized countries. The United States frequently took the position that Mexico and other poor countries expected preferential treatment without granting advanced nations reciprocal trade favors in return.

U.S. negotiators became especially frustrated with Mexico's reluctance to join GATT (General Agreement on Tariffs and Trade), rejecting Mexico's reasons for nonparticipation. Mexico claimed that bilateral agreements were a better alternative to GATT because the GATT system favored the interests of industrialized countries more than those of developing economies. Mexicans pointed to lack of guarantees in GATT against "dumping," a practice that advanced countries had utilized against poor nations in previous decades. Joining GATT not only would hurt Mexico economically, argued the Mexican government, but it would also cause serious internal political problems because powerful sectors of Mexican society viewed U.S. pressures on this issue as attempts to strip Mexico of its freedom to pursue independent economic policies. U.S. leaders responded that Mexico was getting a "free ride" because of its inclusion as a "most favored nation" among U.S. trading partners, and also because Mexico benefited from Washington's participation in the U.N.-created generalized system of tariff preferences (GSP) policy of permitting importation into advanced countries of select products from the Third World totally or partially duty-free. The GSP agreement dated from 1968, but the United States only began implementing it in 1976. Mexico indeed benefited from "most favored nation" status. Without belonging to GATT, Mexicans received whatever reductions in tariffs the United States granted to other countries that belonged to GATT. And many Mexican products entered the United States duty-free under the GSP program; such goods amounted to 7 percent of all U.S. imports from Mexico by the late 1980s. Yet Mexico felt the United States exaggerated the benefits of the GSP program, pointing out that, like other developing countries, Mexico at most derived modest gains because many of its products were excluded from the GSP list and those that did qualify frequently were quickly phased out or were subjected to quotas and other nontariff restrictions. For years Mexicans felt that U.S. products had far greater access to Mexican markets than Mexican products had to U.S. markets.[53]

Contraband Trade

The rise in legal trade spurred by the post-1920 improvement in U.S.–Mexico relations also precipitated a significant increase in contraband trafficking. Expansion of Mexico's middle class by the 1950s boosted the black market demand for many U.S. products, including foodstuffs, whisky, wines, cigarettes, clothing, furniture, appliances, automobiles, radios, televisions, record players, cameras, watches, calculators, and sundry luxury goods. The illicit merchandise that constantly entered Mexico seriously undermined the government's import substitution industrialization (ISI) regimen, the intent of which was to maintain a protectionist wall against unwanted foreign products through the use of prohibitions, restrictions, high tariffs, and import licenses. "At virtually every customs port in Mexico, be it seaport, airport or border crossing, contraband is as common as conversation," reported the *New York Times* in 1970. "So widespread is commerce beyond the law that many a legitimate importer has been forced into another line of business simply because he cannot compete...."[54]

On the U.S.-Mexico border, many shady business concerns and contraband rings from Brownsville-Matamoros to San Diego-Tijuana supplied local people as well as clientele from deep in Mexico with a great variety of smuggled goods at prices well below those of legally-imported merchandise. Trucks loaded with bulky bootleg products like ranges, refrigerators, freezers, washing machines, and television sets made regular runs from the border to cities like Monterrey, Saltillo, Torreon, Mexico City, and many others. Former Minister of Foreign Relations Jorge Castañeda recalled in 2010 how, like so many other Mexicans, a few decades earlier his family would make periodic trips to the U.S. borderlands that included shopping with nefarious intent.

> One of the main purposes of [these journeys] was to purchase *fayuca*: contraband electronics, food, clothes, gadgets of all sorts, unavailable in Mexico and quite accessible, price-wise, in the United States. Instead of the obsolete TV sets manufactured in our country, we could buy Sony Tinitrons; instead of rancid peanut butter, we could obtain Skippy; instead of highly flammable Terlenka windbreakers, we could don Members Only jackets. The only problem was how to get them into Mexico without paying duties (they were onerous) or excessive bribes (moderate ones were okay). The car or station wagon would be filled to the brim, with maybe a small television on top of everything, highly, even ostentatiously, visible. When we stopped at the secondary customs inspection, some twenty miles into Mexico, the on-duty official would make believe he was searching for drugs, guns, money, or high-value contraband, and all of a sudden, lo and behold, he would discover the small TV. With deep regret and shame, he would convey to us his irreversible decision to confiscate it, together with a stern warning to refrain from introducing forbidden goods into the county, since they took jobs away from Mexicans, and besides, "Lo hecho en México está bien hecho" (loosely translated: Mexican stuff should be good enough for you). And we would be on our way, with our *fayuca*, or American stuff, nicely stashed away under blankets, children, coats, and suitcases.[55]

Thousands, if not millions, of Mexicans, especially those living in the Mexican border cities and other parts of northern Mexico, have similar anecdotes. In his classic book *On the Border*, Tom Miller described the pervasiveness of the contraband business in Laredo, Texas, during the 1970s. Mexican customers who wished to have consumer goods delivered to their homes in Mexico simply paid an extra fee to cover the cost of smuggling and transportation. It cost $315 dollars to deliver a $1,125 television set and $150 to deliver an electric typewriter worth $825 to Mexico's interior. According to Miller, about 70 percent of all sales of television sets in Laredo in 1978 involved smuggling. After crossing the border clandestinely, merchandise made its way to different destinations in Mexico via highways and railways and, for high-cost luxury contraband, even onboard private airplanes owned and piloted by rogue Americans.[56] One of my informants from Sonora confided that just prior to their marriage in the mid-1970s, he and his fiancée followed the custom of many Mexican couples. They bought most of their household furnishings in a department store in Nogales, Arizona, and arranged for delivery directly to their new home in Guaymas, Sonora. Along with the cost of the goods, they paid a "transportation" fee that included bribes to be given to Mexican customs agents at the port of entry and at the interior checkpoint some twenty kilometers from the border. He added that every middle- and upper-class family he knew in Sonora furnished their homes mostly with U.S. products. Appliances, televisions, and some furniture pieces were particularly popular.[57]

Repeating an old familiar story that dated back to the early nineteenth century, Mexican business and industrial leaders complained time and again regarding the harm that smuggling did to their interests, insisting that the federal government had to do more to address the problem. And Mexico City responded as it had in previous generations, periodically cracking down on the contraband trade by firing corrupt customs agents, tightening up regulations, increasing vigilance in the nation's ports of entry on land and by the sea, and enacting "buy Mexican" campaigns. The Mexican government even "declared war" on smugglers in 1971. Officials estimated that half of the illicit goods that found their way into Mexico originated in the United States. Finance Minister Hugo Margain used the term "unpatriotic" to refer to the smugglers and their accomplices, including crooked customs agents who allowed contraband to enter Mexico in exchange for bribes.[58]

Notwithstanding government declarations, things changed very little, and contraband continued on as before. Popular new products like VCRs, movie videos, stereos, and audio cassettes were added to the growing list of smuggled merchandise. Tepito, the massive and notorious open-air marketplace in Mexico City, was the best place for consumers to obtain most of these items, and many others, at wholesale prices. Newspaper accounts from the late 1970s document the thriving black marketeering in Tepito and other places in Mexico.[59]

Trade Liberalization, 1980 to the Present

Conventional Trade

The structural conditions that had long shaped U.S.–Mexico bilateral trade changed radically when the historic economic crisis of the 1980s compelled Mexico to embrace neoliberalism and embark on the path toward free trade with the outside world. Between 1982 and 1985 the Mexican government slashed the maximum tariff rate from 100 percent to 25 percent and greatly reduced the number of imports subject to permits.[60] Then Mexico joined GATT in 1986 and dropped the average tariff rate to 10 percent two years later. The biggest step in trade liberalization took place in 1993, when Mexico became a partner of the United States and Canada in the tri-country North American Free Trade Agreement (NAFTA). In the ensuing decade Mexico entered into additional free-trade agreements with thirty other countries.

Trade liberalization has transformed Mexico's economy. Whereas in 1985 foreign trade (exports plus imports) accounted for only one-fifth of the nation's GDP, by 2010 it had grown to three-fifths of GDP and had become the major engine of growth.[61] Open trade has brought some impressive benefits to Mexico, including greater access to U.S. markets, significant diversification of exports, unprecedented growth in the export of manufactures, and expanded influx of foreign direct investment. During the decade and a half following the enactment of NAFTA, Mexican exports to the United States more than quadrupled, and U.S. imports into Mexico tripled. Most significantly, manufactures comprised more than 80 percent of Mexico's exports, confirming the success of Mexico's strategy of making industrial products the bulk of its exports. By comparison, agricultural products and food made up only 7.2 percent and fuel and ores only 11.5 percent of all exports respectively. Trade liberalization has also led to a drop in prices for many imported goods, benefitting especially middle- and upper-income consumers. Additionally, free trade has created new jobs in select regions of Mexico and brought prosperity to well-placed entrepreneurs, investors, brokers, and executives of companies connected to the U.S. economy.[62]

While the benefits of the new trade paradigm are numerous, there have been significant disappointments as well. Trade liberalization has done little to spur real GDP per-capita growth. The share of manufacturing in GDP actually dropped from over 23 percent in the late 1980s to under 19 percent in 2008 and, between 2000 and 2009, Mexico lost over 1 million manufacturing jobs.[63] The volume of NAFTA-related jobs has fallen far short of expectations, with maquiladoras absorbing too few of the unemployed or new workers entering the labor force. Most of the job growth that has taken place in Mexico is actually in microbusinesses, where employees earn low pay and enjoy few benefits, and in the informal sector, where "self-employed" individuals run makeshift businesses and others struggle to survive by shining shoes, hawking newspapers, or selling food, trinkets, cigarettes, and other such items. Wages in the formal sector have remained pitifully low, while unemployment has remained high. Between 1993 and 2007, the real minimum wage in Mexico fell by about 25 percent, and the gap between U.S. and Mexican manufacturing wages grew wider.[64]

NAFTA has also hurt small and independent farmers in Mexico and displaced large numbers of rural workers, many of whom joined the stream of undocumented migration to the United States. Poultry and hog farmers were particularly hard hit as U.S. companies captured significant shares of Mexican markets through the importation of U.S. animal products and also through the acquisition of existing Mexican operations. By 2001–2002 U.S.-based Tyson and Pilgrim's controlled 41 percent of Mexico's chicken production, while by 2010 Smithfield Foods captured 25 percent of pork sales in Mexico as tons of cheaper U.S. pork flooded the Mexican market, driving at least a third of Mexico's hog farmers out of business and eliminating 120,000 hog-growing jobs.[65] One study concludes that between 1997 and 2005 Mexican producers of eight key crops endured losses of nearly $13 billion dollars as a result of "dumping" of subsidized U.S. products on the Mexican market.[66] Mexican corn farmers were the hardest hit, absorbing almost half the losses. It is estimated that corn imports have resulted in the loss of 2 million jobs in Mexico. Disturbingly, imported food made up half the food consumed by Mexicans in 2002 and 43 percent in 2014.[67]

At a more generalized level, NAFTA has deepened Mexico's subordination to the United States. In 2006, 88 percent of Mexico's exports went to the United States, but only 14 percent of U.S. exports went to Mexico; 56 percent of Mexico's imports came from the United States, but only 11 percent of U.S. imports originated in Mexico.[68] The extremely high level of export reliance on one country means that Mexico's economic health is more dependent than ever on the fortunes of the powerful neighbor to the north. Mexicans often say that "when the United States sneezes, Mexico catches pneumonia." The truth contained in that statement was evident during the recessions of 2000 to 2001 and 2008 to 2010, when the Mexican economy endured severe declines triggered by depressed conditions in the United States. Another problem with NAFTA is that because the pact is full of trade restrictions and loopholes, in reality it has not given Mexico free access to the U.S. economy. American producers, particularly agricultural growers in California and Florida, have continued to employ nontariff protectionist measures such as import quotas, sanitary regulations, and exaggerated transportation safety requirements to block or diminish the entry of Mexican products into the U.S. market. Of course Mexico, too, has engaged in protectionist actions to mitigate negative impacts from NAFTA and has responded in kind to unfavorable measures enacted in the United States. In the most serious recent retaliatory action, Mexico imposed tariffs on thirty-six U.S. agricultural and fifty-three industrial products in early 2009 in response to the U.S. government's decision to cancel the pilot program that allowed Mexican trucks unrestricted use of American highways.[69]

As if conducting trade with the United States were not challenging enough, lately Mexico has faced aggressive competition from China's growing economic prowess. After China joined the World Trade Organization (WTO) in 2002, many of Mexico's manufacture exports, including high-technology exports, came under threat from the Chinese economy.[70] With wages more than 200 percent higher in Mexico than in China, numerous companies took their operations out of Mexico and into China. Mexico also lost market share to China in products imported by the United States, with China capturing 19 percent of the U.S. market by 2010, compared to Mexico's 12 percent. But then Mexico became much more wage-competitive with China and companies began returning to Mexico, illustrating the ever-present chase by the transnational corporations for countries that offer the lowest production costs.

A related problem is that Chinese-made goods entered Mexico in increasing amounts despite whopping Mexican tariffs on products such as shoes, apparel, and textiles. Between 2001 and 2011 Mexico tried to stop the flood of Chinese goods by imposing duties as high as 1,000 percent. However, Mexico's efforts did not work. In a few short years a highly unequal trade relationship developed between the two countries, exemplified by the fact that in 2004 Mexico imported $14 billion dollars worth of Chinese products, but China bought only $1 billion worth of Mexican goods.[71] "In the warren of stalls that spread out from the center of Mexico City, Chinese-made products abound—from illuminated wall plaques of Mexico's patron saint, the Virgin de Guadalupe, and children's backpacks to hair accessories and cosmetics," wrote journalist Jan Bussey in 2006.[72] Cheap Chinese imports have displaced hundreds of Mexican businesses and have forced many factories to shut down, with the textile, apparel, shoe, toy, and electronic industries absorbing the heaviest losses. The Mexican textile industry alone lost 35 percent of its jobs between 2000 and 2006. With the expiration of extant trade agreements with China at the end of 2011, Mexican duties dropped dramatically in 2012 to the 15 to 30 percent range. Vast quantities of formerly illicit Chinese goods began immediately to enter Mexico legally, intensifying the external pressures on Mexican manufacturing. By 2012 the value of Mexican exports to China stood at 10 percent of the value of Chinese exports to Mexico.[73]

Contraband Trade

When Mexico joined GATT in 1986, the government reduced tariffs on imports and removed many foreign products from the prohibited list, causing smuggling to assume a different character compared to previous eras. As duties were lowered to an average of 10 percent or less by 1988, consumers no longer had to resort to purchasing many foreign goods on the black market because these could now be bought legally at competitive prices. Imported toys from the United States, for example, became more popular than ever, much to the consternation of domestic manufacturers who found it very difficult to compete with U.S. toy companies. By late 1992 almost a third of Mexico's mainstream toy-making companies had gone out of business, "victims of Barbie Dolls, Cabbage Patch Dolls, Ninja Turtles and the like."[74] Contraband merchants across Mexico adjusted to the new reality, finding ways of offering customers a mix of illegal and legal items.

With the enactment of NAFTA in 1994, Mexico opened the door more widely to U.S. and Canadian merchandise, but countless items remained on the unauthorized list or remained subject to the payment of tariffs. For example, duties on foreign corn, sugar, and beans would not be phased out until 2008, and such goods continued to be smuggled from the United States into Mexico. In 1998 Mexican chicken growers loudly protested the illegal importation of chicken parts from the United States. The incentive to smuggle derived from the fact that under NAFTA importers had to pay a 240 percent duty for frozen or fresh chickens. "It's getting worse and worse," stated a poultry famer from Chihuahua. "We have watchers on the frontier who saw 15 trailers of the [illegal] stuff going through [the border] in two days."[75]

Used motor vehicles made in the United States continued to be imported illegally on a massive scale after the NAFTA signing in 1993, given that the easing of regulations pertaining to automobiles and trucks were not scheduled to take effect until 2006. That time lag caused the well-established black market trade in foreign vehicles to remain undisturbed, especially in the border area. The magnitude of the used car problem became clear in May 2000 when, following the enactment of a new policy authorizing the duty-free importation of ten-year old trucks, the owners of 300,000 cars and trucks that had previously entered Mexico as contraband openly demanded that their vehicles also be legalized—without penalty.[76] In response to the pleas of car owners and to relieve confusion at the border, in 2005, a year earlier than anticipated, the Vicente Fox administration started the process of removing extant restrictions against the importation of used vehicles into Mexico. By 2009 vehicles up to fifteen years old began to be imported under liberalized terms and in accordance with the NAFTA timetable.[77] The changes in the rules unquestionably benefitted consumers. Yet used car contraband trafficking did not end because remaining import duties, value-added taxes, and miscellaneous fees, as well as having to deal with dreaded bureaucratic procedures, still encouraged smuggling.

The textile sector provides another example of post-NAFTA contraband activities. The policy of allowing foreign fabrics to enter duty-free into Mexico for processing in export-oriented maquiladoras was easily abused. Mexican manufacturers, for example, complained in 2003 that unscrupulous importers were legally bringing in large amounts of loose fabric ostensibly destined for the maquiladora sector, when in fact the untaxed fabric wound up illegally in the hands of domestic manufacturers who then used it to make clothing for sale in Mexico.[78]

The proliferate and complex policies enacted to administer rapidly rising amounts of imports and exports have stimulated contraband as well. Regulations favorable to some sectors but unfavorable to others have encouraged many traders that lack free trade or "most favored nation" privileges to pay bribes to move their merchandise in and out of Mexico untaxed. Apart from having to master confusing regulations and variable tariffs that apply to different categories of importers, harried customs officials must also keep track of specialized rules such as those pertaining to import permits and "dumping."[79] Such a complex system guarantees circumvention of trade regulations.

Throughout the NAFTA period, the meaning of "free trade" has puzzled Mexican consumers who still encounter restrictions on the kind and amount of merchandise that they can import tax-free into Mexico. For example, in 2012, taxation on foreign liquor and tobacco products continued just like in the pre-NAFTA era, while such items as eggs, fresh fruits and vegetables, pet food, and live animals still appeared on the prohibited list. The duty-free importation allowance for foreign merchandise into Mexico's border areas was $75 dollars per person, except during the Christmas and Easter seasons, when the amount went up to $300, meaning there was often still a great cost to trade. During the periods of liberalized importation, individuals could introduce miscellaneous goods valued up to $3,000 ($4,000 for computers); using the $3,000 figure, the $300 duty-free allowance reduced the taxable amount to $2,700, which was subject to the standard value-added tax of 16 percent. Thus, in 2012 a consumer had to pay $432 for the privilege of importing $3,000 worth of foreign merchandise into Mexico.[80] Such restrictions, limits, and levies assured that the incentive for smuggling both on a large and small scale would remain a fact of life on the border.

China has also added to Mexico's contraband woes. U.S. soil has been used to smuggle many cheap Chinese component products (such as rolls of fabric) into Mexico, passing these off at border crossings as NAFTA-approved duty-free goods supposedly destined for maquiladoras. In addition, illegal Chinese merchandise has made its way into Mexico via the well-established corrupt pipeline in the Pacific seaports. Textiles, shoes, and toys have stood out among popular Chinese bootleg merchandise. To keep such items out of Mexico, between 2001 and 2011 the government enacted extremely high tariffs against Chinese products, exceeding 1,000 percent on some of them. Officials also cracked down on corrupt customs agents and their collaborators. The Vicente Fox administration replaced most of the seaport directors and fired about 80 percent of customs service employees. In addition, the government increased the budget of the customs service tenfold, raised employee salaries, and upgraded port inspections with sophisticated technology. Manzanillo, the main entry port for merchandise from China, received special attention because of its well-known reputation for pervasive smuggling. The Lázaro Cárdenas port is another facility overrun with illegal activity, prompting the government to send federal troops to oversee port operations in 2013.[81]

As protectionist agreements between the Mexico and China expired, duties against Chinese goods dropped drastically in Mexico in 2011. Remarkably, formerly surreptitious flows became normal legal trade by 2012.[82] During the decade that Mexico imposed the extraordinarily stiff tariffs on China, the profitability of Chinese merchandise was enormous, and of course that encouraged more smuggling. The amount of contraband confiscated by Mexican customs agents during the "crackdown" years represented but a fraction of the illicit merchandise that had entered Mexico not only from China but other countries as well. Referring to government efforts to stamp out smuggling, José Guzman Montalvo, the head of Mexico's customs service, commented in 2003: "We're like sweepers in [New York's] Central Park in the fall. We sweep all day but by the end of the day, the leaves have piled up again where we swept."[83]

Arms smuggling is another major contemporary concern for Mexico. Weapons can be openly purchased in the United States and easily taken into Mexico. Over the last two decades, and especially after 2006, when the Mexican government launched its all-out war on drugs, the importation of illicit U.S. arms proliferated. As pointed out earlier, arms smuggling on the U.S.–Mexico border has existed for generations. Foreign guns largely determined the course and outcome of the Mexican Revolution a century ago. Today illicit foreign guns, especially high-powered rifles and assault weapons such as AR-15s and AK-47s, give the advantage to Mexican drug cartels and other criminal organizations over the Mexican military and law enforcement agencies. The strictness and severity of Mexican gun laws have been totally ineffective in the face of the ready availability of ordinary handguns as well as combat weapons in the U.S. borderlands, and the ease with which these can be purchased and taken to Mexico. Mexican officials, as well as the U.S. Bureau of Alcohol, Tobacco, and Firearms, have estimated that between 80 and 90 percent of the guns used by Mexican criminal organizations originate in the United States, where practically anyone can buy weapons because of lax gun laws in many states. Such laws are grounded in the long-held popular belief in the United States that the U.S. Constitution gives all Americans the right to bear arms, an interpretation that has been upheld by the U.S. Supreme Court. As a result, U.S. gun sales and trafficking are big business—and plenty of weapons are smuggled into Mexico. After an exhaustive year-long investigation, the *Washington Post* identified in 2010 the top twelve dealers in the United States that supplied guns that eventually wound up in the hands of Mexican criminals. One was based in California, three in Arizona, and eight in Texas.[84] The ubiquitous contraband weapons have made Mexico's war on drugs far more violent and deadly than anyone expected, resulting in the destabilization of many regions of Mexico and the death of perhaps as many as 100,000 people during the period of 2007 to 2011.[85] Potent weapons have also strengthened the ability of criminal organizations to stay in business and to keep corrupting many of the public servants charged with maintaining order, including judges, prosecutors, and the police, especially at the municipal level. Low salaries make such employees, in particular the police, easy targets for corruption. Under these circumstances it is not hard to understand why the rule of law has collapsed in much of Mexico.

Conclusion

Foreign trade, both legal and illegal, has been a major driver of Mexico's economy since the country achieved independence in 1821. From that point on through the late nineteenth century, Mexico's exports consisted almost exclusively of agricultural products and precious metals, while its imports were dominated by capital goods and manufactured products, including consumer and luxury items. That pattern began to change in the 1890s when protectionism enhanced Mexico's capacity to produce more industrial goods, thus lessening the country's reliance on imported finished products. The strategy of replacing imported manufactures with Mexican-made merchandise continued for many decades, achieving significant success between the 1940s and 1970s, when Mexico managed to make notable strides in its efforts to industrialize and to satisfy many domestic consumer needs.

The structure of trade between Mexico and the United States was transformed when Mexico began to adopt the neoliberal model in the early 1980s. The near-collapse of the Mexican economy during the debt crisis and oil bust drove the government to abandon import substitution industrialization, to lower tariffs, and to join the world trading community through GATT. Free trade became institutionalized in 1994 with the enactment of NAFTA, a watershed pact that deepened Mexico's ties to the United States. With NAFTA, previously prohibited or highly taxed U.S. products could now enter Mexico legally, either completely duty-free or subject only to low taxes, while Mexico could now supply the U.S. market with an increasing number of Mexican-made goods under similar terms. Mexican consumers have benefitted from the easier availability of American products, but many Mexican firms have gone out of business because they cannot compete with cheaper foreign imports. NAFTA also made it easier to move component parts and other materials back and forth across the border for the benefit of the export-oriented maquiladora sector. Maquiladoras have become the backbone of Mexico's export industries, thereby contributing significantly to the nation's economy.

Contraband has been a major problem for Mexico for generations. In the nineteenth century rampant smuggling from both Europe and the United States held back advances in textile manufacturing and other sectors. With the passage of time, the United States became Mexico's leading trade partner—and its major source of smuggled goods. For most of the twentieth century illicit U.S.-made weapons, foodstuffs, clothing, technology, machinery, automobiles, appliances, furniture, entertainment products, electronic gadgets, and many other items kept domestic industries in an underdeveloped condition, reduced demand and profits for honest Mexican merchants, and deprived the Mexican government of considerable revenues. In the globalization age, NAFTA has reduced the smuggling of consumer merchandise into Mexico, but the problem has not been eliminated. Many U.S. and Mexican products not covered by NAFTA have continued to make their way across the border illegally.

Mexico's latest preoccupation comes from China, the rising Asian giant that has injected itself into Mexico's trade universe in an ominous way. Some of NAFTA's benefits to Mexico have been reduced by the growing Chinese success in attracting foreign investment to China and gaining market share in the United States for precisely the products that Mexico exports. Most alarmingly, China's recent legal as well as illicit penetration of Mexican markets has contributed to deindustrialization in key sectors of the Mexican economy such as apparel, footwear, and toys. Through 2011, before Mexico drastically reduced its tariffs on Chinese goods, vast amounts of smuggled Chinese merchandise penetrated Mexican markets via the U.S.–Mexico border and through Mexico's seaports. If Porfirio Díaz were alive today, he just might say, "Poor Mexico, still so far from God, still stuck in the orbit of the United States, and now facing the fire of the Chinese dragon."

Notes

1 Williamson (2011), 125.
2 Bernecker (1997), 129–135, 152–154.

3   Bernecker (1997), 155; Ibarra Bellon (1998), 114.
4   Bernecker (1993), 394–395; Bernecker (1994), 19.
5   Poinsett quote from Bernecker (1993), 396, 402.
6   Weber, (1982), 150; Stacy (2003), 761; Findlay and O'Rourke (2007), 400.
7   Boyle (1997), chapter 4; Weber (1982), chapter 8.
8   Quote is from a letter written by a British diplomat, cited in Bernecker (1994), 46.
9   Bernecker (1993), 399–400; Mayo (1987), 393.
10 Quoted in Salvucci (2009), 717 (bracketed text inserted by Salvucci).
11 Chang (2002), 17, 24–27.
12 Quoted in Salvucci (2009), 717.
13 Salvucci (2009), 716, 718.
14 Jones (1921), 194–197, 201.
15 See Márquez Colín (2002), 83–90.
16 Quote appears in Márquez Colín (2002), 88, footnote 25 (my translation).
17 Salvucci (2009), 722.
18 Memoria de la Dirección de Colonización e Industria. Año de 1849, México, 1850. Cited in Bernecker (1994), 118 (my translation).
19 Bernecker (1993), 400–401 (my translation).
20 Bernecker (1994), 84–87.
21 Adams (2008), 85–86.
22 Tenenbaum (1986), 92.
23 The clash between the center and the periphery over the issue of the handling of illicit trade in the 1850s in Northeastern Mexico even contributed to an aborted separatist movement that sought to create a new "country" dubbed the "Republic of the Sierra Madre." On the Contraresguardo, see Hernández (1997).
24 Mayo (1987), 409.
25 Bernecker (1993), 395, 398, 417.
26 Tinker Salas (1997), 114–116, 119.
27 Text of portions of the decree are found in Romero (1892).
28 Márquez Colín (2002), 92.
29 King (1970), 4.
30 Kuntz Ficker (2002), 170.
31 Quoted text appears in Márquez Colín (2002), 313.
32 King (1970), 6.
33 Keremitsis (1973), 172–174; Haber (1992), 10–26; Haber (1989), 39–42.
34 The value of exports rose from $16 million dollars to $106 million dollars and the value of imports increased from $6 million dollars to $57 million during that thirty-year period (Beatty 2000, 404–405).
35 Colegio de México (1960), 467, 481; Cumberland (1968), 227–229; Jones (1921), 201–202, 209–214.
36 Coatsworth (1981), 180–181.
37 Jones (1921) 217–219; Lerman Alperstein (1989), 164–167.
38 Cumberland (1968), 249.
39 Romero (1892), 469.
40 *Los Angeles Times* (June 7, 1918), 15. See also Díaz (2015).
41 Harris III and Saddler (2009), 87.
42 México, INEGI (1985), II:479, 666; Avella Alaminos (2010); Haber (1992), 28.
43 México, INEGI (1985), II:666.

44 Izquierdo (1973), 236, 247–248; Cline (1963), 389–390; Haber et al. (2010), 42–43; Horn and Bice (1949), 181.
45 Esquivel and Márquez (2007), 340.
46 Horn and Bice (1949), 243.
47 Cline (1962), 292–294; Freithaler (1968), 47–50; Morton and Tulloch (1977), 97.
48 Katz (1976), 235–250.
49 Weintraub (1984), 67–68; Pastor and Castañeda (1988), 205.
50 The oil and gas controversy is discussed in Pastor and Castañeda (1988), 99–110.
51 *New York Times* (November 13, 1977), E3; Pastor and Castañeda (1988), 205–207.
52 Bagley (1981), 19–20.
53 Cline (1963), 389–391; Pastor and Castañeda (1988), 205–207; Coote (1996), 8–9, 107–108; Armendáriz E. (1982).
54 *New York Times* (August 12, 1970), A2.
55 Castañeda (2011), 154–155.
56 Miller (1981), 49–60.
57 Anonymous interview conducted in April 2013.
58 *Washington Post* (September 9, 1971), F6.
59 See, for example, *New York Times* (December 2, 1976), 45; *New York Times* (November 11, 1977), 8.
60 Kose et al. (2004), 11.
61 Falck and López Jimenez (2012), 9.
62 Kose et al. (2004).
63 Peters (2009), 28–29.
64 Zepeda et al. (2009), 10–14; Haber (2008), 79, 81, 84, 92.
65 Schwartzman (2012), 114, 115, 119–120, 126, 136; *The Progressive* (July 27, 2013).
66 The eight products are corn, soybeans, wheat, cotton, rice, beef, pork, and poultry. U.S. government support for the eight crops totaled $11.5 billion per year between 1997 and 2005, with corn receiving more than a fourth of the subsidies (Wise 2010, 165; Wise 2009, 33).
67 McClatchy Newspapers (February 2, 2011); *Excelsior* (May 5, 2013). See also Ruíz (2010), 222.
68 The rising reliance on U.S. markets is reflected in the fact that in 1980 Mexico sold 66 percent of its exports to the United States, a figure far below the 88 percent recorded in 2006 (Amsden 2001, 183; Cañas et al. 2006, 11).
69 *The Seattle Times* (March 19, 2009).
70 Gallagher and Porzecanski (2010), 56, 68–69.
71 Hernández (2012), 65–96, data on 77; Knight Ridder Newspapers (January 29, 2006).
72 Knight Ridder Newspapers (January 29, 2006).
73 *Juarez-El Paso Now* (January 2012), 35; Mexico Business Blog (September 26, 2011).
74 *New York Times* (August 28, 1992), D1.
75 *Wall Street Journal* (June 24, 1998), 1.
76 *Business Mexico* (May 2000, 14).
77 *Los Angeles Times* (February 16, 2008).
78 EIU ViewsWire (March 20, 2003).
79 López Córdova and Zabludovsky K. (2010), 721–722.
80 Information on Mexican importation rules and procedures extracted on March 22, 2012, from various government websites. See www.aduanas.gob.mx www.senasica.gob.mx, and www.paisano.gob.mx.

81 *Washington Post* (November 30, 2013).
82 *Juarez-El Paso Now* (January 2012), 35; Mexico Business Blog (September 26, 2011).
83 *Los Angeles Times* (September 23, 2001), A27; *New York Times* (June 5, 2003) (includes Guzmán Montalvo's comment).
84 *Washington Post* (December 13, 2010).
85 Official statistics from INEGI, as reported in the *El Paso Times* (September 10, 2012), 1A.

10
DRUGS, LIQUOR, TOBACCO, AND MIGRANTS

Illicit smuggling of vice products and undocumented migration of people have long been staple activities along the U.S.–Mexico border. These flows dramatically demonstrate the weaknesses of the Mexican economy and the great reliance of large numbers of Mexicans on the United States for making a living.

The best known of Mexico's vice industries with transnational significance is the notorious illegal narcotics trade, which, over the last century, has generated high monetary returns for Mexico but at the same time has precipitated enormous domestic lawlessness and endless disputes with the United States. Viewed in a larger context, the narcotics contraband mirrors what usually happens along borders where unequal countries lie in juxtaposition to one another: illicit drugs flow from the poor country to the affluent country.[1] The drug trade has been a big industry in Mexico because the largest and most lucrative drug market in the world is situated next door.

Trafficking in illegal alcohol from Mexico to the United States is another controversial activity in the history of the border. Liquor bootlegging peaked during the 1920 to 1933 Prohibition Era in the United States. After Prohibition ended, the illicit transborder alcohol business went into a decline, but liquor contraband did not disappear because U.S. and Mexican liquor quotas, levies, and taxes remained in place, guaranteeing continued profits for smugglers.

The least known and least contentious long-term contraband flow is trafficking in illegal tobacco products, a practice also sustained by the imposition by both countries of quotas, levies, and taxes. Cigarette smuggling continues to generate profits on the border, although probably on a smaller scale than contraband liquor.

And finally, undocumented migration of people across the border has been a thorny issue between Mexico and the United States for almost a century. This problem strongly reflects the uneven development in Mexico and the need for cheap labor in the United States. Given the current condition of the Mexican economy and the rising integration between the two neighbors, the smuggling of people will generate friction for years to come.

The Drug Trade

In the early twentieth century both Mexico and the United States enacted prohibitionist laws and restrictive policies against opium, opiates, marijuana, and cocaine. Such initiatives spawned illegal drug trade activity in both countries, and the Mexican border area emerged as an important distribution center for controlled or forbidden substances. The volume of contraband drugs exported from Mexico to the United States increased many-fold through the years and, as public alarm grew, the two countries responded with harsher laws and stricter policies. The United States created numerous federal domestic antidrug agencies, subsidized local police departments, and gave aid to other countries so that they could fight domestic producers of drugs more aggressively. In Mexico, inadequate budgets and widespread corruption hampered that country's efforts to diminish the domestic production and distribution of drugs. Thus large-scale smuggling operations into the United States continued unabated.

In the second half of the twentieth century, drug trafficking assumed greater importance in the U.S.–Mexico relationship as the demand for and production of narcotics grew rapidly. Hard drugs, especially cocaine, flowed more freely into the United States. Tougher antidrug laws enacted in the United States over several decades and sterner law enforcement seemed not to make much of a difference in curbing either drug consumption among Americans or drug trafficking. On the border, soaring profits gave rise to many drug bands, rings, gangs, and syndicates before the days of the narco cartels.

By the 1960s the influx of illegal narcotics into the United States had become such a vexatious issue that it prompted the Richard Nixon administration to formally declare a "War on Drugs." The central elements of the "war" included draconian prison sentences for drug users and dealers, greater militarization of the border, and unprecedented undercover work by American agents in Mexico. Periodically the U.S. government stepped up border inspections to express dissatisfaction with Mexico's ineffectiveness in fighting drug trafficking. Two well-publicized U.S. drug "crackdowns" at the border, one in 1969 and the other in 1985, precipitated micro diplomatic and economic crises. In both instances onerous and time-consuming inspections by U.S. agents at the border slowed down international traffic and adversely affected commerce, especially in Mexican border communities. The month-long 1969 campaign, dubbed "Operation Intercept," signaled Nixon's resolve to fight the drug trade. Mexico protested the humiliating interrogations of its citizens at the border as well as the economic losses endured by Mexican businesses as a result of the traffic slowdown. During the shorter 1985 episode, Mexican officials voiced similar complaints and accused the United States of using the drug issue to pressure Mexico into supporting Washington's interventionist policies in Central America.

From the late 1980s to the mid-2000s, an alarming escalation of violence linked to the drug trade occurred in Mexico. Powerful Mexican drug-trafficking organizations that had supplanted existing gangs and syndicates asserted de facto control over many areas, especially on the border. Corruption of public servants and the breakdown of the rule of law reached extraordinary levels. As drug-related lawlessness worsened, the U.S. government periodically issued official warnings to Americans to refrain from traveling in Mexico, triggering angry responses from the Mexican government.

Fighting between rival drug cartels became more frequent in Mexican border cities. One shooting incident in 1997, which occurred in one of my favorite restaurant/bars in Ciudad Juárez, resulted in several deaths. That brought home the realization that public spaces in that city were becoming increasingly dangerous. More and more innocent *juarenses* found themselves at the wrong place at the wrong time and got caught in the crossfire in shootouts between traffickers or between traffickers and the police. Casualties mounted rapidly. I cut back on my visits to Juárez. When I did cross the border to visit friends or to patronize restaurants I exercised extra caution. Lots of El Pasoans simply stopped going to Juárez, and the city's tourist industry started to plummet.

Drug-related violence kept increasing as the twentieth century gave way to the twenty-first century. By early 2007 conditions in Mexico began to spin out of control. President Felipe Calderón declared an all-out war on the Mexican drug cartels, using the military and the federal police to go after drug traffickers in a coordinated manner. Pleased by that policy, the United States extended approximately $1.5 billion dollars in aid to Calderón for the purpose of carrying on the drug war. Calderon's government had hoped for a bigger aid package, but it welcomed the additional help at a time when the effectiveness of Mexico's antidrug campaign remained highly doubtful. The Mexican cartels responded to Calderón's offensive by fighting ferociously to safeguard their interests, with the result that the drug war turned Mexico into one of the most violent countries in the world.

At the end of his administration in 2012, President Calderón claimed the drug war had been a "success," citing the disruption of cartel activities, the capture or execution of some top drug lords, the seizure of large quantities of drugs, and the confiscation of many weapons. Most Mexicans, however, saw the drug war as a colossal failure. The government had to spend substantial resources fighting a war that to most observers yielded few results and precipitated many serious problems. Mexican governmental, judicial, and law enforcement institutions were seriously corrupted and performed poorly in trying to restore order. Citizen confidence in public officials, the army, the police, and the courts plummeted. Worst of all, the drug war led to an estimated 100,000 drug-related homicides during the six-year Calderon presidency. Extortion of businesses skyrocketed, with over 50,000 complaints filed with the Mexican government in 2008. Moreover, the drug war seriously destabilized the northern border region and other parts of the country. In early 2012, Juárez, Acapulco, Torreon, Chihuahua, and Durango all appeared on a list of the ten most violent cities in the world.[2] Drug-related murders, kidnappings, carjackings, extortions, and general lawlessness exacted a horrendous toll in the border urban areas. Thousands of businesses closed and hundreds of thousands of people left the region in search of safety elsewhere. Large numbers of U.S. tourists likewise stopped visiting trouble spots in Mexico. In Juárez, daily shootouts, assassinations, kidnappings, disappearances, extortion of businesses, and destruction of property generated a reign of terror and a local economic crisis of major proportions. The embattled border city recorded 1,623 homicides in 2008, 2,754 in 2009, and 3,622 in 2010. Reportedly almost 11,000 local businesses had shut down in Juárez from 2008 to 2010 and between 200,000 and 400,000 people had abandoned the city.[3] For many Mexicans, such pandemonium cancelled whatever gains the Calderón government claimed were accomplished in the effort to stamp out the drug trade.

Wars always generate winners and losers, and so it was with Calderón's drug war. Some cartels in Mexico lost power while others increased theirs, and the chaos produced new criminal organizations seeking a piece of the drug profits. Communities across the country lost a great deal as a result of the war on drugs. Yet in some parts of Mexico the influx of billions of drug-generated dollars into the Mexican economy continued to stimulate both the informal and formal sectors while giving direct employment to upwards of half a million people. A significant percentage of the drug profits wound up as investments in agriculture, ranching, mining, logging, oil and natural gas, transportation, security, money exchange houses, entertainment, tourism, restaurants, shopping centers, real estate, and a variety of small businesses.[4] It is impossible to know the exact value of the drug trade, but estimates from informed sources provide a general idea. A U.S. Congressional Research Service report released in 2012 calculated that Mexico's drug cartels received between $19 and $29 billion dollars every year from their nefarious activities, while knowledgeable observers in Mexico estimate that the drug industry may generate as much as $50 billion dollars annually.[5]

In retrospect, the 2006 decision by the Mexican government to wage a unilateral full-scale war against drug cartels appears to have been a terrible mistake. Such a war cannot be won without a similar all-out war inside the United States against that country's own drug-trafficking organizations. Absent decisive action by the U.S. government, Mexico's only realistic hope of quelling drug-related lawlessness is to find more effective and nonviolent ways of diminishing the drug trade. But, trapped as it is by geography, Mexico cannot do that by itself. Real success is contingent upon substantially greater efforts by U.S. authorities to reduce drug use in the United States and a stronger commitment to blunt the flow of U.S. drug money and weapons to the cartels in Mexico. Since the U.S. federal government seems unlikely to make any sweeping changes in its drug policies anytime soon that would parallel the trend toward legalization of marijuana in U.S. states (eighteen states by 2012), Mexico is left with four, far from ideal options: do nothing, continue the drug war, legalize drugs, or reach an accommodation with the cartels. Whatever Mexico's eventual policy choice, there is no reason to believe that the drug trade will disappear anytime soon. Drugs will continue to torment Mexico and contribute to the country's dependent status vis-à-vis the United States in a significant way.

Trafficking in Alcohol

Liquor bootlegging was a well-established activity along the border before U.S. states like Arizona and Texas began to adopt prohibition-type laws in the years prior to the enactment of federal Prohibition in 1920. In the 1910s newspapers frequently carried stories of trafficking in Mexican *mescal, sotol, tequila*, and *aguardiente* into the U.S. borderlands.[6] In a 1916 *New York Times* article, for instance, correspondent W.D. Hornaday noted the ease with which these illicit products entered the United States in defiance of the law: "One of the most annoying features of Federal court proceedings in Laredo, Brownsville, Del Rio, and El Paso is the large number of mescal smuggling cases that have to be disposed of at each term," wrote Hornaday. "It is a petty lawlessness that the border custom officers and river guards have never been able to suppress."[7]

From a relatively minor irritation, liquor smuggling from Mexico to the United States became a major problem after the approval of the eighteenth amendment to the U.S. Constitution in 1919 and the passage of the Volstead Act by the U.S. Congress in 1920. The Volstead Act prohibited the manufacture, transportation, and sale of liquor throughout the United States. Communities along the Mexican border quickly jumped at the opportunity to supply Americans with liquor. Distilleries, saloons, casinos, and related establishments proliferated in Tijuana, Ciudad Juárez, and other Mexican border towns, drawing large numbers of Americans who wished to consume alcohol and at the same time enjoy gambling and other forms of border-style entertainment. As demand for alcohol grew in the United States, transnational smuggling became a larger and better organized enterprise.

Inevitably acrimony broke out between Mexico and the United States over the violation of the law by liquor smugglers. Frequent confrontations and shootouts involving bootleggers and U.S. law enforcement officers fueled violence and constantly disrupted border life and triggered diplomatic incidents. After almost a decade and a half of border troubles caused by liquor trafficking, a measure of tranquility returned to the borderlands when repeal of U.S. Prohibition finally occurred in 1933.

The relegalization of alcohol in the United States relegated liquor-smuggling activities on the border to relative insignificance, but liquor contraband did not disappear. For the United States the challenge shifted from trying to keep illicit alcohol completely out of the country to one of regulating how much foreign liquor could be legally imported and, at the same time, to making sure that taxes were paid at the ports of entry. U.S. federal officials worked with state agents along the border to enforce the collection of federal and state levies. In contrast to the pre-1933 period, when U.S. border law enforcement battled organized liquor-smuggling syndicates, after Prohibition most of the targets became small gangs, petty traffickers, and casual tax dodgers. U.S. authorities reported in 1935 that of the 672 seizures of liquor contraband over the previous year, two-thirds had taken place along the border with Mexico.[8]

The practice of charging federal and state taxes on foreign liquor has remained in place in the United States to the present day, and that has kept alive the incentive for smuggling. An interesting twist in the contraband game involves liquor that is purchased in U.S. tax and duty-free shops as an "export" product with the understanding that it is bound for Mexico. Frequently the discounted liquor slips into the Mexican market without paying Mexican duties and, perhaps as often, some or all of the liquor surreptitiously finds its way back into the United States for resale to U.S. consumers at reduced prices. In 2012, taxes on distilled spirits entering Texas from Mexico amounted $3.50 dollars and $5.50 for a pint and gallon respectively, and $3.25 each for a fifth of wine and six twelve-ounce containers of beer.[9] These levies have kept liquor smugglers in business. For example, in July 2012 a man driving a tractor-trailer was arrested in Ciudad Juárez for smuggling from the United States 18,000 bottles of whiskey worth over $146,000 dollars.[10]

Trafficking in Tobacco Products

Cross-border illicit tobacco trafficking has been driven by the same forces that stimulated the post-1933 smuggling of liquor—quotas and excise and sales taxes. By the early twentieth century, stories in U.S. newspapers often mentioned the unlawful introduction of cigars and cigarettes into U.S. soil, a trade carried on by professional traffickers as well as ordinary people intent on evading duties. Smugglers used a variety of techniques and devices to fool the authorities. One gang hollowed out the insides of loaves of bread and stuffed them with cigars. Even respectable, well-dressed American women engaged in cigar and cigarette smuggling, hiding these products on their persons. But they did not always escape detection from sharp-eyed inspectors, resulting in considerable embarrassment for the offenders.[11] By 1935 Texas smokers who did not wish to pay levies on cigarettes could make purchases from bootleggers on either side of the border, while budget-minded smokers could buy cheaper Mexican-made cigarettes that closely imitated U.S. brands.[12] Smuggling of tobacco products went on with the general tolerance of officials, who considered the activity relatively harmless in an economic or political sense. That changed in the 1970s, when awareness of the health hazards of tobacco coincided with pressures on authorities to tap into new sources of tax revenues. Different U.S. government jurisdictions targeted tobacco for such taxes, and levies on tobacco products started going up sharply. But the higher the taxes, the more lucrative cigarette smuggling became. Inevitably tax avoidance escalated, leading to losses of significant revenues for the government. In 1977 U.S. officials estimated that the federal government lost $7 million dollars annually in uncollected levies, while Texas lost $14 million and Arizona lost $1 million.[13]

At the border wily entrepreneurs fashioned a system whereby they purchased untaxed American cigarettes in bulk from U.S. duty-free export shops under the pretense that all the cigarettes would be taken to Mexico. Escorted by U.S. customs agents, the buyers transported the cigarettes across the border. But they avoided paying Mexican levies by either bribing Mexican customs agents or by circumventing the customs houses entirely. Either way, the imported merchandise typically was split into two parts, with some of the smuggled cigarettes destined for sale in Mexico and others for resale in the United States—as untaxed contraband. I witnessed the clever antics of one band of cigarette smugglers some years back at an international bridge in Ciudad Juárez–El Paso. Using hand trucks, four smugglers hauled about a dozen cardboard boxes containing large quantities of cartons of U.S.-bought cigarettes toward Mexico. Once they crossed the dividing line the smugglers hurried to a spot above the river bank perhaps 100 feet from the Mexican customs house. They quickly tossed the boxes, one at a time, over the bridge railing. Collaborators situated some forty feet below skillfully hauled in the boxes using large canvases, much like firefighters who catch people who jump from buildings. The catchers placed the payload onto a raft that they then proceeded to float on the Rio Grande, presumably to a secluded spot where they could safely parcel the boxes for delivery to dealers in both cities. No one bothered the smugglers on the bridge; they simply walked into Mexico. I figured that either the Mexican customs agents had been paid off or they did not consider going after cigarette smugglers worth the trouble.

In the late twentieth century making cigarettes more expensive became an important part of the strategy in antismoking campaigns in both countries. That trend continued in the twenty-first century. In Mexico, taxes on a pack of cigarettes, whether foreign or domestic, added up to almost 61 percent of the price in 2009.[14] In the United States, the federal excise tax alone on a pack of cigarettes was $1.01 dollars in 2010, while states imposed their own levies in addition. The state tax in Arizona that year was $2.00, in New Mexico $1.66, in Texas $1.41, and in California $0.87. Beyond the U.S.–Mexico borderlands, the states with the highest excise taxes on cigarettes were: Rhode Island at $3.46, Connecticut at $3.00, New York at $2.75, and New Jersey at $2.70. New York City tacked on another $1.50 on top of the state levy, bringing the total tax there to $4.00. By contrast, taxes in U.S. tobacco-producing southern states remained much lower than in northern states. South Carolina, for example, placed a miniscule tax of $0.07 on a pack of cigarettes. Thus the long-standing domestic cigarette-smuggling industry continued to thrive in the United States, with busy Interstate 95 most likely serving as the main corridor for transporting bootleg cigarettes from South to North.[15] On the U.S.–Mexico border, profit margins were not as high as those in New York City and other major U.S. urban areas, but even at lower levels the continuing profitability of cross-border cigarette smuggling kept the industry alive. On the same day in July 2012 that a man was arrested for smuggling 18,000 bottles of whiskey into Juárez, another man was charged with smuggling 12 million cigarettes worth nearly $1.8 million dollars, also imported from the United States in a tractor-trailer.[16]

Impact of Trafficking in Vice Products

Viewed historically and from an economic perspective, cross-border trafficking in cigarettes, liquor, and drugs has had a much greater impact on Mexico than on the United States. Just like everyday U.S. consumer goods that enter Mexico illegally and harm domestic industries and deprive the government of tariff revenues, illicit cigarettes and liquor do likewise. One might imagine that the effect is similar in the United States, but that is not the case, certainly not in magnitude. Because the U.S. economy is infinitely stronger than the Mexican economy, the impact of the influx of illicit cigarettes and liquor from Mexico has not been felt as much by Americans. Trafficking in illicit narcotics is another matter entirely. While the drug trade has been an engine of economic activity in its own right, it has been extraordinarily problematic for both countries in other ways. Mexico has benefitted significantly from the influx of billions of "dirty" dollars, but the lawlessness attendant to drug trafficking has seriously undermined the authority of the state, has required large expenditures for military and law enforcement operations, and has produced catastrophic levels of violence. For the United States there have also been economic benefits because the circulation of drug money is unquestionably a component of the U.S. marketplace. And, as in Mexico, illicit narcotics have had many undesirable social consequences for Americans, including lawlessness and violence in numerous cities. Fighting the drug war and incarcerating drug traffickers and users in the United States has been extremely costly for American taxpayers as well.

Human Migratory Flows

We leave the subject of trafficking vice products and turn to the topic of Mexican migration to the United States, an intractable issue in Mexico's relationship with the United States. The exodus of millions of Mexicans to the neighboring country over the past century points out two fundamental realities about Mexico: it demonstrates in a dramatic way that the Mexican economy has not been able to provide sufficient opportunities for the masses, and it underscores Mexico's deep-seated dependence on the United States.

The historical periods that stand out in the history Mexican migration to the United States are as follows: 1910 to 1940, when hundreds of thousands fled the Mexican Revolution and its aftermath, followed by pressures in the United States during the Great Depression that drove between half a million and a million Mexicans back to their homeland; 1940 to 1965, when World War II and the Korean Conflict created labor shortages in the United States and needy Mexicans were encouraged to seek U.S. jobs in great numbers; and 1965 to the late 2000s, when, despite the passage of restrictive immigration laws in the United States and growing American opposition to the influx of Mexican immigrants, migrants continued to cross the border in greater numbers than ever before.

According to official U.S. statistics, between 1820 and 2009 7.6 million Mexicans immigrated legally to the United States and millions more immigrated illegally. The vast majority of these immigrants left Mexico after 1980. Credible sources have calculated that in the early 1980s roughly 5 million people lived illegally in the United States and, of those, an estimated 3 million were from Mexico.[17] In 2007, surveys based on improved data and better methodology yielded estimates up to 12 million total undocumented people, with Mexicans assumed to number about 7 million. The Great Recession of 2008 to 2010 slowed migration significantly and the estimate of the undocumented population dropped to 11 million in 2009–2010, with the number of Mexicans calculated at approximately 6.5 million.[18]

One other number—that is, the total Mexican-origin population living legally in the United States—is instructive for understanding the scale of the exodus from Mexico. By 2011 that number was calculated at 33.5 million persons, with slightly over one-third born in Mexico.[19] With that statistical sketch, let us now look at highlights of the cross-border human flow over the last century.

Migration Trends, 1910 to 1940

Prior to World War I, Mexican immigrants crossed the U.S.–Mexico border with relative ease because few bureaucratic barriers existed.[20] But that situation began to change in 1917 when the U.S. Congress passed a law that imposed a literacy test and a head tax and restricted foreign-labor contracts in the United States to six months. These requirements, coupled with anxiety felt by many Mexican nationals during World War I that they might be drafted into the U.S. military, resulted in a sudden downturn in immigration and a shortage of workers in the United States. The U.S. government quickly suspended the restrictive provisions of the immigration law and assured Mexican nationals that they would not be drafted into the military. To give some structure to the flow of labor, the U.S. government established the Temporary Admissions Program, a guest worker initiative that mandated wages, working conditions, and length of stay in the United States. The World War I–era government program, which lasted from 1917 to 1921, would serve as a precursor to the much larger Bracero Program initiated during World War II.

The steady rise in the flow of Mexican workers across the border in the 1920s caught the attention of U.S. anti-immigration groups worried about the impact that higher numbers of Mexicans would have on U.S. society. During and after the recession of 1921 U.S. labor unions complained that Mexican workers depressed wages and interfered with unionization efforts. Americans concerned about social problems argued that Mexicans did not have the capacity to assimilate into the U.S. mainstream population, and racists centered their attacks on alleged detrimental consequences of biological mixture between dark-skinned mestizos and whites. The inflammatory rhetoric of the anti-Mexican forces, however, could not overcome the lobbying power of U.S. corporations and agricultural growers who needed a steady supply of low-wage immigrant workers. With the collaboration of institutions in American society sympathetic to Mexico, including the executive branch of the U.S. government and various religious denominations, employers convinced the U.S. Congress to exclude Mexico and other countries in Latin America from the immigration quotas contained in the U.S. Immigration Acts of 1921 and 1924. Thus, despite much opposition in U.S. society, the influx of Mexican workers into the United States went on with minimum interruption. The anti-Mexican forces in the United States, however, continued to lobby for immigration restrictions and kept the debate alive, while the creation of the U.S. Border Patrol in 1924 led to tighter controls at the border.

The Great Depression, which began in 1929, strengthened the anti-immigrant movement in the United States and spawned an unprecedented campaign to rid the nation of "undesirable" foreigners. As before, Mexicans became the principal target of the attacks, this time resulting in massive deportations and repatriations. In the 1930s between half a million and 1 million Mexicans reluctantly departed the United States under great duress, among them an undetermined number of U.S. citizen spouses and children who accompanied deported Mexico-born heads of households. Many people in Mexico saw the returnees as an unwelcome burden for their impoverished country and often treated them with disdain.

Contract Labor and Undocumented Migration, 1940 to 1965

Immigration restrictions in the United States eased substantially when World War II created serious labor shortages in the U.S. economy. Americans opened the border to returning Mexican repatriates and also welcomed first-time entrants. Mexican workers took advantage of the favorable climate and entered the United States in large numbers under the bilateral Mexican Farm Labor Supply Program, which was enacted in 1942. Also known as the Bracero Program, the initiative lasted over two decades and allowed millions of Mexican men to obtain seasonal work in the United States under contract with private employers. Although continuous disagreements emerged between the two governments over policy, structure, and execution of the Bracero Program, the benefits derived by both countries trumped all the problems and served to prolong the arrangement. Eventually, after numerous renewals and changes in the manner in which the Bracero Program functioned, the accord came to an end in 1964. The efforts of U.S. labor unions and other opponents of the program succeeded in convincing the U.S. Congress to terminate a labor system deemed harmful to the interests of American workers. For Mexico, the end of the Bracero Program meant higher unemployment rates at home, increased poverty and, inevitably, more undocumented migration to the United States.

During the years that the Bracero Program was in operation, illegal migration remained a thorny issue between Mexico and the United States because many workers preferred to be on their own rather than be tied down by contract to specific employers. By the 1950s rising numbers of undocumented Mexican immigrants became a national concern in the United States, precipitating action by U.S. authorities to force mass "voluntary departures" of Mexicans back to their homeland. The U.S. Immigration and Naturalization Service conducted a multiyear quasi-military campaign known as "Operation Wetback" that involved roundups, detentions, and expulsion of illegal "aliens." Millions were deported or left "voluntarily" in the early and mid-1950s. While the Mexican government resented the treatment of its citizens in the United States and their forced return home, it nonetheless cooperated with U.S. authorities for the sake of maintaining good relations as well as to ease the reentry of the expelled migrants back into Mexican society.

For several years during this period my father labored as a legally admitted bracero in the United States, but he worked as an undocumented immigrant as well for an even longer span, until he became a legal U.S. resident in 1957. That phase of his life illustrates how multitudes of needy people in Mexico reoriented their economic lives away from their homeland and became permanently tied to the U.S. economy. Few opportunities existed for my father in his home state of Jalisco during the late 1930s and early 1940s. After working for meager pay in a variety of dead-end jobs, he landed a more permanent position with a mining company in San Francisco del Oro, Chihuahua. That was the best job he ever had in Mexico in terms of wages. But the work in the mine was backbreaking and dangerous, so he set his sights on the United States. He signed up as a bracero five times between 1945 and 1950, working mostly in the agricultural fields of California. His dissatisfaction with the onerous requirements for obtaining bracero contracts eventually drove him to become a freelance undocumented immigrant for the next seven years. He picked crops in New Mexico, Kansas, Washington, Idaho, and California, and worked on the railroad in Colorado. During the years of Operation Wetback, it became tougher to evade detection by U.S. immigration authorities, and he was caught on several occasions, placed in detention for weeks at a time, and in each instance he was deported back to Mexico. In 1950, in the midst of a railroad stint that my father had in Pueblo, Colorado, my mother and their six children, including myself, snuck across the border and joined him. My parents intended for the family to live in Pueblo permanently. But that was not to be. Within a year immigration agents discovered our illegal status, and we were all shipped back to Mexico—in an unmarked grey bus with bars across the windows.

That disastrous episode and other deportations did not discourage my father. He continued crossing the border without documents in order to keep earning dollars to support his family, now back in Ciudad Juárez. The nightmare of illegal migration and frequent family separations ended when we all immigrated legally to the United States in 1957. In researching the history of cross-border migration I have learned that during that era many other people had the same kinds of experiences as my own family.

Escalation of the Exodus from Mexico, 1965 to the Present

In 1965, a landmark U.S. law expanded the extant system of priorities for prospective immigrants wishing to enter the United States legally, with greater preference given to relatives of U.S. citizens and to foreign professionals and businesspersons. After the new law took effect in 1968, working-class immigrants with no relatives in the United States had almost no chance of obtaining residency visas. Thus, both ex-braceros and a new generation of poor Mexicans desirous of working in the United States resorted to illegal entry, incurring the wrath of U.S. anti-immigrant groups and conservative politicians. Data reveal that, while the number of Mexicans who immigrated to the United States legally increased modestly after 1965, those who entered without documentation skyrocketed. Yearly U.S. apprehensions of undocumented migrants surpassed a million by the late 1970s, reaching an all-time high of 1.3 million in 1985. The high apprehension numbers fueled alarm regarding the size of the undocumented population residing in the United States. Some U.S. public officials spoke of an ongoing "illegal alien invasion" of the country. In Mexico, government-sponsored studies undertaken by the Centro Nacional de Información y Estadística del Trabajo (CENIET) rejected the U.S. numbers as exaggerated and emphasized the seasonal, temporary, and circular nature of cross-border migration.

Mexico grew increasingly uneasy with the anti-Mexican rhetoric in the American media and in the halls of the U.S. Congress. Recurring incidents along the border led to more friction between the two countries. A high point in the international quarrel over immigration took place in late 1978 during the "Tortilla Curtain" episode, when a plan became public that the United States would build military-like fences along the border to keep undocumented immigrants and drug smugglers from entering the country. Objections to the Tortilla Curtain quickly surfaced in Mexico and among Mexican Americans and other groups in the United States concerned with humanitarian issues. On the defensive, INS officials scaled back the original menacing design of the fences, removing from the plans the objectionable razors that might cause physical harm to immigrants. In addition, INS reduced the length of the fences planned for El Paso and San Ysidro (directly across from Tijuana).[21] As borderlanders grew accustomed to the new barriers, the INS in subsequent years added more fencing in those two communities and in other parts of the border as well. But, because the post-1979 structures lacked the dangerous designs that had brought notoriety to the Tortilla Curtain, the work proceeded with relatively little controversy on either side of the border.

While the Tortilla Curtain drama played out, the larger debate over the need for immigration reform continued in the executive and congressional branches of the U.S. government. President Jimmy Carter had introduced an immigration reform proposal in 1976, but upon seeing that his plan would not make it into legislation, he joined the Congress in 1978 in creating the Select Commission on Immigration and Refugee Policy. The commission's recommendations formed the basis for more immigration proposals that surfaced in the House of Representatives and the Senate. The new momentum would lead to the passage of the Immigration and Reform Act of 1986 during the second term of the Ronald Reagan administration. The major provisions of the 1986 law included the awarding of amnesty to undocumented people already residing in the United States, enactment of sanctions against employers of illegal workers, and strengthening the enforcement capacity of the U.S. Border Patrol.

During the prolonged period of debate that led to the landmark 1986 law, Mexican officials grew frustrated over the U.S. policy of addressing the immigration problem exclusively as a domestic issue, leaving Mexico without a voice in the formulation of policy affecting so many of its citizens. The Mexican government also took offence over the unilateral U.S. militarization of the border and the consequences that resulted from a tougher U.S. approach to immigration matters. In 1993 the U.S. government began building new and stronger fences and walls and implemented "blockades" in El Paso, San Diego, and other urban zones along the border. These measures had the effect of driving migrants to remote and dangerous areas such as the Sonoran desert to attempt the border crossing. For thousands of migrants, death in the desert brought on by the punishing sun tragically ended the dream of a better life in the United States. To avoid the increasing problems and dangers of crossing the border, many undocumented people simply settled permanently in the United States, thus breaking the traditional circular pattern of labor migration between the two countries.

The U.S.–Mexico border assumed even greater significance following the terrorist attacks in New York City on September 11, 2001, as traumatized Americans, egged on by opportunistic politicians and conservative media pundits, demanded that a formidable border wall be built to deny entry to unauthorized immigrants and drug traffickers and at the same time keep terrorists from entering the United States through Mexico. Meanwhile states and municipalities throughout the United States enacted anti-immigration laws and ordinances and voters passed anti-immigration initiatives, all of which were primarily aimed at Mexicans. Arizona led the way in the creation of an unwelcoming climate for immigrants with the passage of the infamous Senate Bill 1070 and other legislation in 2010. Although most of SB 1070 was struck down by the U.S. Supreme Court in 2012, the provision that empowered the police in Arizona to ask suspects for their immigration "papers" was upheld. Mexican Americans and civil rights advocates denounced that part of the court's decision, charging that it validated racial profiling specifically directed at people of Mexican origin.

Consequences of Mexican Migration to the United States

Having surveyed the story of Mexican migration to the United States, let us return to the matter of impact. How has Mexico been affected by the massive exodus of its people to the United States? Mexico has benefited in two ways. First, outmigration has long served as a safety valve, sparing Mexico of social pressures and tensions that would otherwise arise if the migrants stayed home. Second, over the generations Mexicans working abroad have sent large amounts of money to their homeland in the form of remittances, and this has greatly helped millions of families and boosted the Mexican economy. Mexico received some $43 billion dollars in the 1990s and about $227 billion dollars in the 2000s from Mexicans living in the United States.[22] On the negative side, millions of Mexican families have become dependent on remittances, a risky situation indeed given the challenges that breadwinners have confronted crossing the U.S.–Mexico border and the uncertainties they have faced finding and holding jobs in a U.S. economy subject to recurring recessions. Moreover, the separation of families for prolonged periods has created serious social problems and led to delinquency among young people who have grown up in households with absentee fathers. The exodus of so many workers from Mexico has also spawned labor shortages in agriculture and other sectors of the Mexican economy. Further, Mexican workers have been subjected to exploitation, discrimination, and physical abuse in the United States. Worst of all, over the last two decades, thousands of undocumented migrants have died from exposure attempting to cross dangerous stretches of the U.S.–Mexico borderlands, including the Rio Grande region, the Arizona desert, and arid and mountainous sections of Southern California. Another disturbing trend is the exodus from Mexico of large numbers of young, well-educated individuals. Between 2001 and 2014, reportedly over 530,000 such migrants left for Canada, Europe, and other countries.[23] Finally, from 2006 to 2010, during the height of Mexico's drug war, violence drove an estimated 265,000 Mexicans to seek refuge abroad, mostly in the United States.[24] (Undoubtedly these figures include some double counting of the same individuals.)

For the United States there have been pluses and minuses as well. Studies reveal that Mexican migrants have made enormous contributions to the U.S. economy, particularly in sectors like agriculture, mining, transportation, urban manufacturing, construction, and various service industries. U.S. consumers have also benefited from low prices for foodstuffs and other goods produced by migrants who work for low wages. Government entities at all levels have likewise profited from taxes paid by undocumented immigrants. With respect to income and social security taxes, most migrants claim no benefits because of their fear of detection and deportation, and that reality represents a net gain for the U.S. government and for U.S. taxpayers. But the research also shows that U.S. taxpayers at the state and municipal levels have had to pay for public services utilized by the migrants, especially in the health and education sectors. In addition, local authorities have seen their law enforcement costs rise as they deal with crimes committed by some of the migrants. At the federal level, the U.S. government has maintained a large and costly law enforcement apparatus designed to prevent illegal border crossings and to expel people apprehended without documents.

Americans have been so preoccupied with the influx of Mexicans into the United States that they have seldom considered that over many generations hundreds of thousands of U.S. citizens have made *Mexico* their home. The U.S. State Department has estimated that the number of Americans living permanently in Mexico soared from around 200,000 in the mid-1990s to perhaps a million by the mid-2000s. A large percentage of those expatriates have purchased property in Mexico, and many of them take advantage of benefits available there. For example, those who have lived in Mexico for more than three years qualify for government-subsidized health care, and any American can obtain dental services and prescription drugs at a fraction of what they would have to pay in the United States. Low housing and low labor costs also make it possible to live comfortably on modest incomes such as U.S. social security benefits. In addition, Americans can import vehicles with U.S. license plates without having to pay registration and license fees. All this illustrates the symbiotic and reciprocal nature of the U.S.–Mexico relationship.

Conclusion

This chapter has highlighted the flow of illicit vice products and the migration of people from Mexico to the United States. As we have seen, these movements have impacted both countries negatively and positively. Good or bad, such forms of cross-border interaction are outcomes of the asymmetry that developed long ago between the two countries. As the dependent partner in a relationship sealed by geographic proximity, Mexico has relied heavily on the trafficking of drugs, alcohol, and cigarettes to generate income and employment for substantial segments of its population. Mexico's dependence is also manifested in the outmigration to the United States of millions of its citizens and the remittances that the exiles have sent back to the homeland. In their totality these activities reflect the incapacity of Mexico to absorb large segments of the labor force in well-paying legitimate work. This situation has never been good for Mexico's image or for the self-esteem of the Mexican people.

In an ideal world, Mexico would have the kind of foundational factors that are strong enough to sustain an economy that makes it unnecessary for so many Mexicans over so many generations to engage in unsavory work or to take considerable risks crossing the U.S.–Mexico border just to make a living. Of course, that ideal world has never existed. The vastly inadequate economic opportunities that have been present in Mexico have left the masses behind. Like people anywhere who face difficult circumstances, disadvantaged Mexicans have sought to make a better life for themselves wherever opportunity presents itself, whether in their own country or abroad.

Notes

1. Moré (2011), 24.
2. San Pedro Sula, Honduras, was identified as the most violent city on earth. Ciudad Juárez ranked second (having slipped from the top spot the previous year), Acapulco fourth, Torreon seventh, Chihuahua eighth, and Durango ninth. The list was compiled by Mexico's Citizen's Council for Public Security and Justice (*Global Post*, January 17, 2012).
3. Molloy (2013); *El Diario de El Paso* (January 18, 2010), (March 1, 2010), B1; *Wall Street Journal* (March 20, 2010); *Juárez-El Paso Now* (May 2010), A43.
4. Toro (1995), 53–54; press reports (various dates).
5. As reported in the *El Paso Times* (February 19, 2012), 1A; *Mexico Now* (November–December 2014, 26).
6. Mescal and tequila are made from the "pineapple" extracted from the agave plant. Sotol comes from the sotol or Desert Spoon plant. Pulque is made from maguey, or the century plant. *Aguardiente* is a generic term for alcoholic drinks and can be made from grains, fruits, vegetables or, more commonly, sugarcane.
7. *New York Times* (August 6, 1916), 15.
8. *New York Times* (March 17, 1935), E7, (April 19, 1935), 32.
9. Texas Alcoholic Beverage Commission. www.tabc.state.tx.us.
10. *El Paso Times* (July 13, 2012), 2B.
11. *Los Angeles Times* (July 22, 1896), 3, (August 19, 1907), 13; *New York Times* (January 16, 1911), 1.
12. *New York Times* (December 15, 1935), 51.
13. *New York Times* (September 27, 1977), 30.
14. Waters et al. (2010), 2.
15. National Conference of State Legislatures (2010); U.S. Federation of Tax Administrators (2010); ATF (2011).
16. *El Paso Times* (July 13, 2012), 2B.
17. U.S. Department of Homeland Security (2009), Tables 33 and 34; Corwin (1982), 227, 282.
18. Estimates based on studies conducted by the Pew Hispanic Center, as reported in *The Washington Post* (September 1, 2010); Passel and Cohn (2011), 12.
19. Pew Research Center (2013).
20. Much of the historical narrative on Mexican migration to the United States presented here draws from Martínez (2001, 2011).
21. *El Paso Herald Post* (October 25, 1978), A1; Stoddard et al. (1979), 20–22.
22. Castañeda (2011), 244; Geo-Mexico website (post dated November 23, 2013). www.//geo-mexico.com.
23. *Dallas Morning News* (February 14, 2014).
24. Rios Contreras (2014), 209.

CONCLUSION
Lessons Learned

This book has examined the roles that five foundational factors have played in shaping the uneven development of Mexico. In the Introduction we began the analysis by raising questions about traditional interpretations regarding development issues and then introduced the foundational factors approach followed in this book. In Part I the comparative historical surveys of the United States and Mexico provided a general view of the forces that have molded both economies. Our inquiry of internal inequalities revealed that wealth concentration and poverty have been long-standing problems in both countries. With that background, Parts II and III examined in detail the context in which Mexico's economy has evolved, with a focus on the impact of the natural environment, the resource endowment, population dynamics, and external relations. The role of the state in structuring production was noted throughout the book. By identifying the building blocks underlying the mixed performance of Mexico's economy and by drawing comparisons with the United States, we are now better able to understand the challenges that Mexico has confronted.

The information and interpretations provided here yield a more satisfactory answer than conventional theories to age-old questions that many have asked: Why has Mexico, being such a large country and having such a robust resource endowment, not been able to achieve a higher level of development? Why has Mexico lagged so far behind the United States? This book has shown that, in comparison to the experience of the United States, Mexico's uneven development is overwhelmingly rooted in the dual nature of the country's foundational factors—partly favorable, mostly unfavorable. In other words, Mexico's difficulties derive fundamentally from the predominance of the adverse side of the milieu that has shaped the national economy. The same can actually be said about many developing countries that have been subjected to the kinds of disadvantages found in Mexico.[1]

By highlighting unfavorable conditions that have worked against Mexico, it has not been my intent to exonerate Mexicans from any blame for the country's problems. Rather, the aim has been to point out the vital importance of context. Mexico's uneven development cannot be explained simply by focusing on corruption, erratic policy-making, or malfunctioning institutions. Such maladies have their origin largely in unfavorable conditions created by a problematic context.

Below is a summary of how foundational factors have impacted Mexico, followed by comments regarding the validity of comparisons that are often made between Mexico and other countries. The book ends with remarks on recently enacted reforms in Mexico and a final word regarding the need for bolder state action on behalf of the Mexican people.

Foundational Factor #1: The Natural Environment

The natural environment, encompassing climatic conditions, physical geography, and locational attributes, constitutes a foundational force of great significance in the shaping of Mexico. In the aftermath of the land loss following the U.S. expansionist war of 1846–1848, Mexico was left with a much smaller territory, a territory that had a mix of tropical, semitropical, and dry climates and a predominance of mountainous terrain. Such conditions greatly reduced the number of favorable areas available to the Mexican people. Unlike the United States, whose ubiquitous favorable spaces support population and economic agglomeration in many places, Mexico is limited to one large, excellent space—the Central Highlands—and a few additional smaller and scattered good spaces throughout the country. Most of the population in the United States lives in coastal areas and along internal waterways, reflecting the auspicious coincidence that many of that country's favorable spaces are located adjacent to bodies of water that can be used for transportation. But, in Mexico, a country that has few internal navigable waterways and whose hot, humid, and generally unhealthy coasts are not ideal living spaces and lack good hinterlands, most of the population is concentrated in the interior. Mexico's coastlines are also deficient in good harbors, having only a few suitable places that can physically host deep-water ports from which transoceanic trade can be conducted. The funnel-like shape of the country, combined with the physical arrangement of the major mountain ranges, gives rise to a predominant north-south axis that long ago locked the main transportation and communication corridors into narrow spaces situated between rugged landscapes. North-south movement of products and people is natural, but east-west movement has always been highly problematic as a result of mountain blockages. The difficult land surface has meant high transportation costs. Added together, the unfavorable features of the landscape, along with the excessively wet and dry climates that dominate large areas of Mexico, have made an enormous difference in how the country's economy has evolved.

Foundational Factor #2: Natural Resources

Up until the 1980s Mexico's economy was highly dependent on minerals, agriculture, and other raw materials. The view predominated that Mexico should be a much more prosperous country because of its supposedly abundant natural resources, especially its silver and oil deposits. In the minds of foreigners and Mexicans alike mismanagement and government corruption explained Mexico's substandard economic performance. Indeed Mexico's resource endowment has been substantial, but the notion that natural resources can propel any economy toward great heights is seriously flawed. Advanced development cannot occur if an economy relies mostly on primary products. Apart from the usual disconnectedness between the raw material sector and the rest of the economy typical of developing countries, the internationally driven "resource curse" is a constant menace. Mexico has felt the force of that curse on various occasions, and the consequences have been severe. As is the case in resource-dependent countries generally, Mexico has had difficulty utilizing its mineral base to develop a sizable domestic manufacturing sector. The troublesome geography has been a major problem, as it has undermined the building of transportation infrastructure capable of overcoming the intrinsic linkage problems between the raw materials sector and industry.

Mexico has been deficient in agricultural production due to climatic conditions, uneven rainfall patterns, and the shortage of good land. The fact that so much of the country is taken up by mountains, deserts, and jungles means that only 10 to 13 percent of the land is suitable for cultivation. The problem with agriculture in Mexico is compounded because the well-watered, technology-friendly good land is not amply concentrated in propitious locations as it is in various areas of the United States. To be sure there are some large favorable agricultural spaces in Mexico, but much of the cultivable land is scattered in small amounts in many isolated plains and valleys. By necessity farming is also done on hillsides, where the soil is poor and irrigation and the use of machinery are difficult. In addition, a large percentage of Mexico's best agricultural land is used to grow export crops rather than to satisfy local needs. Mexico's weighty agricultural problems are reflected in the need to import large amounts of food from the United States.

With all its limitations, Mexico's endowment of natural resources has made important contributions to the nation's economic growth. But the long era of pronounced resource dependency made clear that raw materials would not suffice to bring about high-level development. Advocates of the neoliberal model like to point out that commodity dependence is a thing of the past in Mexico. However, in view of the fact that the government continues to rely on oil for a substantial portion of its revenues, and given the reality that Mexico continues to have a U.S.-dependent economy that is predominantly driven by low-cost human labor, the validity of that claim is questionable.

Foundational Factor #3: Population Dynamics

Population pressures have troubled Mexico since the country achieved independence in 1821. At the time, underpopulation posed a serious problem, given that the country extended northward from Central America to the Canadian border and included today's U.S. Southwest. Many parts of the national domain were sparsely populated or not populated at all, especially in the North. This contributed to security vulnerabilities that eventually played into the hands of the United States during the era of American expansionism, which culminated in the U.S. detachment of Mexico's far northern frontier. Another major challenge for Mexico was how to integrate the millions of linguistically and culturally diverse indigenous groups scattered throughout the country. The difficult geography exacerbated the problem because so many Indian groups were pushed by Spaniards and Mexicans into remote locations. Even today a significant percentage of the Mexican population is still physically isolated and living in resource-deficient areas, lacking access to modern transportation, drinking water, education, health services, adequate housing, and good jobs. More construction of paved roads, highways, power lines, and water lines, as well as the delivery of an array of basic services, are needed in many underserved regions. All require large outlays of public expenditure. These circumstances have greatly complicated the already difficult task of alleviating poverty and pushing forward the nation-building agenda.

Consistent with the general pattern in developing countries, the demographic transition began much later in Mexico than in the United States or Western Europe. By the early twentieth century, underpopulation in Mexico abated as birth rates increased, child mortality declined, and life spans went up. Improvements in health services, better diets, more education, and urbanization brought about these changes, triggering gradually accelerating population growth. By the mid-twentieth century Mexicans began to worry about creeping overpopulation. But the government, still driven by old security concerns and convinced that the economy could sustain a much larger population, continued to promote large families. Mexico was not alone in encouraging population growth. Many countries in Europe and elsewhere followed a similar path, especially in the post–World War I and post–World War II periods. As social conditions continued to get better in Mexico, the fertility rate climbed higher and higher, and by the 1960s the country had to confront the reality that the era of overpopulation had arrived. Mexico's economy simply could not satisfy all the needs of a population that was growing at over 3 percent annually and doubling every twenty years. Despite some economic progress, huge numbers of poverty-stricken people found it difficult to make a living, much less to climb the social ladder into the middle class. The crisis that ensued compelled Mexico to abandon pro-growth policies in the 1970s and to initiate a comprehensive family planning program. In the decades that followed, the population program worked exceedingly well, bringing down fertility rates from 6 children per woman in her child-bearing years in 1975 to 2.3 children by 2011, and overall annual population growth rates down from 3.0 percent in 1974 to 1.1 percent in 2010. Despite the success, however, growth momentum has caused the population to continue to rise, even if more slowly. Unemployment and underemployment remain critical problems. In sum, the size, makeup, distribution, and growth trends of the population have had a deep effect on how Mexico has evolved economically.

Foundational Factor #4: External Relations

The evidence strongly supports the proposition that external relations constitute another foundational force of the first magnitude in the evolution of Mexico. Without question the interaction that Mexico has carried out with other countries has played a major role in determining internal development. One must first consider that Mexicans were not born a "free" people. As a colony of Spain for 300 years, Mexico lost a considerable portion of its natural wealth as the Europeans extracted large amounts of silver and gold. Mexico's indigenous population was subjected to brutal labor exploitation and also suffered a catastrophic demographic decline from smallpox and other deadly diseases introduced by the Spaniards. Poor mestizos were likewise exploited and marginalized. Colonialism ended with independence in 1821, but serious problems with foreigners would continue during the next century.

The old saying, "Poor Mexico, so far from God and so close to the United States," reveals a great deal about Mexico's mixed fortunes of being situated next to the world's major superpower. Since 1821 interaction with the United States has dominated Mexico's foreign relations. The worst outcome of that relationship for Mexico is the calamitous U.S. expansionist war of 1846–1848, which resulted in the loss of half Mexico's territorial holdings, including the extremely valuable provinces of Texas and California. The war truly shaped Mexico's destiny because what remained territorially was a much smaller space and one that had formidable geographic constraints. After 1848 Mexico's prospects for achieving a high level of development dwindled. For decades friction with the United States continued as numerous problems along the new border led to repeated U.S. interventions in Mexican political and economic affairs. Mexico experienced conflicts with European countries as well—namely with Spain, England, and France. Napoleon III practiced imperialism to an extreme, occupying Mexico from 1863 to 1867 with Ferdinand Maximilian as the surrogate "emperor." Serious trouble with the United States resurfaced during the Mexican Revolution of 1910–1920, a turbulent period that spawned numerous U.S. political and military interventions along the border, in the states of Chihuahua and Veracruz, and in Mexico City. In short, aggression against Mexico was rooted in the ambitions of other countries to tap into Mexico's natural wealth. Foreigners used Mexico's defaults on loan payments, its frequent inability to pay foreigners for property losses, and its chronic internal political troubles as pretexts for conquest and intervention. The confrontations with other countries took a heavy economic toll on Mexico.

After 1920 the relationship with the United States improved markedly, and since then bilateral disagreements have been settled diplomatically. While trade with the United States expanded, Mexico managed to make significant strides in fostering domestic industries. Yet Mexico remained largely a supplier of raw materials and an importer of capital goods and consumer products. In the 1980s, with its economy in great trouble and under external pressures, Mexico abandoned import substitution industrialization and adopted neoliberal policies, including trade liberalization. In 1994 Mexico began an unprecedented partnership with the United States and Canada with the enactment of the North American Free Trade Agreement (NAFTA), and later the Mexican government signed free-trade agreements with dozens of additional countries.

The radical economic changes brought about by neoliberalism have, since the 1980s, greatly stimulated Mexico's productivity and created lucrative opportunities for Mexicans well positioned to take advantage of them. Sectors of the middle class and blue-collar workers have also benefitted from expanded employment possibilities and from the greater availability of foreign consumer goods. But the lion's share of the material benefits produced by the neoliberal economy has flowed primarily to the elite sector of society and to the foreign corporations that have proliferated in Mexico. The impoverished masses have seen few of the fruits of free trade and expanded foreign investment. Moreover, select groups such as small corn producers have been devastated by food imports from the United States. Grinding poverty has forced millions of Mexicans to migrate to the United States, continuing a sad tradition that goes back generations.

One must not overlook one other extremely important historical effect of physical proximity to the powerful United States—the undermining of Mexican industry and commerce. Tariffs and other trade barriers imposed by the Mexican government never worked well because of the ease with which foreigners could circumvent them and because Mexico has always lacked the capacity to stop contraband on its porous northern border and its relatively unprotected coasts. Further, elite Mexicans long ago forged partnerships with foreign companies, thus reinforcing the economic subordination of Mexico to the United States. Mexico cannot escape its geographic trap. That reality goes a long way toward explaining why homegrown industries have not thrived in Mexico to the extent they have flourished in China, Japan, South Korea, and India. Such countries have not had to contend with an economic superpower as their next-door neighbor determined to dominate.

Foundational Factor #5: The Structure of Production and Governance

The manner in which Mexico's capitalistic economy has been structured and the way in which economic policy has been carried out cannot be separated from the four foundational factors discussed above. In other words, the production strategies utilized by the Mexican state and the private sector to promote growth have derived from the other factors, with environmental conditions and foreign relations being the most significant building blocks in that process. These strategies are as follows: 1821–early 1940s, exportation of raw materials and select protectionism of domestic industries; early1940s–early 1980s, exportation of raw materials and stepped-up import substitution industrialization; and early 1980s–present, free trade and export-oriented industrialization.

Many analysts have overemphasized the role of government in fostering or inhibiting development in Mexico. Frequently the spotlight regarding the nation's economic ills has been placed on the actions of the state, which is presumed to be all-powerful. In reality, the capacity of the state to keep the economy healthy has often been constrained by powerful forces beyond the control of those who govern. While governance has mattered greatly in the shaping of Mexico's economy, it has not been the deterministic force that many believe it to be. The state has never been an autonomous entity with unlimited capacity to control how the country functions economically. Governmental institutions have not performed well because they have not been well supported; they have not been well supported because there have not been enough financial resources for that purpose; and there have not been enough financial resources because of a predominant unfavorable context over an extended span of time. Corruption is likewise an outcome of the overall unfavorable context as much as it is a product of human greed. If inefficient institutions and inept or dishonest leaders were to disappear by magic in Mexico, it would make a significant difference for the country. But Mexicans would still have to contend with the difficult context that continues to present formidable hurdles to the achievement of genuine development. Overcoming the effects of that tough milieu remains a tall order.

In the last generation government policy has made possible the explosive growth of the manufacturing-for-export industries, with mixed outcomes for Mexico. On the bright side, maquiladoras have expanded their functions from simple assembly to greater complexity and sophistication. Further, an increasing number of Mexican firms are supplying inputs to the maquiladoras, although such activity remains extremely low. In the area of commercial subcontracting, where domestic firms make products from start to finish for foreign retailers, Mexico has also made minute gains in comparison to the heralded achievements of East Asian countries. Mexico has likewise made little headway in the domestic manufacture of consumer products bearing local proprietary brands for sale abroad through well-established retail networks. With the exception of the marketing of a few homegrown Mexican items such as beers, Mexico is decades behind a country like South Korea, whose proprietary brand computers, household appliances, and televisions are sold around the world. Mexican firms have simply not developed the capacity to produce globally competitive durable consumer products. Such weaknesses stem from the laissez-faire approach adopted by Mexico since 1980 as well as the ever-rising dependent relationship between Mexican firms and foreign corporations.

Comparing Mexico to the United States

As detailed throughout this book, Mexico's long-term struggle to develop economically is fundamentally different from the experience of the United States. Several factors underlie the divergence between the two neighbors. To start, the United States is several times the size of Mexico. That bigger U.S. landmass is primarily a result of U.S. expansionism not only in North America but in other parts of the planet as well. Without its massive territorial possessions, the United States would not have become such a prosperous and powerful country. But size is only part of the story. The land that makes up the continental United States is the most privileged space in the world for generating and sustaining economic productivity. No other country rivals the United States in physical advantages that lend themselves so naturally to promoting easy communication, efficient and inexpensive transportation, dynamic trade and commerce, and innovative industrialization. The bountiful gifts of nature bestowed on Americans include a superb geographic location, a very favorable topography, two coastlines approximately on the same latitude with prosperous regions of Europe and Asia, many excellent harbors, climatic diversity, and abundant resources such as agricultural land, precious metals, and industrial minerals. It is not surprising that the United States became the "land of opportunity" and that tens of millions of people have immigrated there from practically every corner of the earth. Population dynamics have likewise worked in favor of the United States in a spectacular manner. In its modern history the United States has had neither an "underpopulation" problem that would threaten the country's sovereignty or an "overpopulation" problem that would lead to significant stresses on natural resources or undermine societal cohesion. Population growth has taken place rather smoothly and in tandem with the needs present in different eras. There has never been another country with a comparable extraordinary capacity to attract massive numbers of talented and hardworking immigrants ready and able to contribute to the building of national wealth. Canada, Argentina, and Australia can be cited as examples of other countries that have attracted significant numbers of European immigrants, but nowhere near the levels of influx experienced by the United States. Nor has humankind seen another society that—even taking into account the historical discrimination against dark-skinned minorities—has so effectively assimilated so many people from so many different nationalities, ethnicities, cultures, and religions. With all these factors working in its favor, it is little wonder that the United States was able to develop a strong and relatively democratic government, efficient institutions, the rule of law, and most of the other positive attributes commonly thought to constitute the kind of human-created environment in which economic development can thrive.

It makes little sense to compare Mexico to the United States without taking into account the vast differences in the natural and human-generated foundations that have shaped each country. Careful examination of how the big-picture context has influenced the history of these two neighbors will yield a more accurate portrait of what forces drive or inhibit nations to develop their economies and will aid in the understanding of the complex workings of our planet. Foundational factors not only matter; they matter the most.

Comparing Mexico to the East Asian "Tigers"

The foundational factors approach goes a long way toward explaining the dramatic economic rise of East Asian countries with which Mexico is often compared—China, Taiwan, Japan, Singapore, and South Korea. Essentially, it is the general context that has prevailed in East Asia that made possible the rapid development of the "tigers." That context is very different from the milieu in which Mexico's economy has functioned. Consider geography and international conditions. Sheer distance from the United States and the excellent physical location of the above mentioned temperate-zone East Asian countries has allowed them to capitalize in a big way on the global trade and manufacturing opportunities that exploded in the post–World War II period and that have carried forward to the present. With the exception of China, which remained a closed economy until the late 1970s, the tigers took advantage of rapidly expanding world trade by utilizing their considerable natural assets, which included plenty of inexpensive labor and most notably excellent coastal areas and easy access to global shipping lanes. International politics during the Cold War also worked in their favor as the United States, in its zeal to stop the spread of communism, not only provided military security to its Asian allies (especially Japan, Taiwan, and South Korea) but also gave them generous economic aid, granted them privileged access to U.S. markets, and made other concessions to ensure their loyalty.[2] Such measures helped the tigers immensely in economic rebuilding following the destruction wrought by World War II and the Korean Conflict. With freedom to remake their industrial economies as they saw fit, the tigers cast aside neoliberal prescriptions promoted by the World Bank and the International Monetary Fund and instead crafted their own brands of state capitalism, put in place protectionist regimes to shield their fledgling industries, engaged in industrial espionage, imitated foreign technologies (mostly through "reverse engineering"), and carefully controlled the influx of foreign investment. They also utilized repressive measures when necessary to keep their workforces in line. In short, from the mid-1940s to the 1970s, Japan, Singapore, Taiwan, and Korea enjoyed exceptional opportunities to build strong industrial foundations in the context of a global milieu that suddenly had turned favorable for them and under a protective military shield and an economically magnanimous umbrella provided by the United States. With their manufacturing and trade regimes on solid footing, the tigers subsequently developed the wherewithal to compete at the highest levels of the world economy.

The rapid economic rise of South Korea merits special attention because it is singularly instructive regarding the roles that favorable internal foundational factors can play to promote development if the right international conditions are present. It is important to understand that the Korean peninsula has always possessed natural attributes that would have allowed it to become a strong independent economy well before World War II. However, that possibility had been forestalled when Korea was a protectorate of Japan from 1905 to 1910 and a Japanese colony from 1910 to 1945. Japanese rule was brutal for the Korean people. Economically, however, Korea derived significant benefits from Japanese development of transportation infrastructure, construction of ports, establishment of factories, expansion of education, and training of engineers, managers, and other professional and skilled workers. By 1945 Korea had an industrial infrastructure and an agricultural system considered to be among the best in the developing world.[3] The division of Korea into two political entities in the late 1940s and the subsequent war between them set back the whole peninsula. In the case of South Korea, however, U.S. intervention and material assistance during and after the war provided an enormous boost for the local economy. When geopolitical and global conditions changed for the better by the 1960s, South Korea could finally use its significant natural assets for economic gain. A temperate climate, the country's peninsular shape, physical location along major seaborne transport routes, and excellent harbors provided substantial advantages for conducting trade. A compact territory relatively unhampered by mountainous terrain facilitated national communication and internal migration, while remarkable population homogeneity encouraged national integration and made it possible for the government to elicit a strong commitment from the people to support the state-directed economic agenda. Population homogeneity also made it easier to persuade ordinary Koreans to embrace family planning, with the result that South Korea effectively curbed accelerated population growth decades before other developing countries could accomplish that important feat. By the early 1980s annual population growth in South Korea stood at an impressive 1.7 percent and the rate of fertility at 2.1, exactly the replacement level. The drastic drop in birth rates increased the proportion of working-age people and produced a "demographic dividend," meaning a demographically linked economic boost caused by a drop in the dependency ratio. Since the 1980s South Korea's population pyramid has mirrored those of developed countries. Today South Korea has a population of about 50 million. All these attributes, plus relative freedom from volcanoes and earthquakes, modest vulnerability to typhoons, possession of adequate arable land, sufficient rainfall, and bold state participation in economic affairs more than have made up for some agricultural problems, severe winters, some rough topography, lack of extensive plains, and shortages of industrial raw materials.

South Korea pursued economic growth through direct state activism once the umbrella of U.S. aid and military protection was in place and the traumas of World War II and the Korean War subsided. For years privileged access to U.S. markets and exchange learning from procurements in connection with U.S. wars in Asia played a central role in the rebirth and rising sophistication of domestic manufacturing. At the same time, South Korean officials promoted development calculated to be in the best interests of the country. They directed or regulated the banks, controlled foreign exchange, imposed a strong protectionist regime, practiced lax enforcement of foreign patent laws, encouraged "reverse engineering," supported autonomous research and development activities, and heavily subsidized strategic industries such as steel, shipping, machinery, electronics, and chemicals. The government favored manufacturers thought to have the best chance of becoming exporters of high-value durable goods to the United States and other world markets. Subsidies and loans flowed to privileged companies (chaebols) such as Samsung, engendering the emergence of conglomerates that led the upward surge of the country. The state also pressured citizens to shun foreign products, even cigarettes. The strategy worked. In a few decades South Korea transformed itself from a developing country into a dynamic independent economy that provided a respectable standard of living for the people.

Could Mexico have followed the example of South Korea and other East Asian countries? That seems inconceivable given the vastly different context in which Mexico's economy has functioned historically. Lacking the geographic attributes and anticommunist political leverage of the tigers, in the post-1950 era Mexico continued its development efforts not only in the shadow of the powerful U.S. economy, but actually under a condition of subordination to U.S. corporations that dated back to the nineteenth century. U.S. corporations had little difficulty in establishing themselves in Mexico, even during periods when the Mexican government placed stiff restrictions on foreign investment. Here again, plenty of Mexican elites who stood to benefit from partnerships with foreigners welcomed U.S. corporations into their homeland and lobbied on their behalf. Physical location next to the United States thus made it very difficult for Mexico to implement independent policies such as those carried on by the East Asian tigers and also to copy or appropriate foreign technologies in violation of patent laws. Mexicans did capitalize on new global opportunities but, given the circumstances at hand, they felt compelled to do so within the confines of a dependency framework that could not be changed.

A Final Word

Neoliberal academics and organizations have for years bombarded Mexico with recommendations on how to improve the country's competitiveness in the global economy.[4] The general message is a familiar one: by focusing on its "comparative advantage" (i.e., low-cost labor), adhering closely to market principles, and limiting government intervention in the economy, Mexico will spur productivity and the benefits of growth will trickle down to all Mexicans. But the model has not lived up to expectations. The reason, neoliberal analysts maintain, is that Mexico has not sufficiently dismantled the old (pre-1980s) system of production and governance. After lengthy debates, the Mexican government indeed recently enacted a number of structural reforms in education, labor, taxation, monopolies, telecommunications, and energy. These initiatives represent positive steps for Mexico, both from the perspective of productivity as well as the well-being of the population. Caution, however, is in order regarding how much the generally mild reforms can actually accomplish. It is far from certain whether the government has the capacity to overcome the strong resistance expected from powerful groups and corporations whose interests are threatened by such policy changes. Given historical antecedents and the circumstances that currently prevail in Mexico, even if all said reforms are implemented effectively, they will hardly suffice to bring about the transformation needed to significantly improve the lives of the impoverished bottom half of Mexican society.

A bolder approach by the state is required, one that elevates the needs of people to the same level as the interests of business and industry. Steps that could be taken in order to at least modestly improve living conditions in Mexico might include the following: mandating meaningful wage increases; raising more tax revenues to expand social programs; providing more state support for domestic research and development; subsidizing homegrown companies engaged in high value-added manufacturing; stepping up assistance to small and middle-sized farmers hurt by free-trade policies; and legalizing drugs to lessen corruption and lawlessness linked to the drug trade. Mexico can do more to mitigate its foundational constraints.

Notes

1 In a separate study in progress, tentatively titled "Rich Lands, Poor Lands: Why Some Nations Are Wealthy but Most Are Poor," I find that the model developed here fits well in the Third World in general.
2 Hersh (1993); Forsberg (2000); Mason (1980); Cummings (1987); Chang (2006).
3 Mason (1980), 90; Cummings (1987), 56.
4 OECD (2007, 2013).

BIBLIOGRAPHY

Acemoglu, Daron, and James A. Robinson (2012). *Why Nations Fail: The Origins of Power, Prosperity, and Poverty*. New York: Crown Publishers.
Adams, John A. (2008). *Conflict and Commerce on the Rio Grande: Laredo, 1755–1955*. College Station: Texas A & M Press.
Aguilar Camin, Hector, and Lorenzo Meyer, translation by Luis Alberto Fierro (1993). *In the Shadow of the Mexican Revolution: Contemporary Mexican History, 1910–1989*. Austin: University of Texas Press.
Aguirre Beltán, Gonzalo (1946). *La población negra de México, 1519–1810: Estudio etnográfico*. México, D.F.: Ediciones Fuente Cultural.
Alanís Patiño, Emilio (1943). "La riqueza de México." *El Trimestre Económico* 10:37 (April–June), 97–134.
Alba, Francisco, and Gustavo Cabrera, eds. (1994). *La población en el desarrollo contemporáneo de México*. México, D.F.: Colegio de México.
Alba, Francisco, and Joseph E. Potter (1986). "Population and Development in Mexico since 1940: An Interpretation." *Population and Development Review*, 12:1 (March), 47–75.
Alexander, John W. (1979). *Economic Geography*. Englewood Cliffs: Prentice Hall.
Almond, Gabriel A., and G.B. Powell (1965). *Comparative Politics: A Developmental Approach*. Boston: Little Brown.
Almonte, Juan Nepomuceno (1925). "Statistical Report on Texas, 1835," translated by C.E. Castañeda. *The Southwestern Historical Quarterly* 28:3 (January), 177–222.
American Association of Port Authorities (2006). "World Port Rankings—2006." www.aapa-ports.org.
Amsden, Alice H. (2001). *The Rise of "The Rest": Challenges to the West from Late-Industrializing Economies*. New York: Oxford University Press.
Apter, David E. (1965). *The Politics of Modernization*. Chicago: University of Chicago Press.
Arizona Daily Star. October 22, 2006; September 6, 2011.
Armendáriz E., Manuel (1982). *A Mexican View of U.S. Protectionism*. Washington, D.C.: Overseas Development Council.
ATF (2011). "Tobacco: The New Commodity for Criminals." www.atf.gov.

Atwood, Wallace Walter (1940). *The Physiographic Provinces of North America*. Boston: Ginn and Company.

Auty, Richard M. (1993). *Sustaining Development in Mineral Economies: The Resource Curse Thesis*. London: Routledge.

Avella Alaminos, Isabel (2010). *De oportunidades y retos: Los engranajes del comercio exterior de México, 1920–1947*. México, D.F.: El Colegio de México.

Ayllón Torres, Teresa (1990). *México: Sus recursos naturales y su población*. México, D.F.: Noriega Editorial Limusa.

Bagley, Bruce M. (1981). "A United States Perspective," in Susan Kaufman Purcell, ed. *Mexico-United States Relations*, 13–24. New York: The Academy of Political Science.

Balderrama, Francisco E. and Raymond Rodríguez (1995). *Decade of Betrayal: Mexican Repatriation in the 1930s*. Albuquerque: University of New Mexico Press.

Ballinger, Clint. (2011, January). "Why Geographic Factors are Necessary in Development Studies." http://ssrn.com/abstract=179112 and clintballinger@cantab.net.

Bamford, C.G., and H. Robinson. (1978). *Geography of Transport*. Estover: MacDonald and Evans.

Banco de México (2008). *Informe Annual 2008*.

Baran, Paul (1957). *The Political Economy of Growth*. New York: Monthly Review Press.

Barker, Eugene C. (1928). *Mexico and Texas, 1821–1835*. Dallas: P.L. Turner.

Barth, Helen (1965). *México, su problema demográfico*. México, D.F.: Ed. De la Sociedad Mexicana de Planificación.

Bassols Batalla, Angel (1959a). "Bosquejo histórico-geográfico del desarrollo de la red de caminos de México." *Investigación Económica*, (UNAM) 19, 645–681.

Bassols Batalla, Angel (1959b). "Consideraciones geográficas y económicas en la confiuración de las redes de carreteras y vías férreas en México." *Investigacón Económica*, (UNAM) 19:73, 41–82.

Bassols Batalla, Angel (1980). *Geografía Económica de México*. México, D.F.: Editorial Trillas.

Bauer, P.T. (1972). *Dissent on Development*. Cambridge, MA: Harvard University Press.

Bazant, Jan (1995). *Historia de la deuda exterior de México, 1823–1946*. México, D.F.: El Colegio de México.

Beatty, Edward (2000). "The Impact of Foreign Trade on the Mexican Economy: Terms of Trade and the Rise in Industry, 1880–1923." *Journal of Latin American Studies*, 32: 2 (May), 399–433.

Beatty, Edward (2001). *Institutions and Investment: The Political Basis of Industrialization in Mexico before 1911*. Stanford: Stanford University Press.

Beatty, Edward (2015). *Technology and the Search for Progress in Modern Mexico*. Oakland: University of California Press.

Benjamin, Thomas (1996). *A Rich Land: A Poor People: Politics and Society in Modern Chiapas*. Albuquerque: University of New Mexico Press.

Benson, Nettie Lee (1989). "Territorial Integrity in Mexican Politics, 1821–1833," in Jaime E. Rodríguez O., ed., *The Independence of Mexico and the Creation of the New Nation*, 275–310. Los Angeles: UCLA Latin American Center Publications.

Benson, Nettie Lee (1987). "Texas Viewed from Mexico, 1820–1834." *Southwestern Historical Quarterly*, 90:3, 219–291.

Berlandier, Jean Louis (1980). *Journey to Mexico During the Years 1826 to 1834*, 2 vols., translated by Sheila M. Ohlendorf, Josette M. Bigelow, and Mary M. Standifer, Introduction by C.H. Muller. Austin: The Texas State Historical Association.

Bernecker, Walther L. (1993). "Contrabando. Illegalidad y corrupción en el México decimonónico." *Espacio, Tiempo y Forma*, Serie V, H. Contemporánea 6, 393–418.

Bernecker, Walther L. (1994). *Contrabando: Ilegalidad y corrupción en el México del siglo xix*. México, D.F.: Universidad Iberoamericana.
Bernecker, Walther L. (1997). "La industria mexicana en el siglo xix. Las condiciones-marco de la industrialización en el siglo xix," in Ma. Eugenia Romero Sotelo, ed., *La industria Mexicana y su historia: Siglos xviii, xix, y xx*, 87–171. México, D.F.: UNAM.
Bernstein, Marvin D. (1964). *The Mexican Mining Industry, 1890–1950*. Albany: State University of New York.
Bloomberg News: February 6, 2012.
Borah, Woodrow Wilson, and Sherburne F. Cook (1963). *The Aboriginal Population of Mexico on the Eve of the Spanish Conquest*. Berkeley: University of California Press.
Bortz, Jeffrey, and Macos Aguila (2006). "Earning a Living: A History of Real Wage Studies in Twentieth-Century Mexico." *Latin American Research Review*, 41:2, 112–138.
Boyle, Susan Calafate (1997). *Los Capitalistas: Hispano Merchants and the Santa Fe Trade*. Albuquerque: University of New Mexico Press.
British Geological Survey (2010). *World Mineral Production 2004–2008*. Keyworth, Nottingham: British Geological Survey.
Brown, Ralph H., and Joe R. Whitaker (1948). *Historical Geography of the United States*. New York: Harcourt, Brace.
Bruchey, Stuart (1965). *The Roots of American Economic Growth, 1607–1861*. New York: Harper and Row.
Business Mexico: May 2000.
Cabrera, Gustavo (1994). "Demographic Dynamics and Development: The Role of Population Policy in Mexico." *Population and Development Review* 20, Supplement, 105–120.
Cabrera, Gustavo (2007). *Obras demográficas selectas*. México, D.F.: El Colegio de México.
Calderón, Francisco R. (1955). *Historia moderna de México: La república restaurada*. General Editor Daniel Cosío Villegas. México, D.F.: Editorial Hermes.
Cañas, Jesus, Roberto Coronado, and Robert W. Gilmer (2006). "U.S., Mexico Deepen Economic Ties." *Southwest Economy*, 11–14, (January/February 2006).
Cárdenas Sánchez, Enrique (2003). *Cuando se originó el atraso económico de México: La economía mexicana en el largo siglo xix, 1780–1920*. Madrid, España: Editorial Biblioteca Nueva.
Cárdenas Sánchez, Enrique, compilador (2004). *Historia económica de México*, segunda edición. México, D.F.: Fondo de Cultura Económica.
Cárdenas Sánchez, Enrique (1996). *La política económica en México, 1950–1994*. México, D.F.: Fondo de Cultura Económica.
Cardoso, Fernando H., and Enzo Faletto (1979). *Dependency and Development in Latin America*. Berkeley: University of California Press.
Carlson, Fred A. (1936). *Geography of Latin America*. New York: Prentice-Hall.
Carter, Susan B. et al., eds. (2006). *Historical Statistics of the United States: Earliest Times to the Present*. New York: Cambridge University Press.
Castañeda, Jorge G. (2011). *Mañana Forever? Mexico and the Mexicans*. New York: Alfred A. Knopf.
Ceceña, José Luis (2007). Ana Esther Ceceña y Raúl Ornerlas, compiladores. *La nación mexicana frente a los monopolios*. México, D.F.: Siglo XXI.
Ceceña, José Luis (1970). *México en la órbita imperial*. México, D.F.: "El Caballito.
Chandler, Tertius, and Gerald Fox (1974). *3000 Years of Urban Growth*. New York: Academic Press.
Chang, Ha-Joon (2008). *Bad Samaritans: The Myth of Free Trade and the Secret History of Capitalism*. New York: Bloomsbury Press.
Chang, Ha-Joon (2006). *The East Asian Development Experience: The Miracle, the Crisis, and the Future*. New York: Zed Books.

Chang, Ha-Joon (2002). *Kicking Away the Ladder: Development Strategy in Historical Perspective*. London: Anthem Press.
Chesnais, Jean-Claude (1992). *The Demographic Transition: Stages, Patterns, and Economic Implications*. New York: Oxford University Press.
Christian Science Monitor. July 15, 1996.
CIA. *World Factbook*: 1981–2012.
Clarkson, Stephen, and Matto Mildenberger (2011). *Dependent America? How Canada and Mexico Construct U.S. Power.* Toronto: University of Toronto Press.
Cline, Howard F. (1962). *Mexico: Revolution to Evolution, 1940–1960*. New York: Oxford University Press.
Cline, Howard F. (1963). *The United States and Mexico*. Cambridge: Harvard University Press.
Clough, Shepard B. (1953). *The Economic Basis of American Civilization*. New York: Crowell.
Coale, Ansley J. and Melvin Zelnik (1963). *New Estimates of Fertility and Population in the United States; A Study of Annual White Births from 1855 to 1960 and of Completeness of Enumeration in the Censuses from 1880 to 1960*. Princeton, N. J.: Princeton University Press.
Coatsworth, John H. (1989). "The Decline of the Mexican Economy, 1800–1860," in Reinhard Lier, ed., *América Latina en la época de Simón Bolívar: La formación de las economías nacionales y los intereses económicos europeos, 1800–1850*, 27–54. Berlin: Colloquium Vertag.
Coatsworth, John H. (1981). *Growth against Development: The Economic Impact of Railroads in Porfirian Mexico*. De Kalb: Northern Illinois University Press.
Coatsworth, John H. (1978). "Obstacles to Economic Growth in Nineteenth-Century Mexico." *American Historical Review* 83:1 (February), 80–100.
Coatsworth, John H., and Jeffrey S. Williamson. (2004). "Always Protectionist? Latin American Tariffs from Independence to Great Depression." *Journal of Latin American Studies* 36:2 (May), 205–232.
Cockcroft, James D. (1998). *Mexico's Hope: An Encounter with Politics and History*. New York: Monthly Press.
Cohen, Michael J. (2011, June 12). *Municipal Deliveries of Colorado River Basin Water*. Oakland, CA: Pacific Institute.
Cole, J.P. (1965). *Latin America: An Economic and Social Geography*. London: Butterworths.
Colegio de México (1960). *Estadísticas económicas del porfiriato: Comercio exterior de México, 1877–1911*. México, D.F.: Colegio de México.
Combined Mexican Working Party (1953). *The Economic Development of Mexico*. Baltimore: John Hopkins Press.
Cook, Sherburne F., and Woodrow Borah (1960). *The Indian Population of Central Mexico, 1531–1610*. Berkeley: University of California Press.
Coote, Belinda, with Caroline LeQuesne (1996). *Trade Trap: Poverty and the Global Commodity Markets*. Oxford, UK: Oxfam.
Corchado, Alfredo (2013). *Midnight in Mexico: A Reporter's Journey through a Country's Descent into the Darkness*. New York: The Penguin Press.
Cordero Melo, Yolanda (1997). *Geografía de la república mexicana*. Mexico: Editorial Herrero.
Cortés, Hernan (1986). *Letters from Mexico*, translated and edited by Anthony Pagden. New Haven: Yale University Press.
Corwin, Arthur F. (1982). "The Numbers Game: Estimates of Illegal Aliens in the United States, 1970–1981." *Law and Contemporary Problems* 45:2 (Spring), 223–297.
Cosío Villegas, Daniel (1949). "La riqueza legendaria de México," in Daniel Cosío Villegas, ed., *Extremos de América*, 154–176. México, D.F.: Tezontle.

Costeloe, Michael P. (2003). *Bonds and Bondholders: British Investors and Mexico's Foreign Debt, 1824–1888*. Westport, CT: Praeger Publishers.
Cotter, Joseph (2003). *Troubled Harvest: Agronomy and Revolution in Mexico, 1880–2002*. Westport, CT: Praeger.
Cue Canovas, Agustín (1970). *Los Estados Unidos y El México olvidado*. New York: Arno Press.
Cuéllar, Alfredo B. (1936). "Railroad Problems of Mexico." *Annals of the American Academy of Political and Social Science* (September), 193–206.
Cueto, Marcos (2007). *Cold War, Deadly Fevers: Malaria Eradication in Mexico, 1955–1975*. Baltimore: The Johns Hopkins University Press.
Cumberland, Charles C. (1968). *Mexico: The Struggle for Modernity*. New York: Oxford University Press.
Cummings, Bruce (1987). "The Origins and Development of the Northeast Asian Political Economy Industrial Sectors, Production Cycles, and Political Consequences," in Frederic C. Deyo, ed., *The Political Economy of New Asian Industrialism*, 44–83. Ithaca: Cornell University Press.
Current History: March 1987.
Cypher, James M., and Raúl Delgado Wise (2010). *Mexico's Economic Dilemma: The Development Failure of Neoliberalism*. New York: Rowman & Littlefield Publishers.
Dallas Morning News, February 14, 2014.
Dana Jr., Richard Henry (1911). *Two Years before the Mast: A Personal Narrative* [originally published in 1840]. New York: Houghton Mifflin Company.
De Grammont, Hubert C. (2003). "The Agricultural Sector and Rural Development in Mexico: Consequences of Economic Globalization," in Kevin J. Middlebrook and Eduardo Zepeda, eds. *Confronting Development: Assessing Mexico's Economic and Social Policy Challenges*, 350–384. Stanford: Stanford University Press.
De la Calle, Luis, and Luis Rubio (2012). *Mexico: A Middle Class Society, Poor No More, Developed Not Yet*. Washington, D.C.: Mexico Institute, Woodrow Wilson Center for Scholars.
Diamond, Jared (1997). *Guns, Germs, and Steel: The Fates of Human Societies*. New York: W. W. Norton.
Díaz, George T. (2015). *Border Contraband. A History of Smuggling across the Rio Grande*. Austin: University of Texas Press.
Díaz del Castillo, Bernal (1955). *Historia Verdadera de la Conquista de la Nueva España* [originally published in 1632]. México, D.F: Porrua.
Dobado González, Rafael Aurora Gómez Galvarriato, and Jeffrey G. Williamson (2008). "Mexican Exceptionalism: Globalization and De-Industrialization, 1750–1877." *The Journal of Economic History* 68:3 (September), 1–54.
Duflot de Mofras, Eugene. (1937). *Duflot de Mofras' Travels on the Pacific Coast*. Translated, edited and annotated by Marguerite Eyer Wilbur, foreword by Dr. Frederick Webb Hodge. Santa Ana, CA: The Fine Arts Press.
Dwyer, John J. (2008). *The Agrarian Dispute: The Expropriation of American-Owned Rural Land in Postrevolutionary Mexico*. Durham, NC: Duke University Press.
The Economist: November 30, 2002; October 30, 2010; August 16, 2014.
El Diario de El Paso: January 18, 2010, March 1, 2010.
El Paso Herald Post: October 25, 1978.
El Paso Times: February 2, 1986; August 7, 2011; January 8, 2012; February 19, 2012; June 13, 2012; July 13, 2012; September 10, 2012; September 26, 2014.
Elizondo, Carlos (1994). "In Search of Revenue: Tax Reform in Mexico under the Administrations of Echeverría and Salinas," *Journal of Latin American Studies* 26 (February), 159–190.

Engerman, Stanley, and Kenneth Sokoloff (2012). *Economic Development in the Americas since 1500: Endowments and Institutions*. New York: Cambridge University Press.

Enock, Reginald (1909). *Mexico*. London: T. Fisher Unwin.

Esquivel, Gerardo (2000). "Geografía y desarrollo económico en México." Inter-American Development Bank, Research Network Working Paper #R-389.

Esquivel, Gerardo, and Graciela Márquez (2007). "Some Economic Effects of Closing the Economy: The Mexican Experience in the Mid-Twentieth Century," in Sebastian Edwards, Gerardo Esquivel, and Graciela Márquez, eds., *The Decline of Latin American Economies: Growth, Institutions, and Crises*, 333–362. Chicago: University of Chicago Press.

EIU ViewsWire (March 20, 2003). www.eiu.com.

Evans, Peter (1979). *Dependent Development*. Princeton: Princeton University Press.

Excelsior. May 5, 2013.

Falck, Melba E., and José Jaime Jiménez (2012). "Qué hay detrás de deficit commercial de México con Asia?" *México y la Cuenca del Pacífico* 15:43 (January–April), 9–14.

Feder, Ernest (1977). *Strawberry Imperialism: An Enquiry into the Mechanisms of Dependency in Mexican Agriculture*. The Hague: Institute of Social Studies.

Federal Writers' Project (1939). *California: A Guide to the Golden State*. New York: Hastings House.

Findlay, Ronald, and Kevin H. O'Rourke (2007). *Power and Plenty: Trade, War, and the World Economy in the Second Millennium*. Princeton: Princeton University Press.

Florida, Richard, Tim Gulden, and Charlotta Mellander (2007). "The Rise of the Mega Region." University of Toronto, The Martin Prosperity Institute (unpublished paper).

FNS (Frontera Norte Sur) News: September 30, 2013; December 22, 2012.

Forbes, Alexander (1973). *California: A History of Upper and Lower California*. New York: Arno Press.

Forbes Magazine (2013). "The World's Billionaires, 2012 List." www.forges.com/billionaires/list/.

Forsberg, Aaron (2000). *America and the Japanese Miracle*. Chapel Hill: University of North Carolina Press.

Frank, Andre Gunder (1967). *Capitalism and Underdevelopment in Latin America*. New York: Monthly Review Press.

Freithaler, William O. (1968). *Mexico's Foreign Trade and Economic Development*. New York: Praeger.

Fuller, John D.P. (1936). *The Movement for the Acquisition of All Mexico*. Baltimore: Johns Hopkins University Press.

Galeano, Eduardo (1997). *Open Veins of Latin America: Five Centuries of the Pillage of a Continent*. New York: Monthly Review Press.

Gallagher, Kevin, and Roberto Porzecanski (2010). *The Dragon in the Room: China and the Future of Latin American Industrialization*. Stanford: Stanford University Press.

Gallagher, Kevin, and Lyuba Zarsky (2007). *The Enclave Economy: Foreign Investment and Sustainable Development in Mexico's Silicon Valley*. Cambridge, MA: MIT Press.

Gallup, John L., Alejandro Gaviria, and Eduardo Lora (2003). *Is Geography Destiny? Lessons from Latin America*. New York: Inter-American Development Bank.

Gallup, John L., Jeffrey D. Sachs, and Andrew D. Mellinger (1998). "Geography and Economic Development." National Bureau of Economic Research, Working Paper #6849 (December).

Garitty, Thomas (2013). *Capital in the Twenty-First Century*. Cambridge, MA: Harvard University Press.

Garza, Gustavo (1976). *El desarrollo urbano de México: Diagnóstico e implicaciones futuras.* México, D.F.: El Colegio de México.
Garza, Gustavo (2003). "The Dialectics of Urban and Regional Disparities in Mexico," in Kevin J. Middlebrook and Eduardo Zepeda, eds., *Confronting Development: Assessing Mexico's Economic and Social Policy Challenges*, 487–521. Stanford: Stanford University Press.
Garza, Gustavo (1985). *El proceso de industrialización en la ciudad de México, 1821–1970.* México, D.F.: El Colegio de México.
Garza, Gustavo (2003). *La urbanización the México en el siglo XX.* México, D.F.: El Colegio de México.
Gauss, Susan M. (2010). *Made in Mexico: Regions, Nation, and the State in the Rise of Mexican Industrialism, 1920s-1940s.* University Park: Pennsylvania State University Press.
Gelb, Alan and Associates (1988). *Oil Windfalls: Blessing or Curse?* New York: Oxford University Press.
Geo-Mexico website. www.//geo-mexico.com: Posts for April 23, 2010; May 3, 2011; May 5, 2012; November 23, 2013.
Gereffi, Gary (1996). "Mexico's 'Old' and 'New' Maquiladora Industries: Contrasting Approaches to North American Integration," in Gerardo Otero, ed. *Neoliberalism Revisited: Economic Restructuring and Mexico's Political Future*, 85–106. Boulder: Westview Press.
Gill, Tom (1951). *Land Hunger in Mexico.* Washington: Charles Lathrop Pack Forestry Foundation.
Glasmeier, Amy K. (2006). *An Atlas of Poverty in America: One Nation Pulling Apart.* New York: Routledge.
Global Financial Integrity (2012). *Mexico: Illicit Financial Flows, Macroeconomic Imbalances, and the Underground Economy.* Washington, D.C.: Global Financial Integrity.
Global Post: January 17, 2012, www.globalpost.com.
Goldprice. www.goldprice.org.
González Casnova, Pablo (1970). *Democracy in Mexico*, translated by Danielle Salti. New York: Oxford University Press.
González Navarro, Moisés (1984). *Historia moderna de México: El porfiriato, La vida social.* Mexico: Editorial Hermes.
González Navarro, Moisés (1974). *Población y Sociedad en México, 1900–1970*, vols. 1 and 2. México, D.F.: UNAM.
González Reyna, Jenaro (1956). *Riqueza minera y yacimientos minerals de México.* México, D.F.: Banco de México, Departamento de Investigaciones Industriales.
Goodrich, Carter (1961). *Canals and American Economic Development.* New York: Columbia University Press.
Goodrich, Joseph K. (1913). *The Coming Mexico.* Chicago: A. C. McClurg & Co.
Gordon, John Steele (2004). *An Empire of Wealth: The Epic Story of American Economic Power.* New York: Harper Collins.
Gottmann, Jean (1961). *Megalopolis: The Urbanized Northeastern Seaboard of the United States.* Cambridge, MA: M.I.T. Press.
Gracida, Elsa (1997). "La industria en México, 1950–1980," in Romero Sotelo, María Eugenia, and Luis Jauregi, coordinators, *La industria mexicana y su historia: siglos xviii, xix, xx*, 419–494. México, D.F.: UNAM.
Graebner, Norman A. (1951). "United States Gulf Commerce with Mexico, 1822–1848." *Inter-American Economic Affairs*, I (Summer), 36–51.
Grant, U. S. (1885–1886). *Personal Memoirs of U.S. Grant*, 2 vols. New York: Charles L. Webster & Co.
Grantz, Margo (1982). *Viajes en México: crónicas extranjeras*, 2 vols. México, D.F.: Fondo de Cultura Económica.

Green, Rosario (1998). *Lecciones de la deuda externa de México, de 1973 a 1997*. México, D.F.: Fondo de Cultura Económica.
Greenberg, Amy S. (2012). *A Wicked War: Polk, Clay, Lincoln, and the 1846 U.S. Invasion of Mexico*. New York: Alfred A. Knopf.
Greenpeace Noticias (July 9, 2009). www.greenpeace.org/Mexico/es/Noticias/2009.
Grunwald, Joseph (1970). *Natural Resources in Latin American Development*. Baltimore: Johns Hopkins Press.
Guerra, Francois-Xavier (1988). *México, del antiguo regimen a la Revolución*, traducción de Sergio Fernández Bravo. México, D.F.: Fondo de Cultura Económica.
Haber, Stephen H. (1992). "Assessing the Obstacles to Industrialization: The Mexican Economy, 1830–1940." *Journal of Latin American Studies*, 24:1 (February), 1–32.
Haber, Stephen, ed. (1997). *How Latin America Fell Behind: Essays on the Economic History of Brazil and Mexico, 1800–1914*. Stanford: Stanford University Press.
Haber, Stephen (1989). *Industry and Underdevelopment: The Industrialization of Mexico, 1890–1940*. Stanford: Stanford University Press.
Haber, Stephen, Herbert S. Klein, Noel Maurer, and Kevin J. Middlebrook (2008). *Mexico since 1980*. New York: Cambridge University Press.
Haggert, Peter (2001). *Geography: A Global Synthesis*. New York: Prentice Hall.
Hammond Incorporated (1984). *United States History Atlas*. Maplewood, NJ: Hammond.
Handbook of Texas Online. www.tshaonline.org.
Hansen, Roger D. (1971). *The Politics of Mexican Development*. Baltimore: Johns Hopkins University Press.
Harlow, Neal (1982). *California Conquered*. Berkeley: University of California Press.
Harris III, Charles, and Ray Saddler (2009). *The Secret War in El Paso*. Albuquerque: University of New Mexico Press.
Hart, John Mason (2002). *Empire and Revolution: The Americans in Mexico since the Civil War*. Berkeley: University of California Press.
Hart, John Mason (1987). *Revolutionary Mexico: The Coming and Process of the Mexican Revolution*. Berkeley: University of California Press.
Hart, John Mason (2008). *The Silver of the Sierra Madre: John Robinson, Boss Sheperd, and the People of the Canyons*. Tucson: University of Arizona Press.
Heilbroner, Robert L., with Aaron Singer (1977). *The Economic Transformation of America*. New York: Harcourt Brace Jovanovich.
Henderson, David A. (1966). "Land, Man, and Time," in Russell C. Ewing, et al. *Six Faces of Mexico: History, People, Geography, Government, Economy, Literature and Art*, 103–160. Tucson: University of Arizona Press.
Hernández, Jorge A. (1997). "Trading across the Border: National Customs Guards in Nuevo León." *The Southwestern Historical Quarterly*, 100:4 (April), 433–450.
Hernández Chávez, Alicia (2006). *Mexico: A Brief History*, translated by Andy Klatt. Berkeley: University of California Press.
Hernández, Roberto (2012). "La política de comercio exterior de China y sus implicaciones para las relaciones comerciales con México." *México y la Cuenca del Pácifico*, 15:43 (January–April), 65–96.
Herrera Pérez, Octavio (2004). *La Zona Libre: Excepción fiscal conformación histórica de la frontera norte de México*. México, D.F.: Secretaría de Relaciones Exteriores.
Hersh, Jacques (1993). *The USA and the Rise of East Asia since 1945: Dilemmas of the Postwar International Economy*. New York: St. Martin's Press.
Higgins Industries (1954). *Estudio sobre México: Economía, transportes, navegación*, 2 vols. México, D.F.: El Banco de México.

Highsmith, Jr., Richard M., and Ray M. Northham (1968). *World Economic Activities: A Geographic Analysis*. New York: Harcourt, Brace & World.
Hilling, David (1996). *Transport and Developing Countries*. New York: Routledge.
Hindle, Brooke, and Steven Lubar (1986). *Engines of Change: The American Industrial Revolution, 1790–1860*. Washington, D.C.: Smithsonian Institution Press.
Holechek, Jerry L. et al. (2000). *Natural Resources: Ecology, Economics, and Policy*. Upper Saddle River, NJ: Prentice Hall.
Horn, Paul V., and Hubert E. Bice (1949). *Latin-American Trade and Economics*. New York: Prentice-Hall.
Hughes, Jonathan, and Louis P. Cain (2003). *American Economic History*, 6th ed. New York: Addison Wesley.
Hunter, Louis C. (1949). *Steamboats on the Western Rivers: An Economic and Technological History*. Cambridge, MA: Harvard University Press.
Hurtig, Mel (1991). *The Betrayal of Canada*. Toronto: Stoddard.
Ibarra Bellon, Araceli (1998). *El comercio y el poder en Mexico, 1821–1864*. México, D.F.: Fondo de Cultura Económica y Universidad de Guadalajara.
International Road Federation (2012). *IRF World Road Statistics*. Geneva, Switzerland: International Road Federation.
Investopedia.com, July 12, 2012.
Iturriaga, José E. (1987). *La estructura social y cultural de México*. México, D.F.: Secretaría de Educación Pública.
Izquierdo, Rafael (1973). "El proteccionismo en México." *La Economía Mexicana*, 4:1, 228–269.
Jáuregui, Luis (2010). "La economía de la guerra de independencia y la fiscalidad de las primeras décadas del México independiente," in Sandra Kuntz Ficker, coordinator, *Historia económica general de México: De la colonia a nuestros días*. 245–274. México, D.F.: El Colegio de México.
Jáuregui, Luis (2004). *Los transportes, siglos xvi and xx*. México, D.F.: Océano.
Jayes, Janice Lee (2011). *The Illusion of Ignorance: Constructing the American Encounter with Mexico, 1877–1920*. Boulder: University Press of America.
Jeter, Jon (2009). *Flat Broke in the Free Market: How Globalization Fleeced Working People*. New York: Norton.
Jones, Chester Lloyd (1921). *Mexico and Its Reconstruction*. New York: D. Appleton and Company.
Journal of Commerce: January 10, 2005.
Juarez-El Paso Now: May 2010; April 2011; January 2012; November 2013; June 2014; August 2014.
Kaplan, Edward S (1996). *American Trade Policy: 1923–1995*. Westport, CT: Greenwood Press.
Kaplan, Robert D. (2012). *The Revenge of Geography: What the Map Tells Us About Coming Conflicts and the Battle Against Fate*. New York: Random House.
Kar, Dav (2012). *Mexico: Illicit Financial Flows, Macroeconomic Imbalances, and the Underground Economy*. Washington, D.C.: Global Finacial Integrity.
Katz, Bernard S. (1976). "Mexico's Tariff Policy: A Study in Alternatives." *American Journal of Economics and Sociology* 35:3 (July), 235–250.
Katz, Michael B., and Mark J. Stern (2001). "Poverty in Twentieth Century America." America at the Millennium Project, Working Paper #7 (November).
Kelso, Paul (1966). "Mexico 1963: Facts, Figures, Trends," in Russell C. Ewing, ed., *Six Faces of Mexico*, 193. Tucson: University of Arizona Press.

Keremitsis, Dawn (1973). *La industria textil Mexicana en el siglo xix.* México, D.F.: SepSetentas.
Kerig, Dorothy Pierson (2001). *El valle de Mexicali y la Colorado River Land Company, 1902–1946.* Mexicali: Universidad Autónoma de Baja California; XVI Ayuntamiento de Mexicali.
Kharas, Homi (2010). *The Emerging Middle Class in Developing Countries.* Paris: OECD Development Centre.
Kim, Linsu (1997). *Immitation to Innovation: The Dynamics of Korea's Technological Learning.* Cambridge, MA: Harvard Business School Press.
King, Timothy (1970). *Mexico: Industrialization and Trade Policies since 1940.* London: Oxford University Press.
Kitco. www.kitco.com/charts/historicalsilver.html.
Kitco Bullion Dealers. http://66.38.218.33/scripts/hist_charts/yearly_graphs.plx.
Klein, Herbert S. (2004). *A Population History of the United States.* Cambridge: Cambridge University Press.
Klein, Naomi (2007). *The Shock Doctrine: The Rise of Disaster Capitalism.* New York: Metropolitan Books/Henry Holt.
Knight Ridder Newspapers: January 29, 2006.
Kose, M. Ayhan, Guy M. Meredith, and Chrisopher M. Towe (2004). "How Has NAFTA Affected the Mexican Economy? Review and Evidence." IMF Working Paper WP/04/59. Washington, D.C.: International Monetary Fund.
Kuecker, Glen David (2008). "Public Health, Yellow Fever, and the Making of Modern Tampico." *Urban History Review,* (March 22), 18–28.
Kuntz Ficker, Sandra (2007). *El comercio exterior de México en la era del capitalismo liberal, 1870–1929.* México, D.F.: El Colegio de México.
Kuntz Ficker, Sandra (2010). *Las exportaciones mexicanas durante la primera globalización, 1870–1929.* México, D.F.: El Colegio de México.
Kuntz Ficker, Sandra, coordinadora (2010). *Historia económica general de México: De la colonia a nuestros días.* México, D.F.: El Colegio de México.
Kuntz Ficker, Sandra (2002). "Institutional Change and Trade in Mexico, 1870–1911," in Jeffrey L. Bortz and Stephen Haber, eds., *The Mexican Economy, 1870–1930: Essays on the Economic History of Institutions, Revolution, and Growth,* 161–204. Stanford: Stanford University Press.
La Jornada, March 12, 2012; December 27, 2013.
Lackey, Earl E. (1949). "Mountain Passes in the Colorado Rockies." *Economic Geography,* 25:3 (July), 211–215.
Latin American Business Chronicle: March 11, 2010.
Latin American Herald Tribune (Caracas, Venezuela): November 1, 2010.
Laxer, Gordon (1989). *Open for Business: The Roots of Foreign Ownership in Canada.* Toronto: Oxford University.
LoPalo, Melissa, and Pia Orrenious (2013). "As Mexico's Social Safety Net Grows, Issues Arise." *Southwest Economy* (Federal Reserve Bank of Dallas, Second Quarter), 12.
Lee, Stacy (2003). *Mexico and the United States,* 3 vols. New York: Marshall Cavendish.
Lempriere, Charles (1862). *Notes in Mexico, in 1861 and 1862; Politically and Socially Considered.* London: Longman, Green, Longman, Roberts & Green.
Lerman Alperstein, Aída (1989). *Comercio exterior e industria de transformación en México, 1910–1920.* México, D.F.: Universidad Autónoma Metropolitana, Unidad Xochimilco, Plaza y Valdez Editores.
Levy, Daniel C., Kathleen Bruhn, and Emilio Zebadúa (2001). *Mexico: The Struggle for Democratic Development.* Berkeley: University of California Press.

Liehr, R. ed. (1989). *America Latina en la época de Simón Bolívar*. Berlin: Colloquium Verlag.
Lingenfelter, Richard E. (1978). *Steamboats on the Colorado River, 1852–1916*. Tucson: University of Arizona Press.
Locklin, David P. (1972). *Economics of Transportation*. Homewood, IL: R.D. Irwin.
López-Alonso, Moramay (2012). *Measuring Up: A History of Living Standards in Mexico, 1850–1950*. Stanford: Stanford University Press.
López Córdova, J. Ernesto, and Jaime Zabludovsky K. (2010). "Del proteccionismo a la liberalización incompleta: Industria y mercados," in Sandra Kuntz Ficker, coordinator, *Historia económica de México: De la colonia a nuestros días*, 705–728. México, D.F.: El Colegio de México.
López de Velasco, Juan (1894). *Geografía y descripción universal de las Indias, recopilada desde 1571 a 1574*. Madrid: Justo Zaragoza.
Los Angeles Times: July 22, 1896; August 19, 1907; June 7, 1918; November 27, 1970; September 12, 1971; June 21, 1982; December 23, 1984; June 21, 1987; November 8, 1987; September 23, 2001; February 16, 2008.
Lubowski, Ruben N., Marlow Vesterby, Shawn Bucholtz, Alba Baez, and Michael J. Roberts (2002). *Major Uses of Land in the United States*. Washington, D.C.: U.S. Department of Agriculture, Economic Information Bulletin No. 14, May 2002.
MacHugh, R.J. (1914). *Modern Mexico*. London: Methuen & Co..
MacLeod, Dag (2004). *Downsizing the State: Privatization and the Limits of Neoliberal Reform in Mexico*. University Park: Pennsylvania State University Press.
Maddison, Angus (2003). *The World Economy: Historical Statistics*. Paris: Development Centre Studies.
Mares, David R. (1987). *Penetrating the International Market: Theoretical Considerations and a Mexican Case Study*. New York: Columbia University Press.
Marichal, Carlos (1989). *A Century of Debt Crises in Latin America: From Independence to the Great Depression, 1820–1930*. Princeton: Princeton University Press.
Márquez Colín, Graciela (2002). *The Political Economy of Mexican Protectionism, 1868–1911*. PhD Dissertation, Harvard University.
Martin, Robert F. (1939). *National Income of the United States, 1799–1938*. New York: National Industrial Conference.
Martín Echeverría, Leonardo (1954). "La leyenda dorada sobre la riqueza de México." *Investigación Económica* (México, Revista Trimestral, Segundo Trimestre), 231–287.
Martínez, Oscar J. (1978). *Border Boom Town: Ciudad Juárez since 1848*. Austin: University of Texas Press.
Martínez, Oscar J. (1983). *Ciudad Juárez: El auge de una ciudad fronteriza desde 1848*. México, D.F.: Fondo de Cultura Económica.
Martínez, Oscar J. (2001). *Mexican-Origin People in the United States*. Tucson: University of Arizona Press.
Martínez, Oscar J. (2011). "Migration and the Border, 1965–1985," in Mark Overmyer-Velázquez, ed. *Beyond La Frontera: The History of Mexico-U.S. Migration*, 103–121. New York: Oxford University Press.
Martínez, Oscar J. (2006). *Troublesome Border*, revised edition. Tucson: University of Arizona Press.
Mason, Edward S. et al. (1980). *The Economic and Social Modernization of the Republic of Korea*. Cambridge, MA: Harvard University Press.
Mayer-Serra, Carlos Elizondo (2006). "Changes in Determinants of Tax Policy," in Laura Randall, ed. *Changing Structure of Mexico: Political, Social, and Economic Prospects*, 140–158. Armonk, NY: M. E. Sharpe.

Mayer-Serra, Carlos Elizondo (2011). *Por eso estamos como estamos: La economía política de un crecimento mediocre*. México, D.F.: Random House Mondadori.
Mayo, John (2006). *Commerce and Contraband on Mexico's West Coast in the Era of the Barron, Forbes & Co., 1821–1859*. New York: Peter Lang.
Mayo, John (1987). "Consuls and Silver Contraband on Mexico's West Coast in the Era of Santa Anna." *Journal of Latin American Studies*, 19 (November), 389–411.
McClatchy Newspapers, February 2, 2011.
McDowell, Carl E., and Helen M. Gibbs (1954). *Ocean Transportation*. New York: McGraw-Hill.
McIlwraith, Thomas F. and Edward K. Muller (2001). *North America: The Historical Geography of a Changing Continent*, 2nd edition. Boulder: Rowman & Littlefield.
McIntosh, C. Alison. (1983). *Population Policy in Western Europe: Responses to Low Fertility in France, Sweden, and West Germany*. Armonk, NY: M.E. Sharpe.
Medina Castro, Manuel (1974). *El gran despojo*. México, D.F.: Editorial Diógenes.
Meinig, Donald W. (1993). *The Shaping of America: A Geographic Perspective on 500 Years of History*, vol. 3. New Haven, CT: Yale University Press.
Menchaca, Martha (2011). *Naturalizing Mexican Immigrants: A Texas History*. Austin: University of Texas Press.
Mexico Business Blog (September 26, 2011). http://bdp-americas.com.
México. *Censos Generales de Población, 1900–2010*.
México, Centro de Estudios Sociales y de Opinion Pública (October 2004). *Análisis comparativo de tarifas en autopistas concesionadas*. México, D.F.: Camara de Diputados.
México, Comisión Intersectarial para el Manejo Sustentable de Mares y Costas (2011). *Política Nacional de Mares y Costas de México*. México, D.F.: CIMARES.
México, Comisión Nacional de los Salarios Mínimos. *Informe de la Dirección Técnica* (November 21, 2012).
México, Comisión Nacional Para el Desarrollo de los Pueblos Indígenas. "Los números—Indicadores Socioeconómicos." www.cdi.gob.mx.
México, CONAPO (2001). *Migración México-Estados Unidos 2001*. Mexico: CONAPO.
México, CONAPO (2004). "La transición demográfica y el proceso de envejecimiento en México." www.conapo.gov.mx/publicaciones/2004/Sdm23.pdf.
México, CONEVAL (2012). *Informe de la evolución de la política de desarrollo social. Evolución del desarrollo social en México, 2012*. México, D.F.: CONEVAL.
México, CONEVAL (2011). *Medición de pobreza en los municipios de México, 2010*.
México, Consejo Nacional de la Industria Maquiladora de Exportación, AC (2006–2007). "Industria manufacturera, maquiladora y de servicios de exportación." www3.diputados.gob.mx/camara.
México, INEGI (2010). *Censo de Población y Vivienda 2010*. México, D.F.: INEGI.
México, INEGI (2013a). "Clases medias en México." Boletín de Investigación. Núm. 256/13, June 12, 2013. México, D.F.: INEGI.
México, INEGI (2005). "Estados Unidos Mexicanos: Densidad de población por entidad federativa." Marco geoestadístico nacional. México, D.F.: INEGI.
México, INEGI (2013b). "Estadística mensual del programa de la industria manufacturera, maquiladora y de servicios de exportación (IMMEX)." México, D.F.: INEGI.
México, INEGI (2007a). *Estadísticas económicas: Industria maquiladora de exportación*. México, D.F.: INEGI.
México, INEGI (1985). *Estadísticas históricas de México*, vols. 1–2. México, D.F.: INEGI.
México, INEGI (1999). *Estadísticas históricas de México*. México, D.F.: INEGI.
México, INEGI (2009). *Estadísticas históricas de México*. México, D.F.: INEGI.

México, INEGI (2007b). "Industria maquiladora de exportación." México, D.F.: INEGI.
México, INEGI (2011). *La minería en México 2011.* México, D.F.: INEGI.
México, INEGI (2004). *La Población Indígena de México.* México, D.F.: INEGI.
México, INEGI (2010). *Principales resultados del Censo de Población y Vivienda 2010.* México, D.F.: INEGI.
México, INEGI (2012). *Sistema de Cuentas Nacionales de México, Producto Interno Brtuto por Entidad Federativa 2007–2011.* México, D.F.: INEGI.
México, INEGI, Banco de Información Económica. "Vista rápida de los datos." http://dgcnesyp.inegi.org.mx/.
México, Instituto Mexicano de Recursos Naturales Renovables (1960). *Mesas redondas sobre los recursos naturals renovables y el crecimiento demográfico de México.* México, D.F.: Ediciones del Instituto Mexicano de Recursos Naturales Renovables, A.C.
Mexico Now: August 7, 2013; September–October 2013; November–December, 2014.
México, Secretaría de Comunicaciones y Transportes website. www.sct.gob.mx.
México, Secretaría de Medio Ambiente y Recursos Naturales (2007). *¿Y el medio ambiente? Problemas en México y el mundo.* México, D.F.: Biblioteca Semarnat.
Meyer, Michael C., William L. Sherman, and Susan M. Deeds (2007). *The Course of Mexican History,* 8th ed. New York: Oxford University Press.
Middlebrook, Kevin J., and Eduardo Zepeda, eds. (2003). *Confronting Development: Assessing Mexico's Economic and Social Policy Challenges.* Stanford: Stanford University Press.
Miller, George J., Almon E. Parkins, and Bert Hudgins (1954). *Geography of North America.* New York: John Wiley and Sons.
Miller, Tom (1981). *On the Border: Portraits of America's Southwestern Frontier.* New York: Harper and Row.
Mitchell, Brian R. (2003). *International Historical Statistics: The Americas, 1750–2000,* 4th ed. Basingstoke: Palgrave Macmillan.
Molloy, Molly. (2013). "The Mexican Undead: Toward a New History of the 'Drug War' Killing Fields." *Small Wars Journal,* (August 21). www.smallwarsjournal.com.
Moré, Iñigo (2011). *The Borders of Inequality: Where Wealth and Poverty Collide.* Tucson: University of Arizona Press.
Moreno Toscano, Alejandra (1972). "Cambios en los patrones de urbanización en México." *Historia Mexicana,* 22:2 (October–December), 160–187.
Moreno-Brid, Juan Carlos (2009). *Development and Growth in the Mexican Economy: A Historical Perspective.* New York: Oxford University Press.
Morton, Kathryn, and Peter Tulloch (1977). *Trade and Developing Countries.* London: Croom Helm.
Murphey, Rhoades (1966). *An Introduction to Geography.* Chicago: Rand McNally & Company.
Nash, Gary B. (1974). *Red, White, and Black: The Peoples of Early America.* Englewood Cliffs, NJ: Prentice Hall.
Nash, Gerald D. (1977). *The American West in the Twentieth Century: A Short History of an Urban Oasis.* Albuquerque: Univerasity of New Mexico Press.
National Atlas. nationalatlas.gov.
National Conference of State Legislatures. "State Cigarette Excise Taxes: 2010." www.ncsl.org.
National Geographic. August 1907; November 2012.
Navarrete Linares, Federico (2008). *Los pueblos indígenas de México.* México, D.F.: Comisión Nacional Para el Desarrollo de los Pueblos Indígenas.
New York Times: January 16, 1911; August 6, 1916; March 17, 1935; April 19, 1935; December 15, 1935; May 30, 1937; November 17, 1944; August 15, 1956; September 7, 1956;

August 15, 1965; August 12, 1970; December 26, 1974; December 2, 1976; September 27, 1977; November 11, 1977; November 13, 1977; November 20, 1977; November 7, 1978; January 4, 1982; December 26, 1988; August 28, 1992; June 8, 1999; September 4, 2002; September 25, 2002; June 5, 2003; December 3, 2003; March 9, 2007; April 21, 2012; April 24, 2012; May 17, 2012; February 27, 2013: November 1, 2013.

Niblo, Stephen R., and Diane M. Niblo (2008). "Acapulco in Dreams and Realities." *Mexican Studies/Estudios Mexicanos*, 24:1 (Winter), 31–51.

Nicolau d'Owler, Luis et al. (1985). *Historia Moderna de Mexico*, v. 7, pt. 1, *El Porfiriato: La Vida Económica*, Daniel Cosío Villegas, general editor. México: D.F., Editorial Hermes.

North, Douglas C. (1965). "The Role of Transportation in the Economic Development of North America," in Colloque International d'Historie Maritime (7 Colloque), *Les Grandes Voies Maritimes Dans Le Monde, XVe-XiXe Sie'cles*, 209–246. Paris: S.E.V.P.E.N.

OECD (2011). "Divided We Stand: Why Inequality Keeps Rising." Paris: OECD. www.oecd.org.

OECD (2007). *Getting it Right: OECD Perspectives on Policy Challenges in Mexico*. Paris: OECD Publishing. www.oecd.org.

OECD (2013). *Getting it Right: Strategic Agenda for Reforms in Mexico*. Paris: OECD Publishing. www.oecd.org.

OECD, Stat Extracts. "Real Minimum Wages U.S.$ PPP." http://stats.oecd.org.

Office of the United States Trade Representative, www.ustr.gov.

O'Neil, Shannon K. (2013a). "Mexico Makes It: A Transformed Society, Economy, and Government." *Foreign Affairs*, 92 (March–April), 52–62.

O'Neil, Shannon K. (2013b). *Two Nations Indivisible: Mexico, the United States, and the Road Ahead*. New York: Oxford University Press.

Ortíz Hernán, Sergio (1994). *Caminos y transportes en México: Una aproximación socioeconómica, fines de la colonia y principios de la vida independiente*. México, D.F.: Secretaría de Comunicaciones y Transportes, Fondo de Cultura Económica.

Ortiz Hernán, Sergio (1968). "Ferrocarriles y caminos mexicanos en el siglo xix." *Comunicaciones y Transportes*, II:1 (July–September), 51–77.

Pacione, Michael (2001). *Urban Geography: A Global Perspective*. New York: Routledge.

Packenham, Robert (1992). *The Dependency Movement*. Cambridge, MA: Harvard University Press.

Passel, Jeffrey S., and D'Vera Cohn (2011). "Unauthorized Immigrant Population: National and State Trends, 2010." Washington, D.C.: Pew Hispanic Center. February 1. www.pewhispanic.org.

Pastor, Robert A., and Jorge G. Castañeda (1988). *Limits to Friendship: The United States and Mexico*. New York: Vintage Books.

Patterson, James T. (1994). *America's Struggle against Poverty, 1900–1994*. Cambridge, MA: Harvard University Press.

Paz, Octavio (1947). *El laberinto de la soledad*. México, D.F.: Cuadernos Americanos.

Peters, Enrique Dussel (2009). "Manufacturing Competitiveness: Toward a Region Development Agenda," in Kevin P. Gallagher, Enrique Dussel Peters, and Timothy A. Wise, eds. *The Future of North American Trade Policy: Lessons from NAFTA*, 27–34. Boston: The Frederick S. Pardee Center for the Study of the Longer-Range Future, Boston University.

Pew Research Center (2012a). "Explaining Why Minority Births Now Outnumber White Births." May 17. www.pewhispanic.org.

Pew Research Center (2013). "Hispanics of Mexican Origin in the United States, 2011." June 19. www.pewhispanic.org.

Pew Research Center (2012b). "Statistical Portrait of Hispanics in the United States, 2010." February 21. www.pewhispanic.org.

Piccinini, Antonio (2001). *Agricultural Policies in Europe and the USA: Farmers between Subsidies and the Market.* New York: Palmgrave.

Picketty, Thomas (2014). *Capital in the Twenty First Century.* Harvard: Harvard University Press.

Pletcher, David M. (1973). *The Diplomacy of Annexation: Texas, Oregon, and the Mexican War.* Columbia: University of Missouri Press.

Pletcher, David M. (1958). "The Fall of Silver in Mexico, 1870–1910, and Its Effects on American Investments." *Journal of Economic History,* 18:1 (March), 33–55.

Poinsett, Joel R. (1969). *Notes on Mexico, Made in the Autumn of 1822.* New York: Praeger.

Polese, Mario (2009). *The Wealth and Poverty of Regions: Why Cities Matter.* Chicago: University of Chicago Press.

Pool, William C. (1975). *A Historical Atlas of Texas.* Austin: The Encino Press.

Population Reference Bureau (2000). *Population Bulletin,* 55:2 (June).

Population Reference Bureau (2006). *Population Bulletin,* 61:4 (December).

Population Reference Bureau (2012). "Fact Sheet: The Decline in U.S. Fertility," PRB World Population Data Sheet 2012. www.prb.org.

Population Reference Bureau, AmriStat (2003). "U.S. Fertility Trends: Boom and Bust and Leveling Off." January.

Port of Oakland website. www.portofoakland.com.

Potash, Robert A. (1983). *Mexican Government and Industrial Development in the Early Republic: The Banco de Avio.* Amherst: University of Massachusetts Press.

Potter, David M. (1954). *People of Plenty: Economic Abundance and the American Character.* Chicago: University of Chicago Press.

Pozas, María de los Angeles (2002). *Estrategia internacional de la gran empreza mexicana en la decada de los noventa.* México, D.F.: El Colegio de México.

The Progressive: July 27, 2013.

"Public Opinion in the United States on the Annexation of Mexico" (Circa 1892). (Copy courtesy of the Bancroft Library, University of California at Berkeley).

Raat, W. Dirk (1992). *Mexico and the United States: Ambivalent Vistas.* Athens: University of Georgia Press.

Ramos, Samuel (1938). *El perfil del hombre y la cultura en México,* 2nd ed. México, D.F.: P. Robredo.

Randall, Laura, ed. (2006). *Changing Structure of Mexico: Political, Social, and Economic Prospects.* Armonk, New York: M. E. Sharpe.

Rappaport, Jordan, and Jeffrey D. Sachs (2003). "The United States as a Coastal Nation." *Journal of Economic Growth,* 8, 5–46.

Reuters: March 21, 2012.

Review of the Economic Situation of Mexico (Mexico: Banamex): April 2007, October 2007.

Reyes, Javier A. (2011). *Latin American Economic Development.* New York: Routledge.

Reynolds, Clark (1970). *The Mexican Economy: Twentieth-Century Structure and Growth.* New Haven, CT: Yale University Press.

Rhoda, Richard, and Tony Burton (2010). *Geo-Mexico: The Geography and Dynamics of Modern Mexico.* Ladysmith, Canada: Sombrero Books.

Riding, Alan (1985). *Distant Neighbors: A Portrait of the Mexicans.* New York: Alfred A. Knopf.

Rios Contreras, Viridiana (2014). "The Role of Drug-Related Violence and Extortion in Promoting Mexican Migration." *Latin American Research Review*, 49:3, 199–217.
Robertson, Ross M. (1973). *History of the American Economy*, 3rd edition. New York: Harcourt Brace Jovanovich.
Rodríguez, Francisco (1999). "Why Do Resource-Abundant Economies Grow More Slowly?" *Journal of Economic Growth*, 4 (September), 277–303.
Romero, Matías (1889). "The Annexation of Mexico." *The North American Review*, 148:390 (May), 525–537.
Romero, Matías (1892). "The Free Zone in Mexico." *The North American Review*, 154:425 (April), 459–479.
Romero, Matías (1898). *Mexico and the United States: A Study of Subjects Affecting Their Political, Commercial, and Social Relations, Made with a View To Their Promotion*. New York: G. P. Putnam's Sons.
Romero Sotelo, María Eugenia, and Luis Jauregi, coordinators (1997). *La industria mexicana y su historia: siglos xviii, xix, xx*. Mexico, D.F., UNAM.
Rosenberg, Nathan (1972). *Technology and American Economic Growth*. New York: Harper and Row.
Rosenzweig Hernández, Fernando (1965). "El desarrollo económico de Mexico de 1877 a 1911." *El Trimestre Económico*, 32:3, 405–454.
Rosenzweig Hernández, Fernando (1963). "La economía novo-hispana al comenzar el siglo xix." *Ciencias Políticas y Sociales*, 3 (July–September), 455–494.
Rostow, Walt W. (1966). *The Stages of Economic Growth*. Cambridge: Cambridge University Press.
Rudolph, James D. (1985). *Mexico: A Country Study*, 3rd ed. Washington, D.C.: Foreign Area Studies, The American University.
Ruíz, Ramón Eduardo (2010). *Mexico: Why a Few Are Rich and the People Poor*. Berkeley: University of California Press.
Russell, Philip (2010). *The History of Mexico: From Pre-Conquest to the Present*. New York: Routledge.
Sachs, Jeffrey D., and Andrew M. Warner (1999). "The Big Push, Natural Resource Booms and Growth." *Journal of Development Economics*, 59, 43–76.
Sachs, Jeffrey D., and Andrew M. Warner (2001). "The Curse of Natural Resources." *European Economic Review*, 45, 827–838.
Sachs, Jeffrey D., and Andrew M. Warner (1997). "Natural Resource Abundance and Economic Growth." Harvard University: Center for International Development and Harvard Institute for International Development, JEL Classification—O4, Q0, F43, November.
Salem-news.com/print/27810: June 30, 2013.
Salvucci, Richard J. (2009). *Politics, Markets, and Mexico's "London Debt," 1823–1887*. New York: Cambridge University Press.
San Diego Union-Tribune: August 14, 2005.
Sanders, E.M. (1921). "The Natural Regions of Mexico." *Geographical Review*, 11:2 (April), 212–226.
Sanderson, Steven E. (1983). *Trade Aspects of the Internationalization of Mexican Agriculture: Consequences for the Mexican Food Crisis*. La Jolla, CA: Center for U.S.-Mexican Studies, U.C. San Diego.
Schaller, Michael (1997). *Altered States: The United States and Japan since the Occupation*. New York: Oxford University Press.
Schwartzman, Kathleen C. (2012). *The Chicken Trail: Following Workers, Migrants, and Corporations across the Americas*. Ithaca: Cornell University Press.

Scott, Ian (1982). *Urban and Spatial Development in Mexico*. Baltimore: Johns Hopkins University.
The Seattle Times: March 19, 2009.
Semple, Ellen Churchill, with Clarence Fielden Jones (1933). *American History and Its Geographic Conditions*. Boston: Houghton Mifflin Company.
Siemens, Alfred H. (1990). *Between the Summit and the Sea: Central Veracruz in the Nineteenth Century*. Vancouver: University of British Columbia Press.
Smith, Justin (1919). *The War with Mexico*, 2 vols. New York: MacMillan.
Solis M., Leopoldo (1967). "Hacia un análisis general a largo plazo del desarrollo económico de México." *Demografía y Economía*, I, 40–91.
Sonnenfield, David A. (1992). "Mexico's 'Green Revolution,' 1940–1980: Toward an Environmental History." *Environmental History Review*, 16:4 (Winter), 28–52.
Spykman, Nicholas J. (1938a). "Geography and Foreign Policy: Part I." *The American Political Science Review*, 32:1 (February), 28–50.
Spykman, Nicholas J. (1938b). "Geography and Foreign Policy, Part II." *The American Political Science Review*, 32:2 (April), 213–236.
Stabler, Herman (1927). "A Nation's Water Power." *Economic Geography* 3:4 (October), 434–446.
Stacy, Lee (2003). *Mexico and the United States*, 3 vols. Tarrytown, NY: Marshall Cavenish.
Stein, Stanley J. and Barbara H. Stein (1970). *The Colonial Heritage of Latin America: Essays on Economic Dependence in Perspective*. New York: Oxford University Press.
Stoddard, Ellwyn R., Oscar J. Martínez, and Miguel Angel Martínez Lasso. (1979). *El Paso-Ciudad Juárez Relations and the "Tortilla Curtain,": A Study of Local Adaptation to Federal Border Policies*. El Paso, TX: Council on the Arts and Humanities, 1979.
STRATFOR (2009). "The Geopolitics of Mexico: A Mountain Fortress Besieged." www.stratfor.com.
STRATFOR (2011). "The Geopolitics of the United States, Part 1: The Inevitable Empire" (August 24). www.stratfor.com.
Sturgeon, Timothy J., and Momoko Kawakami (2010). "Global Value Chains in the Electronics Industry: Was the Crisis a Window of Opportunity for Developing Countries?" in Olivier Cattaneo, Gary Gereffi, and Cornelia Staritz, eds. *Global Value Chains in a Postcrisis World: A Development Perspective*, 245–302. Washington, D.C.: World Bank.
Tamayo, Jorge L. (1962). *Geografía General de México: Geografía Económica*, vol. IV. México, D.F.: Instituto Mexicano de Investigaciones Económicas.
Tamayo, Jorge L. (1964). *El problema fundamental de la agricultura mexicana*. México, D.F.: Instituto Mexicano de Investigaciones Económicas.
Tannenbaum, Frank (1950). *Mexico: The Struggle for Peace and Bread*. New York: Knopf.
Taylor, George R. (1951). *The Transportation Revolution, 1815–1860*. New York: Rinehart.
Tenenbaum, Barbara (1986). *The Politics of Penury: Debts and Taxes in Mexico, 1821–1856*. Albuquerque: University of New Mexico Press.
Texas Alcoholic Beverage Commission. www.tabc.state.tx.us.
Theobald, Robin (1990). *Corruption, Development and Underdevelopment*. London: Macmillan.
Thomson, Guy P. C. (1989). "Continuity and Change in Mexican Manufacturing, 1800–1870," in R. Liehr, ed. *America Latina en la época de Simón Bolivar*, 255–302. Berlin: Colloquium Verlag.
Thornton, Christy, and Adam Goodman (2014). "How the Mexican Drug Trade Thrives on Free Trade." *The Nation* (July 15). www.thenation.com.
Tilly, Chris (2005). "Wal-Mart in Mexico: The Limits of Growth," in Nelson Lichtenstein, ed. *Wal-Mart: The Face of Twenty-First Century Capitalism*, 189–209. New York: New Press.
Time Magazine: January 14, 2013.

Tinker Salas, Miguel (1997). *In the Shadow of the Eagles: Sonora and the Transformation of the Border during the Porfiriato*. Berkeley: University of California Press.

Toro, María Celia (1995). *Mexico's "War" on Drugs: Causes and Consequences*. Boulder: Lynne Rienner Publisher.

Unikel, Luis, Crescencio Ruid Chiapetto, and Gustavo Garza Villarreal (1976). *El desarrollo urbano de México: Diagnóstico e implicaciones futuras*. México, D.F.: El Colegio de México.

Urquidi, Victor L. (1986). "Technology Transfer between Mexico and the United States: Past Experience and Future Prospects." *Mexican Studies/Estudios Mexicanos* 2:2, 179–193.

U.S. Bureau of the Census (2010). "2010 Census Results—United States, Population Density by County or County Equivalent." 2010 Census Redistricting Data Summary.

U.S. Bureau of the Census (1900). *Census of Population 1900*. Washington, D.C.: U.S. Government Printing Office.

U.S. Bureau of the Census (1950). *Census of Population 1950*. Washington, D.C.: U.S. Government Printing Office.

U.S. Bureau of the Census (2010). *Census of Population 2010*. Washington, D.C.: U.S. Government Printing Office.

U.S. Bureau of the Census (2002). *Demographic Trends in the 20th Century*. Census 2000 Special Reports, Series CENSR-4. Washington, D.C.: U.S. Government Printing Office.

U.S. Bureau of the Census (1960). *Historical Statistics of the United States: Colonial Times to 1957, A Statistical Abstract Supplement*. Washington, D.C.: U.S. Government Printing Office.

U.S. Bureau of the Census (1975). *Historical Statistics of the United States: Colonial Times to 1970* (Series Z1–19). Washington, D.C.: U.S. Government Printing Office.

U.S. Bureau of the Census (2006). *Historical Statistics of the United States*, Vol. 3.

U.S. Bureau of the Census (1998a). "Population of the 46 Urban Places, 1810." www.census.gov.

U.S. Bureau of the Census (1998b). "Population of the 100 Largest Urban Places, 1860." www.census.gov.

U.S. Bureau of the Census (1998c). "Population of the 100 Largest Urban Places, 1900." www.census.gov/population/www/documentation/twps0027/tab13.txt.

U.S. Economic and Statistics Administration (2012). *Statistical Abstract of the United States: 2012*. Washington, D.C.: U.S. Census Bureau, 2012.

U.S. Bureau of Economic Analysis (2011). "Gross Domestic Product by State: Advance Statistics for 2010 and Revised Statistics for 2007." www.bea.gov/sch/2011/07July/0711/_gdp-state.pdf.

U.S. Department of Agriculture, Foreign Agricultural Service (May 2011). *World Agricultural Production*.

U.S. Department of Commerce (1932). *Commerce Yearbook*.

U.S. Department of Commerce (1935). *Foreign Commerce Yearbook*.

U.S. Department of Energy. "Energy Efficiency and Renewable Energy." www.1.eere.energy.gov/windandhydro/hydro_potential.html.

U.S. Department of Homeland Security, Office of Immigration Statistics. *2002 Yearbook of Immigration Statistics*.

U.S. Department of Homeland Security, Office of Immigration Statistics. *2008 Yearbook of Immigration Statistics*.

U.S. Department of Homeland Security, Office of Immigration Statistics. *2009 Yearbook of Immigration Statistics*.

U.S. Department of Labor, Bureau of Labor Statistics (2012). "International Comparisons of Hourly Compensation Costs in Manufacturing, 2011." December 19, 2012.

U.S. Department of State, Office of the Historian. "Mexican Expropriation of Foreign Oil, 1938." www.state.gov/milestones/1937–1945/mexican-oil.

U.S. Department of Transportation (2009). "U.S highway map courtesy of Mike Neathary." Mike.Neathary@dot.gov.

U.S. Department of the Treasury (1968). *Report of the Secretary of the Treasury, Albert Gallatin, on the Subject of Public Roads and Canals* [originally published in 1808]. New York: A. M. Kelley.

U.S. Energy Information Administration (March 2009). "Country Analysis Briefs: Mexico." www.doe.gov/emeu/cabs/Mexico/Full.html.

U.S. Energy Information Administration. "Electric Power Annual 2006." http://eia.doe.gov/cneaf/electricity/epa/epa_sum.html.

U.S. Energy Information Administration (2014). "Mexico Overview/Data as of April 24, 2014." www.eia.gov/countries/country-data.cfm?fips=mx#pet.

U.S. Energy Information Administration. "World Coal Production, 1997–2006." www.eia.doe,gov/emeu/aer/txt/ptb1114.html.

U.S. Energy Information Administration. "World Crude Oil Production, 1960–2007." www.doe.gov/aer/txt/ptb1105.html.

U.S. Federal Highway Administration (2012). "Freight Facts and Figures 2012." http://fhwa.dot.gov/freight.

U.S. Federation of Tax Administrators (March 2010). Washington, D.C. www.taxadmin.org

U.S. Geological Survey. Mineral Commodity Summaries: 2007, 2013. http://minerals.er.usgs.gov/minerals/pubs/mcs/2007/mcs.2007pdf.

U.S. Geological Survey. *Minerals Yearbook*: 2005, 2006, 2008, 2009. http://minerals.usgs.gov/minerals/pubs/latin.html#mx.

U.S. Senate, 30th Congress, 1st Session. Message from the President of the United States. July 8, 1848.

U.S. Senate Executive Document 52, 30th Congress, 1st Session. Buchanan to Slidell. November 10, 1845.

USAgold.com. www.usagold.com

Van Cleef, Eugene (1937). *Trade Centers and Trade Routes*. New York: London D. Appleton.

Van Royen, William (1952). *Atlas of the World's Resources*. New York: Prentice-Hall.

Van Royen, William, and Nels A. Bengtson (1964). *Fundamentals of Economic Geography: An Introduction to the Study of Resources*. Englewood Cliffs, NJ: Prentice Hall, Inc.

Venezian, Eduardo L., and William K. Gamble (1969). *The Agricultural Development of Mexico: Its Structure and Growth since 1950*. New York: Frederick A. Praeger.

Vigna, Anna (2008). "Rude Awakening in Mexico." *Le Monde Diplomatique*, March 14. www.indybay.org.

Villagómez, Paloma, and César Bistrain. "Situación demográfica nacional 2008." http://www.conapo.gob.mx/publicaciones/sdm/sdm2008/01.pdf.

Von Humboldt, Alexander (1966). *Ensayo político sobre el reino de la Nueva España* [originally published in 1811]. México, D.F.: Editorial Porrúa.

Von Humboldt, Alexander (1824). *Selections from the Works of the Baron de Humboldt, Relating to the Climate, Inhabitants, Productions, and Mines of Mexico*, with notes by John Taylor. London: Longman, Hurst, Rees, Orme, Brown, and Green.

Walker, Louise E. (2013). *Waking from the Dream: Mexico's Middle Classes after 1968*. Stanford: Stanford University Press.

Wall Street Journal: June 24, 1998; March 20, 2010.

Walton, Gary M., and Hugh Rockoff (1990). *History of the American Economy*. San Diego: Harcourt Brace Jovanovich.

Walton, Gary M., and James F. Shepherd (1979). *The Economic Rise of Early America*. New York: Cambridge University Press.

Washington Post: September 29, 1956; September 9, 1971; December 24, 1978; July 2, 2006; September 1, 2010; December 13, 2010; April 3, 2012; November 30, 2013.

Waters, Hugh, Belén Sáenz de Miera, Hana Ross, and Luz Myriam Reynales Shigematsu (2010). *The Economics of Tobacco and Tobacco Taxation in Mexico*. Paris: International Union against Tuberculosis and Lung Disease.

Watson, J. Wreford (1967). *North America: Its Countries and Regions*. New York: Frederick A. Praeger.

Weber, David J. (1982). *The Mexican Frontier, 1821–1846: The American Southwest under Mexico*. Albuquerque: University of New Mexico Press.

Weigert, Hans W. (1957). *Principles of Political Geography*. New York: Appleton-Crofts.

Weiner, Myron, ed. (1966). *Modernization: The Dynamics of Growth*. New York: Basic Books.

Weiner, Richard (2014). "Antecedents to Daniel Cosío Villegas' Post-Revolutionary Ideology: Justo Sierra's Critique of Mexico's Legendary Wealth and Trinidad Sánchez Santos' Assault on Porfirian Progress." *Mexican Studies/Estudios Mexicanos* (Winter), 30:1, 71–103.

Weintraub, Sidney (1984). *Free Trade between Mexico and the United States?* Washington, D.C.: Brookings Institution.

Weintraub, Sidney (2010). *Un-Equal Partners: The United States and Mexico*. Pittsburgh: University of Pittsburgh Press.

Weisbrot, Mark, Stephen Lefevre, and Joseph Sammut (2014). "Did NAFTA Help Mexico? An Assessment after 20 Years." Washington, D.C.: Center for Economic and Policy Research (February). www.cepr.net.

Werner, Alejandro M., Rodrigo Barros, and Joe F. Ursúa (2006). "The Mexican Economy: Transformation and Challenges" In Laura Randall, ed. *Changing Structure of Mexico: Political, Social, and Economic Prospects*, 2nd ed., 67–90. Armonk, NY: M.E. Sharpe.

West, Robert C., and John P. Augell (1966). *Middle America: Its Lands and Peoples*. Englewood Cliffs, NJ: Prentice-Hall.

Whiting, Jr., Van R. (1992). *The Political Economy of Foreign Investment in Mexico: Nationalism, Liberalism, and Constraints on Choice*. Baltimore: The Johns Hopkins University Press.

Wilkie, James W. (1967). *The Mexican Revolution: Federal Expenditure and Social Change since 1910*. Berkeley: University of California Press.

Williamson, Jeffrey G. (2011). *Trade and Poverty: When the Third World Fell Behind*. Cambridge, MA.: MIT Press.

Wilson, Patricia M. (1992). *Exports and Local Development: Mexico's New Maquiladoras*. Austin: U.T. Press.

Wionczek, Miguel S. (1965). "The State and the Electric-Power Industry in Mexico, 1895–1965." *The Business History Review*, 39:4 (Winter), 527–556.

Wise, Timothy A. (2009). "Agricultural Dumping Under NAFTA: Estimating the Costs of U.S. Agricultural Policies to Mexican Producers." Global Development and Environment Institute Working Paper No. 09–08 (December).

Wise, Timothy A. (2010). "The Impacts of U.S. Agricultural Policies on Mexican Producers," in Jonathan Fox and Libby Haight, eds. *Subsidizing Inequality: Mexican Corn Policy since NAFTA*, 163–171. Washington, D.C.: Woodrow Wilson International Center for Scholars.

Wolf, Eric. (1959). *Sons of the Shaking Earth*. Chicago: University of Chicago Press.

World Bank (2014). "Research and Development Expenditure." www.data.worldbank.org.

World Intellectual Property Organization (2014). "U.S. and China Drive Intellectual Filing Growth in Record-Setting Year." *Annex* 1, Geneva (March 13). www.wipo.int.

World Security Network, Latin America (November 8, 2008). www.worldsecuritynetwork.com/Latin-America/.

Wright, Gavin, and Jesse Czelusta (2004). "The Myth of the Resource Curse." *Challenge*, 47:2 (March–April), 6–38.

Wythe, George B. (1949). *Industry in Latin America*. New York: Columbia University Press.

Yuk, Pam Kwan (April 5, 2013). "Mexican Labour: Cheaper than China." http://blogs.ft.com/beyond-brics.

Yúnez-Naude, Antonio, and Fernando Barceinas Paredes (2006). "The Reshaping of Agricultural Policy in Mexico," in Laura Randall, ed. *Changing Structure of Mexico: Political, Social, and Economic Prospects*, 2nd ed., 213–235. Armonk, NY: M. E. Sharpe.

Zaragoza, José (1996). *Historia de la deuda externa de México, 1823–1861*. México, D.F.: UNAM.

Zeihan, Peter (2014). *The Accidental Superpower: The Next Generation of American Preeminence and the Coming Global Disorder*. New York: Twelve Hachette Book Group.

Zepeda, Eduardo, Timothy A. Wise, and Kevin P. Gallagher (2009). "Rethinking Trade Policy for Development: Lessons from Mexico under NAFTA." Carnegie Endowment for International Peace, Policy Outlook (December).

INDEX

Acapulco, 87, 95–6, 97, 123–4, 127
Acemoglu, Daron, 9, 10, 11
Adams-Onis Treaty, 188
Africans in United States, 22
African slaves, 23, 31
Afro-mestizos, 34
  age of imperialism (U.S.), 185
agiotistas (moneylenders), 210
agricultural institutions, 6–7, 9
agricultural land, 150, 158, 204, 209
agricultural products, 31, 42, 250, 255
agricultural workers, 39
agriculture (Mexico): challenges, 150–2, 158, 279; expansion of, 42; Mexican-American investor partnerships in, 222–3; Mexican Revolution impact on, 39; population actively involved in, 43; regional variations, 32; savings and foreign exchange aided by, 41; during struggle for independence, 33; trade liberalization impact on, 250–1
agriculture (U.S.): building of economy in, 21; in California, 198–9; land available for, 209; predominance of, 22–3; production structures in, 20; success of, 141; in Texas, 197, 198; water resources and distribution for, 141–2, 143–4
airplanes, 27
Alamán, Lucas, 35, 148
Alaska, 184–5
Alberdi, Juan Bautista, 172
Albuquerque, 114

alcabalas (transit fees), 36–7
alcohol, production methods, 264, 275n6
alcohol, trafficking in, 260, 264–5, 274
Almonte, Juan Nepoceno, 191
American (term), xix, xxn2
American business people, 37
American immigrants to Texas, 190–1
American interests, importance of considering, 10–11
American landowners, 219
American migration to Mexico, 274
American national character, 13
amnesty to undocumented people, 272
Anaconda Amalgamated Copper Mining Company, 214
anti-Americanism, 203
anti-immigration sentiment, 13, 268–9, 272–3
antimalaria spraying, 90–1
anti-Mexican sentiment (U.S.), 269, 271, 272–3
antismoking campaigns, 266
Appalachian Mountains, 144
Argentina, railroads of, 121
Arizona, 238, 272–3
Arizona-Mexico border, Colorado River flow from, 142–3
arms smuggling, 243, 254–5
ASARCO, 214
Asia, 28
Asian countries, 28, 283, 285–7
Association for Maternal Health, 176

automated production, 35
automobile industry, 220, 225
automobiles, mass production of, 27

Baja California, 127, 174, 204
Baltimore, 22, 77, 111, 112
Banco de Avío, 35
bandits, 119, 201, 202
banking, Mexican majority ownership required in, 220
Barrio, Francisco, 138
Bear Flag insurrection, 195
Belden, Samuel A., 236
Belize, 95
Berlandier, Jean Louis, 91
Bernstein, Martin D., 11, 12
birth control program (Mexico), 171
Border Industrialization Program, 43, 45
borderlands, water problems troubling, 143
border towns, 237
Borlang, Norman, 41
borrowing (Mexico), 208, 209–12, 226–7
Boston, 111, 112
Boston harbor (U.S.), 77
Bracero Program, 205, 268, 269–70
Brazil, railroads of, 121
British loans to Mexico, 208, 210, 211, 212
broker or shelter companies, Mexican, 64
Bucareli Agreements, 1923, 215
Buchanan, James, 194–5
businesses, extortion of, 262–3

Cabrera, Gustavo, 87, 99–100n28
Calderón, Felipe, 97–8, 262, 263
California: gold, 198; population in, 200; ports, 78–9; U.S. obsession and conquest of, 193–6, 211; value of, 198–200
California Gold Rush, 96, 114
Californios, trade with, 212
Calles, Plutarco Elías, 153, 215–16
Campeche-Laguna Corporation, 215
Canada, 8, 225
canals, 24
Cananea Consolidated Copper Company, 214
Cancún, 97
capital: Mexico, 8, 33, 34, 48; United States, 24, 209. *See also* foreign capital
capitalism, 7–8, 59, 223, 285
capitalist-socialist system, 44, 50
Cárdenas, Lázaro, 172–3, 217, 218–19
Caribbean Coast, 94–5

Carranza, Venustiano, 215
Carter, Jimmy, 272
Caso, Antonio, 173
Castañeda, Jorge G., 12, 13, 63, 224, 248
Catholic Church, 31, 32, 33, 210, 217
Ceceña, José Luis, 220
cell phones, 27
Central America: U.S. interventionist policies in, 262
Central Highlands: agricultural land in, 209; development in, 54; economic benefits to, 41; highways connecting, 119; land forces concentrated in, 81; population of, 168
Central Mexico, *88*
Central Plateau, 99
Centro Nacional de Información y Estadística del Trabajo (CENIET), 271
Chang, Ha-Joon, 11, 14
character studies, 13
Chetumal port, 95
Chiapas, 188
Chicago: economic assets of, 140; location and technologies *versus* climate, 74; Martínez family move to, 101; personal impressions of, 19, 139–40; rise of, 113; waterways serving, 104–5
Chicago River, 140
children in Mexico, 162
Chile, railroads of, 121
China: closed economy of, 285; as economic competitor, 251–2, 256; global expansion of, 224–5; goods smuggled from, 254; trade imbalance with, 28; wages, 61
church-state conflict, 41
cigarette smuggling, 260, 266–7, 274
cities: location of, 140; Mexico, 116–17, 129–34, *131*, 135; most violent in world, 263; United States, xviii, 111–15
Ciudad Juárez: Chicago compared to, 19; economic environment, 101; as Mexican representative city, xvii, xviii; personal recollections of, xvii, 19; poverty, sources of, xviii; water supply, 143
Civil War (U.S.), 13, 24, 25, 239
class warfare, 66
Clay, Henry, 192, 233
climates: Mexico, 82–3, *83*, 98, 148, 168–9; United States, 74, 98
climatic conditions, 14
coal, 149, 153, 157

coastal areas: defined, 75–6, 99n5; Mexico, 89–91, 97–8, 99, 149, 278; United States, 75–6, 98, 284
coastal regions (defined), 87, 99–100n28
Cold War, 285
colonial period (U.S.), 22–3
Colorado River, 106, 135n11, 142–3
Colorado River Land Company, 217–18
Columbia River, 106
commerce: Mexico, 36, 98; United States, 3, 6–7, 20, 22–3
communication, 28, 110–11, 149
communism, 13, 187
competition, 12
comsumer products, 27
comsumer products (United States), 248–9
conflict: aversion to, 12
Consejo Nacional de Población (National Population Council, CONAPO), 176
conservation programs (United States): overview of, 144
consumer goods, 40, 255, 283–4
consumer market, 36
context, 1, 278
Continental Rubber Company, 214
contraband trade: 1980 to present, 252–5; altered border and trade patterns, 235–9; defined, 231; historic conditions, 256; in postindependence period, 232–34; protectionism and industrialization, 1880–1920, 242–3; U.S.-Mexico trade relations, 1920–1980, 247–9; vice products, 260, 267. *See also* drug trade
conventional trade: 1980 to present, 249–52; altered border and trade patterns, 234–5; defined, 231; in postindependence period, 231–2; protectionism and industrialization, 1880–1920, 240–2; U.S.-Mexico trade relations, 1920–1980, 244–7
copper, 146, 147, 149, 157
corruption: alleviating, key to, 14; conditions giving rise to, 278; economic development not impacted by, 14; in Mexican society, xix–xx, 12, 139; Mexico and other countries compared, 11; United States and Mexico compared, 13–14
Cortés, Hernán, 84, 147
cotton, 24, 31, 234
countries, comparing experiences of, 1

country location: Mexico, 81–2, 98, 149; United States, 73–4, 98, 140, 284
countryside, marginalized, 20
cross-border trade, 4
cross-national inequalities, 3
Cue Canovas, Agustín, 196
culture, economic development and, xix, 12–15

deforestation, 144, 152
de la Madrid, Miguel, 44
Delphi Mexico Technical Center, Ciudad Juárez, 45–6
demography, xix, 162, 165, 171–7
Department of Colonization and Industry (Mexico), 236
department stores, 226
dependence: external, 11, 208, 231, 246; in Mexico-United States relations, 21, 241, 251; migration as manifestation of, 274; on resources, 279–80; sustaining, factors in, 14
dependency theory, 3–4
dependent economy, 30
deportations, 270–1
desert communities, 143
developing (term defined), 2, 15n1
developing countries: labor reserves optimized by, 28; national economies, forces shaping, 277–378; resource-abundant, 159; self-sustaining development, challenges of achieving, 139; status, cause of, 2; term, 2, 15n1
development: balanced, obstacles to achieving, 20–1; economic model and, 45; global trade and, 230; opportunities for, 5; process of, 5–7; psychological and cultural interpretations of, 13
Díaz, Porfirio: alcabalas eliminated by, 37; concessions to U.S. made by, 10; conditions, critical assessment during regime of, 150; development projects financed by, 96; economic conditions under, 38–9; foreign creditors, dealings with, 212; foreigner control over Mexico dating back to, 219, 223, 227; land annexation, warnings against, 202; national resources, state control relinquished by, 214; opposition to, 122, 203; "Order and Progress" propagated by, 49; protectionism under, 240; rebellion and election as president, 213;

revolution at end of administration, 61; rich-poor gap under, 56; sayings, 183, 256; United States, attitude concerning, 183; wage deterioration under, 59; Zona Libre (border) established by, 242
Díaz Ordaz, Gustavo, 175–6
Dirección General de Industria (DGI), 35
domestic contexts, 5
domestic goods, 42
domestic industries, 30, 283
domestic market, 9, 24, 26, 34
drought (U.S.), 143
drug cartels, 254–5, 262, 263, 264
drug-related violence, xviii, 96, 262
drugs, legalization pros and cons, 264
drug trade, xviii, 260, 261–4
drug trafficking, xviii, 267, 274
drug war, 263, 264, 273
dual nature of society, 2
Duflot de Mofras, Eugene, 194
duties (for merchandise into Mexico), 236, 239, 243

East Asian countries, 283, 285–7
East Coast (U.S.), 76–7
economic activity: cities as centers of, 101; geography-centered studies of, 72; geography-imposed limitations on, xix; substandard, explaining, 6
economic autonomy, 14
economic circumstances, importance of, 11
economic disparities, 2, 7
economic downturns, xvii, 61
economic gap, U.S.-Mexico, xix
economic growth, 3
economic institutions, geographical factor impact on, 8
"economic miracle" (Mexico), 40–2, 50, 56, 59, 175, 176, 220
economic models, 4–5
economic opportunities, 275
economic organization, xix, 2, 11
economic power, concentration of, 9
economic productivity, spaces for, 74
economic sovereignty, loss of, 10
economies, building and improving, factors limiting, xx
El Aguila Company, 214
electricity, 145, 152–3
elite private sectors, 32
Elizondo, Eduardo, 176

El Paso: Ciudad Juárez compared to, xvii–xviii; Martínez family move to, 101; prosperity, reasons for, xviii; railroad impact on, 114; standard of living in, xvii; water supply, 143
El Segundo Barrio (El Paso neighborhood), 53
encomiendas, 9, 31
energy production, 145
Engerman, Stanley L., 8
England, 8, 36
English immigrants (U.S.), 22
entrepreneurial ethic, 3
environmental constraints, 12, 71
environmental determinism, 72
environmental differences, 3
environmental forces, 8
equal opportunity, United States, ideal *versus* reality, 55
Erie Canal, 104
ethnic discrimination, 34, 54–5
Europe, 26, 28
Europe, Western, 174
European countries as competitors, 28
European culture, assumed superiority of, 12
European immigrants, 163, 165, 190–1
Europeans in United States, 22
evolution, factors behind, 1
export-import paradigm, 231
exports, markets for Mexican, 42
export sector (United States), 26
external blame, pitfalls of overemphasizing, 3–4
external factors in underdevelopment, 12
external forces, 14, 226–7
external trade, 4, 44

factories, 21
family planning initiatives, 162, 176, 281
family size decrease, 162
fast-food eateries, 1
Feder, Ernest, 222
Federal Republic of Central America, 188
Ferdinand Maximillian (Mexican emperor), 120, 201, 211, 234
Fernández Lira, Ingeniero Emilio, 175
First World, 5
food exports, 41, 42
foreign banks, indebtedness to, 10
foreign capital: borrowing, 209–12; economic miracle made possible

through, 50; foreign investment, 208–9, 212–15, 220–3; influx of, 227; need for, 208–9, 226–7; taking back the country, 215–19
foreign creditors, pressures from, 216–17
foreign-dominated industries, 47
foreigners: control over Mexico, curbing, 219; elites with close ties to, 39; fear of, 12; hegemony established by, 30; interests, importance of considering, 10–11; Mexican dependence on, 121; property rights acquired by, 10
foreign firms, 43, 61, 159
foreign investment: drop in, 208; in East Asian countries, 285–6; encouraging, 44; flight of, 48; foreign direct investment (FDI), 223–4, 226; investment capital, 208–9; Mexican economy shaped by, 4; overview of, 212–15; pros and cons of, 227
foreign investors, 10, 41–2, 210, 220–3, 227
foreign manufacturers, 34–5
foreign oil companies, 39
foreign-owned properties, expropriating, 227
foreign relations (general), 9, 14
foreign relations (Mexico): 1848–1920, 200–4; as foundational factor, 5, 281–2; overview of, 183–84; since 1920, 204–5; unequal relationships, 6. *See also* U.S.-Mexico relations
foreign trade (Mexico): boom in, 241; development and, 230; drop in, 210; growth of, 44; postindependence, 231–4; during struggle for independence, 33; U.S. markets as asset for, 30
foreign trade (U.S.), 24, 27, 28–9
forests, 144, 152
formal education, 2
Fort Ross, California, 193
foundational factors: and development process, 5–7; examining, 14; external relations, 281–2; historic framework of, 21; of national economies, 6; natural environment, 278–9; natural resources, 279–80; population dynamics, 280–1; structure of production and governance, 283–4; United States and Mexico compared, 20, 277, 285
Foundation for Population Studies, 176
Fox, Vicente, 253

France: family protections, 174; Louisiana acquisition from, 184, 188; Mexico, intervention and occupation of, 36, 37, 49, 120, 201, 281; war against Mexico, 211
free market economy, 4, 44, 50
free trade, 48, 244, 253–4
free trade agreements, 44, 249, 282. *See also* NAFTA (North American Free Trade Agreement)
free trade zone, 239, 242–3
freight transport, 108–9, 110, 119, 123, 125
Fremont, John C., 195

Gadsden, James, 234
Gadsden Treaty, 184, 200, 234, 238
Gallagher, Kevin, 224
GATT (General Agreement on Tariffs and Trade), 223, 246–7, 249, 252, 256
GDP (defined), 2, 15n3
GDP (Mexico): breakdown of, 2; concentration of, 168; growth, 48, 61; in NAFTA period, 47, 250; per capita, 2, 48, 50, 250; regional distribution of, *169*
GDP (United States), 23, 26
GDP (United States and Mexico compared), 20
GDP-PPP (real GDP) (defined), 2, 15n3
generalized system of tariff preferences (GSP), 247
General Population Law, first, 173
geography (general), 8, 72
geography (Mexico): capital, internal, generating limited by, 209; constraints, lessening of, 42; economic challenges posed by, 14, 279; industrial activity cost driven up by, 38; land loss and, 71
geography (United States), 5, 109, 111
geography, United States and Mexico compared, xix, 5, 29–30, 36, 71–2, 98, 99, 116, 209
German submarines, Mexican oil tankers sunk by, 204
Germany, 174
Gill, Tom, 174–5
Gini Coefficient (Gini Index) (defined), 57, 68n13
Glen Canyon Dam, 142
global economic asymmetries, 3
global economy, 5, 25, 27, 288
globalization, U.S. promotion of, 28
global trade, 20, 28, 98, 99, 230

global warming, 143
GNP (Mexico), 65
gold: Mexico, 149, 154, 155, 238, 281; United States, 24, 145, 198
Gold Rush, 96, 114
governance: advances, requirements for, 11; means of, 7; new system, instituting, 39, 41; structure of production and, 5, 6, 7–11, 15, 283–4
governing, sensible approaches to, 11
governmental apparatus, origin of weak, 20
governmental institutions, xix, 8, 262
governmental structures, 9, 12
government expenditures, 44
government policies, 11, 14
government regulation, 8
governments, downsizing of, 4
Gran Apertura (Great Opening), 43–8
Grant, Ulysses S., 193, 195
Great Depression: international environment after, 50; Mexican national product during, 40; migration spurred by, 268, 269; oil production (Mexico) during, 155–6, 244; protectionism during, 27; U.S. economy, impact on, 26; U.S. investment drop during, 220
Great Lakes, 103, 104, 105, 106
Great Lakes region, 108, 113
Great Recession, 224
Green Revolution, 41, 42, 150, 151
groundwater sources, 141
GSP (generalized system of tariff preferences), 247
Guadalajara, 20, 133, 135, 224
Guatemala, 188
Guaymas, 90
Guerra, Ramon, 239
Guerrero, 123
guest worker initiative, wartime, 268. *See also* Bracero Program
Guggenheim American Smelting and Refining Company (ASARCO), 214
Gulf Coast (Mexico), 91–2
Gulf of Mexico, 43
Gulf of Mexico coastline, 77–8
gulf ports (Mexico), 92–4
Guzmán Montalvo, José, 254

haciendas, 9
Hart, John Mason, 150
Hawaii, 26, 185–6
health sector, advances in, 98
Hearst, William Randolph, 214, 216
high-definition televisions, 27
highways (Mexico): extent and placement, limitations to, 135; growth potential, limited of, 129; historic overview of, 125, *127*; infrastructure, 128; maintenance of, 119
highways (United States), 109–10, *110*, 114
Hilling, David, 115
hinterlands: Mexico, 87, 92, 95, 96, 98; United States, 76, 77, 98
history relationship to nature, 80
Hoover Dam, 142
Hudson River, 106
human environment, xx
human habitation, spaces for, 74
human societies, forces shaping, 1
hydroelectricity, 145, 152–3

ideological paradigms, 4–5
illegal drugs, 14. *See also* drug trafficking; drug war
IMMEX (Industria Manufacturera, Maquiladora y de Servicios de Exportación), 46, 224
immigrants: United States, 13, 25–6, 165, 268–9, 272–3; United States and Mexico compared, 163
immigration reform, 272
imperialistic countries, 3
import controls, reducing, 44
import substitution industrialization (ISI), 40, 44, 223, 240, 255, 282, 283
impoverished masses, policies neglecting, 7
income, 2
Indian raids, trans-border, 201, 202
Indians (Mexico): abuse of, 31; death from disease, 167, 281; Federal District, 169–70; marginalization of, 57; population of, 177–8; racial discrimination against, 178; social status of, 34; Spanish conquest and colonialism impact on, 12; Spanish exploitation of, 31
Indians (United States), 21, 22
Indians, U.S. and Mexico conditions compared, 32
indigenous languages (Mexico), 178
individualism, 12, 13
Indo-mestizos, 34

industrial development, achieving balanced, 14
industrial economy, U.S. building of, 21
industrial innovations, 23
industrialization (international), 38
industrialization (Mexico): challenges, 34–7; expansion, 40; export-oriented, 45; government promotion of, 41; protectionism and, 240–3, 255; wage increase resulting from, 59
industrialization (United States), 24–6, 145
industrial revolutions, 21, 26–7, 144
industrial work (New Spain), 31
industry: Mexico, 3, 41, 43; United States, 20, 22
INEGI (Instituto Nacional de Estadística y Geografía), 46, 63
inequality, 57–8
informal economy, size of, 2
information technology (IT) sector, 224–5, 228n40
infrastructure projects, 42
inland waterways: Mexico, 115, 117–18, 131, 134, 209; United States, 102–6, *105*
inner-city neighborhoods, xviii
institutions: capacity of, 14; defective, xx, 20; derivative nature of, 8; economic ills blamed on, 9; foreign interference with Mexican, 10; formation, factors limiting, 9, 10–11; long-term development required for effective, 11; mega context role in shaping, 9; poverty, role in, 10; uneven growth blamed on, 11; United States and Mexico compared, 10
internal markets, small, 20
international forces (Mexico), 30
International Monetary Fund, 4, 10, 44, 223
international trade, 26, 73
Internet, 27
interstate highway system, 109–10, *110*
inventions, 21, 45–6
investment, external, 4, 48
investment capital into Mexico, 208–9, 212–15, 220–3
investments, U.S., 4
iron, 149
Islamic State, U.S. fight against, 187
Isthmus of Tehuantepec, 127
Italy, 174
Iturbide, Agustín de, 33, 210

Japan, 28
job creation, 227
job growth, 250
job losses (Mexico), 39, 208, 231
job losses (United States), 28–9
jobs, low-wage, xviii, 227, 250
job shortages, 2, 179
Juárez, Benito, 201, 211, 234
Juárez-El Paso disparities, xviii

Korea, 286
Korean Conflict, 268, 285, 287
"Korean time" (expression), 14
Krakauer, Zork, and Moye (firm), 243

labor, 8, 45, 159
labor unions, 40
La Chaveña (Ciudad Juárez neighborhood), 53
Lake Mead, 142
Lake Powell, 142
land: arable, 150, 158, 204, 209; concentration, 9; foreign exploitation of, 10; foreign ownership of, 213–14, 218; reform, 39, 40, 41, 42
land transport (Mexico), 116, 118–20, 123–4, 134
Larkin, Thomas O., 195
Las Vegas, 142
Latin America, U.S. interventionist policies toward, 205
law, disrespect for, 12, 13, 14
law enforcement institutions (Mexico), 262
leftist agenda, radical, 4
Lerdo de Tejada, Sebastian, 213
life expectancy, 2
life-threatening diseases, 92
Limantour, José Y., 240
limited government, U.S. promotion of, 4
liquor bootlegging, 260, 264
liquor smuggling, 264
literacy, 2
littorals (Mexico), 89–91
living conditions, 58–9
loans to Mexico: borrowing, 208, 209–12, 226–7; repaying, difficulty of, 209–10; repayment, immediate demanded on, 227; rescue packages, 4
local economy (U.S.-Mexico border), 242
location, 73, 101, 140. *See also* country location

López Mateos, Adolfo, 175
López Portillo, José, 245
Los Angeles, 101, 114, 142
Louisiana, 184, 187
Lower Rio Grande Valley, 239
low-paid unskilled labor, 45
low-wage jobs, xviii, 227, 250
low wages, 9, 19, 59, 97, 159
low-wage sector, 43, 46
low wage workers, 230
Loyo, Gilberto, 173, 174, 175

machines, innovations in, 27
Madero, Francisco, 203
malaria, 90–1, 92–3, 100n36
malinchistas (term defined), 42, 52n35
manifest destiny, 184
manufacturing (Mexico): advances in, 240; attempts to limit, 35; concentration of, 41; expanding, 40; expertise, expanding, 45; for export, 46, 139, 224; foreign competition in, 231; GDP, share in, 250; government emphasis on, 36; growth in, 37, 41, 43, 61; institutions linked to, subpar performance of, 6–7; low-wage labor sector sustaining, 159; New Spain, 31; product assembly, 230; promotion of, 44; during struggle for independence, 33
manufacturing (United States), 22–3, 24, 26
Manzanillo, 90, 96
maquiladoras: boom and bust conditions, 50; distinctions reduced for, 46; domestic firms not involved with, 45; establishment of, 43, 60, 221–2; expansion of, 283; as export industry backbone, 256; industry, growth of, 64; modification and expansion of, 44; sector, assistance provided to, 64, 68n31; trade liberalization and, 250
marijuana, U.S. legalization of, 264
markets for Mexican exports, 42
Marshall, Edwin Jessup, 214
Martínez, Oscar, childhood in Mexico, 162
Martínez (Oscar) family: deportation of, 270–1; immigration to United States, xvii, 19, 101, 270–1
mass-consumption urban economy, 24
mass-information economy, 21
Mazatlán, 90, 97
McIntosh, C. Alison, 171
McKinley, William, 203

mechanization, 35
mega contexts, 5, 8, 9
megalopolises, 114–15, *115*, 133, 135
Mengel Company, 214
mercantilistic system, Spanish-imposed, 30–1
merchants, rise of, 22
mestizos, Spanish conquest impact on, 12
metals industry, 21
metro areas, largest (Mexico), *132*
Mexicali Valley, 218
Mexican (term), xix, xxn2
Mexican businessmen, U.S. opportunities for, 126
Mexican Central Railroad Company, 121
Mexican economy: boom and bust cycles, 61; crisis, early 1980s, 208, 223–6, 255–6; diversification, 245; foreign control over, 214–15, 220, 225; future direction, 288; historic developments, 29–48, 279; international circumstance impact on, 244; national policies (Mexico), 10, 44; overview of, 29–30; productivity of, 45; progress, 135; railroads as foundation of, 120; reforms, 50; remittances impact on, 273; state control over, relinquishing of, 223; trade liberalization impact on, 250; United States impact on, 183, 280; vulnerability of, 50, 61
Mexican Farm Labor Supply Program, 269
Mexican Foundation for Family Planning, 176
Mexican land lost to U.S.: California, 24, 193–6, 198–200; Díaz, P. attitude toward U.S. following, 183; impact of, 30, 71, 196, 197, 205–6, 278, 281; maps, *186*; population, low blamed for, 171–2, 173, 179; Texas, 184, 190–2, 197–8; U.S. gains from, 23, 24, 196, 197–200; U.S.-Mexico War, 192–3; U.S. westward expansion, 21, 184
Mexican leaders, xx, 11
Mexican peso, 60–1, 153, 219
Mexican Revolution: arms smuggling during, 243; conditions leading to, 39; at end of Díaz regime, 61; impact of, 49–50; land and oil expropriations after, 219; migration spurred by, 267–8; population concerns in wake of, 172; transportation prior to, 125; U.S.-Mexico relations, impact on, 183,

203–4, 215, 216, 281–2; wage increase after, 59; waning of, 204
Mexicans abroad, 171, 173, 180n12
Mexican wars of independence, 33, 93, 119, 153, 231
Mexican workers, plight of, 19
Mexico: attitudes concerning, xviii, 12; constitution, 1857, 37; constitution, 1917–1930, 10, 215, 227; constitutions (general), 33, 50, 176; debts, 201, 223; developed portion of, 20; early influences, 8; environment, attributes of, 80–98; evolution of, 84; foreign invasions, 81, 281–2; French intervention and occupation, 36, 37, 49, 120, 201, 281; French war against, 1838, 211; growth and development, 101–2; health conditions, 90–1; independence from Spain, 32–3, 188, 210; interior of, 86–9, 130, 135 (*see also* United States and Mexico compared: population concentration: coastal *versus* inland); maps, *58, 80, 83, 85, 88, 124, 127, 131, 132, 170, 186, 189*; national character, 12–13; natural riches, legend of, 138–9, 147–50, 158; as new republic, 33–4; original land holdings, 188; other countries, comparison to, 2, 11, 13, 15n1, 30, 287; productivity, decline in, 49; rainfall and flooding, 82–3; Republic of, *189*; Spanish conquest of, 147–8; survival as nation-state, 183, 189–90; U.S. invasions of, 173–4, 203–4; U.S. occupation of, 232; wars and instability, 33, 36, 49; water resources, 142–3, 150; worldwide recession impact on, 48
Mexico City: as developed site, 20; economic prowess in, 135; historic development of, 129; Indians in, 169–70; industrial production dominated by, 37; as manufacturing site, 41; population of, 133, 168; textile industry in, 231; transportation/linkage to, 93, 94, 96, 126, 127
middle class (Mexico), 62–4
middle-class neighborhoods, xvii
migration: consequences of, 273–4; contract labor, 269–70; escalation of, 1965 to present, 271–3; future trends, 177; illegal/undocumented, 260–1, 268, 270–1; later 19th century to early 21st century, 59; Mexican economy shaped by, 4; overpopulation accompanied by, 176, 179; overview of, 267–8; pre-World War II, 268–9; as safety valve, 67
military (Mexico), 41
military-industrial complex, 27
Miller, Tom, 248
mills, water-powered, 145
minerals: Mexico, 10, 42, 149, 157–8; United States, 146–7
minimum salary, real, *60*
minimum wage, deterioration of, 60
mining, institutions linked to, 6–7, 9
mining firms, 10
mining industry, 220
mining production, 31
Mississippi River, 106, 113, 114
Missouri River, 106
Moctezuma (Aztec Emperor), 147
modernization, 39, 41
modernization theory, 2–3
Monterrey, 20, 37, 41, 135
mosquito-borne diseases, eradication of, 92–3, 96
motor vehicles, 109, 253
mountainous terrain, 84–6, 122, 129, 149, 178
mountain systems, 75
multinational corporations: export-oriented assembly manufacturing established by, 50; globalization trends, view of, 29; maquiladora operations set up by, 221–2; Mexican economy portions in hands of, 220; Mexican invention ownership claimed by, 45–6; partnerships with, 64; profit margins of, 27
municipios, poverty rates in, *58*

NAFTA (North American Free Trade Agreement): investment possibilities in U.S. and Canada, 226; maquiladora distinctions reduced following enactment of, 46; Mexican exports to United States after, 250; Mexico signing of, 44, 223, 249, 256, 282; per capita GDP (Mexico) and, 50; pros and cons, 250; tariff reduction mandated by, 151; trade restrictions eased, not gone, 252; U.S. worker opposition to, 28–9
Napoleon III, 281
National Alliance for the Growth of Population, 174

national character, 13–14
national economies, 5, 6, 9, 12
national growth, failure to achieve balanced, 47
national income (United States), 24–5
National Infrastructure Program, 128
national product (Mexico), 41
national security, population role in, 171, 172
nation-states, disparities among, 5
natural assets, 20
natural endowment, 9
natural environment: conditions, defective institution relationship to, xx; divergence in, xix; European influences secondary to, 8; examining, 14; as foundational factor, 5, 278–9; influence of, 15; national economies dependent on, 9; raw material shortage *versus,* 6
natural gas, 153, 245
"natural resource curse" (term), 139
natural resources, 9
natural resources (Mexico): contribution of, 15; economic development, limited role in, 159, 279; examining, 14; exploiting, 38; land, rain, forests, and waterpower, 150–3; metals and minerals, 153–5, 157–8; natural riches, legend of, 138–9, 147–50, 157; oil (*see* oil (Mexico)); overview of, 139–41, 147; sale of, 40; state control over, end to, 10, 214, 227
natural resources (United States), 139–41, 141–5, 145–7
natural resources (United States and Mexico compared), 5
nature, 80, 134
neighborhoods, United States and Mexico compared, 53
neoliberalism: benefits, limited of, 61–2, 279; capitalism system under, 7; East Asian country non-participation in, 285; economic crisis and onset of, 223–6, 249; endorsement of, 44; impact of, 282; implementation of, 47, 50; Mexican economic challenges and, 288; overview of, 4
New England (U.S.), 76–7
New Orleans, 112–13
New Spain, 30–3, 129–30, 147, 231
New York City, 22, 77, 93–4, 111
nini population (defined), 66, 68n38
Nixon, Richard, 261

non-European countries, U.S. trade with, 26
non tax-paying economy, 2
North America, political geography of, *185*
North American culture, 12
Northeast Mexico, trade in, 237, 257n23
northern frontier (Mexico), population of, 171–2, 179
northern states (Mexico), 54

obrajes, 232
Obregón, Alvaro, 172, 215
Oglala Aquifer, 141
Ohio River, 106, 113
oil (Mexico): boom, 61; discovery of, 43, 245; dispute over, 219; economy, changing role in, 48; foreign ownership of deposits, 204; Great Depression impact on, 244; international prices, drop in, 208; Mexican Revolution impact on, 216; overview of, 155–7; pitfalls of dependence on, 208, 279–80; ups and downs, 50, 158–9
oil (United States), 197–8, 199
oil economies, pros and cons of, 43–4
oil firms, 10
oil production, 43
online piracy, 14, 16n18
On the Border (Miller), 248
Operation Intercept, 261
Operation Wetback, 270
Oregon Trail, 113
Ortíz, Tadeo, 148
overpopulation (Mexico): response to, 162, 280–1; underpopulation *versus,* 171, 178–9, 280
overpopulation (United States), 165
Owens Valley, 142

Pacific coast, 95
Panama Canal Zone, 186–7
Partido Revolucionario Institucional (PRI), 138
past, understanding, 1
Paz, Octavio, 12
Pearl Harbor, attack on, 204
PEMEX (Petroleos Mexicanos), 156, 157, 214, 219
people in Mexico, 166–78
people in United States, 163–6
per capita income, 47
Persian Gulf War, 187
personal computers, 27
petrochemicals, 27

petroleum production, 43, 153
Philadelphia, 22–3, 77, 93–4, 111
Philippines, 26, 186
Phoenix, 142
plantations, 9
Poinsett, Joel R., 92, 233
policy-making, 11
policy mistakes, xix–xx
political disputes, mending, 39
Political Essay on the Kingdom of New Spain (von Humboldt), 148
political integration, xix
political policies, 2
political power, concentration of, 9
political sovereignty, 10
Polk, James, 192, 193, 194, 195, 198, 232
poor countries, 4, 5, 9–10
population (Mexico): composition and assimilation, 177–8; control, attempts at, 176–7; demographic trends, 171–7; density, *170*; distribution, 167–70, 179; by ethnicity, *168*; overview of, 166–7; regional distribution, *169*; size, 167
population (United States): composition and assimilation, 165–6; demographic trends, 165; density, *164*; physical distribution, 163–5; regional distribution, *164*; size, 163, 173; water resource pressure due to, 142, 159–60n8
population concentration. *See under* United States and Mexico compared
population dynamics: economic challenges posed by, 14; examining, 14, 15; as foundational factor, 5–6, 280–1; modernist theory ignoring of contrasting, 3; national economies and governmental structures dependent on, 9; in new Mexican republic, 33–4; population growth decline, 67
population patterns, 8
ports: Mexico, 92–4, 97; United States, 76
positive attributes (Mexico), 30
poverty (Mexico): alleviating, challenge of, 280; historic conditions, 62; institution role in, 10; migration to U.S. in wake of, 179; municipios, *58*; neoliberalism failure to diminish, 4; overview of, 56–9; persistence of, 4; sites and overview of, 1–2
poverty (United States), 54, 55–6
poverty (United States and Mexico compared), 54, 67, 277
poverty-stricken urban districts, 20
power concentration, 7

precious metals (Mexico): export of, 235, 255; gold and silver, 153–5; New Spain, 31; observers attracted by, 83
precious metals (United States), 145–6
present, understanding, 1
production: dual structures of, 20; and governance, structure of, 5, 6, 7–11, 15, 283–4; means of, 7, 8, 30, 34; methods, 28; structure as foundational factor, 5
productivity distribution, 20
prohibited imports, 231–2
Prohibition (U.S.), 1920, 264
Prohibitionist Era (U.S.), 260
pronatalist propaganda, 174, 179
pro-population stance (Mexico), 171, 172, 173–5, 179
protectionist policies (Mexico): after U.S.-Mexico War, 237; debates over, 235; elimination, advocacy of, 3; and industrialization drive, 1880–1920, 240–3, 255; instruments, 40
protectionist policies (United States): in 1970s, 28; in Great Depression, 27; in industrial era, 24
public enterprises, 44
public policy, 15
public servants, corruption of, 255
Puerto Isabel, 238
Puerto Rico, 26
Puerto Vallarta, 97
Punta Colonet project, 97–8

quasi-socialist practices, 4
Quay, Matthew, 203
Quintana Roo, 94–5

racial and ethnic diversity, 166
racial discrimination, 54–5
railroads (Mexico): connection to United States, 37; economic progress, role in, 135; expansion efforts, 240; foreign trade, impact on, 241; goods, shipment of, impact on, 238; historic overview of, 120–5; limitations to development of, 42, 124–5, 134; to Mexico City, 96; motorized transport as adjunct to, 128; network, *124*; roads combined with, 134–5; Tampico connections, 93; Veracruz connections, 94
railroads (United States): in California, 114; city development, role in, 112, 114; networks, *108*; overview of, 107–9; proliferation of, 25; westward spread of, 113

rainfall (Mexico), 150, 152, 158
Ramírez, José Fernando, 238
Ramos, Samuel, 12
ranching, 197, 198
raw materials (Mexico): access to, 140; demand for, 38, 40, 50, 240; development, limited role in, 279; exploitation of, 139; export of, 230, 283; extent of, 138; other countries, comparison to, 30; over-reliance on, economic pitfalls of, 159; processing of, 40; railroad role in transport of, 120; shortage of, 6, 34
raw materials (United States), 24
Reagan, Ronald, 272
regions, Mexico division into, 29, 54
religions, 13
remittances to Mexico, 273, 274
repartimientos (term defined), 31, 51n12
Republic of the Sierra Madre, 237, 257n23
research and development (Mexico), 45
research and development (United States), 27
resource constraints, 12
resource endowment, xix, 3, 5–6, 8
resource scarcity, xviii
restaurants, U.S.-owned, 226
Restored Republic, 119–20, 211–12
retailing, 1, 225–6
revenue collection (Mexico), 245
rich and powerful, policies favoring, 7
rich countries, 5
rich-poor gap: Mexico, 4, 7, 39, 41, 67; United States, 55, 56
Rio Grande, 143
risk avoidance, 12
rivers, navigable (Mexico), 118, 136n28, 149
roads: Mexico, 119–20, 125–9, 134–5; United States, 106, 109, 114
Robinson, James A., 9, 10, 11
Rocky Mountains, 109
"romantic nationalism" (term), 174
Romero, Matías, 149, 202–3, 242
"rugged individualism," American, 13
Ruiz Cortines, Adolfo, 175
rule of law, 255, 285
rural community *versus* urban area, 101
Russia, 184–5

Sacramento River, 106
safety net, 8, 67
safety valve, Mexican migration to U.S. as, 273

Salinas de Gortari, Carlos, 44
Sam's Clubs, 226
San Diego, 87–8, 130–1, 142, 143
San Francisco, 114
San Francisco Bay, 79, 80
San Joaquin River, 106
San Joaquin Valley, 142
Santa Anna, Antonio López de, 35, 189, 200, 234
Santa Fe, 114
scientific discoveries, 27
Sea of Cortés, 142–3
seaside cities, 99
Select Commission on Immigration and Refugee Policy, 272
self-created jobs, 2
Senior, Clarence, 174
service economy, 21
services sector, 43
shape of country: Mexico, 83, 98, 132–3; United States, 74–5, 98, 132–3
Sheldon-Payne Arms Company, 243
"shelter" companies, 231
shipbuilding, 22
Sierra Madres, 123
silver: Mexico, 149, 153–4, 155, 158–9, 238, 281; United States, 145, 146
size of country: Mexico, 83, 98; United States and other countries compared, 74, 98
slavery, 24
Slidell, John, 194–5
smuggling into Mexico: 1880–1920, 243; 1920–1980, 247–8, 249; 1980 to present, 256; postindependence, 233–4, 235–6, 237–8, 239; vice products, 260
smuggling of people. *See* migration: illegal/undocumented
social disparities, 53
social inequalities, 7, 14–15
social integration, xix
socialism, 13, 44, 50
socialistic policies, 3
social mobility, 59
social programs, cutting of, 4, 44
social security programs, 8
social stratification, 53
societal upheaval, 61
soil erosion (Mexico), 149
Sokoloff, Kenneth L., 8
South America, 240–1

southern states (Mexico), 54
South Korea, 14, 284, 286–7
space-age communication technologies, 21–2
space exploration, 27
Spain: colonialism, impact of, 12; Florida acquisition from, 184; as global exploration and colonization winner, 72; legacy impact on Mexico, 8; mercantilistic system imposed by, 30–1; Mexico existence to provide wealth to, 31; Mexico wars against, 189; New Spain riches provided to, 32; territory lost to U.S., 21, 23, 186; trade reforms enacted by, 32
Spaniards, Mexico abandoned by, 33
Spanish-American War, 186
"Spanish influenza" epidemic, 172
Spykman, Nicholas J., 73, 86
standard of living, xvii, 2, 21
Standard Oil, 214
state activism (Mexico), 44
state-church relations, 39–40
state-directed economies, 3, 59
state enterprises, privatization of, 4, 64
state entrepreneurship, 41
steamboats (U.S.), 25, 103, 107, 112
steam power, 21, 23–4, 36
Stillman, Charles, 212–13
St. Lawrence River, 113
St. Lawrence Waterway, 102–3, 104, 105–6
stock-raising, 31
supermarkets, 226
Superstores, 226
Switzerland and Mexico mountains compared, 85–6

Tabasco (state), 91
Tamaulipas, 239
Tampico, 87, 90, 92–3
Tannenbaum, Frank, 84
Tarahumara Indians, 152, 170
tariffs, 244
tariffs (Mexico): 1920–1980, 244, 245; 1980 to present, 251, 252, 254; after U.S.-Mexico War, 235, 237; industrialization protection attempts through, 35, 40, 231–2; lowering, 44, 151, 255
tariffs (United States): 1920–1980, 244–5; in 1970s, 28; after U.S.-Mexico War, 234; Depression era, 27; post-World War II, 28; pre-Civil War regional divisions over, 24; World War I and aftermath, 26

taxation (general), 8
taxation (United States), 22
tax system (Mexico), 65–6, 211, 214
technological inventions, 23, 27
technological revolutions, 21
technology, import of, 35
telegraph network (United States), 111
telephones (United States), 111
Tenochtilán, 129
terrorist attacks of September 11, 2001, 13, 272
Texaco, 214
Texas, 184, 190–2, 197–8, 237
textile manufacturing (Mexico): cotton, 31; in industrial era, 37, 38; international markets, obstacles to reaching, 240–1; New Spain, 31, 32, 231; recession, recovery from, 36
textile manufacturing (U.S.), 21
textile mills, 22
textiles, smuggling of, 234, 238, 253
Third World, 3, 4, 5
Third World countries, 165, 227, 277–378, 288n1; U.S. trade with, 26
Third World country (term), 2, 15n1
Third World cultures, 12
Tijuana, 87–8, 130–1, 143
Tijuana River, 143
tobacco products, trafficking in, 260, 265–7
topography: Mexico, 84–6, *85*, 120, 135; United States, 111, 284; United States and Mexico compared, 75, 98
Tortilla Curtain, 271–2
tourism (Mexico), 96, 97, 98–9, 124, 263
towns, small and villages, population of, 169
toy-making companies, Mexican *versus* U.S., 252
trade, 230. *See also* contraband trade; conventional trade; external trade; world trade
trade (Mexico): institutions linked to, subpar performance of, 6–7; liberalization of, 64, 234, 249–55; New Spain, 32; trade balance challenges, 244; U.S. economy, integration with, 30
trade (United States), 20, 21, 23–4, 246
transportation (Mexico): banditry, 119; city integration into, 116–17; geographic challenges of, 101, 278; infrastructure,

134, 149; infrastructure, expansion of, 98; infrastructure, motorized of, 128–9; land transport, 116, 118–20, 123–4, 134; modernization of, 116, 122, 135; overview of, 115–16; pre-railroad, 118–20, 209; transport network lacking, 36; travel through Mexico, 85. *See also* railroads (Mexico)
transportation (United States): city emergence and multiplication aided by, 102; corridors, 75; highway infrastructure, 109; improvements in, 28; inland waterways, 102–6; innovations in, 24, 27; intercity infrastructure, 111; overview of, 102; steam power in, 21
transport costs, drop in, 25
Tratado de Mesilla (Gadsden Treaty), 200
Treaty of Guadalupe Hidalgo, 192, 195, 201
trunk lines, north-south (Mexico), 124, 126
Tucson, 114, 142

underdeveloped (term), 2, 15n1
underdeveloped countries, 3, 10, 28
underdeveloped segment of Mexico, 20
underdevelopment, 2–3, 11, 13, 14, 39–48
underground economy, 2
United Kingdom coasts, 89–90
United States: attitudes concerning, xviii; commonwealths of, 186; early influences, 8; economic conditions, xvii; environmental attributes of, 72–80; expansionist foreign policy, 20, 30, 187, 281; global preeminence, factors behind, 19–20; global superpower, emergence as, 184–7, 206; historic developments, 21–9; industrialization, 23–6; land annexation sentiments, post-1848, 202–3; Mexican migration to (*see* migration); Mexican territory, bid for (*see* Mexican land lost to U.S.); Mexico contiguity with, 71, 81, 98, 282; regional economies, 25; size, shape and topography, 74–5; territorial expansion, 21, 23, 26, 184–7, *186*, 188, 190, 193–6, 284; water resources, 143; wealth distribution in, 8; world supremacy, 26–9
United States and Mexico compared: border towns, 237; capitalism, 7, 8; corruption, ethics and national character, 12, 13–14; development gap, 2; disparities, roots of, xviii; economic gap, causes of, xix; economies, 14, 19, 20–1, 49, 50–1, 206; environmental factors, 74, 75; evolution, 7; foundational factors, 5–7, *6*; geography (*see* geography, United States and Mexico compared); human circumstances, 5; independence and nation formation, 34, 205; indigenous workers, 32; institutions, 10; migration consequences, 273–4; military strength, 192; natural resources, 139; overview of, 284–5; physical differences, 5; population, 162–3, 165, 173; population concentration: coastal *versus* inland, 86–7; raw materials, 138; security and law enforcement, xviii; social disparities, 53; transportation, 106, 109–10, 115, 128; urban systems, 102, 115, 130–3; vice product trafficking, 267; water resources, 143; wealth concentration and poverty, 277
University of Texas at El Paso (UTEP), 208
upper class (Mexico), 64–7
upper-class neighborhoods, xvii
urban areas (United States), *112*
urban centers (Mexico), 116
urban corridors (United States), *115*
urbanization (United States), 26–7, 111–15
urban networks (Mexico), 129–34
urban system (Mexico), 134
U.S. Border Patrol, 269, 272
U.S. Department of Energy, 145
U.S. Immigration and Naturalization Service, 270
U.S. loans, 4
U.S.-Mexico border, 10, 142, 201, 234–9, 272
U.S.-Mexico relations: distrust and suspicion characterizing, 246; drug trafficking impact on, 261; Mexican dependency manifested in, 21; Mexican economy, impact on, xix, 4; Mexican Revolution impact on, 183; post-Mexican Revolution, 184, 204–5, 282; pre-Mexican Revolution, 183; trade-related issues and, 232; trade relations, 1920–1980, 244–9; water disputes, 143
U.S.-Mexico War, 1846–1848, 192–3, 195–6, 200, 235, 281

Valley of Mexico, 133, 135
Van Royen, William, 146
Veracruz, 32, 90, 92, 93–4, 204
vice products, 260, 267
victimization, culture of, 12
Villa, Pancho, 204, 243
Volstead Act, 264
von Humboldt, Alexander, 93, 95, 148

wage exploitation, 31
wages (Mexico): China and Mexico compared, 61; drop in, 39, 61; increase in, 59; low, 9, 19, 59, 97, 159; minimum, 60
Walmart, 225–6
War on Drugs, 261
waterpower, 144–5, 152
wealth concentration, 277
wealth disparity/ies, 3, 7, 54
wealth disparity/ies (Mexico): economic classes, 62–7; eradicating, 14; political and economic power concentration as factor in, 9; poverty and inequality, 56–9; substandard wages, benefits and safety-net coverage, 59–62
wealth disparity/ies (United States), 54–6
wealth distribution, 6, 8, 230–1
wealth redistribution, 67
weaponry, breakthroughs in, 27
well-educated individuals, migration of, 273

western continental United States, 78
Western industrial countries, 2–3
Western Sierra Madres, 96
whites, status and power of, 34
Wilson, Henry Lane, 203
wireless communications (United States), 111
wood, 144
World Bank, 4, 10, 44, 223
world leaders, limitations of, xx
world trade. *See* global trade
World Trade Organization, 28, 251
World War I, 26, 174, 187, 204, 243
World War II: East Asian countries after, 285, 287; economic impact of, 26; Mexican participation in, 204–5, 219; migration during and after, 268, 269; raw materials, demand during, 40, 50; recessions after, 26; U.S. economic conditions after, 20, 27–8; U.S. involvement in, 187
worldwide recession, 2008, 48, 50

yellow fever, 91, 92–3, 100n36
Yucatán, 123
Yucatán peninsula: climate and environment, 91–2

Zapatista rebellion, Chiapas, 48
Zarsky, Lyuba, 224
Zona Libre, 239, 242–3